I would like to dedicate this book to my son, Nicholas Hitoshi,
who managed to make it safely into this world
during the creation of this book.

—David Jung

I would like to dedicate this book to my wife, Devvie,
who tolerated "don't debug me" and other corny jokes
that I tried out on her before I put them in this book.

—Jeff Kent

About the Authors

David Jung has been programming on computers since the early 1980s. A graduate of California State Polytechnic University, Pomona, David has a bachelor of science degree in business administration emphasizing computer information systems. His development expertise is in architecting and constructing cross-platform client/server and distributed database solutions using Visual Basic, XML, Access, SQL Server, Oracle, DB2, and Internet technology.

He is a member of the Pasadena IBM Users Group's technical staff and leads its Visual Basic Special Interest Group. He is also a frequent speaker at seminars and users groups showing how Visual Basic, XML, and Internet technology can be integrated into business solutions.

David has co-authored a number of books on Visual Basic ranging from introductory and reference titles to client/server development, as well as a book on Microsoft Outlook programming. He is also a contributing editor for *Data Communications* (http://www.data.com).

When he's not programming, writing, and presenting, he can be found on bike trails and golf courses in Southern California, or spending time with his wife Joanne, his son Nicholas, and their two dogs (that he pretends he likes).

Jeff Kent is an assistant professor of computer science at Los Angeles Valley College in Valley Glen, California. He teaches a number of programming languages, including Visual Basic, C++, Java, and, when he's feeling masochistic, Assembler, but his favorite is Visual Basic.

Jeff has had a varied career, or careers. He graduated from UCLA with a bachelor of science degree in economics, then obtained a juris doctor degree from Loyola (Los Angeles) School of Law, and went on to practice law. During this time, when personal computers still were a gleam in Bill Gates' eye, Jeff also was a professional chess master, earning a third place finish in the United States Under-21 Championship, and later, an international title. These days, however, Jeff's focus is on computers. In addition to teaching and other college duties, he also manages a Windows NT network for a Los Angeles law firm and, of course, writes. His current interest is the integration of programming languages, applications (such as the Microsoft Office suite), and the Internet technologies to provide solutions for businesses, particularly professional services firms.

Jeff, like his co-author, belongs to the Pasadena IBM Users Group and its Visual Basic Special Interest Group, at which he speaks when they get desperate for speakers.

Jeff does find time to spend with his wife, Devvie, which is not difficult since she also is a computer science professor at Valley College. He also bikes and roller-blades with his daughters, Elise and Emily, who describe him as a stork on skates. His goal is to resume running marathons, since he feels the ability to run fast and far can be important to a programmer, particularly when the program does not work.

Debugging Visual Basic:

Troubleshooting for Programmers

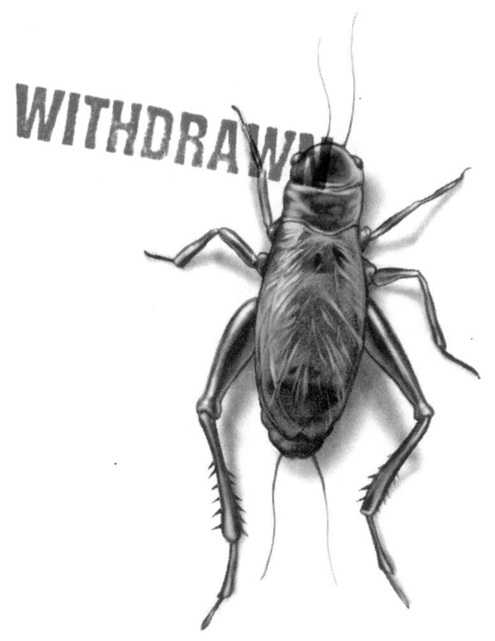

David Jung
Jeff Kent

Osborne/McGraw-Hill

Berkeley / New York / St. Louis / San Francisco / Auckland / Bogotá
Hamburg / London / Madrid / Mexico City / Milan / Montreal / New Delhi
Panama City / Paris / São Paulo / Singapore / Sydney / Tokyo / Toronto

Osborne/**McGraw-Hill**
2600 Tenth Street
Berkeley, California 94710
U.S.A.

For information on translations or book distributors outside the U.S.A., or to arrange bulk purchase discounts for sales promotions, premiums, or fund-raisers, please contact Osborne/**McGraw-Hill** at the above address.

Debugging Visual Basic: Troubleshooting for Programmers

1234567890 VFM VFM 019876543210

ISBN 0-07-212518-7

Publisher Brandon A. Nordin
Vice President and Associate Publisher Scott Rogers
Editorial Director Wendy Rinaldi
Project Editor Janet Walden
Acquisitions Coordinator Monika Faltiss
Technical Editor Bob Noble
Copy Editor Andy Carroll
Proofreader Mike McGee
Indexer David Heiret
Computer Designers Jani Beckwith
Jean Butterfield
Dick Schwartz
Illustrators Robert Hansen
Michael Mueller
Beth Young
Series Design Peter Hancik
Cover Design Dodie Shoemaker

This book was composed with Corel VENTURA ™ Publisher.

Contents at a Glance

Table of Contents

Acknowledgements

Our heartfelt thanks to Wendy Rinaldi, without whose help, guidance, and patience this book in the Debugging series would not exist. A special thanks goes to Monika Faltiss who was very understanding when we said, "We just need one more day."

Thanks to Janet Walden and Andy Carroll for wading through mounds of pages of our manuscript and keeping our writing as honest as it could possibly be.

There are a lot of other talented people behind the scenes who also helped to get this book to press, and, like in an Academy Awards speech, we're bound to forget to mention them. That doesn't mean we don't appreciate all their hard work, because we do.

David would like to personally give thanks to his co-author, Jeff Kent, for his constant encouragement and words of guidance during this endeavor. He would also like to give thanks to his friends and family for putting up with him during the writing of this book and understanding that he "couldn't come out and play." As strange as it may sound, he'd like to thank his dogs for always showing up with toys in the middle of the night to provide a good distraction for all the late night coding sessions. But most importantly, he would like to thank his wife, Joanne, for her enduring love, encouragement, and support. And during this project, she gave birth to their first child, Nicholas Hitoshi.

Jeff would like to personally give thanks to his co-author, David Jung, for yet another interesting book collaboration. He also would like to give thanks to his family for tolerating him while he was grumbling about deadlines or cracking corny jokes about debugging, and for not having him committed when he talks about writing his "next" book.

Introduction

We did not write this book as a road to riches or fame. We are misguided, but not that misguided. We wrote this book because we believe it fills a need. There already are many good "how to" and reference books, and unfortunately also many bad rehashes of Microsoft Visual Basic manuals. By contrast, there are relatively few books that focus on good software development and debugging techniques using Visual Basic.

However, sound software development and debugging techniques are critically important. Writing a program without a sound structure or error-handling routines is akin to backing your car out of your driveway without first taking the time to look down the street. Maybe you'll be lucky and no car will be coming. However, the odds are against you, and the result of a crash often will take more time and money to undo than preventing the problem in the first place with simple precautions. Similarly, programmers taking unwise shortcuts under pressure to shave days off development time end up wasting weeks or more trying to fix a buggy program while fending off irate customers.

Indeed, reliable software development and debugging techniques are important enough for us to risk the anger of neglected spouses and other dangers and write this book for you, the Visual Basic programmer. Which leads us to the next subject.

Who This Book Is for

If your programs always are perfect the first time, every time, then you don't need this book. For the rest of us lesser mortals, this book is for you. We wrote this book so it will be useful to all Visual Basic programmers, whether you're new to Visual Basic or have been programming in Visual Basic for years. The reason, quite simply, is that writing bug-free, crash-proof programs is important regardless of whether the program is at the beginning, intermediate, or advanced level.

Visual Basic is one of the most, possibly *the* most, popular programming languages for the Windows operating system. The very popularity of Visual Basic makes it more difficult to write bug-free code because you may be using Visual Basic in many different ways—developing stand-alone products with Visual Basic, interoperable programs with VBA, or writing Web-based applications with IIS applications and DHTML applications. However, the common denominator among all is that you're bound to run into problems. This book is designed to help identify many of the common and not-so-common bugs that plague developers.

How to Use This Book

This book is divided into four parts, "Coding Development Skills" (Chapters 1-2), "Debugging VB" (Chapters 3-12), "VBA and Automation" (Chapters 13-14), and "VB and the Internet" (Chapters 15-16). Each chapter is self-contained, which allows you to go straight to the chapter without having to read a previous one.

In Part I, "Coding Development Skills," we discuss the theories used in software development, such as coding and naming standards, application specifications, design specifications, and testing procedures. This provides you with a guideline for application development and the factors you should consider before one line of code is written.

In Part II, "Debugging VB," we look at techniques you can use to help debug your applications through the VB development environment, such as the conditional compilation statements and Immediate Watch window. We will also cover, through coding examples, how to trap errors, identify the common and not-so-common places errors occur, and how to handle errors within your applications.

In Part III, "VBA and Automation," we look at how VB is used in making your applications interoperable with VBA-enabled applications, such as Microsoft Office.

In Part IV, "VB and the Internet," we'll discuss Visual Basic's role with Internet development and offer a look into what Microsoft plans for the next evolution of Visual Basic and programming the Internet.

Conventions Used in This Book

All Visual Basic keywords appear in **bold**. Variables, function parameters, control names, and so on are formatted in different ways, such as by being italicized.

The chapters include three special elements:

Error Watch *This is used to indicate areas of programming likely to contain errors. These errors can be of the logical or syntactical nature.*

This is used to indicate programming practices that should be adopted to ensure that your code will be robust, stable, and capable of keeping your application up 24 hours a day, 7 days a week.

Design Tip *These are used to point out better programming practices and help you avoid developing bad coding habits. They are usually used to guide you around poorly designed, but working, code.*

Contacting the Authors

We enthusiastically welcome gushing praise. We also are receptive to comments, suggestions, grunts, groans, and yes, even criticism. The best way to contact us is via e-mail; you can use **books@vb2java.com**. Or, you can visit our Web site, **http://www.vb2java.com**, which contains resources and updated information about the code and contents of this book.

We hope you enjoy this book as much as we enjoyed writing it.

PART I

Coding Development Skills

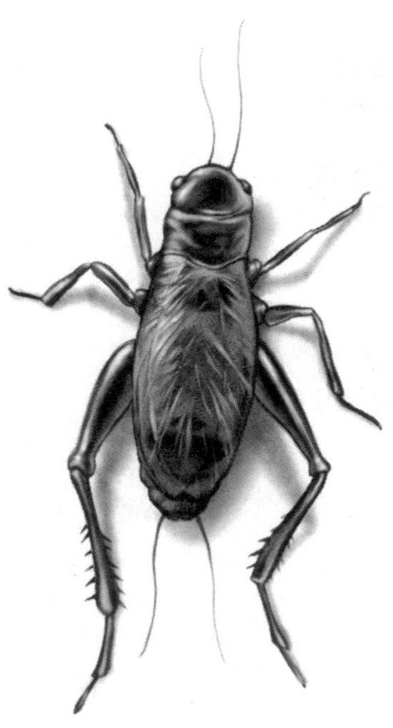

CHAPTER 1

Program Design and Management

Visual Basic is one of the computer industry's most popular programming environments. Based on the BASIC (Beginner's All-purpose Symbolic Instruction Code) programming language, Visual Basic allows programmers to develop Windows-based applications by drawing the user interface for an application while writing the code behind it.

Prior to the introduction of this concept in Visual Basic, you had to draw the form completely by writing code. You wouldn't know if your interface looked right until you compiled and ran it. If a button was misplaced, or you missed a text box, you would have to add the code, recompile it, and re-run it. This was a very tedious and time-consuming process. You also had to have a good understanding of the Windows Software Developers Kit (SDK)—it spelled out all the resource files and support hooks.

When it was first introduced in 1989, Visual Basic was considered a lightweight development tool compared to other languages like C/C++, Pascal, or even (gasp!) Assembler. Over the years, it has been much improved and has gained respect. It has become more than just a rapid application development tool. It has become an integral part of Microsoft's Windows DNA. It is used to develop components that can be used for Web development, transaction processing, and message queuing.

Planning Your Application

Whether you are developing your application in Visual Basic, C/C++, Pascal, Java, or COBOL, you should take the time to consider application design. If adequate time is not spent on general application design prior to beginning work on development, you can expect to pay the price down the road. The planning of an application is almost always overlooked or scheduled with inadequate time. That is because most programmers consider design boring, and they would rather start developing as soon as they get their assignments.

"Any color—so long as it's black." —Henry Ford

Whether Henry Ford really said this or not isn't relevant. What's relevant is the sentiment. Often in software development, programmers believe that they know what the users want better than the users do. "We can develop the program for you, so long as it's to our specifications," could be what a programmer says to a user. Sometimes programmers have attitude because they can program a computer and their customers can't. But what good is a custom program if it's not what the customer wants?

Software development requires two-way communication between the developers and the users. When you first meet with the users, you should be attempting to determine the project scope, get a program definition, and identify the user community for the application; it is very important that you establish communication with everyone involved. One of the most important things you need to communicate to the users is that they must take ownership for their part of the project. Software development can't pit the programmers against the users, and the programmers can't be responsible for everything. Your team is responsible for implementing the business rules in the application, but if the users don't take ownership of their part of the requirements, there is a good probability that the project will not succeed. There are a lot of users out there who feel that because they aren't techies, they only have to give you some requirements, sit back, and let you do all the work. Without the user's involvement, commitment, and sense of ownership to the project, the project will more than likely fall short of expectations and the finger-pointing will more than likely be pointed in your direction.

"A fool and his tool is a faster fool." —Unknown author

In general, when developers start writing applications just because they want to finish more quickly, the applications take longer to complete than they would if they were properly designed and clearly specified. Applications for which development time was invested up-front will be easier to maintain and will work much better than will applications that are thrown together hastily. Everyone who has developed applications for any period of time has horror stories to tell about development projects that failed. Basically, it is better to take your time to build a system on a strong foundation than to quickly complete a system on a weak one.

"A stitch in time saves nine." —Unknown author

Joint application development (JAD) meetings are a good way to bring developers and users together for application-requirement gathering. To hold a JAD meeting, you need a meeting facilitator, a scribe (note-taker), and both users and developers. During these sessions, application ideas are discussed. Technology should not be brought into the discussion during the first few meetings. The first few meetings should focus on gathering requirements and formulating ideas. After the meeting, the scribe should compile the notes into a document that will help serve as a historical reference of the meeting. In addition, the scribe should create an outline of feature and functionality requirements. Everyone in the JAD meeting should review the outline. By having a clear set of ideas in writing, features and functionality can be prioritized and grouped. Once that has been completed, analysts can take the information and derive functional specifications from them. If something isn't clear in the outline, subsequent meetings should be held until all the questions are answered. You're not going to get all your questions answered, but the more ambiguity you clear up, the cleaner your design will be.

The functional specification document should serve as a living document that captures all the information that is required for the system and it should be updated as progress is made. It should be void of specific names when defining roles and responsibilities because organizations change, people leave, and so on. If names should be used, generic names should be used so they don't get confused with people currently in the company. John Doe is a good example.

Identifying Users

"Because every person knows what he likes, every person thinks he is an expert on user interfaces." —Paul Heckel

As trivial as it may sound, identifying who the users are is a step that is often overlooked in software development. By identifying the users, you can gain insight on how the application is going to be used, how sophisticated the users are, how sophisticated the application is going to be, and how the user interface of the application needs to be.

When you develop an application, you can build a great one that makes the programmers at Microsoft envious, but if no one can use it, it's worthless. In order to make sure that people use it, you have to make sure to keep your user community in mind. In order to do that, you first need to find out who will be using the application. Say you have been asked to develop an application to track diabetic patients for the optometry department for the hospital. When developing the application, you will capture and report on data differently than if the application were being designed for general practitioners studying diabetic patients. By knowing the user base, you can get an idea as to the type of data that will be captured, how the user interface should be designed, and the way the system is going to be used.

Also, by identifying the users, you get an idea how sophisticated the user base will be. An application built for biostatisticians can be designed with more mathematical interfaces and entry points than can an application designed for physicians conducting research on a medical device. Knowing your user base can help you determine the appropriateness of various interfaces.

When you know your user base, you will also discover the full scope of the application. At first, one department may request the application, but later you might discover that several departments really need to integrate their information with the application. Without knowing that, you might have built an application that did not lend itself to interoperability. You might have designed it with the one group that requested it in mind, and you would have had to reconstruct it to allow the other departments to interact with the application.

Project Scope

Project scope. There's a nebulous term that project managers sometimes throw around during development and staff meetings. In reality, what they are trying to do is ensure that you're not doing more than you need to, or that what you're building fits into the grand scheme of things. Essentially it's the big picture of how your application is going to be used, and it should be identified when the functional specification document is being created.

When defining the scope of the project, you should get the answer to the following questions:

- What is the program's purpose?
- What are the application boundaries or scope?
- Who is the user community?
- What is the timeframe for designing, developing, and implementing the program?
- When should the users be trained?

When developing applications with tools like Visual Basic, documenting the application is often overlooked. Once programmers think they know the application they need to build, they want to start coding. The keyword in the last sentence is "think." How many times do you think you know what someone wants, and then you realize you didn't even come close, or you came close but you left out some really obvious features.

In software development, it's important to identify what you are trying to build. In order to do that, you need to meet with the users, identify what the application is supposed to accomplish, determine whether it's replacing an existing application or process, and find out how it fits into the department's or users' workflow.

By identifying what the application is supposed to do, you will get an idea as to whether the application is supposed to be a stand-alone system or whether it will integrate with other systems. This can be important when trying to figure out how broad or narrow you need to make the application.

Context Diagram

The "picture is worth a thousand words" cliché definitely helps in application development and in designing functional specification documents. When considering application design, whether you're new to programming or you've been programming since punch cards, it's a good idea to diagram your application into workflow processes. In order to get an image of the entire scope of the project, you can use a diagramming method called a context diagram. A *context diagram* is used to help display the high-level interaction in a system. In the center of the diagram, you simply define an object as "the system." Surrounding the system are external entities that will interact with the system. The external entities can be either people or other systems. A context diagram is a great reference if you are building an integrated system because it identifies the other applications that will be interacting with the system you're commissioned to build. Figure 1-1 is an example of a context diagram for a hotel reservation system.

Program Definition

If you find out that the application is supposed to replace an existing system, you will want to know which features of the original system the users liked and disliked. You should find out why the existing system is being replaced, as well, and what they expect to gain from the new system.

When interviewing the users about how the new system will work in their daily operations, you will discover how sophisticated the application needs to be. For example, if the application is going to be used by every user in the

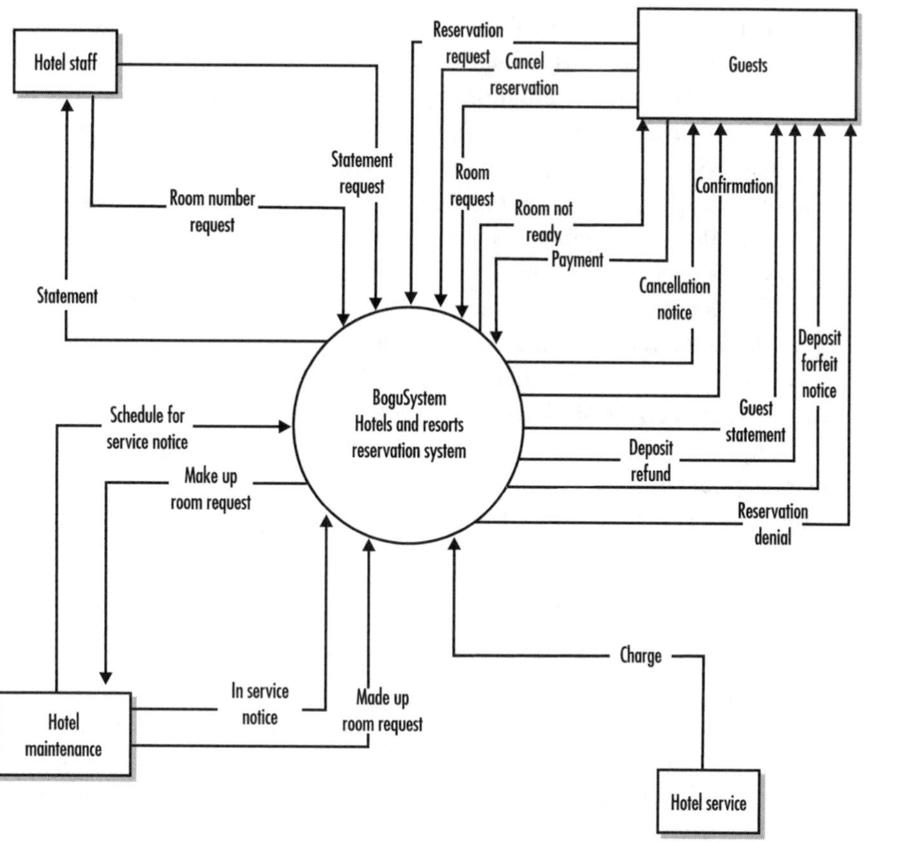

Figure 1.1 Context diagram for a hotel reservation system

department to input orders for the Home Shopping Network, you'll have to code in a lot of transaction-processing routines and business-rule components to handle all sorts of transaction validations. The user interface should be extremely easy to use with immediate error handling and data validation so the user can get immediate feedback if any information is incorrect, and so on.

You might be building a similar application to be used by traveling sales representatives, and the application would be installed on notebook computers. A lot of the same functionality would be needed, but is the urgency for incorporating transaction validation as important in this situation? Probably not, because all the transactions are going to be processed in a batch mode; therefore, certain data-validation routines won't have to be too exact. In an online transaction environment, you will want to know immediately whether an order quantity is available. In a disconnected ordering system, like a sales force automation system for traveling sales representatives, you won't know if the exact quantity is available. Rather, you would implement rules like "a customer cannot order more than 20 units per item."

When documenting the application, don't go overboard on details. However, in trying to keep the documentation light, you also want to make sure you don't leave any gaping holes, either. Documenting the specification will also help identify any unclear or impossible application goals. More often than not, users will request features that they've seen in other applications that are completely inappropriate to the application you're building. By eliminating them up-front, your developers won't have to waste their time trying to fit those square pegs into the round holes. This brings us to gathering the functional requirements.

Dataflow Diagrams

As you start defining the application, you might want to start flowcharting some of the logic. However, it's still too early for that. The next diagramming phase after the context diagram is the dataflow diagram (DFD). Flowcharting comes later, when you start designing how your logic will flow.

Dataflow diagrams are used to show, in detail, how the external entities interact with the system. DFDs are a set of multiple layered illustrations, with each one becoming more granular than the previous one. It starts with Level 0, which displays all the different elements that make up a system. Figure 1-2 illustrates Level 0 of a dataflow diagram. For each interaction that's identified in the context diagram, there is a one-to-one relationship with the processes identified in Level 0 of the dataflow diagram. Each business process is identified as a circle. Data stores represent a logical data storage interaction.

Each process is numbered, and the next diagram level, Level 1, is used to illustrate further interactions of a given process. Figure 1-3 illustrates Process 1—Manage reservation. Just as in the context diagram and Level 0 of the DFD, there is a one-to-one relationship between the inputs and outputs of Level 0 and Level 1.

All this diagramming may seem time consuming, but in the long run it will help your developers get a better understanding of the users' requirements. It will

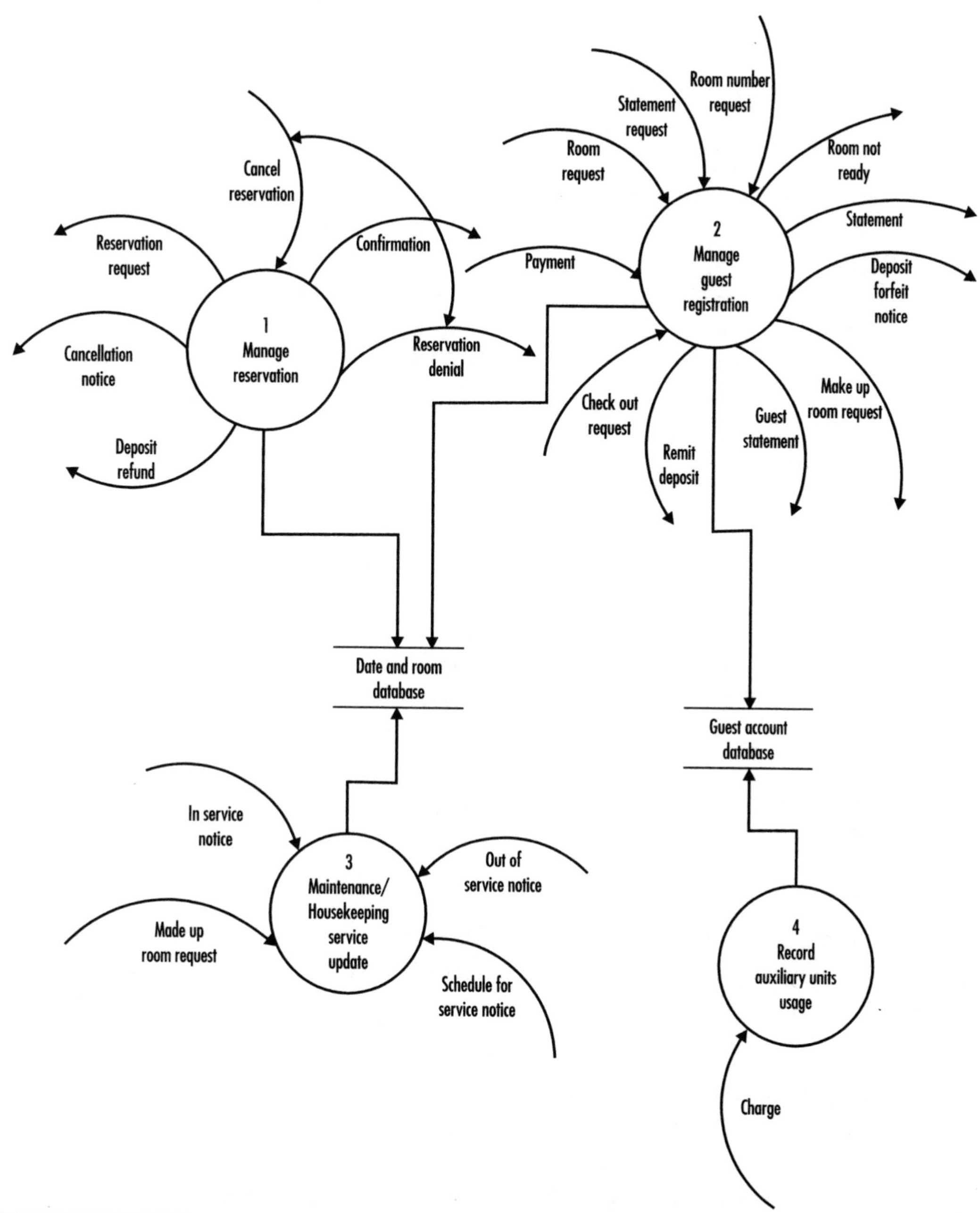

Figure 1.2 Dataflow diagram showing how an external entity interacts with a system

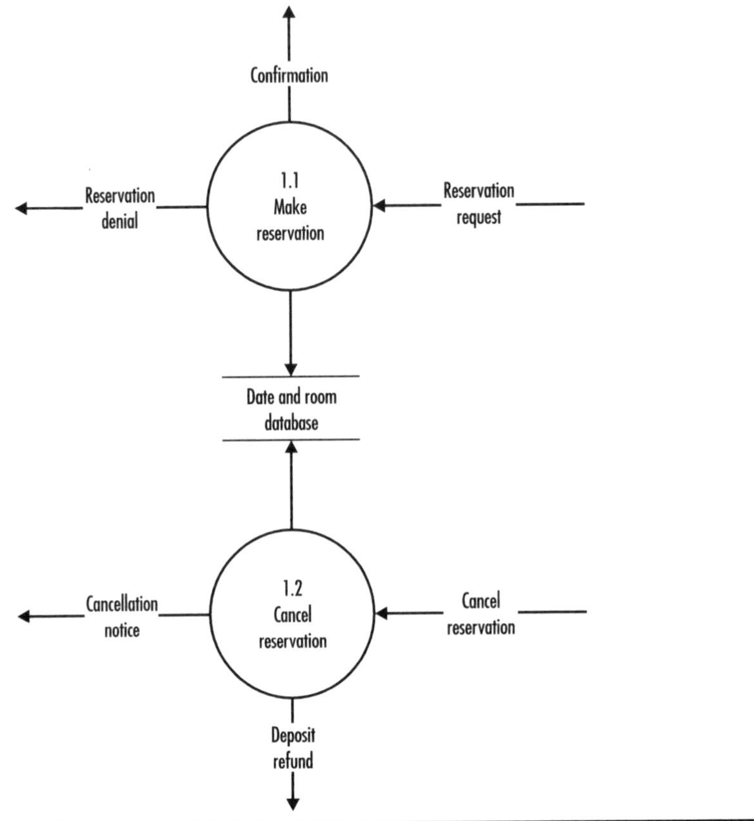

Figure 1.3 Dataflow diagram, Level 1, Process 1

also help ensure that the users understand the business rules they are asking the developers to create for the system. You don't have to make your diagrams so elaborate that they take up all of your analysts' time, but there should be enough detail to describe what's going on and what processes need to be looked at.

Analysis Techniques and Prototyping

There are two techniques developers use when analyzing and designing systems. They are the structured development life cycle (SDLC) and rapid application development (RAD). Using the SDLC technique is a lot more tedious and methodical than using RAD techniques. SDLC is best used when you're trying to design a system that both the users and developers have a good idea of what the general system requirements are, what the program is supposed to accomplish, and when there is adequate time to plan. SDLC is a more methodical process of software development broken down into four phases: planning, analysis, design, and construct and testing. Since both the users and developers have a good idea of what is to be designed, each phase has a number of takes to be accomplished and milestones to achieve.

RAD is best used if the client or end users have an idea of their requirements but can't really put it into words. This is where Visual Basic can help. It can be used to quickly come up with a prototype, which is a mock-up or facsimile of what the users might think they want. If the users are unclear on what they want and they see something that reflects their thoughts, you can quickly find out exactly what the requirements of the system are. However, you need to explain to the users that the prototype may not represent what a completed system would look like. Often a client will see a prototype with basic functionality, and they will think that a completed system is not far behind. However, there is no business logic programmed into a prototype. It's strictly designed for interface navigation. It is very probable that the final product may look nothing like the prototypes you have been previewing. By letting them know this ahead of time, you will avoid any undue expectations the customer might have about the program.

One key aspect of RAD that developers sometimes overlook is that they still need to do analysis work. Developers tend to build a prototype, show the prototype, receive feedback on the prototype, update the prototype, and start this cycle over again. They get so caught up in building the perfect prototype that they lose sight of the application and its business functions, their milestones, and their project deadlines.

Designing Your User Interface The user interface (UI) is the portion of the application that the user sees. It is critical that the interface be designed properly and that it be intuitive and consistent. There are many good books on UI design, so we are not going to teach it in this book. However, there are a few rules that you should follow:

- *Keep the design really simple.* Cutting-edge button and field design is great, but chances are that you will be the only one who knows how they work. Unless you enjoy support calls, keep the cool and obscure controls to a bare minimum.

- *Stick to the basics.* Do not go overboard on having controls move around, change sizes, and so forth. Try to standardize the location of your command buttons, label your accelerator keys, and so on. Don't have OK and Cancel buttons on one screen and then have Cancel and OK buttons on another. Keep it simple and consistent.
- *Use a role model.* One of the advantages of using a graphical user interface (GUI) is that you can present a common look and feel. By making your applications look and function like other GUI applications, the time it takes your users to learn your application will be minimal. Look at Microsoft Word, Excel, and other successful GUI applications, and use them as patterns in your applications.
- *Do not use a bunch of crazy colors.* Think back to when you used your first word processor. The first document you created probably had bold and italic type everywhere, and ten different fonts displayed on each page. It was probably difficult to read, and not very appealing to look at. User interfaces tend to suffer from the same disease. If you are going to use color, make sure it is effective, and get input early in the UI design from other developers and your target audience. You also need to take into consideration that users have a tendency to change the appearance of their screens. Some of the colors you choose for your application might not show up well if the users change their appearance preferences.
- *There are times when it is desirable and highly appropriate to deviate from the norm.* It might be appropriate to completely break the Windows UI standards. Your task might be to create an application that is designed around a long-standing manual process or form, such as a check-writing or employee-expense report. It can be advantageous to create an interface that mimics the manual process of the form, because it will give your users instant identification and comfort with the application. However, even though you might digress from the Windows norm, you should also try to include as many Windows standards as possible, such as tab stops, accelerator keys, and so forth. Just because the data entry form doesn't look like a typical windows application, it should still behave like one. By incorporating some of the Windows standards, the users will feel comfortable with your application because they will not have to learn a new way of navigating through the application, like getting to the menus or selecting information from a list. Be smart about your UI design, and it will improve the usability of the application. Remember that the UI is the only thing the user will ever see.

- *Use accelerator keys, keyboard combinations, and tab orders efficiently.* Accelerator keys are field labels that have an underscore under one of the letters and require the user to press the ALT key plus the underscored letter to move the field or activate a menu. For example, ALT-F is a common one for activating the File menu. Keyboard combinations provide further shortcuts for performing tasks. Pressing the CTRL and S keys is a common combination for saving a file or record. Tab orders refers to the sequence in which the cursor moves through the user interface when the user presses the TAB key. When you develop a UI that requires a lot of data entry, the last thing you want your data entry associates to do is waste time using the mouse to move from field to field. The WIMP (Windows, Icon, Menu, and Pointer) interface is user-friendly and pleasing to look at, but when speed and accuracy are the top priority for an application, you want to make the operator be as efficient as possible without having their hands leave the keyboard. Take WordPerfect for DOS as an example. It was not the most elegant program to look at, but for transcribers who really knew the menu system, which relied heavily on keyboard combinations, it was more efficient than Microsoft Word for DOS, which relied mainly on strict menu operations, because their hands didn't need to leave the keyboard for formatting. With Microsoft Word for DOS, the transcriber could do minor formatting through keyboard combinations, but any real formatting had to be accomplished through a series of menus that didn't have any accelerator keys for quick access.

Lowest Common Denominator As part of a development group, your computing power is probably just short of a Cray supercomputer with super-high-quality graphics and almost unlimited hard drive space. Your application will run at light speed on your system, but when you deploy your application to the enterprise, your application may run as slow as a turtle.

You need to consider your audience. Just because you have the latest and greatest computers in your organization, that does not mean that your end users will. If you're developing an application for a group that only has SVGA display capabilities, then do not develop your UI to be larger than their screen capabilities.

Developing for lower resolutions used to be a problem, but there is a tool that is part of the Visual Basic IDE (Integrated Development Environment) that can assist in keeping your user interface well within the screen resolution. This tool is called the Form Layout window, and it is shown in Figure 1-4. To display the Form Layout window, select it from either the View menu or click its icon on

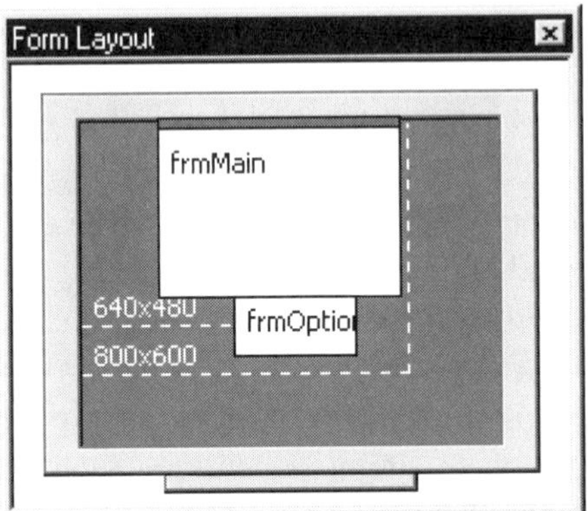

Figure 1.4 Form Layout window displaying the position of two forms

the IDE's toolbar. The window serves two purposes. It allows you to visually position your forms at design time, which will allow you to see where the form will appear when your application runs, assuming your forms don't call any positioning routines as they are displayed, such as a CenterForm routine. Also, you can visually see if the form will fit within the screen resolution you are designing for.

Scope "Creep"

One of the biggest dangers for the success of any project is scope "creep"—it needs to be detected early during the development process. What is scope creep? It is when, during the development cycle, your client requests an additional feature that wasn't originally agreed upon. The feature sounds easy enough to implement and shouldn't affect the schedule, so you add it to your list of things to do. Then another person asks you for another feature. One or two features that weren't originally agreed upon won't affect the overall schedule, but if too many features are asked for, the schedule will slip and the delivery date will be missed. After all, you still need to test the features that were not in the original scope. If the test team isn't aware of what the features are supposed to do when they write their test plans, they will have to figure out how to test them as well as determine whether they are functioning correctly.

This may sound like it would only happen to development groups that produce commercial software. Unfortunately, it happens to every developer and project manager in any size company at one stage or another.

"Killer App" Syndrome

Another type of scope creep is when, during the development process, someone comes across a program that does something similar to the one your group has been asked to build, and they ask you to take a look at it. You try the demo software and discover that it has a lot of the features your program will have, and there are features you will have but it does not, and it has features that you, your development team, and the users never thought of before. Now that people have seen the other product, your group is told that the extra features in the other program have to be included in this release of your program, because the user believes that these are essential features that were overlooked.

As the project manager (or project lead, lead developer, or other title that describes someone who can make a decision about the development schedule), you know that this is a bad idea. You might be surprised to know how many times people just can't say "no," or how many people won't take "no" for an answer. A simple word like "no" can cause a lot of problems. In the case of project schedules, not saying "no" to additional features once development has started is detrimental to the delivery schedule and ultimately to the success of the project. Make sure that everyone is clear on the ramifications of implementing features and functions that weren't originally agreed upon. If possible, convince them that these features will be investigated and included in future releases. A phased release is the best way to ensure the success of the project.

One way to ensure that you've captured enough information in your documentation and reduced the risk of scope creep is to have the primary user or owner of the new system sign off on the requirement document. This does not require a full legal contract to be drafted, but having them sign a cover letter stating that they read the document and believe that it describes what they want in the new system helps avoid misunderstandings.

Development Schedule

Now that you know what you need to build, which features are needed, and who you're designing it for, you need to consider the development schedule. There are many tools, seminars, and methodologies to help you formulate a schedule. Is one better than another? It really depends on the project manager, the development team, the client, the work environment, and so on. When devising the schedule, you need to take all these into consideration.

If you've ever studied physics in any great detail, you will have learned that in a balanced structure, if you remove one of the critical elements that supports a structure, it will topple. A simple example is a three-legged stool. Each leg is designed to support the top of the stool and the weight placed upon it. Remove one of the legs and the stool will topple. If you shorten one of the legs, the stool may not be able to sustain the weight placed upon it and may become unstable.

The same holds true in software development. Everyone involved supports the entire project. If you remove one of the parties or restrict resources—such as people, equipment, or time—you weaken the foundation and undermine the overall success of the project.

However, unlike the stool, not all the resources are constant to begin with. Developers leave projects for other assignments, for time off, and so on. The same holds true for the client. With changing resources, how can anyone make an accurate schedule? It's important to create an aggressive development schedule, but it shouldn't be so aggressive that it doesn't account for the human factor, meaning that you cannot assume that people are going to be on the project 100 percent of the time, working 80 hours a week, and not taking any time off for vacation or illness. People's work quality will lessen over time, and enthusiasm will diminish.

Though you don't want to make the schedule too aggressive, you also don't want it to be too easy-going either. If the schedule isn't aggressive enough, people will lose the sense of urgency, as well as losing focus on the project itself.

When scheduling a due date for version releases, it must be understood that these dates should be used as milestone marks, or as good-faith gauges for delivery and not as absolute delivery dates. All too often clients want hard due dates, and delivery slippage is not acceptable. This is not good for morale. Giving people "guilt trips" about being over budget or missing their deadlines is more harmful than helpful. If the client is aware that the delivery dates may slip, you help to manage their expectations and allay their anxiety. However, when you do miss delivery dates, you need to make sure that the product is of the same or better quality than if it had been delivered on time.

Code Review and System Testing

Something that is commonly overlooked in systems development is properly testing a system before deploying it to the user community. In the publishing world, a common adage is "never proofread your own mistakes." This means that the person who wrote or typeset a manuscript should not proofread it because that person will not be as objective in looking over his or her own material as someone else might be. The same holds true with application development. Two things that you should consider as part of your development strategy are code review sessions and system testing.

A *code review session*, also known as a *structured walkthrough*, is not a new concept in software development. Many development methodologies include this as part of the development requirements. The purpose of a code review is not to go through the developer's code line by line. It is designed to ensure that the developer designed a module, component, interface, or application to meet the business specifications. Code reviews should be frequent, non-threatening, and informal. By holding these sessions, it makes it easier to ensure that the developer understands the design specifications and helps everyone see if there are any "glaring" holes in the development process. It is better to catch errors in the general structure of an application early on rather than after the application has been put into production.

The participants of a code review should be the developer's peers, as well as any analysts who are familiar with the business process the code is designed to solve. Before a session is held, it is a good idea to distribute a hard copy of the code to all parties involved in the review. A review session is not very effective if people are seeing the code for the first time at the review.

With development tools like Visual Basic, it is easy for developers to perform functional testing as they code. This means they can ensure that their code compiles and that it meets the required business specifications. The developer may understand the fundamental business logic he or she is developing for, but might not understand the context in which it will be used in the completed system. Therefore, it is important that someone who understands the system requirements test the application or component(s) before the system gets put into production.

Historically, most systems do not get thoroughly tested before they reach the user community. No matter how much beta testing you do, you can never guarantee that all the errors are going to be caught before the application rolls out—Microsoft can attest to that. By performing your own testing first, you have a higher probability of catching a lot of the minor errors and bugs up-front. Also, testing can help ensure that the business rules are implemented correctly, or at least that they are functionally correct according to the design specifications.

There are a number of third-party tools that can help analyze system deficiencies and perform error tracking within your applications. For example, CompuWare's NuMega DevPartner Studio, FMS's TotalStatistics, and AdvantageWare's VB Advantage come with tools that generate statistics on functions that are called within your application and how many times they were accessed. This information can help you identify any procedure or function in your program that is not being used either because it's obsolete or it's part of your application framework that isn't being referenced. Also, this information helps you identify if a procedure or function is being called more times than you think it should be. With a situation like that, you might be able to determine why a process is taking longer than you think it should.

Regression testing is also something you should look into when developing an application testing strategy. This is usually accomplished by using an automated testing tool like Rational Software Corporation's SQA Suite or Mercury Interactive's WinRunner. Regression testing is important because when it comes to maintaining an application, it can help ensure that you did not introduce new bugs into areas of code that were working before. The last thing a developer wants to do is break something that was working just fine.

Holding code review sessions and implementing system testing can help you reduce the chance of distributing a bad system.

Version Control

When working on large projects, you will usually be developing in teams. Since a Visual Basic project is composed of different modules, it is possible to have developers working on different modules at the same time. You want to make sure that all the developers are using the latest versions of every form and module and that they are not modifying the code that someone else is working on. In order to ensure this, you should consider using version control software, such as Microsoft Visual SourceSafe or PVCS Version Manager and Version Manager Plus.

Version control software is nothing new to a lot of software developers. It has been used on mainframe and mid-range computers for years. By using version control, you can ensure that only one person is working on a component at a time. You can also share components across applications so that if you make a change to a shared component in one application, the other applications will also see the change. Trying to do this manually, without the assistance of software, can get out of hand in a hurry.

Rollout Deployment

Often in software development, people get caught up in the notion that everything should be in the first version in order for the project to be successful. If that was truly the case, companies like Microsoft, Symantec, and Oracle would never have shipped their products. Combining the information you gathered from the specifications and requirements, you can start ranking the features and requirements that positively have to be part of the core application. Everything identified should be scheduled to be included in version 1.0 of the release. When the time comes, you can examine the features and functions that are held off in version 1.0 and determine whether they should be in version 2.0 or not, and so on. It's easier to manage a project that has milestones and successful incremental versions than trying to get out the best application with everything in it, only to find out later that things just don't work.

Writing Good Code

In many ways, software development is an art. As software developers, like artists, we are asked to create something simply from one's idea. A lot of times, we won't know how it's going to turn out until the project is complete.

In the process of making your creation, there are some fundamental things you should keep in mind to make your work easier. No matter what computer language you use, these pointers will help you become a more conscientious developer.

Object-Oriented Programming

When developing your applications with Visual Basic, you cannot help but think about objects. Microsoft has begun embracing the idea of object-oriented programming (OOP) in all their development products. One thing to keep in mind about OOP is that a solid understanding of its theory and a structured implementation method is needed in order to make an OOP project a success. There have been too many horror stories of how an OOP project failed because the developers were so caught up with developing the perfect objects that the objects were unusable. OOP is not for everyone, but it can be useful when implemented properly.

Programmers, Start Your Coding!

Before there were rapid application development tools like Visual Basic, developers would never just start to write code, compile it, test it, rewrite it, recompile it, retest it, and so on. Computer time was expensive, and so was storage space; therefore, developers would create flowcharts, write a lot of pseudo code, hold code reviews, and so on before sitting down to a keyboard and typing one line of code. Nowadays, developers are so anxious to start their projects as soon as they receive their assignments that they start into the development environment and start coding. There are some developers who are very talented and can start programming without running into too many problems. However, the majority of developers will discover that they aren't as efficient as they could be, had they just stopped and written out an algorithm or two, or even drawn a flowchart to determine how the logic would flow.

Coding Style

Whether you're an independent developer or part of a development group, your program's code may at some point have to be connected or integrated with another project or system. On the surface, this sounds easy enough, but when you get a group of developers together, they will have different programming backgrounds and different coding styles. It doesn't sound like a big deal, but when you try to integrate each other's code, the people trying to piece all the components together will probably think differently.

Let's start with a writing analogy. You're part of a group that needs to put together a report for the annual shareholders meeting. Your organization has standardized on Microsoft Word 97, and it's your responsibility to merge all the submissions and make the whole report look consistent. A week before the report is due, you receive documents from the other team members, and as you start to merge the documents together, you find that half the group used the NORMAL.DOT template, three used the DEPT.DOT template, and two people didn't use a template at all. Merging them all together is the easy part. Trying to format them to look consistent is where the real work begins, because the heading styles, paragraph indenting, and so on will be inconsistent.

The same problem arises when you try to merge programs or parts of other people's source code into your code when they use a different coding style than you. So how do you make people code like you do? That's simple, you don't. What you do is make everyone agree on one coding style that you all will use. It could be based on your style, your cubicle neighbor's style, a style based on an article someone has read, and so on. The objective is to have everyone's code look the same, so that someone in the group can easily understand it and be productive almost immediately with it.

One of the things you should come to agreement on is how to format the code. Formatting the code does nothing for the performance of the application you build. It's strictly for code readability for debugging and logic analysis. It has been said that "spaghetti is nice to eat, but it's not fun to program through."

Going through code that was not formatted, that has variables defined on the fly, and that isn't commented is a painstakingly difficult process. It's like taking a bowl of spaghetti and trying to follow where each noodle starts and ends. That's why unstructured, unformatted, uncommented code is often referred to as "spaghetti code."

Indent Code

One of the most obvious code-formatting techniques is to indent the lines of code into logical groups. The following is an example of bad code formatting:

```
If question = "Yes" Then
For x = 0 To 100
DoSomething = x * 186232
If DoSomething > 3205420 Then
MsgBox "You are here"
Else
MsgBox "You are there"
End If
Next x
Else
MsgBox "Later"
End If
```

The next example shows good code formatting:

```
If answer = "Yes" Then
    For x = 0 To 100
        DoSomething = x * 186232
        If DoSomething > 3205420 Then
            MsgBox "You are here"
        Else
            MsgBox "You are there"
        End If
    Next x
Else
    MsgBox "Later"
End If
```

By indenting your code, you can immediately see how the logic is grouped. The **For-Next** loop is enclosed within the first half of the **If-Then** statement. Within the **For-Next** loop, you will find another **If-Then** statement. In the code that is not indented, you can see that the logic is harder to follow, and if the entire application were written this way, imagine how long it would take you to debug.

Comment as You Go

This sounds really obvious, but you would be surprised at how many developers don't like to comment their code. The attitude is "since I wrote the code, of course I'll remember how it works." But what about the other developers in your group? If someone else has to look at your code, will they know what you did and why? Is your code really so good that you don't need to write any comments?

It's better to comment your source code as you go, rather than to comment after the fact. Just like writing documentation, if you don't do it up-front, it will never get done. Also, if you comment your code as you go, you might just stumble across a solution to a problem that had been eluding you.

Developers often write comments into their code simply for the sake of keeping notes. This can be helpful in some cases, because the source code could be seen by more than a dozen programmers over the life span of an application. Over that period of time, you may encounter a lot of comments that are no longer relevant. It's a good practice to clean up any comments that have become stale and outdated.

Naming Your Data Types

All too often, developers will name their variables as whatever comes to mind, and they complete their program without thinking of the consequences down the road. If the developer is a sole developer, then naming standards might not be critical. In a collaborative team environment, making sure that everyone is using the same naming conventions is essential for seamless code integration.

In team development, the functional areas of a program will be divided amongst the teams. It's important that each team agrees on how they are going to name their data types. It's especially important that the team leaders communicate with each other how the teams name their data types so that when it's time to integrate each area together, there are no surprises.

Hungarian Naming Convention

The *Hungarian naming convention* provides a naming convention and several other advantages. Since so many names are standard, there are fewer names to remember in a single program or routine. The Hungarian naming convention, also known as *Hungarian notation*, gets its name because names that follow the convention look like a foreign language, and the creator of the convention was originally from Hungary. The naming convention is composed of three parts:

- A base type
- One or more prefixes
- A qualifier

Of the three parts, two are mandatory. The combination is either base type and qualifier, or prefix and qualifier—notation is never defined as a base type and prefix. Each part is described in greater detail in the following sections.

Base Types The base type is the data type of the variable you are trying to identify. A base type name generally does not refer to any of the predefined data types offered by the programming language—it is usually a more abstract data type. It might refer to entities such as windows, screen objects, and such. Examples of some base types and their meanings can be found in Table 1-1.

Prefixes The prefix takes a variable name to the next level of definition by denoting the data type of the variable. Unlike base types, which are abstract data types, prefixes refer to standard data types. Table 1-2 provides a list of prefix notations and their meanings. Depending on the programmer, the prefix notations

Base Type	Meaning
btn	Button (common among C++ and Java developers)
chk	Check box
cmd	Command button (used by VB developers)
fra	Frame control
frm	Form
lbl	Label box
opt	Option button or radio button
scr	Screen region
txt	Text box

Table 1.1 Examples of Base Type Notation

Prefix	Meaning
a	Array
dt	Date
dbl	Double
g	Global variable
f	Form-level variables
h, hnd	Handle
i, int	Integer
l, lng	Long
m	Module-level variables
n	Number
s	String
sgl	Single
v	Variant

Table 1.2 Examples of Prefix Notation

may vary; therefore, it's important that all developers be in agreement about the prefixes that are to be used. Table 1-3 illustrates what some base types would look like with prefix notations.

You might have noticed the prefix notation using "i", "l", and "n" to depict number variables. Explicit definitions are good if you are absolutely sure that the variable is never going to change. You might be thinking that you're never going to change a data type once your program is in place, and in many cases this is true.

Variable Name	Meaning
miCounter	Module-level variable for holding integer values
nCounter	Generic variable for holding a number value
gvStudentInfo	Global variable for holding a variant value, often used for variant arrays
dtDOB	A date/time value for date of birth

Table 1.3 Examples of Variable Names with Prefixes

However, in applications that deal with calculations and financial information, this might happen. For example, suppose you develop an application to help managers forecast their departments' expenditures on a monthly and quarterly basis. You design all your variables as integers. This seems reasonable, since the integer data type can handle values up to 32,767, and you are displaying all your values in millions of dollars; therefore, if the application shows 125 in a cell, it really means $125,000,000. But what happens when you perform a calculation that exceeds the 32,767 limit? Your users will start experiencing calculation errors. The solution to this is to change all the data types from integer to long. This sounds simple enough, until you look at your variable's prefix notations, which all start with "i". Not only do you need to change your data types, but you also need to update all the prefix notations. Had you defined the prefix notation with an "n" to denote a number, you would only have to change the data type of the variable and you could leave the notation alone.

Qualifiers The qualifier is the descriptive part of the name that will make up the entire name. It should be combined with prefixes and base types. For example, txtLastName is a text box for the last name, fraCreditCardType is a frame that will contain information about types of credit cards, and gdtAudit is a global date variable for an audit.

Working with Variables

Just like other programming languages, Visual Basic allows developers to create variables that store information about the current state of the running program. Each variable refers to a location in memory and is referenced with a specific data type that determines how the data is stored and what it represents.

Not to reiterate what every Visual Basic book covers regarding variables, but there are a few rules you might not be aware of.

Use Option Explicit

When you first install Visual Basic, the option to require that all variables be defined is not marked by default. Select Options from the Tools menu and check the Require Variable Declaration check box, as shown in Figure 1-5. What this means is that the key phrase **Option Explicit** will be placed in the General Declaration section of every module. This means that every variable within your

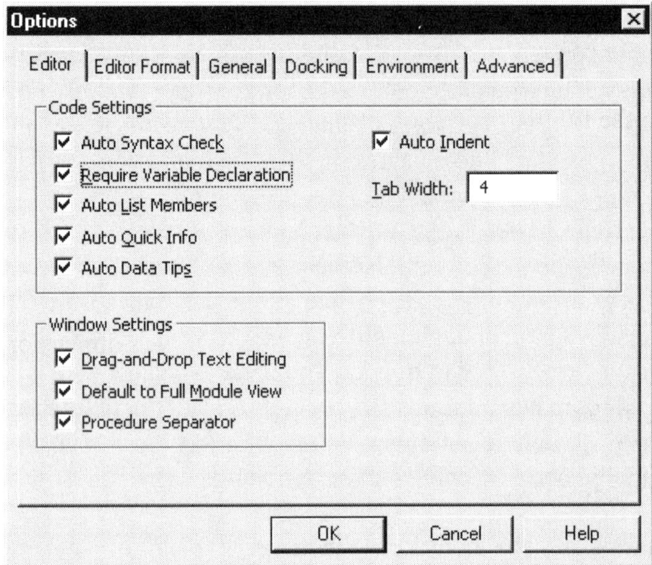

Figure 1.5 The Options dialog window where Require Variable Declaration resides

application needs to be defined. This is helpful, because when you compile your application, if you've used a variable that has not been previously defined, or you've mistyped a variable, the compiler will detect the error. It's better to find simple mistakes like this before the program compiles versus finding them at run-time.

Arrays Start at Zero

An array is a group of common elements accessed through a common variable name. Each element is referenced with a number called an index. Array elements start with zero (0). When you define your array, it would look something like this:

```
Dim sStudentName(10) as String
```

This defines the variable sStudentName to contain 11 elements. Why 11 instead of 10? Since arrays start with 0, that element is included in the total number of elements. In other words, it's 0 to 10 inclusive.

Why is this important to know? When you work with controls like the list box or combo box, every element contained within them is part of an error. To find out how many elements are in one of those controls, you use the **ListCount** property of the control. This returns the number of elements in the array. Now when you use that value within a **For-Next** loop to process array information as in the following code, you're going to received a "Subscript out of range" error.

```
For x = 0 To lstStudents.ListCount
    If sStudentName(x) = txtStudentName Then
        MsgBox "The Student is Enrolled"
    End If
Next
```

That's because the sStudentName array was dimensioned to 10, not 11. The way to avoid the error is to subtract one from the total returned from the **ListCount** property, as shown in the following code:

```
For x = 0 To lstStudents.ListCount - 1
If sStudentName(x) = txtStudentName Then
        MsgBox "The Student is Enrolled"
    End If
Next
```

Watch Your DIM Statements

A common error when defining variables occurs when you put several variables on one line. For example:

```
Dim nVar1, nVar2, nVar3 As Integer
```

You might think that all the variables will be assigned as an integer data type, but the reality of it is that only the last variable, nVar3, is an integer. The other two are defined as variant data types. A variant data type is an undeclared data type. They act like any of the Visual Basic data types, such as string, Boolean, and currency, but they can also contain objects, Null, and Empty.

The correct way to define variables on one line would be like this:

```
Dim nVar1 As Integer, nVar2 As Integer, nVar3 As Integer
```

For code readability, this is not a recommended coding format. It would be better to define each variable on its own line.

Dollar Signs in Functions

If you've looked through some existing code, either in books, articles, or programs, you might have noticed some functions that have the dollar-sign character as part of the function name, like **Left$**, **Right$**, and **Mid$**. If you peruse through more recent manuals and documentation, you will find that these functions are still referenced, but the references don't use the dollar-sign character. The core feature of the functions is the same, which is to process the information and return a value. The significant difference is the value that is returned. If the function without the dollar-sign character is used, for example, **Mid**, it takes a variant argument and returns a variant. The function with the dollar-sign character (**Mid$**) takes a string argument and returns a string.

Having the functions accept variant arguments and return variant values is useful for client-side Internet development, because both JavaScript and VBScript only accept variant data types. However, for Windows-based application development, having information stored as a variant and used by string data types might cause confusion during development, as well as affect application performance. If the data types of the input and the resulting output variables don't match the type of function, the compiler may need to perform a data-type conversion before and after the function is used.

Summary

Applications are usually developed to solve a problem. To determine how sophisticated the user interface needs to be, you need to identify who the users are going to be.

After finding out who is going to use the application, you need to scope it out. Find out what it is going to be used for, why it is being created, whether it is replacing an existing process or application, and what functions are necessary. Build a document that lays out the information so that everyone involved is on the same page regarding the application requirements. By documenting this information, you reduce project scope "creep." It is important for you to stay focused on the functions and features at hand, and not to try to make the best application in the world. That will come over time during the life span of the application.

When creating the development schedule, it should be aggressive but not so overwhelming that you set unreasonable expectations from the client's point of view or that you make your developers work harder than they probably already are.

Following these guidelines will not guarantee you will have a 100 percent successful project, but it will help identify fallacies in your current development process and areas where you might need improvement.

CHAPTER 2

Software Release Methodology

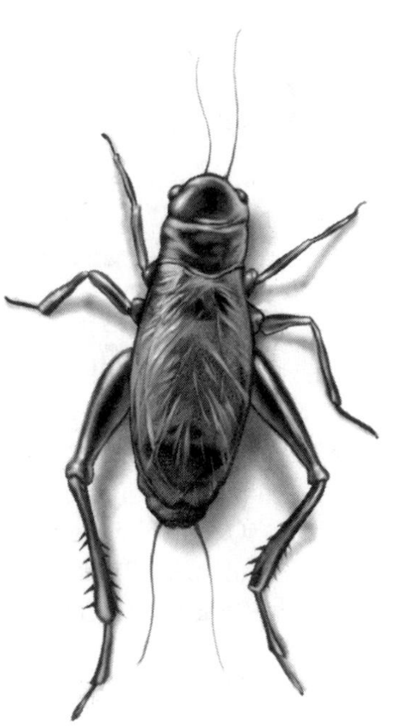

You and your team slaved for the last several months on your product. Before coding began, you actually took the time to gather requirements from the user community, held JAD (joint application design) sessions, prototyped the application and removed all the gray areas from your design document, and constructed your application. Your team held impromptu and formal meetings when necessary. All of the developers agreed on the coding style and naming convention before one line of code was written. You held your code reviews, you met with the users on design issues, and you had them test the program for several months. The users who tested the software became satisfied with the product, and they gave the "go-ahead" to install and deploy it on the server and signed off on your approval document. You scheduled time with the network administrator and database administrator and told them that your project that was residing on the test application and database servers was ready to be moved to the production server after hours. The application was then moved into production without a problem, and everyone gave each other a "high-five" and went home happy.

The next day your customers come in and they receive an e-mail informing them that the long-awaited application is ready for them to use. The e-mail includes instructions on how to access and use the program, and mentions that formal training will occur in a couple of days. Shortly after everyone starts using the application, though, your team starts getting phone calls about why feature "X" doesn't seem to be working, or why feature "Y" isn't giving the right calculation back. Some people are complaining that the program won't launch on their systems. All of a sudden you want to be a two-year-old, holding your hands to your ears and yelling "No! No! No! No!" up and down the halls. Your best laid plans just took a nosedive. So what do you do?

First, remember the infamous phrase from Douglas Adams' *The Hitchhiker's Guide to the Galaxy*, which is "Don't panic." Panicking never does any good. It might feel good for a moment, but the problem will still persist. Take a step back and wonder what could have gone wrong. Tactically, you did nothing wrong. You made sure that all your developers where in sync with the project plan and scope. During the code reviews everything eventually turned into very readable and sound code. You had a handful of key users test the software. They found some problems with the program, but your team eventually got them resolved. The key users used the system the way they would have, had the program been in production. So what did you miss?

One of the most overlooked software deployment strategies is doing a phased implementation. A phased implementation is when you have both the existing system and the new system running in tandem for several months, so you can ensure that the new system is capturing and producing the same results as the existing system. Also, by having the two applications running in tandem, people get used to the application and they use it as it was intended. They will make mistakes on it, ask questions about how things work, and so on. If you restrict testing to the key users, chances are that they won't use it like a "real" user would. When experts use a beta application, they have a tendency to handle it with kid gloves. They don't make mistakes in data entry, click the Commit button when the form isn't completely filled out, and so on. Why do you think companies like Microsoft spend thousands of dollars to have people beta test their applications for them? Regardless of the number of developers and testers that they have, they can't possibly test every feature of an application. Even their system is not foolproof, but the majority of the errors will be detected.

In this chapter, we will discuss topics you should consider during your software deployment cycle. Figure 2-1 provides a visual representation of the development hierarchy. There are essentially four phases to a development cycle: planning, analysis, design, and construction and testing. Each section in the figure represents the amount of time that should be taken for each phase. As described in Chapter 1, planning your application before any development is done is crucial for the success of the project. If sufficient planning is done up-front, analysis should take less time. The design phase of the application should be easy to accomplish if enough information is uncovered during the planning and analysis phases. The construction and testing phase, theoretically, should not take any longer than your design phase. Unfortunately, this hierarchy would be better represented as a volcano rather than a pyramid. Anyone who has been part of software development for any period of time knows that when you reach the construction and testing phase, the volcano blows its top. As the application gets released to the user community, things get scattered in different directions, and feedback on the application starts trickling down like lava.

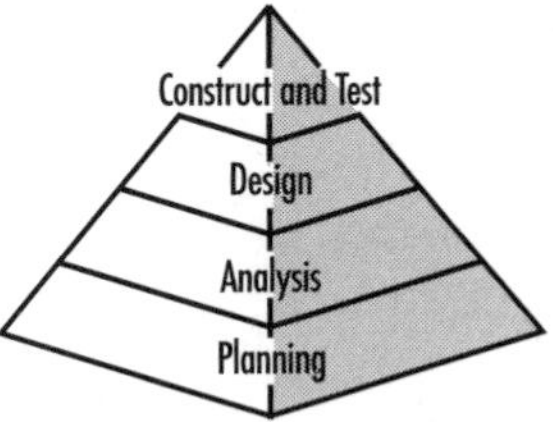

Figure 2.1 Software development hierarchy

When Things Go Wrong

"Programs do not acquire bugs as people acquire germs, by hanging around other buggy programs. Programmers must insert them." —Harlan Mills

According to a leading authority on software quality, a bug is introduced once in every 100 lines of code in small applications. In large applications, the rate at which bugs get introduced into your system is increased. Armed with this knowledge, you shouldn't be too surprised if users encounter problems with your application. It's not an attack on you or your team, however it's still disheartening to find out that no matter how hard you tried to ensure you released a bug-free application, problems still happen.

Knowing that problems are bound to happen, the best thing you and your team can do is prepare for them, which means having a plan of attack. The following four topics will be discussed, which will help prepare you for the problems calls you might receive:

- Error tracking
- Iterative construction and testing
- Testing your software three different ways
- Using alpha and beta versions before releasing a production version

Error Tracking

Often during the development process, unavoidable errors occur. When errors occur, the big question all developers ask themselves is "Is this a logical error or an environment error?" Most logical errors are due to incorrect formulas, wrong seed number (such as when you use February 29, 1999 instead of February 28, 1999), and so on. An environment error is caused by something other than the code itself. For example, the program could be working, but the application didn't install all the necessary resource files onto the customer's system. Or, the user could have entered a wrong value and the program didn't handle the exception correctly. Or, the program shows 1900 instead of 2000 in the year whenever a calendar look-up occurs, which could be due to the Windows operating system's Regional Settings being set for a two-digit year instead of four-digits.

Regardless of the nature of the error, you need to identify whether the error is reproducible. Having to reproduce unexpected software behavior is a time-consuming, tedious, and very difficult task. During the reproduction process, software developers must try to emulate the user's actions, data, and environment.

When the errors are reproducible, diagnosing how they occurred becomes easier. It's when you can't replicate the error that you start feeling like you're looking for a needle in a haystack.

Software Problem Requests

As the user community starts to use the application, errors and issues with the application will start to arise. Your help desk will start to get a flood of calls for assistance. Shortly after you release the application, the questions are going to range from "How do you use this program?" to "I'm not getting the results that I was expecting."

The first reaction most developers have when they hear that there are problems with their system is disbelief. "How can anything possibly have gone wrong?" is a common response. After the initial shock wears off, developers and analysts calm down, collect the problems and issues, and then attempt to provide fixes for them.

One problem with this technique is that there usually isn't an easy way to track the activities of the developers and analysts. In order to avoid having developers issue quick fixes or "code bandages," planning is required. The first thing that you need to identify is the nature of the problem. A number of problems are user-related, others might be related to an actual problem in the application, and others might be simply the result of user expectations, and should be categorized as feature requests.

Most information systems departments have a help desk in place to track problem requests. This is a great first level of defense for routing complaints to the technicians, keeping track of calls that have been opened and closed, and building a knowledge base for frequently asked questions. The terms "open" and "closed" calls are help-desk jargon that relate to the state of the problem call assigned to a technician. If a call is open, it means the technician is aware of the problem and is in the process of getting it resolved. If the call is closed, the technician has resolved the issue and no further follow-up is needed. The problem and the resolution, along with any other support information, should be documented for each call. With this information entered into the help-desk system, you build a central repository of troubleshooting knowledge. If a problem call comes in that is similar to another one that has been resolved, its possible that the help-desk person might be able to assist the caller without involving a technician.

As problems come in to the help desk, the problem requests are triaged and assigned to the appropriate technician. The technician will contact the user to get more information about the problem and then determine the course of action for

resolving the issue. Often, the technician assigned to the problem call is one of the developers. When Microsoft releases a new version of a product, many of the developers are required to handle the support phones for the product for the first two to three months. Who's better equipped to understand what might be wrong with the application than the developers who wrote it? The developers can find the answers to the following questions:

- Is the problem the result of user error?
- Is the problem replicable, and is it truly an application error?
- Is the problem really a misunderstanding by the user (should the "problem" be classified as a feature request), or was a feature or function not implemented completely?

A help-desk system is a great way to keep track of open and closed issues. It provides a repository for building a knowledge base of solutions to problems that have been identified and resolved. However, if the problem is an actual application problem or a feature request, these systems tend to fall short. Generic help-desk systems are designed to be open-ended with no real direction other than capturing problem requests and their resolutions. Many do not have any functionality for bug, defect, or feature-request tracking.

A solution that a lot of organizations implement is a software problem request system. A software problem request (SPR) system's focus is different from a help-desk application, though its interface may capture similar information. SPR systems capture information like who originated the call, to whom was it assigned, what was its severity, and so on. Figure 2-2 shows an example SPR system built using Microsoft Access. In addition, they manage bugs, features, and request tracking, and many can be linked with your software version control tool.

If it's a true problem with the application, and you can identify the developer who worked on that part of the code, you can assign the SPR to that developer. You would provide information on how to replicate the error, what the expected results should have been, and what the results actually are. You can also assign a level of importance indicating how urgently the correction is needed.

Using a system like this will help you keep track of the software problems that have been logged, but it will also make sure that the problems are getting closed in a timely manner. You can also determine which developer is getting the most trouble calls assigned to them.

Why is tracking the software problems so important? This information should be used as part of your lessons-learned follow-up meetings. The information captured should provide you with enough feedback to determine whether ample

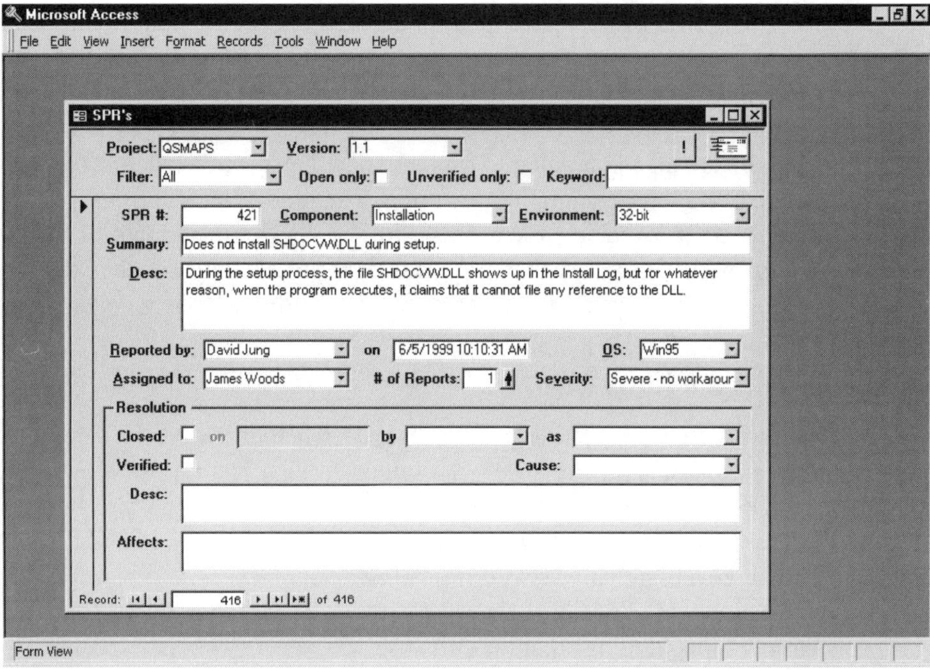

Figure 2.2 An example interface for a software problem request system

functional, unit, and regression testing was done, whether the developers understood what they were coding, whether the problems were related to user complications, and so on.

Iterative Construction and Testing

At one point during the development cycle, milestones should be set so that all the components that are being worked on can be tested. The developers should be testing them during this time, so the individual components should be error-free. This phase is an integration test to ensure that all the components that are being worked on still work when combined together. The reason to periodically construct and test the application during this cycle is to ensure that the application still works. It's easier to detect errors and fix them early on than to wait until the entire application is completed. When you catch the errors early, the code is still fresh in the developer's mind, and he or she can resolve the issue more quickly than when trying to remember what they did months earlier.

Using Microsoft as an example, during the development cycle, whether it's a major release or a feature release, at the end of the day all the developers are instructed to check their code into the main file server. In the middle of the night, automated systems build new executables that are sent to the test servers. The test servers are then instructed to run automated test scripts against the application and generate reports on the execution. The reports are distributed to the program managers, who review the results with the development team. If there are any problems at this point, they are identified immediately and they can be resolved before the bugs get integrated too deeply within the source code.

Testing All Software Three Ways

When it comes to testing your software—whether it's before a company-wide release or a revision release—it's important that you follow your standard testing procedures. The first thing you should do is *regression testing*. Its purpose is to make sure that the software works the way it's supposed to and that you didn't break anything that was working before.

Another kind of testing is *stress testing*. This type of testing is where you throw input at things that the software was never explicitly specified to handle. Here are some ideas for stress testing:

- If a field can hold 10 characters, type 20 characters or none.
- If a field is supposed to hold a number, enter characters.
- Enter punctuation where none is expected, especially in name fields.
- Enter reserved characters, including plus signs, ampersands, and equals signs.
- If a number is supposed to be positive, make it negative or zero.
- Enter numbers with embedded commas or dollar signs.
- Bring in people who don't like computers, and let them work out their frustrations.

This may sound absurd, but you would be surprised how many errors you can prevent by employing this technique.

The third kind of testing is *load testing*. This only applies if your application is going to be used by multiple people at the same time. It's rare that a business application that goes through a formal development process is built solely for a single user, or is not to be used in concurrency at some point. During this type of testing, you might be able to gauge where potential bottlenecks in your code might be, or where network resources are really going to be depleted. Here are some ideas for load testing:

- Have a group of users search for a number of records.
- Have some testers do data entry while others are doing data queries.
- Have some testers do data entry while reports are being generated.
- Try having two people click the Commit button at the same time, and see what happens.

In a multiuser, multicenter environment, this form of testing is often overlooked because of time and resource limits.

Releasing Alpha and Beta Test Versions

Once the product seems to work, and it passes the developer's tests, give it to a friendly in-house test team. Depending on the software, the testers can be administrative staff, fellow developers, and so on. Ask them to interact with the software and try to break it. A bunch of twelve-year-olds are an excellent resource for alpha test teams. They can usually figure out most systems and can break nearly anything.

Keep written records of the defects found during alpha testing, as well as recommendations from the testers for improvements. Fix the problems and run a full set of regression tests to make sure nothing broke in one part while you were fixing another part.

After you and your alpha testers are satisfied that the product works, you are ready to move on to the next phase, the beta test. If you're working on a package that your company is planning to sell, offer it to one client at a discounted rate. Otherwise, release it to a very small group of potential users of the program. Make it absolutely clear that this software is going out for its first test. Give the client some customer trouble reports (CTRs) and make sure they know how to fill them out. Consider putting the CTR online, so visitors can report problems and so you can integrate the information into your SPR system. Analyze the error log daily, to see whether the software is malfunctioning.

If you have ever been on a software company's beta testing team, you'll know that it can be a lot of work. The more of the error-reporting and error-tracking function you can automate, the easier it will be. Make sure that you offer technical support to your testing community. Remember that they are helping you make a better product.

When you select the people to be beta testers, it's a good idea to take the types of computers they are using into account. Even though you might be within the same organization, and the company has a policy that you should not install any unauthorized software on the computer, strange configurations tend to creep in anyway. These unusual configurations often cause havoc when it comes to troubleshooting, because there's an unknown element involved.

Software Rollouts

When it comes to rolling out your software, you need to consider how to integrate all of the features in each release. The first release of the software should include the entire feature set that you promised to the clients. During the analysis phase, you should have identified which features are part of which components, rather than just lumping them all into one program. The common method is to combine your functions into components and integrate them into one main controlling program. However, if you integrate the software in the wrong order, it will become difficult to code, test, and especially debug. If the application doesn't work, you need to figure out where it doesn't work. The more intricate the components, the more time it will take you to track down coding problems.

There are two different methods of handling feature and component integration: phased integration and incremental integration. The *phased integration* method historically has been the most common method. The process was to design, code, test, and debug each component that the program required, then combine them into the main program stub, and then test and debug the entire system. The problem with this approach was that even though each component might have worked during the individual unit tests, unforeseen problems would inevitably occur during integration. The most common problems would generally be variable declarations, passing arguments to functions, and error trapping.

When the client/server method of software development was made popular, back in the mid-1990s, it became apparent that the phased integration approach wasn't the best method of software integration after all. They realized that their mainframe developer counterparts were right all along with the *incremental integration* method. This method is basically a one-component-at-a-time approach to software development. Basically, developers build small, functional components, test and debug them as thoroughly as they can, and then integrate them into the main stub program that holds the entire application together, one at a time. Each component is then tested and debugged against the main stub. Once the integration of one component is completed, the next component is integrated into the application and the testing and debugging process is done all over again.

The incremental integration approach definitely has its place in software development, and if the project manager plans it carefully, you can build the application in a shorter time period than a phased approach. Errors are easier to localize to the particular function and they can be corrected quickly. Each unit of the system is tested a lot more thoroughly than during a phased integration approach, and when one component is being integrated and tested, you can save time designing the next part of the system with lessons learned from the previous component's construction. The caveat is that the testing and debugging might take longer than expected, thus producing a bottleneck and slowing down the next step. Regardless of what integration approach you choose, it's important that you keep track of each build and release number.

Release Numbering

Release numbering is a mechanism for identifying the product's functional state. There is no standard release numbering technique used in the industry. For example, Microsoft originally released the products that made up Microsoft Office at different times, so their release numbers were different. When Microsoft Word for Windows was first released, its release number was 1.0, and then it became 1.1 due to some corrections, and version 2.0 then added a whole new feature and functionality set to the program. When Microsoft released Office 4.0, all the version numbers of the products leaped from whatever they were before to version 6.0. Microsoft did this because they wanted all of their Office products to have the same release number. They chose 6.0 because Microsoft Excel for Windows was at version 5.0 before Office 4.0 was released.

Numbering Syntax

Each individual release of a product is viewed as a unique state in the product's life, so each release should have a different number. The most commonly accepted numbering syntax is to break the release number into three parts: major release number, feature release number, and defect repair number. Major release numbers identify a major increase in the product's functionality for the customer. A change of the major release may be due to the introduction of a new set of functionality that makes the product seem like a new product.

The feature release number gets incremented to identify when a product feature has been added or significant modifications to the original specifications have been made. This is sometimes referred to as a minor release. If you're developing commercial software, feature releases can be an important mechanism for keeping up with competing products between major releases.

Defect repair numbers are used to identify the level of defect maintenance that has been performed on a release. Defect repair releases are important for getting fixes to your clients and for minimizing the customer's support calls.

Incrementing the Release Number

Incrementing release numbers is a very subjective process. Not every developer or software publisher agrees on how it should be done. Traditionally, a release number starts with setting the major release number as 1 (for the first release), followed by a 0 for the feature number and 0 for the defect repair number, resulting in release number 1.0.0. If a new release is issued due to defects, the defect repair number should be incremented by 1, resulting in release 1.0.1. As more defects are found and fixed, the defect repair number should be incremented. To avoid incrementing the defect repair number for each defect fixed, the best process is to increment it only when a group of defects are corrected, unless only one defect is corrected in the new release. When a new feature is added to the program, the second field should be incremented by 1, and the defect repair number should be reset to 0. The new release number would then be 1.1.0.

When a new release is issued, the release number is incremented to the next number. However, there is debate as to what the feature release number should be. Most developers adopt the strategy of resetting the feature release number to 0 because they argue that you really are "resetting" the features of the program. There are developers and software publishers who feel that a major release doesn't constitute a reset of feature releases, though. Therefore, if the release number of a program was 1.1.0 and a new major release was issued, they would have the release number become 2.2.0. The philosophy behind this is that a major release introduces features that were not in the original specification, almost making it a completely new product. The feature release number is incremented because a major new release adds new features.

Within Visual Basic, you can set the release number of the application in the Make tab of the Project Properties dialog box, as illustrated in Figure 2-3. You can either set the release number for the project manually or mark the Auto Increment check box so that the release number increments each time you generate a new executable.

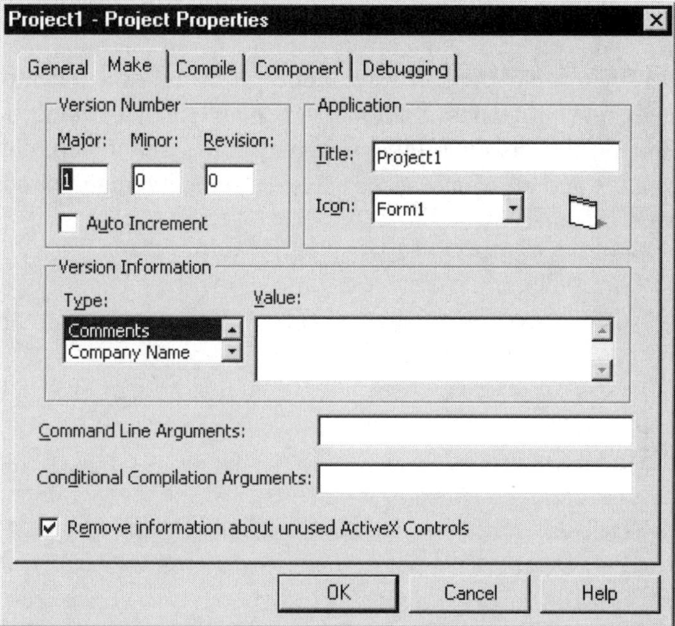

Figure 2.3 The Project Properties Make tab, displaying the Version Number information

Summary

The process of issuing software releases to your clients needs to be planned by the project manager just like any other phase of the project. Once the software has been introduced into the user community, you will need to keep track of any trouble calls that come in to your help desk. Many help desk systems are great for capturing basic trouble calls, but when it comes to tracking problems within a program and assigning them to technicians or developers, they fall short. Software problem request (SPR) systems, like PVCS Professional and SQA Suite, help you track feature problems and issues with each release.

As you correct and deploy fixes and patches, it's important that you keep track of them by recording the release number in your SPR system as a milestone. This way you can trace fixed errors within a given release.

When deploying software, it doesn't matter how much planning and testing you and your team does, it's never enough. What you need to keep in mind is to not panic, to fix the problems as they come, and to deploy patches and fixes as quickly and efficiently as possible, to avoid having your customers lose faith in your product.

PART II

Debugging VB

CHAPTER 3

Debugging Tools

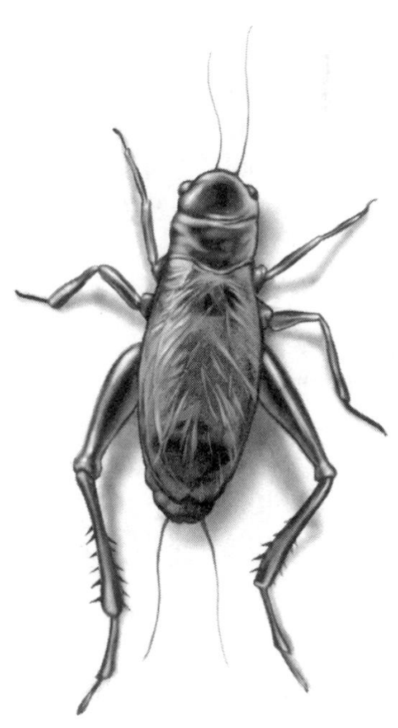

"Don't debug me, man." —Corny joke by anonymous bug

If your code works the first time, every time, then you do not need to read this chapter. In fact, you do not need to read this book. However, we lesser mortals who have not attained code-writing perfection often need to figure out why our code does not work. This chapter will teach you how to "debug" your code so that you can quickly diagnose and fix the problem.

The term "debugging" means, as the prefix "de" and the included word "bug" suggest, ridding your program of "bugs." A "bug" is simply an error in your code. The consequences of the error may be that your application produces illogical results (2 + 2 = 22), terminates prematurely, or does not run at all.

The origin of the term "bug" is in dispute. One story is that during the pre-PC era, when mainframe computers ruled the earth, a mainframe was producing illogical results. The programmers checked and rechecked their punch cards but could find no errors. In desperation, they opened up the mainframe. Inside they saw a small bug fried on one of the circuits.

While we have found loose bolts rolling around in computers we have purchased, it is unlikely that a bug fricassee is the cause of your code not working (although it is a good excuse to give your boss). Fortunately, Visual Basic gives you many debugging tools for finding the bugs in your code. However, as you were warned in Chapter 1:

"A fool and his tool is a faster fool." —Unknown author

Indeed, debugging tools, like other tools, only have value in skilled hands, or in the case of programming, skilled minds. Debugging is detective work. The debugging tools make your detective work easier and faster. Therefore, this chapter will explain not only the Visual Basic debugging tools but also strategies for using them.

When Bugs Bite

How do you know if your code has a bug? Like bed bugs in your bed, bugs in your code are generally undetectable until the bug announces its presence by biting you. Bugs can bite at any time, but usually show themselves at one of the following three successive stages of code development:

- **Stage 1** Your code will not compile. This often is because the name of a variable or control is misspelled or because of a mistake in syntax.

- **Stage 2** Your code will compile, but when you run your application, it terminates due to an unhandled run-time error. For example, your code is supposed to loop through a list box, removing, one at a time, six people listed in the list box. However, the program terminates with the error "array index out of bounds."
- **Stage 3** Your code compiles and your application runs, but a logical error occurs. For example, your code is supposed to print out the names of six people in a list, but instead it prints the first name in the list six times.

Debugging tools are used in stages 2 and 3. You cannot use the debugging tools until your code compiles and runs, at least for one statement. Chapter 1 explains how to avoid the misspelling of variables (by using the **Option Explicit** statement) and other problems that may cause your code not to compile.

In this chapter, we'll look at three debugging examples. Freeze-frame debugging shows you how to debug a program that has stopped, usually due to a run-time error. Real-time debugging shows you how to debug a program while it is running, either to find the bug before it causes a run-time error or to determine why a logical error is occurring. Step-by-step debugging shows you how to step through your code, statement by statement, if necessary, to diagnose the cause of a run-time or logical error.

Visual Basic Debugging IDE

All three debugging examples access the debugging tools through the Visual Basic Integrated Development Environment (IDE). The Visual Basic IDE has three menus and one toolbar that you will often use to debug your applications. These are the Run, Debug, and View menus and the Standard and Debug toolbars.

Figure 3-1 shows the Run menu and the Standard toolbar.

Table 3-1 lists the commands and corresponding functions of the Run menu. The Standard toolbar has controls, similar to those on the VCR, for start/continue, break, and end.

Figure 3-2 shows the Debug menu and the Debug toolbar. The Step Into, Step Over, Step Out, Set Next Statement, and Show Next Statement commands on the Debug menu are described in Table 3-5 later in the chapter, and are used in the step-by-step debugging example. Breakpoints stop program execution, and they are discussed in the real-time debugging example. The Toggle Breakpoint command creates a breakpoint at the statement where the mouse cursor is, or if a breakpoint is already there, it removes it. Clear All Breakpoints does exactly

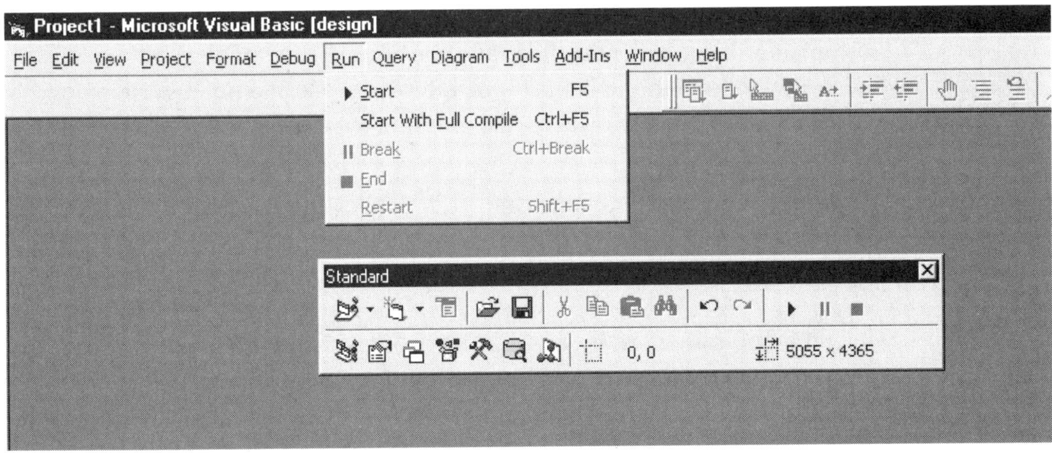

Figure 3.1 The Run menu and Standard toolbar

what its name suggests. The Watch commands are used to view the values of variables or properties. Add Watch, Edit Watch, and Quick Watch are discussed and used in the step-by-step debugging example.

The Debug toolbar has, in addition to the buttons corresponding to items on the Debug menu, the VCR-like controls for start/continue, break, and end. If the Debug toolbar does not appear, you can make it visible by selecting Toolbars from the View menu and checking Debug, as shown in Figure 3-3.

Finally, the View menu has commands to display the Immediate window, Locals window, Watch window and Call Stack window.

Command	Function
Start or Continue	Starts execution of the program. The command changes from Start to Continue when the Break command (described below) is executed.
Start With Full Compile	Starts execution of the program after compiling the entire program, not just the portion necessary to commence execution of the program.
Break	Halts execution of the program. Program execution can be started again with the Continue command.
End	Stops execution of the program.
Restart	Restarts execution of the program from the beginning.

Table 3.1 Run Menu Commands

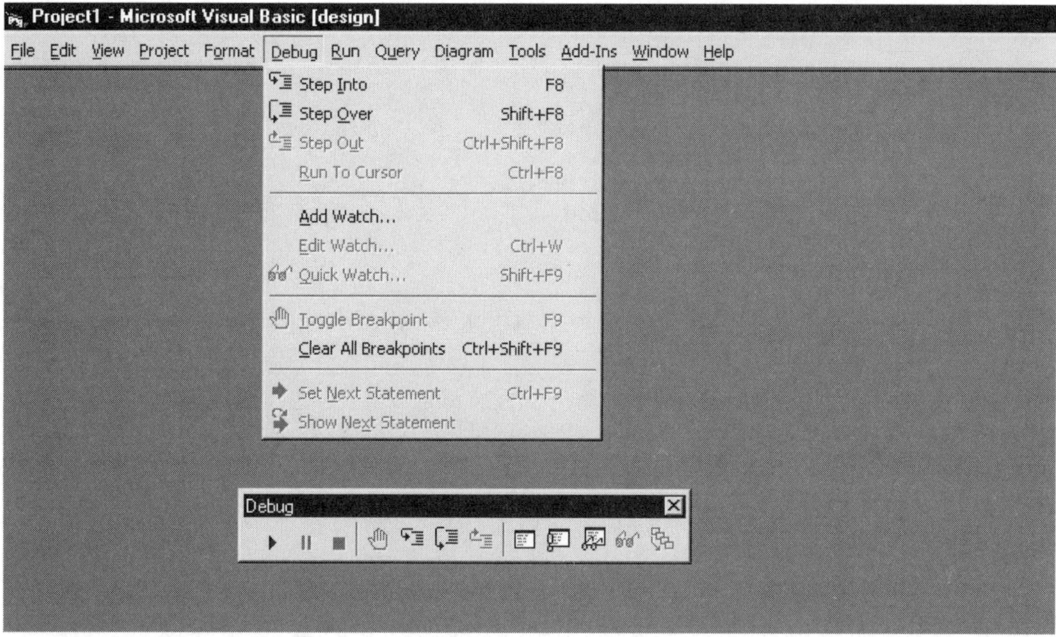

Figure 3.2 The Debug menu and Debug toolbar

Freeze-Frame Debugging

The title of the main form of this project, "Welcome to Error-Free Programming," is a wish, not a warranty. This program has more errors per line of code than most. However, debugging it will demonstrate Visual Basic's debugging tools and some strategies for using them effectively.

Build the Project

The number of steps required to build this project are far fewer than the number of errors it contains:

1. Start a new project, Standard EXE.
2. Add to the default form the controls described in Table 3-2. Figure 3-4 shows how the form appears in design mode.
3. Add the following code to the load event of the form to populate the list box with the names of six people:

```
Private Sub Form_Load()
    With lstPeople
        .AddItem "Al"
        .AddItem "Bill"
        .AddItem "Chuck"
        .AddItem "Dave"
        .AddItem "Ed"
        .AddItem "Fred"
    End With
End Sub
```

4. Add the following code to the Click event of the **cmdRemove** command button:

```
Private Sub cmdRemove_Click()
    lstPeople.RemoveItem lstPeople.ListIndex
End Sub
```

That's all it takes to build the project. Figure 3-5 shows the project in run mode.

Synopsis of the Project

The **RemoveItem** method of the list box removes, from the list box, the item whose index is its parameter. The **ListIndex** property of the list box contains the index of the item in the list box that has been selected. This index is zero-based. Thus, the index of the first item is 0, the index of the second item is 1, and so on. If the user of your application selects the second item, the parameter 1 is passed to the **RemoveItem** method, which then removes the second item. Indeed, when you run the project and select the second item and click the Remove command button, poor Bill (not Gates of course) disappears from the list box.

The Bug

One of your first lessons as a programmer is that your application's users often do not even read, much less follow, instructions, or perform tasks in the right order. Therefore, you have to anticipate possibilities, such as the user clicking the Remove button without first selecting an item in the list box. If you do this, you

Name	Type	Purpose
lstPeople	List box	Lists people
cmdRemove	Command button	Removes the selected item from the list
cmdRemoveAll	Command button	Removes all items from the list

Table 3.2 Form Controls for Remove Project

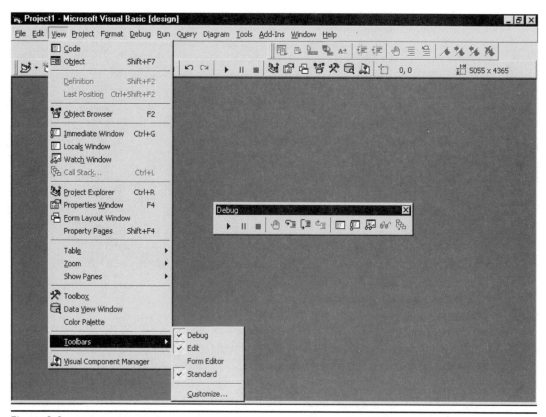

Figure 3.3 Making the Debug toolbar visible

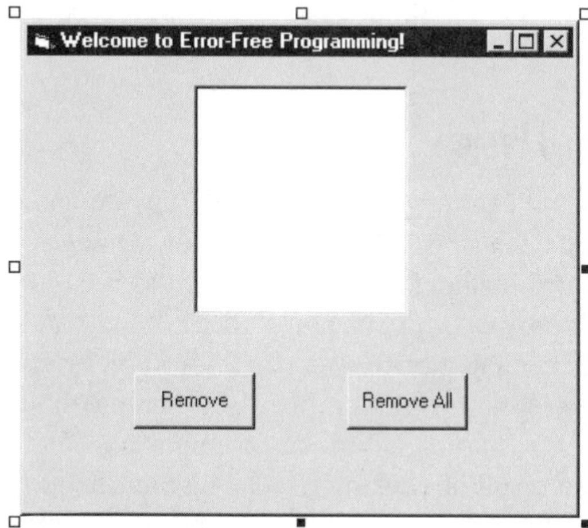

Figure 3.4 The form in design mode

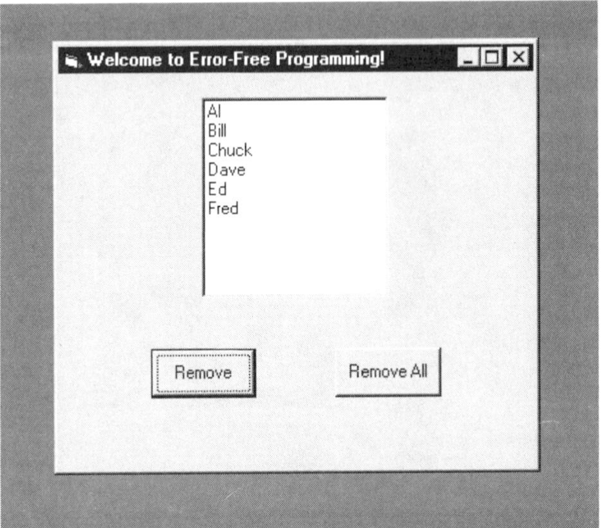

Figure 3.5 The form in run mode

will find that your application terminates with the message, "Run-time error '5': Invalid procedure call or argument," as shown in Figure 3-6.

Distributing applications that terminate with run-time errors will not put you first in line for the Programmer's Hall of Fame. More likely, it will put you in the unemployment line. This is not a problem if your idea of the "Great Outdoors" is standing at the end of a freeway off-ramp with a cardboard sign proclaiming your willingness to program for food. Otherwise, you will want to rid your program of this bug.

Debugging a Halted Project

Now that you are properly motivated, how do you debug a program that has come to a dead stop? As usual, the error message is not much help. You already know that something in the code is invalid because the program terminated with the error. However, the message does not tell you what is invalid.

The error dialog box gives you three choices: End, Debug, or Help. End just ends the program with no further information about the error. That does you no good. Help, as usual, is little or no help at all. That leaves Debug. Figure 3-7 shows the result of clicking the Debug button: the line of code in the **cmdRemove_Click** procedure that calls the **RemoveItem** method of the list box is highlighted.

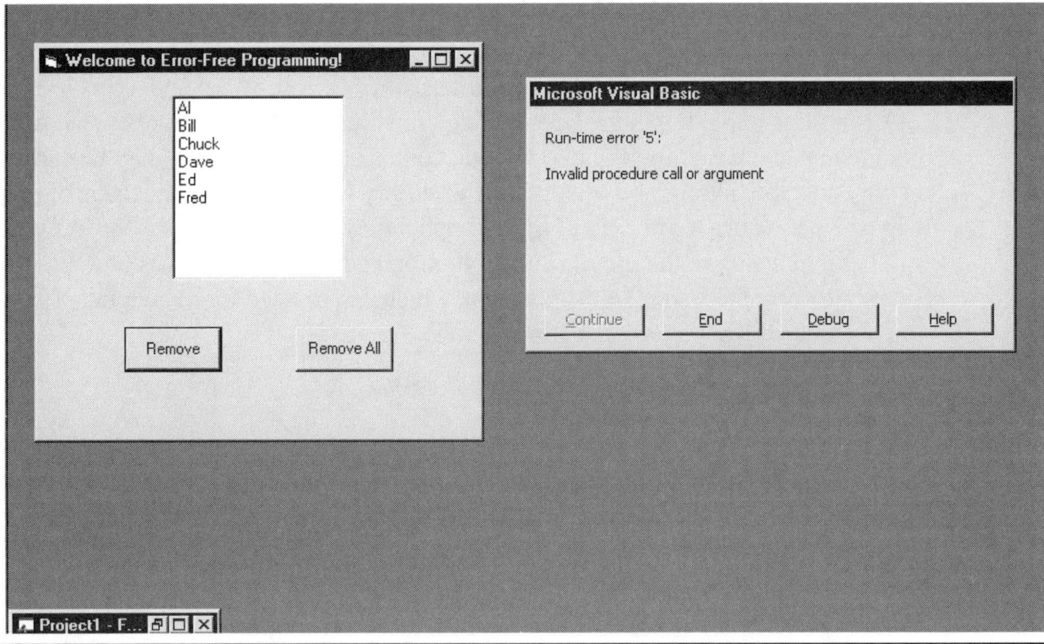

Figure 3.6 Error message when Remove button is clicked without selecting an item

Project1 - Form1 (Code)

cmdRemove | Click

```
Private Sub cmdRemove_Click()
    lstPeople.RemoveItem lstPeople.ListIndex
End Sub

Private Sub cmdRemoveAll_Click()
Dim j As Integer, x As Integer
For j = 0 To lstPeople.ListCount - 1
    Debug.Print j
    Debug.Print lstPeople.ListCount
    lstPeople.RemoveItem j
Next
```

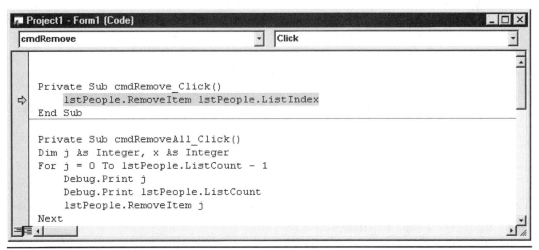

Figure 3.7 Code highlighted after clicking the Debug button in the run-time error dialog box

Now what? The syntax of the highlighted line of code is correct. Otherwise, the code would not have compiled. Yet something is wrong, or the program would not have terminated with a run-time error.

Visual Basic highlights the line of code on which the error occurred. That does not mean that the highlighted line of code contains a bug. The bug may be earlier in the code; the highlighted line of code is simply where the consequences of the bug (the premature termination of your application) took place.

The termination of the program at the highlighted line of code gives us a snapshot, or freeze-frame, of the program, which can be used for debugging. The statement at which the program stopped was:

```
lstPeople.RemoveItem lstPeople.ListIndex
```

The logical starting point of our investigation, therefore, is to determine what the value of the **ListIndex** property of the list box was when this statement executed. This value can be determined using Auto Data Tips, the Immediate window or the Locals window.

Using Auto Data Tips

Auto Data Tips are easy to use but often overlooked. Their function is similar to a ToolTip. A ToolTip is a small text box that describes the purpose of the toolbar button under the mouse pointer. Similarly, an Auto Data Tip displays a small text box that contains the value of a property, variable, or other statement under the mouse pointer.

You enable the Auto Data Tips feature by choosing Options from the Tools menu to open the Options dialog box, and then on the Editor tab check Auto Data Tips, as shown in Figure 3-8.

Figure 3-9 shows that when you hold the mouse pointer over **lstPeople.ListIndex** after the program stops, the Auto Data Tip gives the value as –1.

This explains why the error occurred. The parameter of the **RemoveItem** method specifies the index of the item to be removed. An error results if the index is not valid, and an index is not valid if there is no item at that index. Since the index of items in a list box is zero-based, there is no item at –1.

The value of the **ListIndex** property is –1 because no item is selected in the list. Therefore, passing **lstPeople.ListIndex** as a parameter to **lstPeople.RemoveItem** when no item is selected results in an error.

Using the Immediate Window

You also can use the Immediate window to determine the value of **lstPeople.ListIndex**. The Immediate window is identified by its highly original caption "Immediate," as shown in Figure 3-10.

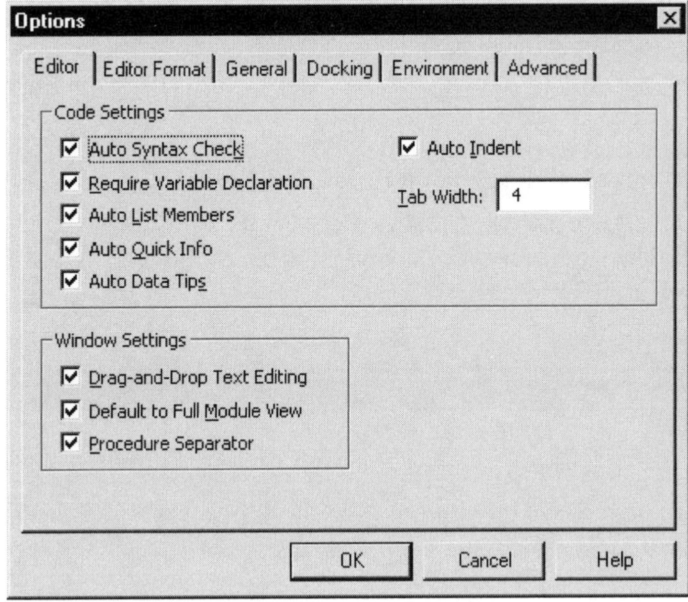

Figure 3.8 Enabling Auto Data Tips

You can open the Immediate window either by choosing Immediate Window from the View menu, by pressing the keyboard shortcut CTRL-G, or by clicking the Immediate Window button on the Debug toolbar.

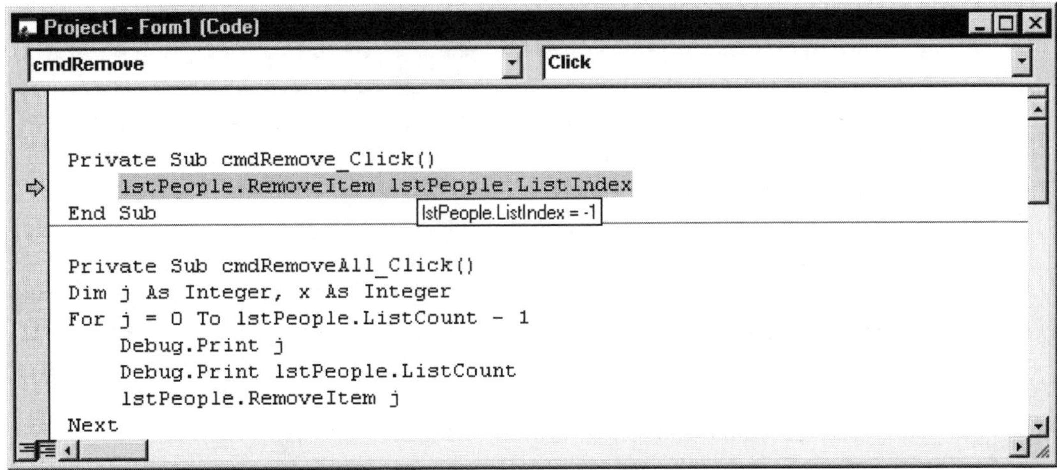

Figure 3.9 Auto Data Tip

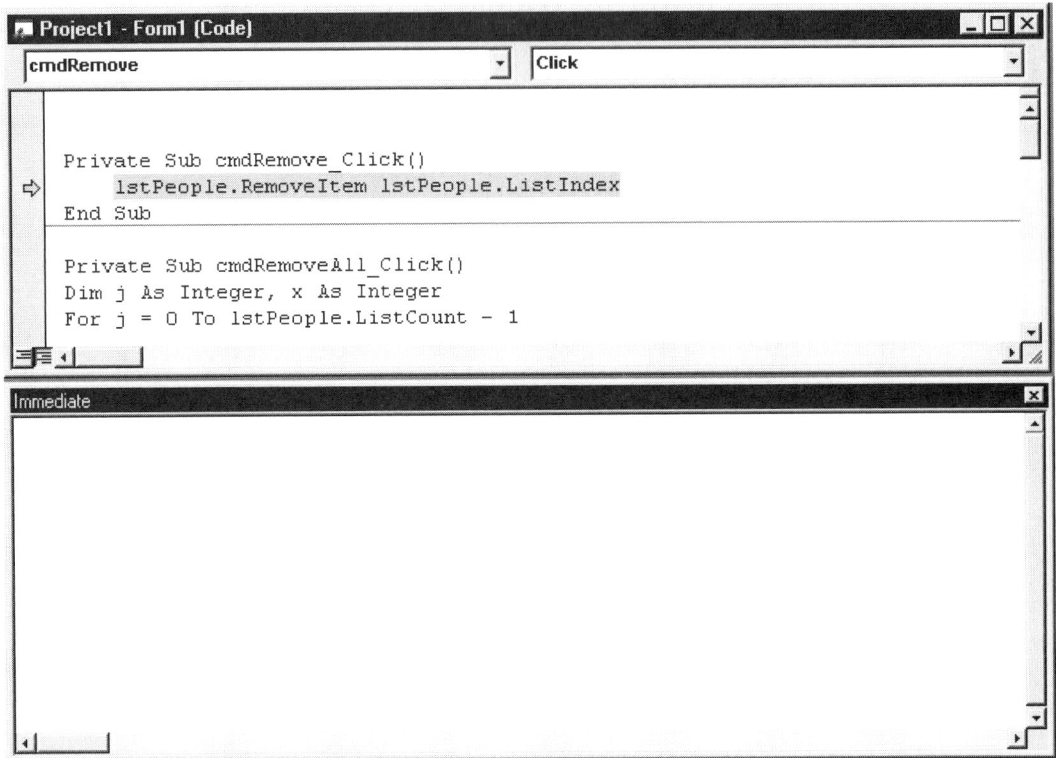

Figure 3.10 The Immediate Window

You can open the Immediate window before you run your program or after it has stopped. You can use the Immediate window to determine the value of a property or variable once the program has halted. In this example, the program halted due to a run-time error. Later in this chapter you will learn how to halt a program at a place of your choosing by setting a breakpoint.

When the program has halted, you can query the value of a property or variable by typing a question mark character (?) followed by the variable or property. In our example, you would type **?lstPeople.ListIndex** in the Immediate window and then press ENTER to determine the value of **lstPeople.ListIndex**. As Figure 3-11 shows, the value of **lstPeople.ListIndex**, –1, will display on the next line of the Immediate window.

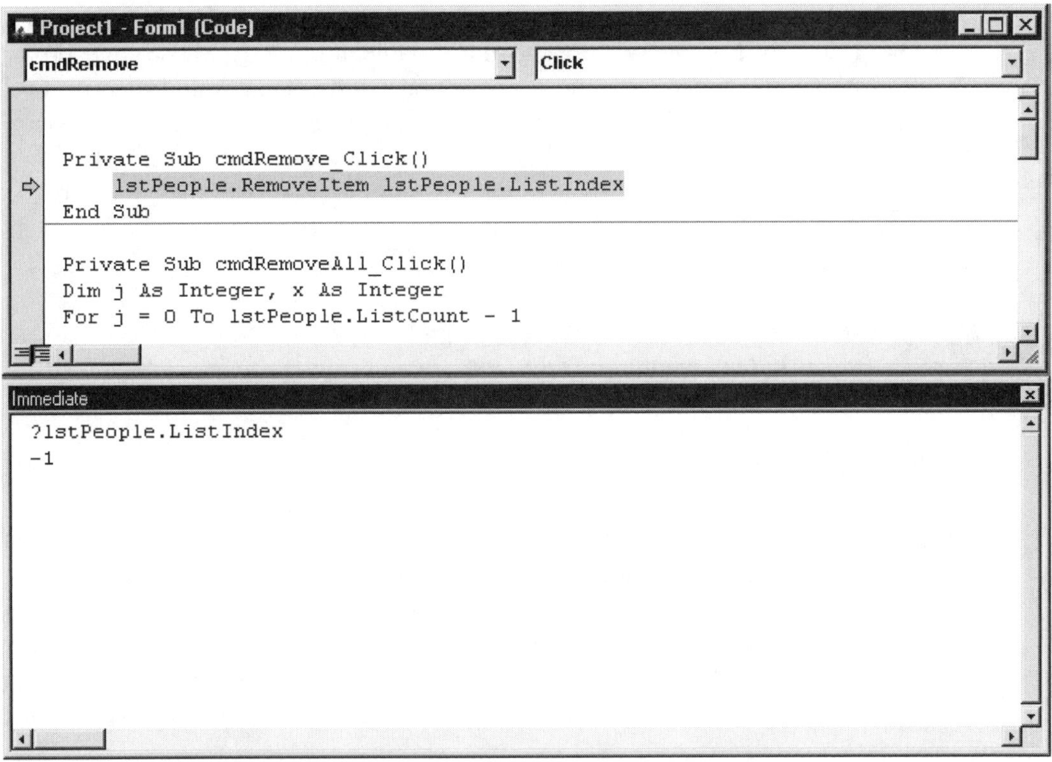

Figure 3.11 Value in the Immediate window

Note *You can use the Print statement as an alternative to the question mark character to query the value of a property or variable in the Immediate window:*

```
Print lstPeople.ListIndex
```

While the ability to query variable or property values in the Immediate window is a nice feature, you may wonder why you would use this feature when you can perform the same task with Auto Data Tips simply by holding the mouse pointer over the variable or property. Actually, if you can perform the same task with either Auto Data Tips or the Immediate window, it probably is quicker and easier to use Auto Data Tips. However, the usefulness of the Immediate window is not limited to querying the value of a variable or property appearing in a procedure.

One debugging task you can perform in the Immediate window but not with Auto Data Tips is to query the value of a variable or property whose name does *not* appear in the procedure. For example, you could not use Auto Data Tips to query the value of the **ListCount** property of the list box. That property does not appear in the procedure, so you cannot hold your mouse pointer over it. By contrast, you can query the value of the **ListCount** property of the list box in the Immediate window simply by typing the question mark character followed by the **ListCount** property and then pressing ENTER.

Note *There also are other debugging tasks you can perform in the Immediate window but not with Auto Data Tips. The Immediate window is used later in the chapter to view trace statements, and it can also be used to call a procedure.*

Using the Locals Window

You can also use the Locals window to determine the value of **ListCount** and **ListIndex** when the program terminated. The Locals window displays the current value and data type of all local variables—hence its name "Locals." However, the Locals window also displays the current value and data type of the properties of the current form and of the form's constituent controls. Figure 3-12 shows the Locals window, which is displayed by selecting the Locals Window command on the View menu or clicking the Locals Window button on the Debug toolbar.

Locals

Project1.Form1.cmdRemove_Click

Expression	Value	Type
Me		Form1/Form1
[_Default]	<Wrong number of arguments or in	Object
ActiveControl		Control/CommandButton
Appearance	1	Integer
AutoRedraw	False	Boolean
BackColor	-2147483633	Long
BorderStyle	2	Integer
Caption	"Welcome to Error-Free Programmir	String
ClipControls	True	Boolean
cmdRemove		CommandButton/CommandButton
cmdRemoveAll		CommandButton/CommandButton
ControlBox	True	Boolean
Controls		Object

Figure 3.12 Locals window

The first item in the Locals window is "Me." The Visual Basic IDE is not being egocentric. Rather, **Me** is a keyword, indicating the current form. Below **Me**, in a tree-view metaphor, are properties and controls of the current form. Locate **lstPeople** by scrolling down. You can view the properties of **lstPeople** by clicking the plus sign next to it. Figure 3-13 shows the entries for **ListCount** and **ListIndex**.

Remove the Bug

Of course, using Auto Data Tips, the Immediate window or the Locals window to obtain the values of properties and variables is not the goal, but rather the means to the end of ridding your program of a bug. These tools simply assist you in quickly determining the reason for the error so that you more easily reach the goal of removing the bug.

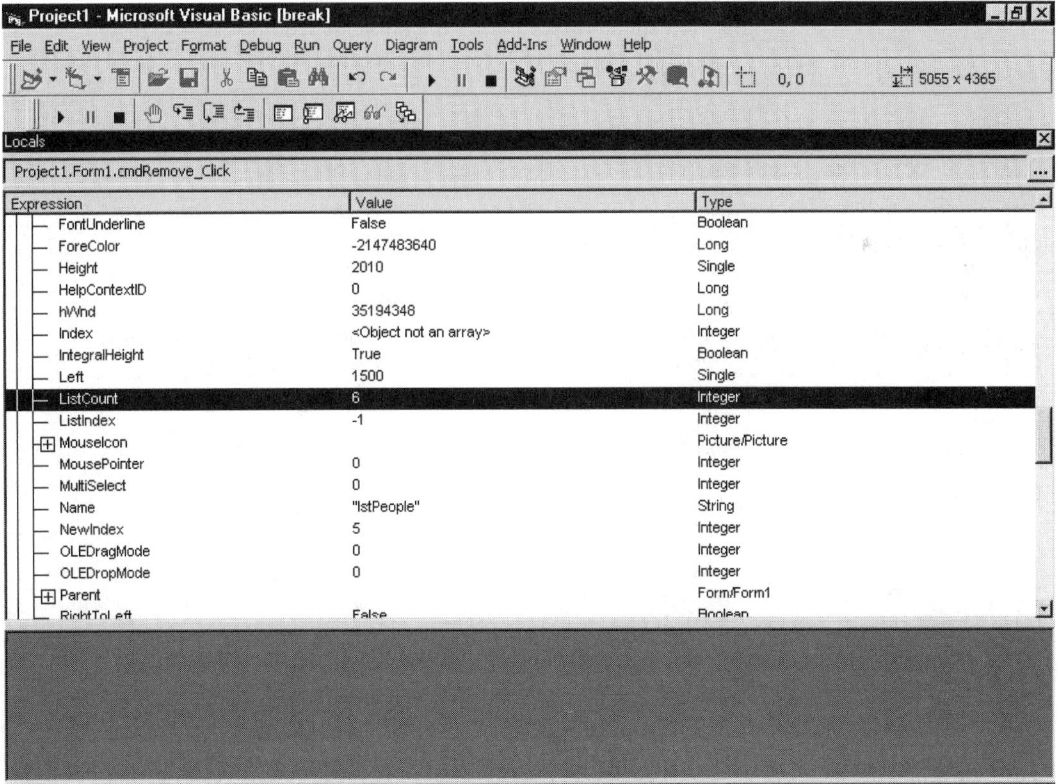

Figure 3.13 Locals window entries for properties of the list box

One way to remove this bug is to have your code first to test to see if the value of the **ListIndex** property is –1, and if it is, warn the user and exit the subroutine:

```
Private Sub cmdRemove_Click()
If lstPeople.ListIndex = -1 Then
        MsgBox "Must select item"
        Exit Sub
    Else
        lstPeople.RemoveItem lstPeople.ListIndex
    End If
End Sub
```

Another solution is to set the **Enabled** property of the **cmdRemove** command button to False when the **ListIndex** is –1. The choice of cure is up to you. The point is that you are now aware of the bug and know why it is occurring.

Real-Time Debugging

The first debugging example looked at a snapshot, or freeze-frame, of the program when it *stopped*. This next debugging example will watch and check values while the program is *running* in real time. In this example, you will use other capabilities of the Immediate window, namely to view trace statements and call procedures.

Build the Project

Building this project won't take long. Simply add to the previous project the following code for the Click event of the **cmdRemoveAll** command button:

```
Private Sub cmdRemoveAll_Click()
    Dim j As Integer
    For j = 0 To lstPeople.ListCount - 1
        lstPeople.RemoveItem j
    Next
End Sub
```

Synopsis of Project

This code is intended to loop through the list box, removing one item at a time. The number of loops equals the number of items in the list, which is the **ListCount** property. Since the index of items in the list box is zero-based, the loop goes from zero to the value of **ListCount** less one, instead of from one to the value of **ListCount**. The **RemoveItem** method of the list box removes the item whose index is its parameter. Since the loop will be from 0 to 5, the

Value	Index	Removed When Counter Variable Equals
Al	0	0
Bill	1	1
Chuck	2	2
Dave	3	3
Ed	4	4
Fred	5	5

Table 3.3 Concept of Code in **cmdRemoveAll_Click**

expectation is that all six items in the list box will be removed. Table 3-3 summarizes the concept.

The Bug

There is one minor problem. The code does not work. When you click the Remove All button, you receive the message shown in Figure 3-14: "Run-time error '5': Invalid procedure call or argument."

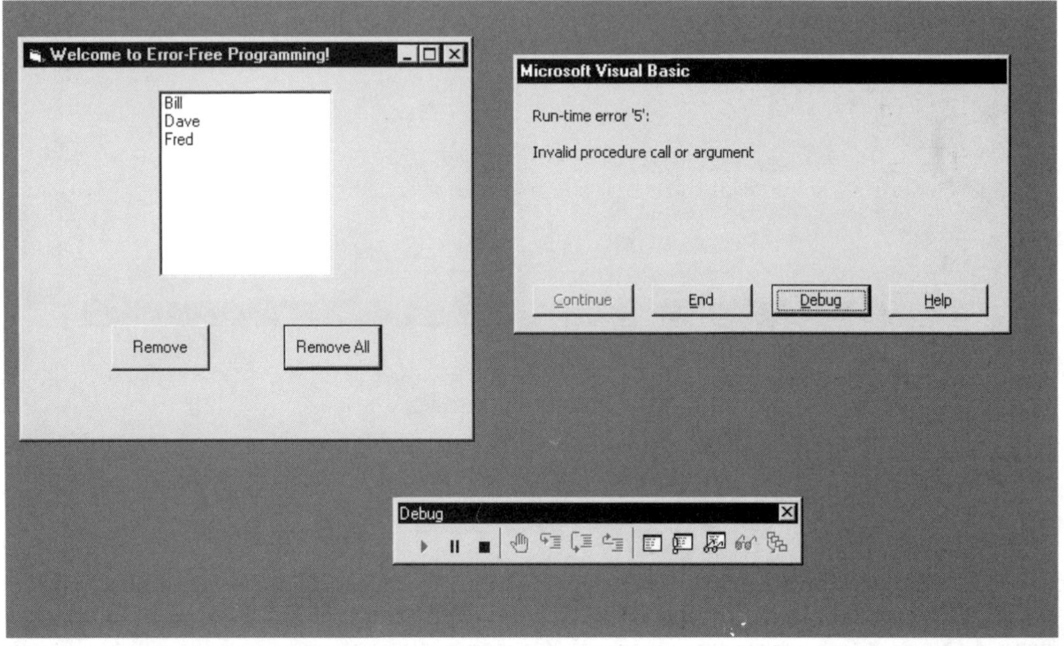

Figure 3.14 Error message when Remove All button is clicked

Debugging a Project in Real Time

Click the Debug button to highlight the line of code at which program execution stopped. The debugger highlights the statement that calls the **RemoveItem** method inside the **For** loop:

```
lstPeople.RemoveItem j
```

As Figure 3-15 shows, you can use Auto Data Tips or the Immediate window to determine that the value of the counter variable **j**, which represents the index of the item being removed, is 3. The Immediate window is used to determine that the value of ListCount also was 3. Figure 3-16 shows the use of the Locals window to determine the value of **j**.

The fact that the values of the counter variable and **ListCount** both are 3 explains why the program ended. The **RemoveItem** method attempted to remove the item at the index whose value was that of the counter, 3. However, since the value of **ListCount** is 3, the value of the highest index is 2, the index being zero-based. Since there is no item at index 3, trying to remove an item at that

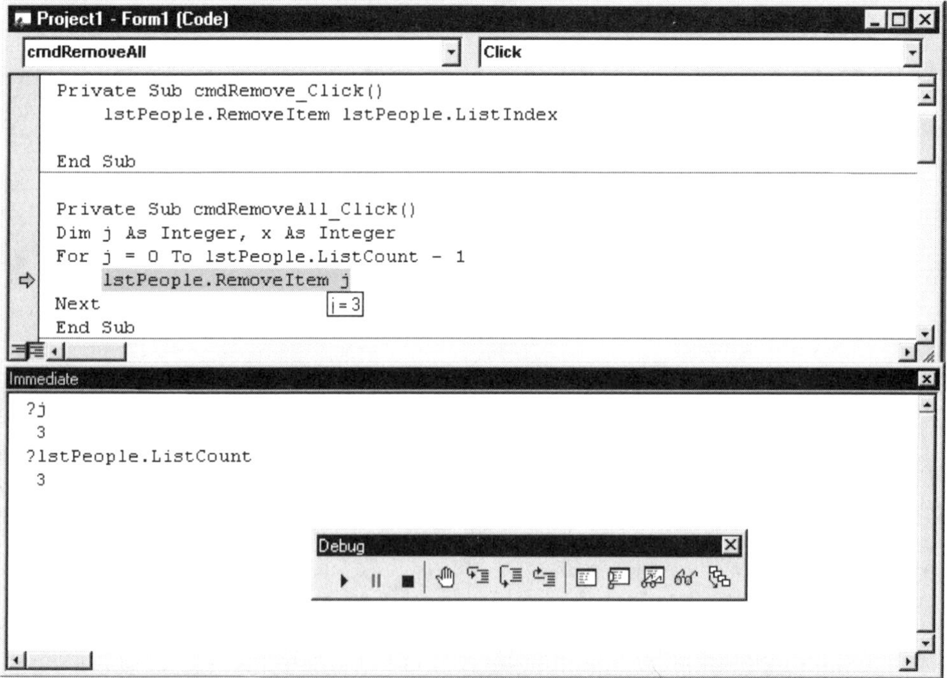

Figure 3.15 Value of counter variable and **ListCount** property

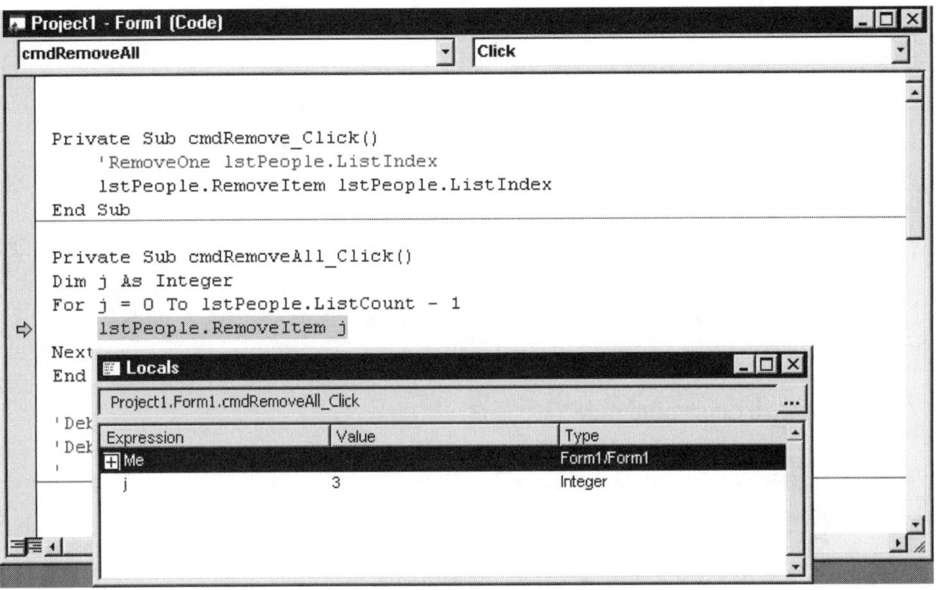

Figure 3.16 Value of counter variable in Locals window

index will result in a run-time error just as surely as trying to remove an item at index –1, as in the last example.

The value of the counter variable **j** being 3 indicates that the error occurred in the fourth loop (**j** having the values 0, 1, 2, and 3). This explains why three items were left in the list box. Of the original six items, one was eliminated in each of the three loops that took place before the program ended. However, Figure 3-14 shows that Bill, Dave, and Fred were the three items left in the list box. These were not the last three items. Instead, they were the second, fourth, and sixth items. The first three loops eliminated, respectively, Al, Chuck, and Ed, the first, third, and fifth items. This is contrary to the expectation that the first three loops would eliminate the first three items.

This puzzle becomes even more puzzling. Since the loop was only supposed to occur from 0 to **lstPeople.ListCount – 1**, the value of the **ListCount** property being 3 suggests that there should only have been three loops (**j** having the values 0, 1, and 2). Yet, the error occurred in the fourth loop.

Our debugging so far has looked at a snapshot, or freeze-frame, of the program when it is *stopped.* To solve this puzzle, we need to see watch and check values while the program is *running* in real time.

Using Tracing

You can place statements in your code that will output values to the Immediate window while the program is running. This is known as *tracing*. Indeed, Microsoft Visual C++ has a TRACE macro that outputs values to a debug window. However, this is not Visual C++, fortunately for those of you who have not had the dubious pleasure of tackling that difficult language. In Visual Basic you use the **Print** method of the **Debug** object to output the value of a variable or property to the Immediate window. Here, two **Debug.Print** statements, inserted in the **cmdRemoveAll_Click** code, output the values of the counter variable **j** and **ListCount**, respectively, to the Immediate window:

```
For j = 0 To lstPeople.ListCount - 1
    Debug.Print j
    Debug.Print lstPeople.ListCount
    lstPeople.RemoveItem j
Next
```

The output in the Immediate window is as follows:

```
0
6
1
5
2
4
3
```

The output ended when the program terminated.

This output, while useful, would be more useful if it stated in English (or whichever other language you speak) the names of the properties or variables that the values correspond to. This code modifies the **Debug.Print** statement accordingly:

```
Private Sub cmdRemoveAll_Click()
    Dim j As Integer, x As Integer
    For j = 0 To lstPeople.ListCount - 1
        Debug.Print "In loop " & j + 1 & " the value of j is " & _
        j & " and the value of ListCount is " &
lstPeople.ListCount
        lstPeople.RemoveItem j
    Next
End Sub
```

The output of the Immediate window now is more readable:

```
In loop 1 the value of j is 0 and the value of ListCount is 6
In loop 2 the value of j is 1 and the value of ListCount is 5
In loop 3 the value of j is 2 and the value of ListCount is 4
In loop 4 the value of j is 3 and the value of ListCount is 3
```

Design Tip *Once you perfect your program, you do not have to remove* ***Debug.Print*** *statements before compiling it into an executable. The compiler ignores* ***Debug.Print*** *statements, so they do not become part of the compiled executable.*

Using Breakpoints

So far, our example programs have halted because Visual Basic has told them to halt because of a run-time error. However, by the time the program has halted, it may be too late to figure out what happened. The program has already gone past that point. Therefore, there are circumstances when you may want to halt the program before the run-time error occurs, whether to examine the values of variables or properties at that time, or to observe the sequence of code.

You can specify where a program halts by setting a breakpoint. You set a breakpoint by clicking on a line of code and then choosing Toggle Breakpoint from the Debug menu or pressing the shortcut key F9. Alternatively, you can click the gray vertical bar to the left of the line of code on which you want execution to halt. Either way, a red bar will highlight the line of code, as shown in Figure 3-17. In this example, a breakpoint will be set at the line of code in the **For** loop where the program terminated: **lstPeople.RemoveItem j**.

Note *You can delete a breakpoint simply by repeating the same action that set the breakpoint, since the command toggles the breakpoint on and off.*

The program will not halt when you first run it. Setting a breakpoint at a line of code will not halt the running of the program until the program reaches that line of code. The line of code at which the breakpoint was set, in this case, will not be reached until the user clicks the Remove All button.

When the user does click the Remove All button, the code will halt at the **lstPeople.RemoveItem j** statement where execution of the program terminated. However, the program will halt at the first iteration of the loop, not the fourth where the program terminated. As Figure 3-18 shows, at this point you can use either Auto Data Tips or the Immediate window to determine that the value of **j** is 0, and you can use the Immediate window to determine that the value of **ListCount** is 6. Both values are the ones expected for the first iteration of the loop.

Continue with the execution of the program by choosing Continue from the Run menu or by pressing the shortcut key F5. Once again, the code will halt at the

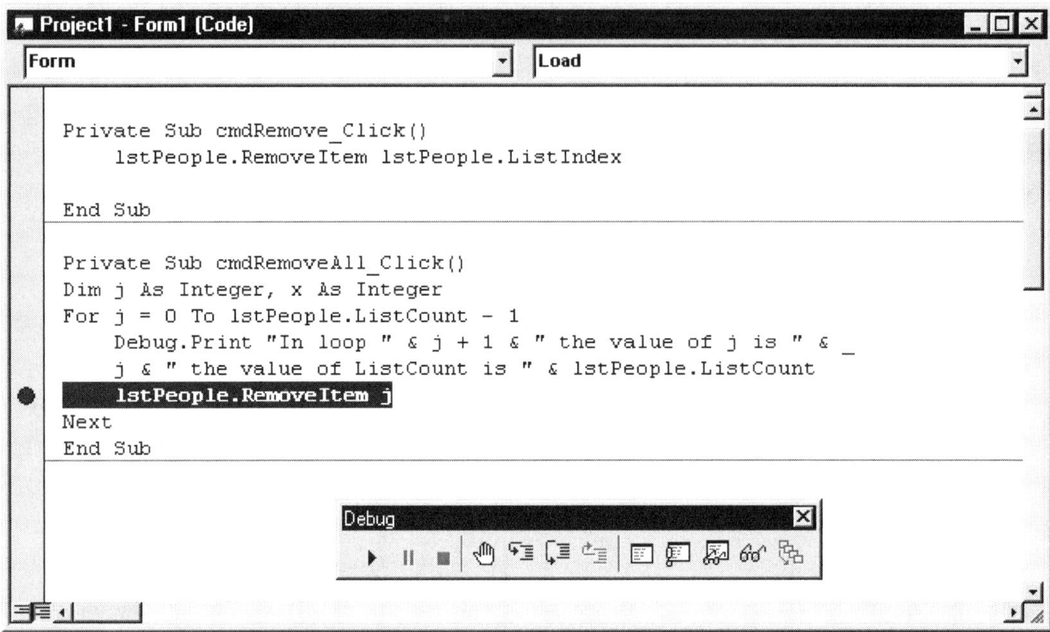

Figure 3.17 Setting a breakpoint

lstPeople.RemoveItem j statement, this time at the second iteration of the loop. You can determine using Auto Data Tips and the Immediate window that the value of **j** is 1 and the value of **ListCount** is 5. Continue with the execution of the program. During the next (third) iteration, the value of **j** is 2 and the value of **ListCount** is 4. When you continue the program until it again stops at the breakpoint, during the following (fourth) iteration the value of **j** is 3 and the value of **ListCount** also is 3. When you continue the program, it terminates.

Note that the program did not terminate when it reached the **lstPeople.RemoveItem j** statement in the fourth iteration of the loop, and only terminated when you ran the program from that statement. The reason is that when a program reaches a breakpoint, the statement at which the breakpoint was set has not yet been executed.

By setting a breakpoint, you were able to determine the values of **j** and **ListCount** listed in Table 3-4 for each iteration of the loop.

Of course, this is the same information that you obtained earlier using the **Print** method of the **Debug** object. Here, as so often in programming, there is more than one way of accomplishing the same result. Which is better? The usual helpful answer: It depends. Breakpoints give you a real-time view of what is

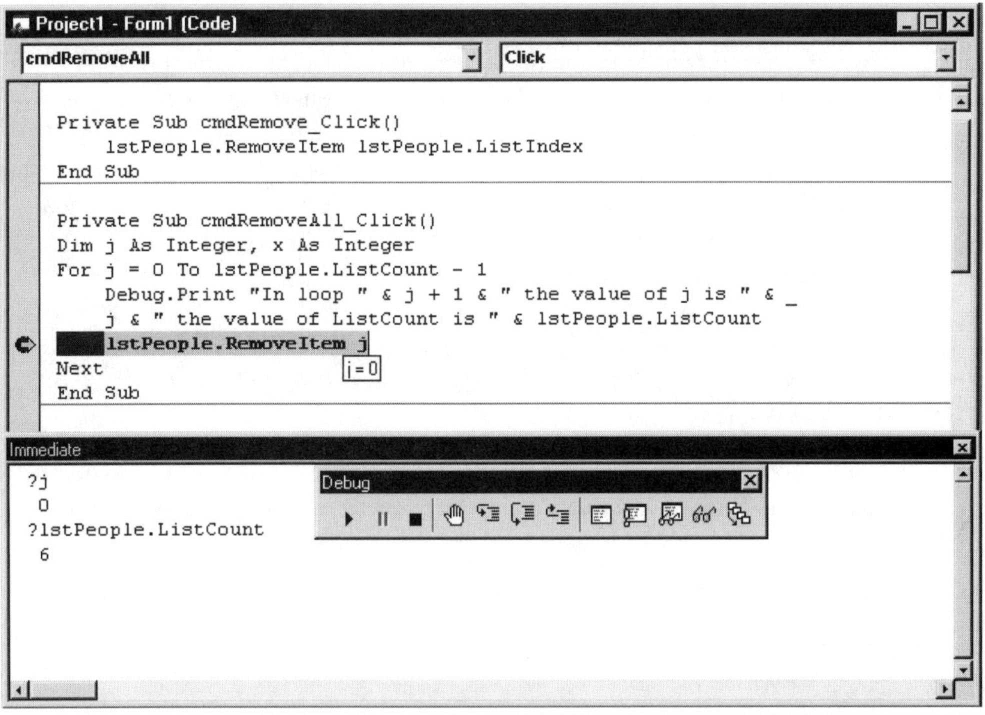

Figure 3.18 Values at the first iteration of the loop

going on in your program. On the other hand, trace statements are faster because your program doesn't stop and you don't have to record the interim values of properties and variables, because they are already recorded in the Immediate window.

Using Assertions

Visual Basic also enables you to set a breakpoint that only stops the program if the condition you specify is no longer True. As discussed previously, the

Iteration	Value of j	Value of ListCount
1	0	6
2	1	5
3	2	4
4	3	3

Table 3.4 Information Determined from Breakpoints

program ran as long as the counter variable was less than the value of **ListCount**. Once the counter variable equaled or exceeded **ListCount**, the program terminated because the index to be removed was out of range.

Previously you used the **Print** method of the **Debug** object to output information to the Immediate window. This time you will use the other method of the **Debug** object, **Assert**. The **Assert** method has one argument, which evaluates to True or False, and stops execution of the program in the Visual Basic IDE if the condition becomes False.

Note *Like the **Print** method, the **Assert** method only works in the Visual Basic IDE and is ignored by the compiler when your program is compiled into an executable.*

This code uses the **Assert** method to stop execution of your program when the value of the counter variable **j** equals or exceeds the value of **ListCount**:

```
Private Sub cmdRemoveAll_Click()
Dim j As Integer, x As Integer
For j = 0 To lstPeople.ListCount - 1
    Debug.Assert j < lstPeople.ListCount
    lstPeople.RemoveItem j
Next
End Sub
```

Run the program and click the RemoveAll button. The program will break at the **Debug.Assert** statement instead of terminate. When you check the values of **j** and **ListCount** after the program breaks, both will have values of 3.

Removing the Bug

Regardless of which way you obtained the values of the counter variable and ListCount at each iteration of the loop, you learn from the information that the decrease in the value of **ListCount** did not affect the number of iterations of the **For** loop. The **For** loop had six iterations because that was the value of **ListCount** when the loop started. A decrease in the value of **ListCount** after the loop begins does not decrease the number of loops. Therefore, the program executed a fourth loop even though the value of **ListCount** had decreased to three. Thus, the concept of using the **For** loop to remove one item at a time from the beginning to the end of the list does not work.

There are several solutions. One is to use the **For** loop, but to remove the items from the end of the list:

```
For j = 4lstPeople.ListCount - 1 To 0 Step -1
    lstPeople.RemoveItem j
Next
```

Another is to always remove the first item in the list:

```
For j = 0 To lstPeople.ListCount - 1
       lstPeople.RemoveItem 0
Next
```

In either case, the solution is relatively simple once you have diagnosed the problem. The ability to view the values of the counter variable and **ListCount** during each iteration of the loop by using a breakpoint enabled you to quickly detect the problem.

Step-by-Step Debugging

Setting the breakpoint permitted you to examine the running of the program through each iteration of the loop. However, sometimes to debug a program you need to examine the running of the program one line at a time. Visual Basic provides you with four commands, all accessible from the Debug menu: Step Into, Step Over, Step Out, and Run to Cursor. Visual Basic also provides you with a Watch window to watch the value of properties and variables and a Call Stack window to view the procedure stack, where one procedure calls another procedure.

Build the Project

This example will require three changes to the existing code:

1. Add the following **IsValidIndex** function, which will be used to check if an index is valid (0 or higher) or invalid (such as –1):

   ```
   Public Function IsValidIndex(idx As Integer)
       IsValidIndex = (idx >= 0)
   End Function
   ```

2. Add the following **RemoveOne** subroutine, which removes the item at the specified index if **IsValidIndex** returns True:

   ```
   Public Sub RemoveOne(idx As Integer)
       If IsValidIndex(idx) Then
           lstPeople.RemoveItem idx
   ```

```
    Else
        MsgBox "Index invalid"
    End If
End Sub
```

3. Change the body of **cmdRemove_Click** so that it calls **RemoveOne**:

```
Private Sub cmdRemove_Click()
    RemoveOne lstPeople.ListIndex
End Sub
```

Synopsis of Project

The additional code implements the suggestion of the freeze-frame debugging example and checks if the value of **ListIndex** is –1 before it removes an item. The implementation is spread over three procedures so that the Call Stack window and other features of the debugging tools can be demonstrated.

Using the Step Commands

Set a breakpoint at the **RemoveOne lstPeople.ListIndex** statement in **cmdRemove_Click**. Run the program and then click the Remove button without selecting an item in the list. Program execution will halt where you set the breakpoint. You can determine that the value of **ListIndex** is –1 by using either Auto Data Tips or the Immediate window.

Press F8, the shortcut key for Step Into. As Figure 3-19 shows, code execution will jump to the **RemoveOne** procedure.

Continue to press F8. Code execution will continue with the next line, which calls **IsValidIndex**. You now have the choice of two different debugging commands:

- **Press F8** Code execution jumps to **IsValidIndex** (as shown in Figure 3-20), just as it jumped from **cmdRemove_Click** to **RemoveOne**. Continuing to press F8 will step you through each statement in **IsValidIndex**. Instead, press CTRL-SHIFT-F8, the shortcut key for Step Out. The debugger will execute, without stopping, the remaining statements in **IsValidIndex**, and return to **RemoveOne**.
- **Press SHIFT-F8** This is the shortcut key for Step Over, and code execution will execute the call to **IsValidIndex** but not stop at that function. Instead, code execution will continue to the next statement in **RemoveOne**, the **Else** statement (as shown in Figure 3-21), since **IsValidIndex** returned False.

Assuming you chose Step Into and are now at the first line of **IsValidIndex**, you might decide not to step through the remaining code in that function but

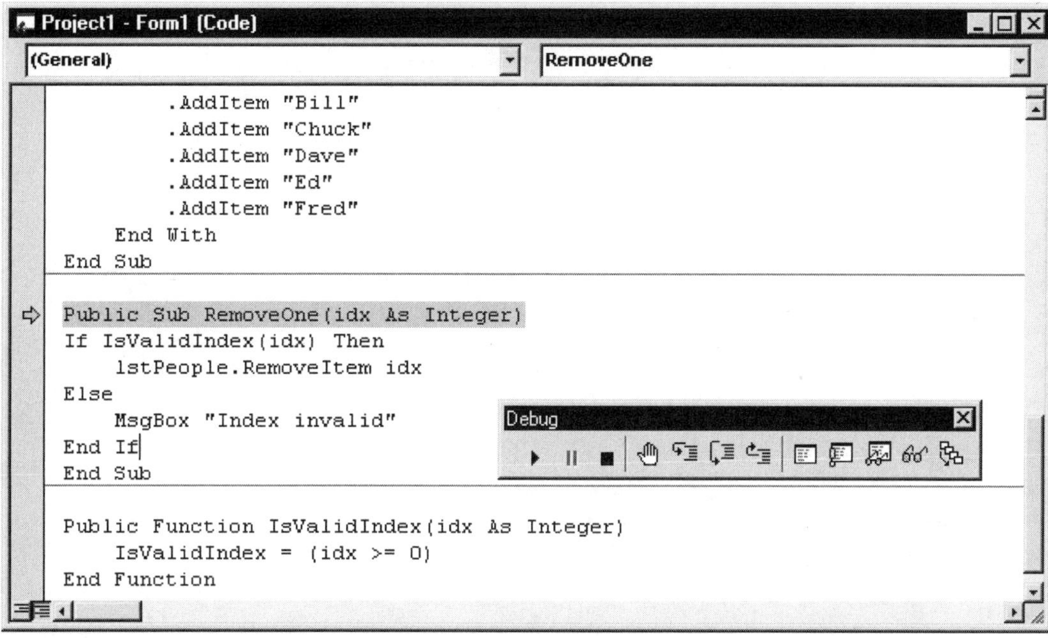

Figure 3.19 Using Step Into to jump to a called procedure

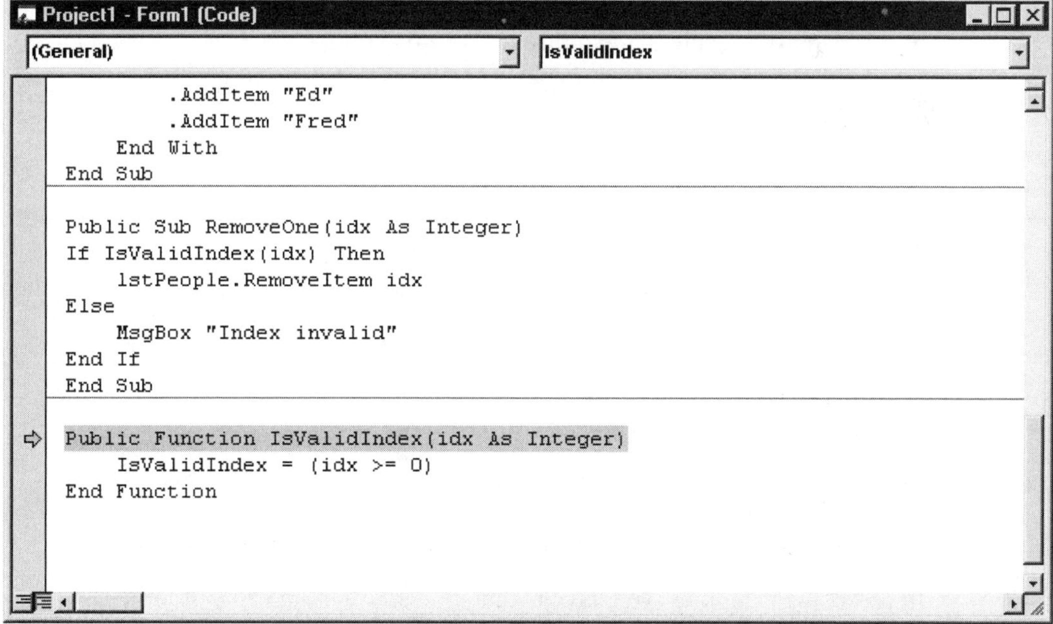

Figure 3.20 Using Step Into moves the debugger to the called procedure

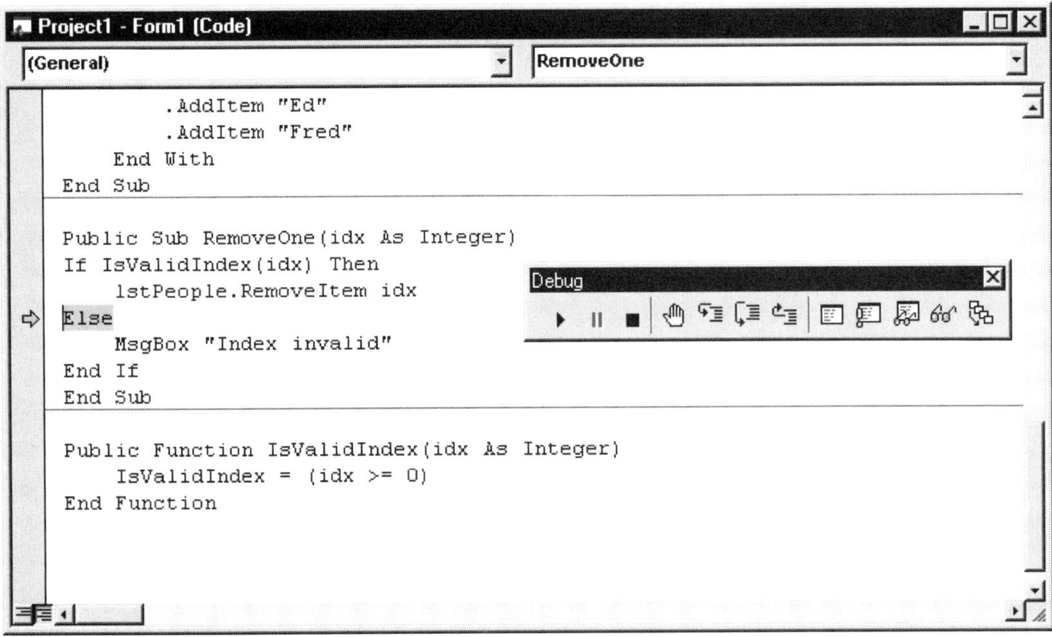

Figure 3.21 Using Step Over executes the called procedure but moves the debugger to the next line of the calling procedure

instead simply execute it and return to **RemoveOne**. You can accomplish this result with the debugging command Step Out. Table 3-5 summarizes these debugging commands and when you would use them.

Visual Basic gives you several choices in debugging commands to make your debugging more efficient. You use Step Into when at first you may need to investigate the problem statement by statement. Later you may use Step Over or Step Out to save time when you are able to eliminate a called procedure or code within it as the culprit. Still later in the process you may use Run to Cursor, when you know exactly where you want your investigation to begin.

Note *Although stepping through code often is done in conjunction with the setting of breakpoints, you can step through your code from the beginning without setting any breakpoints. You simply start your program with Step Into instead of Run.*

Using the Watch Window

In preceding examples, you have manually inspected the value of properties and variables using Auto Data Tips, the Immediate window, and the Locals window.

Command	What It Does	When To Use It
Step Into	Executes the current statement. If the statement calls another procedure, then the debugger goes to the first line of the called procedure.	Used when you don't know if the error is in the called procedure.
Step Over	Like Step Into, Step Over also executes the current statement. Unlike Step Into, if the current statement calls another procedure, the debugger does not go to the first line of the called procedure, but rather executes the called procedure and then goes to the next statement of the calling procedure.	Used when you are satisfied that the bug is not in the called procedure, so you don't want to waste the time of stepping through the called procedure.
Step Out	Executes the remaining statements in a called procedure and then moves to the next statement of the calling procedure.	Used when you have already investigated the statements in the called procedure with which you were concerned and want to return to the calling procedure.
Run to Cursor	Executes all statements before the one in which the cursor is located.	Used when you know exactly where you want to start your investigation.
Set Next Statement	Specifies the next statement, which must be within the current procedure, at which execution continues.	Used to skip statements in the current procedure that, for current debugging purposes, you don't want to execute.
Show Next Statement	Transfers the cursor to the next line to be executed.	Used in conjunction with Set Next Statement.

Table 3.5 Debugging Commands

You can also use the Watch window to keep track of property and variable values for you as your program is running. Figure 3-22 shows the Watch window, which you display by choosing Watch Window from the View menu or by choosing the Watch Window button on the Debug toolbar.

You use the Watch window to see the value of properties and variables that are in scope. Unlike the Locals window, you have to add variables to the Watch window to watch them. You can add a variable to the Watch window by double-clicking and then dragging and dropping the variable into the Watch window. If, like the authors, you find dragging and dropping a major coordination challenge (akin to walking and chewing gum at the same time) the Add Watch window is a welcome alternative to drag-and-drop. Figure 3-23 shows the Add Watch window, which you display by choosing Add Watch from the Debug menu.

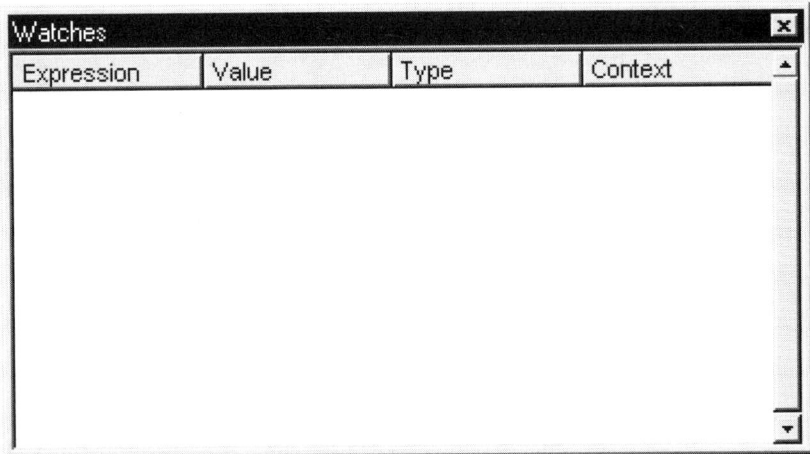

Figure 3.22 The Watch window

The Add Watch window has the following controls:

Expression The variable or property to watch. You can type the name in the Expression text box, or you can highlight a variable or property before choosing Add Watch, and that variable or property's name will appear in the Expression text box.

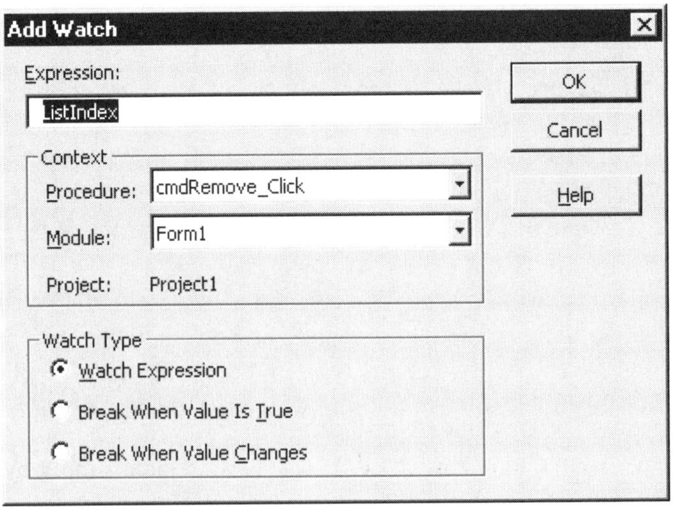

Figure 3.23 The Add Watch window

Procedure The procedure in which the property or variable is located. You also can choose All Procedures from the drop-down box for properties or global variables.

Module The procedure in which the property or variable is located. You also can choose All Modules from the drop-down box for properties or global variables.

Watch Type There are three choices:

- **Watch Expression** Adds the property or variable listed in the Expression text box to the Watch window.
- **Break When Value Is True** Program execution breaks, as if a breakpoint were reached, when the value of the property or variable becomes True.
- **Break When Value Changes** Program execution breaks, as if a breakpoint were reached, with each change in the value of the property or variable.

This example will add **ListIndex**, **ListCount**, and the counter variable **j** to the Watch window. The two properties have scope throughout the form module, so choose All Procedures in the Procedure drop-down box. The counter variable is local to the **cmdRemoveAll_Click** subroutine, so for that variable, choose that subroutine in the Procedure drop-down box. Finish by choosing, for all three, Form1 in the Module drop-down box (Form1 is the only module in this project) and Watch Expression for Watch Type. Figure 3-24 shows the resulting Watch window.

Note *Properties like **ListIndex** and **ListCount** must be prefaced with the name of the control, as in **lstPeople.ListCount**.*

The Watch window has four columns. The Expression column shows the property or variable being watched. The Value column lists the value of the expression. The Type column shows the data type of the expression. The Context column identifies the scope of the expression being watched, as selected from the Procedure and Module drop-down boxes in the Add Watch window. In Figure 3-24, the Value column shows "<out of context>" and the Type column shows "Empty" because the program has not yet started.

You can delete a watched property or variable simply by highlighting it and pressing DELETE. You also can edit information in the Watch window by, you guessed it, using the Edit Watch window. Figure 3-25 shows the Edit Watch

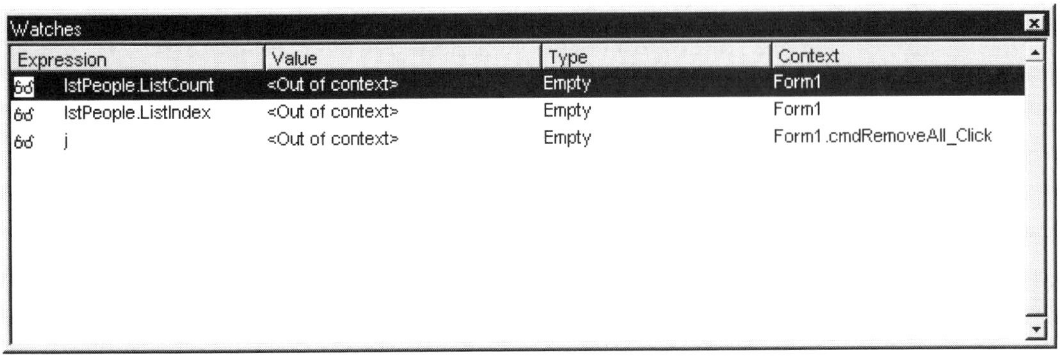

Figure 3.24 Watch window with properties and variables

window, which you can display by choosing Edit Watch from the Debug menu or by right-clicking a property or variable in the Watch window and choosing Edit Watch from the context menu.

The Edit Watch window is identical to the Add Watch window, except that the caption is "Edit Watch" instead of "Add Watch." Use the Edit Watch window to make changes, and then click OK and your changes will be reflected in the Watch window.

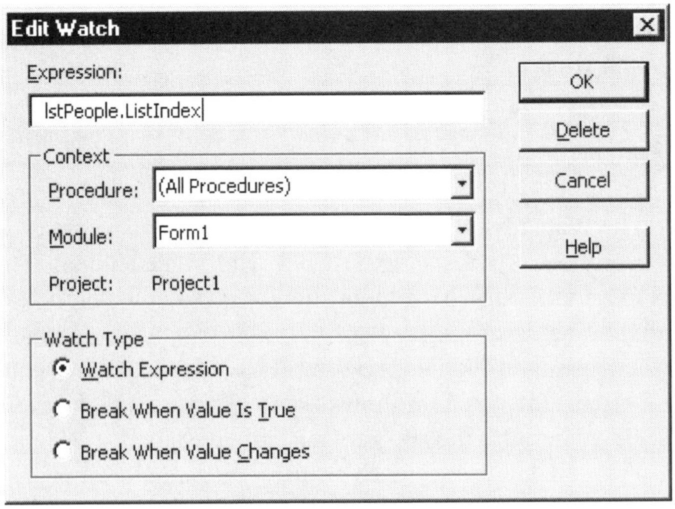

Figure 3.25 The Edit Watch window

Run the program, setting a breakpoint in the **cmdRemoveAll_Click** procedure, on the **lstPeople.RemoveItem j** statement, as before. Figure 3-26 shows the values of the watched properties and variables during the first iteration of the loop, and Figure 3-27 shows them during the second iteration.

You also can use the Quick Watch window to watch an expression's value on the fly. Figure 3-28 shows the Quick Watch window, which you display by highlighting the expression and then selecting Quick Watch from the Debug menu or the Debug toolbar.

Using the Call Stacks Window

Often your programs have one procedure call another, which calls another, which calls another... (enough already). Indeed, in this example, **cmdRemove_Click** called **RemoveOne**, which in turn called **IsValidIndex**. If keeping this information in your brain while you are dealing with other issues of your program overtaxes your mental RAM, no problem. Visual Basic keeps this information for you in the Call Stack window.

Place a breakpoint on the **RemoveOne lstPeople.ListIndex** statement in **cmdRemove_Click**, run the program, and click the Remove button. Step into the

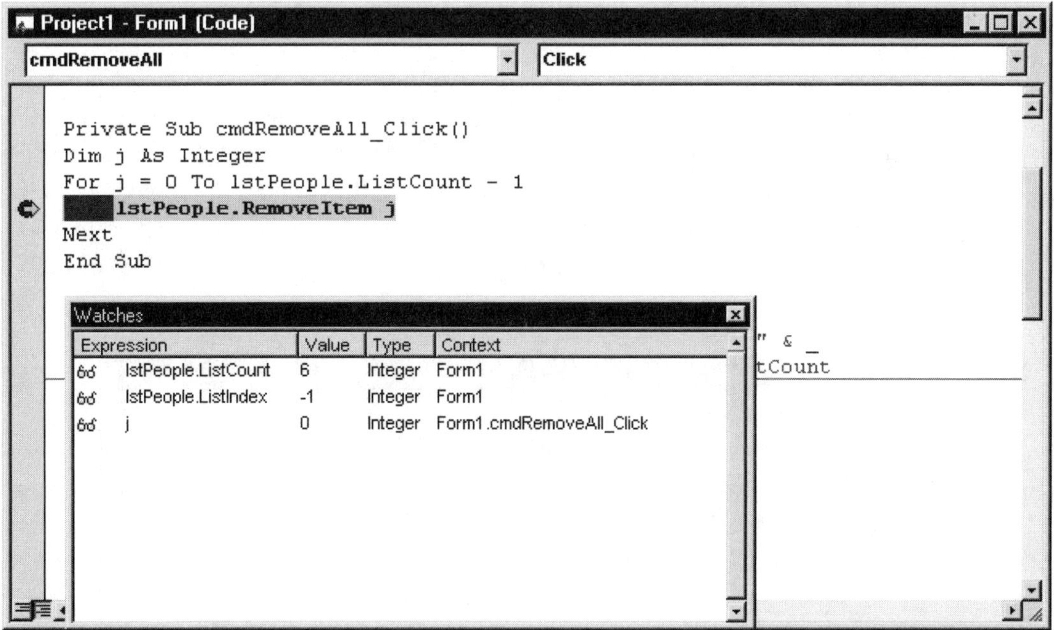

Figure 3.26 Values of watched properties and variables during the first iteration of the loop

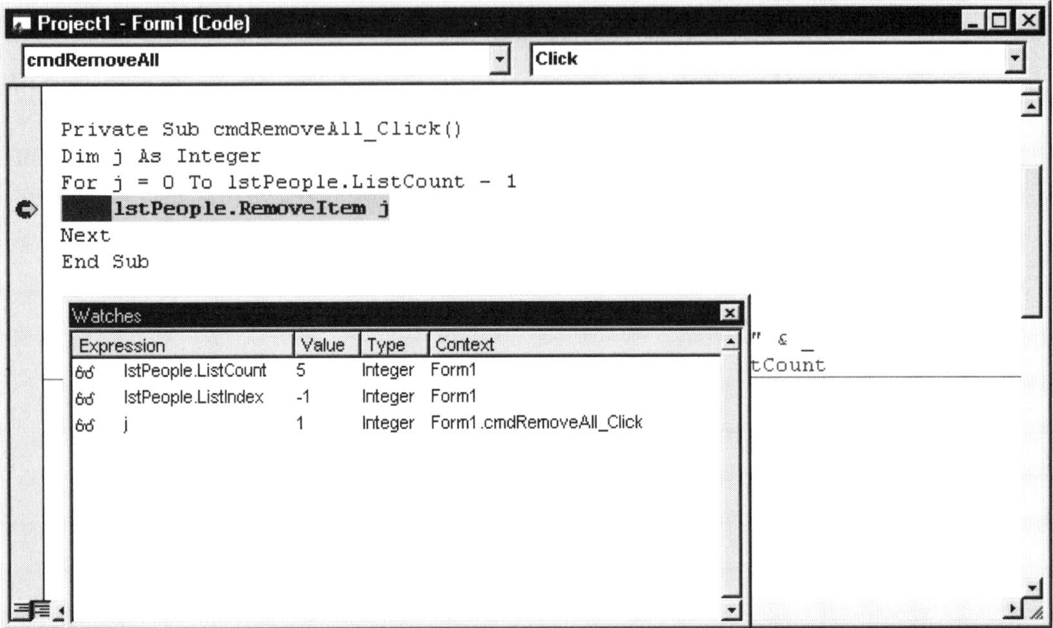

Figure 3.27 Values of watched properties and variables during the second iteration of the loop

code by clicking F8 until you come to the **IsValidIndex** function. Display the Call Stack window by selecting Call Stack from the View menu or from the Debug toolbar. Figure 3-29 shows the resulting Call Stack window.

The procedure listed on top, **IsValidIndex**, is the procedure being called. The procedure listed next, **RemoveOne**, is the procedure that called **IsValidIndex**. The procedure listed last, **cmdRemove_Click**, is the procedure that called **RemoveOne**.

Quick Watch

Context: Project1.Form1.cmdRemoveAll_Click

Expression: lstPeople.ListCount

Value: 5

Add | Cancel | Help

Figure 3.28 Quick Watch window

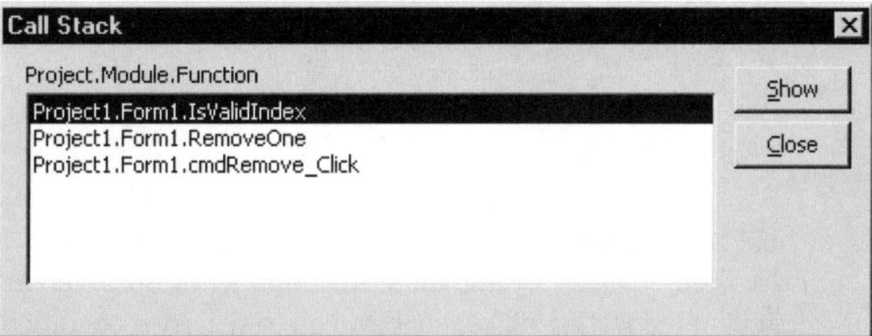

Figure 3.29 Call Stack window

Figure 3-30 shows the result of highlighting **IsValidIndex** in the Call Stack window and clicking Show. A triangle (green in color) points to the statement that called **IsValidIndex**, in this case the **If IsValidIndex(idx) Then** statement in **RemoveOne**.

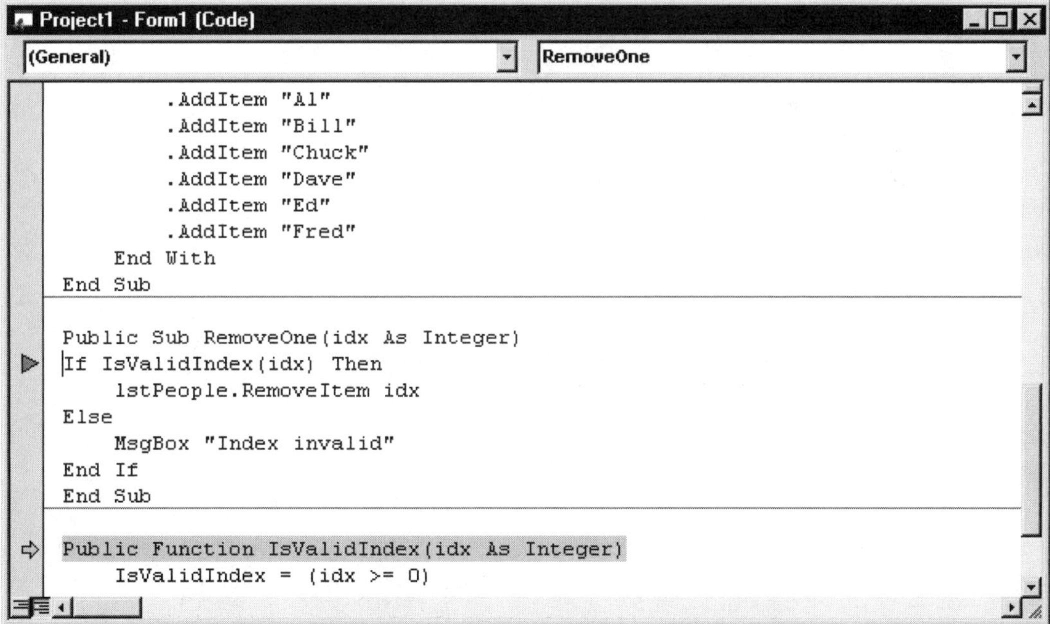

Figure 3.30 Using Show in the Call Stack window to find the statement that called the procedure

Note *You also can display the Call Stack window by pressing the "..." button in the Locals window.*

Summary

Visual Basic provides you with a number of debugging tools. Breakpoints enable you to specify where a program's execution will stop, whereas the **Assert** method of the **Debug** object enables you to specify a condition that will cause a program to stop. Step Into and the other step commands allow you to run your program more interactively, going literally one step or statement at a time, if necessary. You can use Auto Data Tips, the Immediate window, and the Locals window to determine the value of variables and properties when a program has stopped. While your program is running, you can use the Watch window to view the value of variables and properties, and the Call Stack window when one procedure calls another.

CHAPTER 4

Errors

In Visual Basic, as in most programming languages, an unhandled run-time error will terminate your program. However, Visual Basic is less forgiving than many other programming languages about what constitutes a run-time error. For example, in Visual Basic, attempting to access the tenth element in a five-element array is a run-time error. Not so in C++.

Visual Basic's strictness about what constitutes a run-time error is for your protection. The ability in C++ to attempt to access an out-of-bounds array element without generating a run-time error makes it possible for you to overwrite valid data with invalid data, or worse. The run-time error generated in Visual Basic protects you from these consequences.

Visual Basic's strictness about what constitutes a run-time error also enables you to debug your program more thoroughly. However, while you should expect to generate run-time errors while you are writing and debugging your code, your long-term job prospects will not be enhanced if the users of your application experience program crashes accompanied by cryptic messages such as "Run-time error 91 - Object variable or With block variable not set."

Run-time errors do not crash programs—*unhandled* run-time errors do. You handle an error by *trapping* it. The word *trapping* gives the empowering connotation that you are no longer the victim of errors, but instead the hunter. However, before you feel too empowered, keep in mind that hunting errors, like hunting bears or boars, needs to be done carefully, lest you become the casualty.

Trapping a run-time error involves two steps. The first step is to anticipate, in your code, the occurrence of the error. The second step is to write code that deals with the error. For example, a run-time error results if your application's user attempts to save a file to their "A" drive but forgets to put a floppy in the drive. If your code does not anticipate that error, then the program will crash ingloriously with the message "Run-time error 71 - Disk not ready." However, if your code anticipates that error, then the program will not crash. Instead, the user will be asked if they want to retry, in which case they are prompted to insert a floppy disk and try again, or to cancel, in which case the procedure (or application) ends.

Sometimes the nature of the error does not permit such an easy recovery, and indeed may be fatal to the continued running of the application. For example, despite the local computer store salesperson's advice that 32MB of RAM should be plenty to run Windows 2000, Office 2000, and Visual Studio at the same time, your user may experience an out-of-memory error. If your program abruptly ends with the cryptic message "Run-time error 7 - Out of memory," the user may blame you instead of the computer salesperson who the week before was selling used cars and the week after probably will be. Instead, your program should warn the user that the computer is low on memory and suggest that they try to free up memory (and buy more RAM).

Error Watch *An out-of-memory error does not always mean that the application is indeed out of memory. Sometimes Visual Basic returns this error because the actual error is of a nature that does not fit precisely within any built-in error code, so Visual Basic chooses the out-of-memory error on the theory that it is "close enough for government work." If your error-handling code takes steps to resolve a non-existent out of memory problem, the cure may turn out to be worse than the disease.*

Even in the worst case, when the error is unrecoverable, the error handler may permit the program to terminate "gracefully." For example, the error handler would permit the user to save their unsaved work and record information about the error to an error log that you could access when the user calls your application's technical support. This is not only good programming, it is also good business, as the user is less likely to blame you and is more likely to blame the used car/computer salesperson who sold the user an underpowered computer.

This chapter will show you how to use the **Err** object and **On Error** statement to handle errors. The **Err** object tells you which error occurred, and the **On Error** statement enables error handling and determines how the error is handled.

While handling errors is important, the only errors that your code handles are those that you anticipate. The ability to anticipate errors improves with experience. However, just as it is difficult for authors to proofread their own work (believe us, we know), it is difficult for a programmer to crash-test their own code. Let others do that. The crash-testers do not have to be experienced. Indeed, sometimes it is better if they are not, for then it is more likely that they will make the type of errors that will be made by inexperienced users.

Err Object

When an error occurs, Visual Basic uses the **Err** object to store information about that error. The **Err** object is built into Visual Basic, so you do not need to create an instance of it in your code. Rather, it is always available from anywhere in your code.

Note *While the **Err** object always is available, it can only contain information about one error at a time. Each time an error occurs, any existing information in the **Err** object is replaced with information about the new error. Consequently, if you wish to have a record of handled errors, you should save information about each error as it occurs, for example, to a log file.*

Properties of the Err Object

The properties of the **Err** object contain information about the error, such as the number Visual Basic assigns to that error, a description of the error, and the module or object in which the error occurred. Table 4-1 lists the properties of the **Err** object.

The **Number** property is the default property of the **Err** object. The value of the **Number** property is 0 if there is no error.

The **Number** and **Description** properties are paired for Visual Basic run-time errors. There are a number of predefined Visual Basic errors, each with its corresponding number and description. The list of Visual Basic run-time errors is too long to be reproduced here. They can be found on the MSDN Library CD under "Trappable Errors." Table 4-2 lists some common ones.

Property	Description
Description	String describing the error, such as "Division by zero" if you try to divide by zero
HelpContext	String containing the context ID for a topic in a help file, identified by the **HelpFile** property
HelpFile	String containing the path to a help file
LastDLLError	A system error code returned from a call to a dynamic-link library (DLL)
Number	Number containing the numeric value of the error, such as 11 in the case of division by zero
Source	String identifying by name the object or application that originally generated the error

Table 4.1 Properties of the Err Object

Code	Message
7	Out of memory
9	Subscript out of range
11	Division by zero
13	Type mismatch
28	Out of stack space
51	Internal error
52	Bad filename or number
53	File not found
54	Bad file mode
55	File already open
57	Device I/O error
61	Disk full
62	Input past end of file
71	Disk not ready
75	Path/file access error
76	Path not found
91	Object variable or With block variable not set

Table 4.2 Common Run-Time Errors

The **Number** property is often used in **Select Case** statements in error handlers to differentiate among various possible errors:

```
ErrorHandler:
   Select Case Err.Number
      Case 71:
         MsgBox "Put a floppy disk in the floppy drive"
         Resume
      Case 61:
         MsgBox "Floppy disk full. Put another disk in floppy drive"
         Resume
      'Case statements to handle other errors
      Case Default:
         MsgBox "Error Number" & Err.Number & ", " & Err.Description
   End Select
```

Note *This example only reads the* ***Number*** *and* ***Description*** *properties. However, you can also write to them, as discussed later in this chapter in the context of user-defined errors.*

The **Source** property identifies the name of the object or application that originally generated the error. The **Source** property returns the project name for errors that occur in a standard or form module, and *projectname.classname* for errors that occur in a class module. The **Source** property is useful for errors that occur outside your application. For example, if your application uses OLE automation to access Microsoft Word, and an error occurs in Word, the value of the **Source** property would be Word.Application.

If your application calls a DLL, and an error occurs in the DLL code, then the DLL will return an error number. However, the error number will not be one of the predefined Visual Basic error numbers, so using Err.Number will not work—DLLs generally have a return value that indicates success or failure. If the value indicating failure is returned, then your code should immediately check the **LastDLLError** property, which will reflect the particular error. The **LastDLLError** property applies only to DLL calls made from Visual Basic code. This property is discussed in Chapter 6 on the Windows API.

The **HelpContext** property is used to automatically display a particular topic in the help file designated by the **HelpFile** property. The **HelpContext** property is similar to a bookmark in Microsoft Word.

If no help file is specified, Visual Basic will check the value of the **Number** property. If that value corresponds to a Visual Basic run-time error value, then the Visual Basic Help context ID for that error is used. If the **Number** value doesn't correspond to a Visual Basic error, the contents screen for the Visual Basic Help file is displayed. Since Visual Basic knows how to display its own help for its built-in error numbers, generally the **HelpFile** and **HelpContext** properties are used for custom objects that have their custom errors.

Methods of the Err Object

The **Err** object also has two methods: **Clear** and **Raise**.

The **Clear** method clears all property settings of the **Err** object. Its syntax is

```
Err.Clear
```

The **Clear** method has no arguments.

The following scenario illustrates the purpose of the **Clear** method. If your code attempts to divide by zero, the **Number** property will be assigned the value 11, and the **Description** property will be assigned the value "Division by zero." Your code would then handle the error, for example, by warning the user that division by zero is not allowed, and by not permitting the division by zero to continue. Your application would then continue to run. However, the **Number** property would remain 11 and the **Description** property would remain "Division by zero"; the handling of the error would not automatically reset the **Number** property to 0 or the **Description** property to a blank string. If these properties, particularly the **Number** property, were not reset, then your code might later be fooled into thinking that there was a division by zero error because the value of the **Number** property was 11.

Visual Basic makes your job easier by automatically calling the **Clear** method when your code executes any of the following statements: **Resume**, **Exit Sub**, **Exit Function**, **Exit Property**, and **On Error**. Therefore, you generally need to call the **Clear** method explicitly only after an **On Error Resume Next** statement.

The **Raise** method generates a run-time error. The response of many programmers when first hearing about purposely creating an error condition is: "Are you nuts?" However, the **Raise** method is quite useful. It often is used to raise for the second time an error that an error handler has failed to resolve, so that the error, instead of terminating the application, can be handled further up the call stack. You also can use the **Raise** method in classes you create in order to report, as an error, a condition that is not among the predefined Visual Basic errors but that you wish to treat as an error condition.

The syntax of the **Raise** method is

```
Err.Raise number, source, description, helpfile, helpcontext
```

The arguments correspond to the **Err** object properties of the same name. Only the **number** argument is required.

As just discussed, the **Raise** method is used both with errors already defined by Visual Basic, such as division by zero, and user-defined errors, such as error conditions in classes you create. If the error is one already defined by Visual Basic, then the values of the remaining arguments are also predefined by Visual Basic. For example, if the **description** argument is not specified, and the

number argument can be mapped to a Visual Basic run-time error code, the string that would be returned by the **Error** function is the value of the description argument.

Note *During the debugging process, the* ***Error*** *function may be useful in reporting a description of an error. The* ***Error*** *function returns the error message that corresponds to an error. It has one optional argument, a number that represents an error number. If the number argument is supplied, the* ***Error*** *function returns the error message that corresponds to the error number. For example, the return value of* ***Error(11)*** *is "Division by zero." If the number argument is omitted, then the* ***Error*** *function will return the error message that corresponds to the most recent run-time error, or if no run-time error has occurred, a zero-length string (" ") will be returned.*

You must assign a number for user-defined errors. Visual Basic errors use the **vbObjectError** constant with error numbers. Visual Basic errors, both Visual Basic–defined and user-defined, are in the range **vbObjectError** + 0 to **vbObjectError** + 65,535. The range **vbObjectError** + 0 to **vbObjectError** + 512 is reserved for Visual Basic–defined errors. Therefore, the range from **vbObjectError** + 513 to **vbObjectError** + 65,535 is available for user-defined errors.

Error Watch *While you need to steer clear of the* ***vbObjectError*** *+ 0 to* ***vbObjectError*** *+ 512 range, that might not be sufficient to prevent conflicting error numbers if your program uses third-party controls. You need to determine the error numbers used by these controls so you don't inadvertently use the same error numbers for the objects you create.*

The **Error** statement can be used as an alternative to the **Raise** method to generate run-time errors. The syntax of the **Error** statement is

```
Error number
```

The **number** argument is any valid error number. The **Error** statement is supported only for backward compatibility. The **Raise** method is preferable because its additional, optional arguments enable you to specify the source of the error and online help. This is particularly important with user-defined errors.

Magic Error Numbers

Deborah Kurata, a Visual Basic object-oriented programming guru, coined the term "magic error numbers" for user-defined errors such as **vbObjectError** + 1,001. Her point is that there is nothing magic about 1,001; it's just a number in the valid range, and not at all descriptive of the error. For code documentation purposes, you should assign a constant with a descriptive name for each user-defined error:

```
Private Const MyLousyClassFunctionBombed = vbObjectError + 1001
```

You should include the optional arguments **source** and **description** when raising a user-defined error to provide a more intelligible error description. The source argument uses the format *ProjectName.ClassName* for objects and *ProjectName.ProcedureName* for procedures. The following code snippet illustrates raising a user-defined error:

```
Err.Raise myLousyClassObjectFailed, Source: = myProject.myLousyClass, _
   Description: = "CreateObject didn't create an object"
```

For errors being raised from classes you create, you may also want to include a help file, because, for your custom classes, Visual Basic Help will be no help at all. If you are providing custom help, then you would include the optional arguments **helpfile** and **helpcontext**.

On Error Statement

An **On Error** statement is required to handle a run-time error. Without an **On Error** statement, any run-time error is fatal.

The **On Error** statement usually enables an error-handling routine, though it also can be used to disable a previously enabled error-handling routine. The **On Error** statement is declared in a procedure; it cannot be placed in the General Declarations section of a module. When it enables an error-handling routine, it also specifies the location of the error handler, which must be in the same procedure as the **On Error** statement.

While the scope of an **On Error** statement is limited to the procedure in which it is declared, an **On Error** statement can be used to handle an error that was raised in a different procedure. Unhandled errors migrate up the call stack. Therefore, if Procedure A calls Procedure B, and an error is raised but not handled in Procedure B, the error can be handled by an error handler in Procedure A. The reason for this is that the unhandled error in Procedure B returns execution to the statement in Procedure A that called Procedure B, raising the error in Procedure A, which has the error handler.

There are three types of **On Error** statements:

- **On Error GoTo *line***
- **On Error Resume Next**
- **On Error GoTo 0**

Both the **On Error GoTo *line*** and **On Error Resume Next** statements enable an error-handling routine in the procedure in which the statement is located. In both cases, if a run-time error occurs, control goes immediately to the error handler. The difference between them is where in the procedure the error handler is located. With the **On Error GoTo *line*** statement, the error handler is at the location designated by the line label or number specified in the **line** argument. With the **On Error Resume Next** statement, the error handler is located at the statement immediately following the statement where the error occurred.

In contrast to the **On Error GoTo *line*** and **On Error Resume Next** statements, which *enable* an error-handler, the **On Error GoTo 0** statement *disables* a previously activated error handler. While the form of the **On Error GoTo 0** statement is similar to **On Error GoTo *line***, **On Error GoTo 0** doesn't specify line 0 as the start of the error-handling code, even if the procedure contains a line numbered 0.

On Error GoTo *Line*

The **On Error GoTo *line*** statement performs two functions. First, it enables an error-handling routine. Second, it specifies, with its **line** argument, the line label or number at which the error handler is located. These days, line numbers are rarely used, so usually the argument refers to a label rather than a line number.

The following code fragment shows how the **On Error GoTo *line*** statement works:

```
Private Sub Whatever()
   On Error GoTo Handler
   'code here does whatever
   Exit Sub
   Handler:
   MsgBox "Error #" & Err.Number & ", " & Err.Description
   'Resume, Resume Next, Err.Raise, or Exit Sub statement goes here
End Sub
```

The **Exit Sub** statement immediately before the **Handler** label is both typical and necessary. It is necessary to prevent the code from continuing into the error handler, even though no error has occurred. For functions or property procedures, you would use an **Exit Function** or **Exit Property** statement, respectively, immediately before the error-handling routine.

The specified line label, **Handler**, is in the same procedure as the **On Error** statement; otherwise a compile-time error will occur. Since the **Handler** label is the argument of the **On Error GoTo *line*** statement, if a run-time error occurs, control jumps to the **Handler** label. The error-handling code following the **Handler** label displays a message box showing the error number and description.

Normally you would not end the error-handler code with an **End Sub** statement. Instead, you have several choices:

- Resume execution in the current procedure with a **Resume** or **Resume Next** statement. This is the most common alternative, adopted when the error either has been resolved by the error handler or can be ignored.
- Raise an error with the **Raise** method of the **Err** object. You will do this when the error handler in the current procedure cannot handle the error, so you want the error to migrate up the call stack to be handled by the procedure that called the current procedure (or by the procedure that called the procedure that called the current procedure, and so on).
- Terminate the execution of the current procedure with the **Exit Sub** (or **Exit Function** or **Exit Property**) statement. The **Exit Sub** statement is used when the procedure cannot resolve the error and must end. However, the

Exit Sub statement also is used when the procedure has accomplished what it needs to accomplish and therefore may end.

Design Tip *Even if you are not going to resume execution in the current procedure or raise an error, it is good programming practice to terminate your error handler with an* ***Exit Sub*** *statement rather than just fall into an* ***End Sub*** *(or* ***End Function****) statement. One reason is that if later you add another error handler, the* ***Exit Sub*** *statement will prevent you from inadvertently falling into one error handler from another.*

While the error handler must reside in the same procedure as the **On Error** statement, the error may not have been raised in the current procedure. As discussed previously, unhandled errors migrate up the call stack. Therefore, the **On Error** statement can be used to handle errors that are raised in the current procedure (the procedure where the **On Error** statement resides) and also to handle errors that are raised in another procedure that is called by the current procedure.

Resume

The **Resume** statement has the following syntax:

```
Resume line
```

The **line** argument is optional. When used, it serves the same purpose as the **line** argument on the **On Error GoTo** ***line*** statement: it specifies a line number or label. In the case of the **Resume** statement, the specified line number or label is where execution will continue.

When the optional **line** argument is not used, which is usually the case, the **Resume** statement continues execution at the statement that raised the error. Whether or not the optional **line** argument is used, it is not necessary to invoke the **Clear** method of the **Err** object before the **Resume** statement, because the **Resume** statement automatically calls the **Clear** method.

Continuing execution at the very statement that caused the error could result in an infinite loop if the problem that caused that statement to raise the error still exists. Therefore, the **Resume** statement should not be used unless the error handler could have fixed the problem that caused the error.

The **Resume** statement is commonly used in the situation where the user tried to read or write a file from a floppy drive and no floppy disk is in that drive. The error handler in the following subroutine advises the user of the problem and asks if the user wants to retry or cancel. If the user chooses retry, it is assumed that the user followed directions (always a dangerous assumption for a programmer to make) and placed a floppy disk in the floppy drive before choosing retry. Placing the disk in the floppy drive solves the problem that caused the error. Therefore, the statement that generated the disk-not-ready error should not generate that error again.

```
Sub OpenFile(ByVal strFile As String)

On Error GoTo ErrorHandler
Dim nFileNum As Integer
nFileNum = FreeFile
Open strFile For Input As nFileNum
'More code
ErrorHandler:
   Select Case Err.Number
      Case 71:
         Dim answer As Integer
         answer = MsgBox("Put disk in floppy drive", vbRetryCancel)
         If answer = vbRetry Then
            Resume
         Else
            Exit Sub
         End If
      'Case statements to handle other errors
      Case Default:
         MsgBox "Error Number" & Err.Number & ", " & Err.Description
   End Select
End Sub
```

Unfortunately, our intrepid user has made another mistake. The file the user is trying to open is not on the floppy disk. Therefore, you should add code to the error handler that advises the user of the problem and asks if the user wants to continue. If so, the user is presented with a common dialog control from which a file can be selected to open. The user's selection of an existing file solves the problem that caused the error. Therefore, the statement that raised the file-not-found error should not generate that error again.

```
Case 53: 'File not found
      Dim answer As Integer
      answer = MsgBox("File not found. Want to find it?", vbYesNo)
      If answer = vbNo Then Exit Sub
   Form1.CommonDialog1.ShowOpen
   Resume
```

The preceding examples involved only one procedure. However, programmers usually do not, and should not, put all their code in one procedure. Rather, they divide their code logically among different procedures so that each procedure handles a discrete unit of work, with procedures calling each other. While dividing code logically among different procedures is good programming practice, it does raise additional issues in error handling. When all of the code is in one procedure, errors necessarily will occur in that procedure. Therefore, the error handler also will be in that procedure. However, when one procedure calls another, although the error may be raised in the called procedure, the seeds of the error may have been planted in the calling procedure.

As discussed previously, unhandled errors migrate up the call stack. Therefore, you have a choice of handling the error in the called procedure, or not handling it there and instead permitting it to be handled by the calling procedure.

Design Tip *Whether it is best to handle the error in the called procedure or in the calling procedure depends, of course, on the circumstances. As a general rule, error handling should be delegated to the procedure in which the problem that caused the error first arose. Thus, if Procedure A calls Procedure B, and an error was raised in Procedure B because of an invalid parameter passed by Procedure A, generally the error should be handled by Procedure A.*

If the error occurred but is not handled in the called procedure, then a **Resume** statement in an error handler in the calling procedure resumes execution at the last statement executed in the calling procedure, namely the statement that called the procedure in which the error was raised. Since that's a mouthful, the following code example may be illustrative:

```
Sub cmdOpen_Click ()
Dim strFile As String
Dim answer As Integer

On Error GoTo cmdOpenError
strFile = txtFile.Text
OpenFile strFile

cmdOpenError:
   Select Case Err.Number
      Case 71:
         answer = MsgBox("No disk in floppy drive", vbRetryCancel)
         If answer = vbRetry Then
            Resume
         Else
```

```
            Exit Sub
         End If
      Case 53: 'File not found
         answer = MsgBox("File not found. Want to find it?", vbYesNo)
         If answer = vbNo Then Exit Sub
           Form1.CommonDialog1.ShowOpen
           strFile = CommonDialog1.FileName
      Case 0: 'File not found
           Exit Sub
      Resume
      Case Default:
         MsgBox "Error Number" & Err.Number & ", " & Err.Description
   End Select
End Sub

Sub OpenFile(ByVal strFile As String)
Dim nFileNum As Integer
nFileNum = FreeFile

Open strFile For Input As nFileNum
End Sub
```

The statement in the **OpenFile** subroutine

```
Open strFile For Input As nFileNum
```

will raise a run-time error number 53, "File not found," because the value of **strFile** does not reflect a valid filename and path.

Since **OpenFile** does not have an error handler, execution will return to the **cmdOpen_Click** subroutine, specifically to the last statement in the **cmdOpen_Click** subroutine that executed: **OpenFile strFile**. That statement was the one that called the **OpenFile** procedure in which the error occurred.

The error that occurred in the **OpenFile** procedure has not cleared. The **Clear** method of the **Err** object was not explicitly called, and it was not automatically called because there was no **Resume**, **Exit Sub**, **Exit Function**, **Exit Property**, or **On Error** statement in the **OpenFile** procedure after the error occurred. Therefore, the program would terminate if the **cmdOpen_Click** subroutine did not have an error handler. However, it does.

The error handler in the **cmdOpen_Click** subroutine corrects the value of **strFile** to reflect the path and name of a valid file, and then ends with a **Resume** statement that returns execution to the **OpenFile strFile** statement. Since the error handler in the **cmdOpen_Click** subroutine has corrected the problem that caused the error in the **OpenFile** procedure, program execution should continue smoothly.

Resume Next

The **Resume Next** statement continues execution at the statement immediately following the statement that raised the error. The **Resume Next** statement is named similarly to the **On Error Resume Next** statement, but the two statements are quite different. The **Resume Next** statement is used inside an active error handler to specify where control should continue. By contrast, the **On Error Resume Next** statement activates and specifies the location of an error handler.

One way you can use the **Resume Next** statement is when you can ignore the error and proceed with your code. One situation where you can do this is when the error results from your code creating a duplicate of something that you need one, but only one, of. If the error is that you already have what you need, you can ignore the error and proceed with what you already have.

Another situation where you can ignore the error and proceed with your code is when you are looping through a collection and the error indicates that the member which is the subject of the current iteration can be skipped. The **FindText** function in the following code example looks for whether the **Text** property of at least one of the controls in a form matches the search string that is the function's one argument. **FindText** returns True if there is a match, and False if there is no match. The code checks for a match by looping through the form's **Controls** collection using the **For Each ... Next** statement. There is one problem. While many controls, such as the **ComboBox**, **ListBox**, and **TextBox**, support the **Text** property, other controls, such as the **CommandButton** and **Label**, do not. Invoking the **Text** property of a control that does not support the **Text** property will raise error number 38, "Object doesn't support this property or method." The error handler, by using **Resume Next** for this error, in effect states that if the object doesn't support the **Text** property, skip it, because it couldn't provide a match anyway.

```
Function FindText(strSearch As String) As Boolean
On Error GoTo Handler
Dim bError As Boolean
Dim ctl As Control
bError = False
For Each ctl In Form1.Controls
   If ctl.Text = strSearch Then
      If bError = False Then
        FindText = True
        Exit Function
```

```
        Else
          bError = False
        End If
     End If
Next
FindText = False
Exit Function
Handler:
Select Case Err.Number
Case 438 'Object doesn't support this property or method
     bError = True
     Resume Next
Case Else
'more code
End Select
End Function
```

This code example does not need to clear the **Err** object before returning to the loop. As with the **Resume** statement, it is not necessary to invoke the **Clear** method of the **Err** object before the **Resume Next** statement, because the **Resume Next** statement automatically calls the **Clear** method.

If the error occurred in the called procedure, and the called procedure does not have an error handler, then a **Resume Next** statement in an error handler in the calling procedure resumes execution at the statement in the calling procedure immediately following the statement that called the called procedure. In essence, the called procedure is ignored, as if it was never called at all.

Err.Raise

The **Resume** and **Resume Next** statements in the error handler in the calling procedure normally would not be reached if the called procedure had an error handler. Errors migrate up the call stack in search of an active error handler. If the called procedure has an active error handler, then the error is handled there and never reaches the error handler in the calling procedure. Therefore, if the error handler in the called procedure cannot handle the error, then the result will be program termination, unless there is a way of having the error migrate up the call stack despite the presence of an error handler in the called procedure.

There is a way. The solution is to raise an error within the error handler itself, using the **Raise** method of the **Err** object. This newly raised error, having been raised within the error handler itself, is not within the scope of an active error handler and therefore will migrate up the call stack to the error handler in the calling procedure.

Error Watch

*You should not attempt to shift control out of an error handler that did not successfully handle an error by placing an **On Error GoTo** statement inside the error handler. The flaw in this concept is that control would not shift from the first error handler to the second. Instead, the second error handler would only become effective when the first error handler finishes and returns control to the current procedure. Then control would shift to the second error handler if there were further errors in the current procedure (as opposed to errors in the first error handler), which was not the intent. Therefore, use the **Raise** method if you want to shift control out of an error handler that did not successfully handle an error.*

In the following example, the called procedure, **OpenFile**, has an error handler. That error handler is designed to resolve the situation where the disk is not in the floppy drive. It does not resolve any other errors. Yet, other errors are within the scope of the **OpenFile** error handler and therefore will not go up the call stack to be handled by the error handler in the calling procedure, **cmdOpen_Click**. The solution for this is, if the error in **OpenFile** is not number 71 (the one raised if the disk is not in the floppy drive), then the error is raised in the error handler by the **Raise** method. This permits the error to go up the call stack to be handled by the error handler in the calling procedure, **cmdOpen_Click**.

```
Sub OpenFile (ByVal strFile As String)
On Error GoTo OpenFileErr
Dim nFileNum As Integer
nFileNum  = FreeFile
Open strFile For Input As nFileNum
'further code
OpenFileErr:
Select Case Err.Number
   Case 71 'disk not in floppy drive
      Dim answer As Integer
      answer = MsgBox("Need to put disk in floppy drive", vbRetryCancel)
      If answer = vbRetry Then
         Resume
      Else
         Exit Sub
      End If
   Case Else
      Err.Raise Err.Number
End Select
Exit Sub
End Sub
```

Error Watch *If your procedure has an active error handler, call the **Raise** method inside the error handler and not in the code that precedes the error handler. If you call the **Raise** method in the code that precedes the error handler, then control may not shift to the calling procedure as you intend, but rather will stay inside the called procedure. The **Raise** method will shift execution to the specified line label in the case of an **On Error GoTo*** **line** *statement and to the next statement in the case of an **On Error Resume Next** statement.*

On Error Resume Next

The **On Error Resume Next** statement is named similarly to, but should not be confused with, the **Resume Next** statement. The **Resume Next** statement resides within an error handler and determines where control continues after the error handler finishes. By contrast, the **On Error Resume Next** statement activates an error handler that is located immediately following the statement that raised the error. With the **On Error Resume Next** statement, the error-handling routine is located just after where the error would occur, as opposed to some other location (identified by a line label or number) within the procedure. In other words, an **On Error Resume Next** statement utilizes inline error handling; that is, it checks and handles errors immediately after the code that might generate the error is executed.

There is another important difference between the **On Error Resume Next** statement and the **Resume Next** statement. The **Resume Next** statement automatically calls the **Clear** method of the **Err** object. By contrast, with the **On Error Resume Next** statement, the handling of the error does not invoke the **Clear** method. Instead, you have to explicitly call the **Clear** method or assign the value of the **Number** property to 0:

```
Function OpenFile(ByVal strFile As String) As Boolean
On Error Resume Next
Dim nFileNum As Integer
nFileNum = FreeFile
Open strFile For Input As nFileNum
If Err.Number = 53 Then 'file not found
   OpenFile = False
   Err.Clear
   Exit Function
End If
'continue with opening file
End Function
```

The **On Error Resume Next** statement often is used with common dialog controls that are displayed for the user to choose a file to open. In the following procedure, designed to open a file chosen by the user from a common dialog control, the code needs to address the possibility that the user chooses cancel rather than OK, for in that event, no file is opened. In this situation, you can use run-time errors as your friend rather than as your enemy. The **CommonDialog** control has a **CancelError** property, which, when set to True, raises a run-time error if the user chooses the Cancel button. The code uses this error to determine if the user chose the Cancel button:

```
Sub OpenFile()

On Error GoTo OpenFileError

Dim nFileNum As Integer, strFile As String
nFileNum = FreeFile
cdlOpen.CancelError = True   'cdlOpen is the CommonDialog control
cdlOpen.ShowOpen

OpenFileError:
If Err.Number = cdlCancel Then
   Exit Sub
ElseIf Err.Number <> 0 Then
   'some other error, to be handled here
End If
strFile = cdlOpen.FileName
Open strFile For Input As nFileNum
'More code
End Sub
```

Visual Basic Help points out, for once helpfully, "The **On Error Resume Next** construct may be preferable to **On Error GoTo** when handling errors generated during access to other objects. Checking **Err** after each interaction with an object removes ambiguity about which object was accessed by the code." This is an important advantage when your application accesses objects outside your applications, such as custom controls and classes. With **On Error Resume Next**, you know exactly which object generated the error—the one accessed in the preceding statement. By contrast, you could arrive at an error handler activated by **On Error GoTo *line*** from any one of several places in your code.

On Error GoTo 0

The **On Error GoTo 0** statement turns off an error handler. The reason you would want to turn off an active error handler is to handle an error further up the call stack. Less obvious is why you would have activated an error handler in the first place just to turn it off. The reason is that you may want some errors handled in the current procedure but others handled further up the call stack. The following code shows the error handler being turned off:

```
Sub OpenFile()
On Error GoTo OpenFileError
Dim nFileNum As Integer, strFile As String
nFileNum = FreeFile
cdlOpen.CancelError = True   'cdlOpen = CommonDialog control
cdlOpen.ShowOpen
OpenFileError:
If Err.Number = cdlCancel Then
   Exit Sub
ElseIf Err.Number <> 0 Then
   'some other error, to be handled here
End If
On Error GoTo 0 'turn off error handler.
                'Error handled further up call stack

strFile = cdlOpen.FileName
Open strFile For Input As nFileNum
'More code
End Sub
```

Best Practices

The term "best practices" has become the business world's sugarcoated phrase for the lessons learned from that educational institution which we have long attended but likely will never graduate from, the "College of Hard Knocks." Differences in lingo aside, there are certain practices that just are a good idea. Let's look at some programming design tips.

Handle Errors That Occur in Error Handlers

You may be rolling your eyes at this one. Error handlers are supposed to take care of your troubles by resolving errors, not adding to your troubles by raising new ones. Yet, it happens; sometimes errors occur in an error handler. When this happens, the new error migrates up the call stack. This new error has to be handled before the error handler can continue. The result may be that the following code in the error handler may never execute, and the unexecuted code may be critical to the health of your application, and its failure to execute could cause further problems.

In an ideal world, the solution would be to ensure that errors don't occur in your error handlers. Of course, in an ideal world you wouldn't need an error handler. In any event, errors occurring in an error handler are a reality, and when you think about it, they are not surprising. Error handlers don't run under the best of circumstances. Indeed, almost by definition, error handlers do not execute unless something already has gone wrong. By the time an error handler is activated, your application, or even worse, the operating system, may be unstable.

You can reduce the risk of errors occurring in an error handler by reducing the complexity of the error handler. The less complicated the error handler, the less likely it is that the error handler itself will raise an error.

The complexity of the error handler depends on the complexity of the procedure in which it resides. This suggests that error handlers that handle "dangerous" errors—errors that can propagate other errors—should be placed in procedures that are devoted to the single purpose of handling dangerous operations. Such procedures must completely handle their own errors. Otherwise, these errors will migrate up the call stack, defeating the whole purpose of the procedure.

Ensure That Errors Are Handled Somewhere

Given the fatal consequences of unhandled run-time errors, hopefully just to your application and not to you as well (users of an application that continually crashes and burns do get irate), errors need to be handled somewhere. Since errors migrate up the call stack, you can ensure that errors will be handled if you put error handlers in your main subroutine (assuming your project starts from **Sub Main**) and in event handlers (such as **cmdDestructButton_Click()**).

Restore Last Good Status

Database applications have transactions, and transactions adopt an "all or nothing" approach to an attempt to take an action. For example, an automatic teller transaction should not succeed unless both the account is debited and the account holder receives the cash (although we wouldn't mind if only the latter occurred). If either fails, both should fail, and the transaction is "rolled back" to its status before the ATM transaction was attempted. Similarly, if an error occurs that cannot be fully resolved, variables and properties should be restored to the values they had before the operation that gave rise to the error was attempted.

Compartmentalize Your Application

You may have seen movies about battles at sea in which sailors manning submarines and other ships taking on water seal off portions of the ship by closing watertight doors. This isolates the problem to a portion of the ship and prevents the rest of the ship from being flooded and the ship from sinking (although it is a bit rough on anyone who didn't get out of the sealed-off portion of the ship in time). Similarly, you can isolate the effects of an error on your application. For example, if clicking a button starts a chain of events that results in an irresolvable error, handle the error so that the user is advised that the desired task cannot be performed, and then restore the program to its condition before the button was clicked.

Log Errors

Sometimes you cannot resolve an error. In such sad cases, you can make the best of a bad situation by at least recording the error. You should pass three parameters to the procedure that logs the error: the number, description, and source of the error. The error number and description can be passed as **Err.Number** and **Err.Description**, respectively. The error source can be passed manually, such as by passing the name of the procedure.

Summary

While it would be nice not to have to worry about errors distracting you from developing an application, the unfortunate reality is that errors are, well, an unfortunate reality. Additionally, poor error handling can make an otherwise well-constructed application look poorly built. Indeed, in this instance, appearances would not be deceiving. Given the consequences of unhandled run-time errors, an application that does not handle errors well is not a well-written application.

This chapter showed you how to use the **Err** object and the **On Error** statements. The **Err** object gives you critical information about the error that has been raised. The **On Error GoTo** ***line*** and **On Error Resume Next** statements activate and specify the location of error handlers. Within an error handler, the **Resume** and **Resume Next** statements and the **Raise** method of the **Err** object determine where control passes when the error handler finishes.

Error handling should not be viewed as a menial task that gets in the way of "real programming." It *is* real programming, in some ways more difficult than usual because you have to anticipate and visualize. Additionally, good error handling is a case where the life (or at least the job) you save may be your own. If you make error handling an organic part of your application instead of an afterthought, you will have made a major stride toward being recognized as a pro by your fellow programmers.

CHAPTER 5

Conditional Compilation and Compiler Options

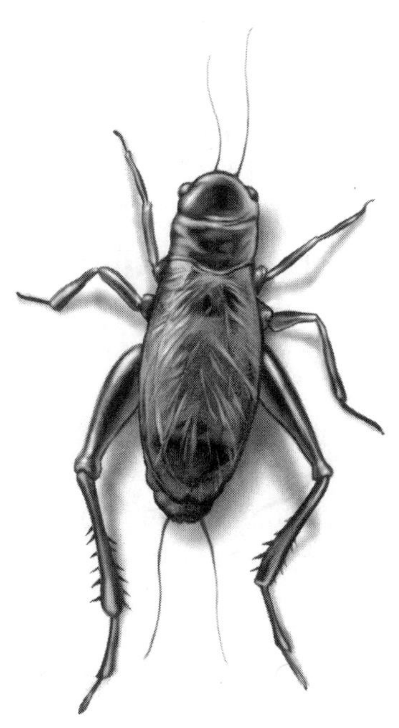

While you are developing applications, you likely will—if you haven't already—encounter situations where the code you want to execute depends on the target customer. For example, when developing your product, you will probably have an internal beta version, a special version with extra error handling for external beta testers, and then your final solution. Rather than keeping different versions of your source code, you can use conditional compilation. Like the **If-Then** control statement, conditional compilation will execute different blocks of code depending on the conditions when the program was compiled.

Whether conditional compilation is necessary or not, eventually it will be time to compile. Compiling for many programmers is essentially automatic. A program won't execute until it is compiled, so the programmer compiles the program so it can be run. Compiling is simply a necessary means to the end of running a program.

You certainly can compile a program in one easy step, simply by choosing Make EXE from the File menu. By doing this, you accept the default compiler settings. However, just as a "one size fits all" suit may not fit you unless you happen to have the build for which the suit was designed, the default compiler settings may not be the best for your application. For example, speed versus size is a common trade-off in application development. You may have to optimize the compilation for speed in one situation and for size in another. Visual Basic gives you the ability to tailor the compile options to fit your situation.

Choosing the correct compilation options is important. The best-written code won't execute optimally if the wrong compile options are chosen. While tailoring the compilation options to your situation is more work, the reward is a better application.

Conditional Compilation

When developing an application, there are times when you will want functions or fragments of code statements to be excluded from your application's execution. You also might want certain segments of your code to execute during the development and testing of your application and not to be available for distribution versions. Using the conditional compilation statements allows you to instruct the compiler to include and exclude segments of your code. For example, in your program, you may have some statements that are relevant to beta candidates of your program because they write a log of every procedure that is executed in the order in which they are executed. You would use the conditional compilation statements to separate code that will be compiled into the various release versions. If it weren't for the conditional compilation statements, you would have to use comment tags to prevent their execution, which would be very time consuming and not very efficient.

The following listing illustrates a use of the conditional compilation statement.

```
#If ReleasedVersion then
    frmRegOption.Show vbModal
#Else
    Call WriteLog("DisplayOptionsDialog",ProcName)
    frmOption.Show vbModal
#End If
```

If you're still using Visual Basic 4.0 to write and maintain 16- and 32-bit applications, using conditional compilation can help you maintain one set of source code for two sets of operating systems. In version 4.0, the conditional compiler constants **Win16** and **Win32** were built into the run-time module. In version 5.0 or later, these constants were removed because 16-bit development is no longer supported.

As you can see from the listing example, the conditional compilation statement is not very difficult to use, and it can be used for a number of things. The syntax for it is based on the standard **If-Then** statement. The main difference is that a pound (#) symbol is placed in front of the **If-Then** statements.

#Const Statement

There are three ways to declare conditional compilation constants. You can embed a constant within your code by using the **#Const** statement, you can add the arguments within the Make tab of the Project Properties dialog box, or you can use the **/d** (or **/D**) flag when compiling a project from the command line.

Defining a conditional compilation constant is very similar to defining a standard constant. You assign a value to the name of the constant, and the value can be a combination of a literal value, other conditional compilation constants defined with the **#Const** statement, and an arithmetic or logical operator. If you use the **#Const** statement within your application to define the variable, you will need to do so within each module. **#Const** statements have a scope of private.

When defining the expression assigned to the constant value, make sure you don't define it more than once per module. If you do, the compiler will produce a "Compile Error: Duplicate Definition" error message. Also, when you define the expression, be careful if you use an intrinsic function that does not return a numeric value, like **Chr**. If you do, you will receive a "Compile Error: Variable Not Found" error message. Conditional compilation constants can only be defined one per line, whereas many regular constants can be defined on one line, separated by colons, within a 255-character line limitation. You can follow the definition of a conditional compilation constant with a comment. The following are a couple of examples of conditional compilation constants.

```
#Const c_Str = "Conditional String Constant"

#Const c_Registered = True
```

In order to define a conditional compilation constant to be global throughout the application, you need to define it either in the Project Properties dialog box or at the time you compile the application through the command line. To set the conditional compilation constant within the Project Properties dialog box, select the Make tab in the Project Properties dialog box, as shown in Figure 5-1.

To define the conditional compilation constant from a command line, you need to be within a MS-DOS window or at the Start menu's Run dialog box. From the command line, execute the Visual Basic executable using the **/make** (or **/m**) flag, the project file you wish to compile, and the **/d** (or **/D**) flag followed

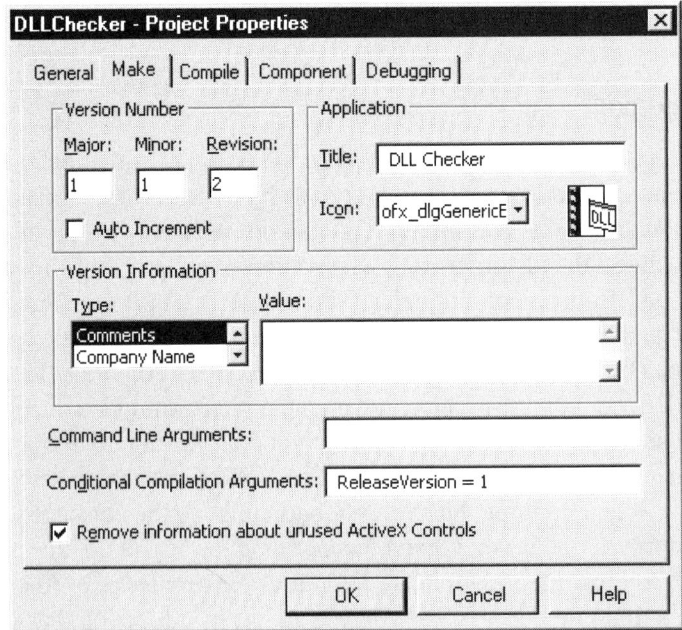

Figure 5.1 Set the Conditional Compilation arguments in the Make tab of the Project Properties dialog box

by the constant declarations. An example of defining the conditional compilation constant at the command line would be as follows:

```
vb6.exe /m dllchecker.vbp /d ReleaseVersion=1
```

In order for this to work, the directory that contains the Visual Basic executable must be in the MS-DOS path, or you need to fully qualify the path.

A caveat you should be aware of is the order in which conditional compilation constants are assigned. Conditional compilation constants assigned within modules have precedence over all other ones assigned in the Project Properties dialog box or at the command line. Defining these constants at the command line has precedence over the Project Properties dialog box. What does this mean? Just like when you define the scope of the regular variables and constants, you need to take care when defining the conditional compilation constants and be mindful of their scope.

Conditional Compilation's #If-Then Statement

The use of conditional compilation's **#If-Then** statement allows you to selectively compile portions of your code to create variations of your application. A lot of developers might think that this would be useful when creating applications for multilanguage applications. For simple multilanguage applications, this might be a method of choice, but you really should consider using Resource files for that. For more information about using the Resource file, refer to the Microsoft Developer Network CD that comes with Visual Studio.

You can also use the **#If-Then** statement to include debugging code within your application. Starting with version 5.0 of Visual Basic, the **Assert** method was built into the **Debug** object. By using this **Assert** method, you can programmatically suspend execution of your application when a certain condition is met. This method is automatically stripped from the application when it is made into an executable. The **Assert** method is fine for stopping execution, but it's hardly efficient. The **#If-Then** statement allows you to segment your code. The format is as follows:

```
#If <switch value> Then
    ' To Do
#ElseIf <switch value> Then
    ' To Do
#Else
    ' To Do
#End If
```

Just like in the standard **If-Then** statement, you can use **#ElseIf** and **#Else** as optional test conditions. The **<switch value>** is a constant or any mathematical equation defined in the **#Const** statement. If the **<switch value>** is zero, which is also **False**, the code that follows is not executed. By default, all undefined switch values are set to zero. Only the condition that is true can be executed.

Although the **#If-Then** is similar to its **If-Then** counterpart, the **#If-Then** statement cannot be used by itself. It must be followed by an **#End If**. Also, unlike the **If-Then** statement, you can only set a breakpoint within the condition that will be executed. Take the following code for example:

```
#Const ccDBG = 1
#If ccDBG then
    MsgBox("You're in Debug Mode")
#Else
    MsgBox ("You're in Production Mode")
#End If
```

If you try setting a breakpoint on the code contained within the **#Else** clause, you will receive a "Breakpoint not allowed on this line" error message. That's because the **ccDBG** constant is True. If you set the constant to False, you will be able to set a breakpoint.

Design Tip *Be mindful of how you define your conditional compilation constants. Remember that True and –1 are the same. Don't define a constant to be 1 thinking it means True. You will encounter problems if you use the* ***Not*** *operator.*

Using the conditional compilation arguments, you can test out a lot of different code routines within a procedure. One method that is not used as often is placing the conditional compilation **#If-Then** before a function or procedure name. If you find yourself using two or more conditional compilation **#If-Then** statements within the same function or procedure, you might want to consider using this method. It can help make your code a lot more readable and maintainable.

```
#If ccDBG Then
    Sub Function DoSomething(sVal1 As String, sVal2 As String) As String
    ...
    End Function
#Else
    Sub Function DoSomething(sVal1 As String) As String
    ...
    End Function
#End If
```

Design Tip *A really good time to use **#If-Then** statements is when you are developing Automation-based applications. By using it, you can include both the early and late binding information to an object in your project.*

Compile on Demand

When you first install Visual Basic, the Compile on Demand option is enabled. What Compile on Demand does is tell the compiler to only compile the code that is needed, allowing the application to start sooner within the development IDE. Rather than the compiler checking every inch of code for syntax errors before the program starts, it only compiles the code necessary to start the program. This means that you'll have to wait until run-time to get any errors that may otherwise be caught by the compiler. As you test your program in this manner, the rest of your code will be compiled and then executed on the fly.

When the Compile on Demand option is enabled, you have the option to select whether you want background compilation to be performed during idle processing or not. This option is called Background Compile. For example, suppose you're working on two functions in a program, and each function is contained within its own form. When you run your application from within the IDE, you can only really test one feature at a time. When you enable Background Compile, while you're looking at one feature, the IDE will compile the other feature in the background. If you choose the Start with Full Compile command on the Run menu, Visual Basic ignores the Compile on Demand setting and performs a full compile.

With computers being as fast as they are today, compiling segments of your program in the background this way is really inefficient and not recommended. It's best to make sure that your program at least passes all its syntax checks before compilation. This will save you a lot of time performing minor debugging.

Compilation Choices

As mentioned in the introduction to this chapter, you can compile your application simply by selecting Make EXE from the File menu. However, you might not always want to do that—after all, not every size fits all. There are a lot of compiler options that enable you to customize your executables to meet a variety of specific needs. This is handled through the Compile tab of the Project Properties dialog box.

The Compile Tab

The Compile tab, shown in Figure 5-2, is found in the Project Properties dialog box and allows you to change specific attributes of your project when you compile. The most significant compiler option you should be concerned with is the distinction between *p-code* and *native code*.

P-Code vs. Native Code

P-code is short for pseudo-code. The definition of p-code here is different from the one you're probably familiar with. Most people think of p-code as generic programming logic or algorithms. In Visual Basic, p-code is a special kind of executable code that will run on a variety of processors, such as Motorola 68000, DEC Alpha, and the Intel x86 family of processors, provided a Visual Basic translator or run-time resource is available. Any time you run a p-code application, there is an intermediate step involved during the application's execution. The operating system translates the p-code into native code that the processor running the application can understand.

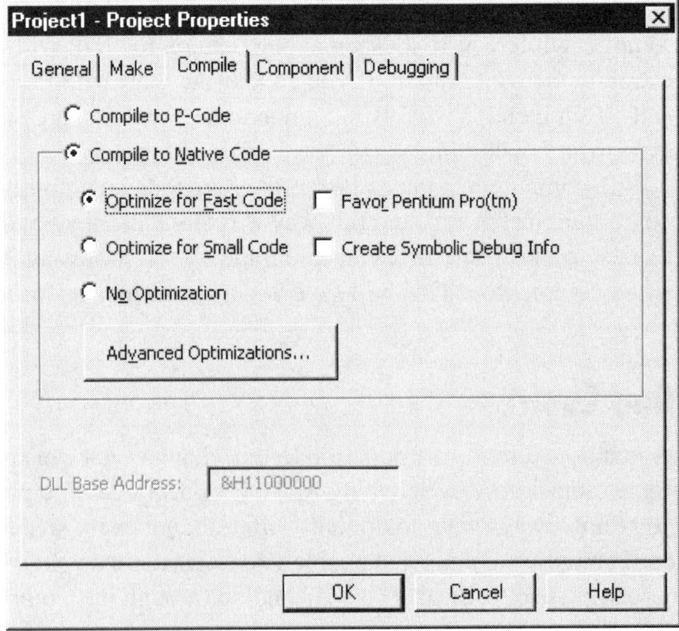

Figure 5.2 Compile tab in the Project Properties dialog box

Native code is real machine code, the native instructions for the processor chip. This is similar to the code that Visual C++ generates. Native code is faster than p-code because the latter is interpreted code. However, native code tends to be larger; therefore, the tradeoff is speed versus size. Indeed, p-code often may be the better choice. Often a decision can be made only after compiling and running the component or program. One guideline is that the speed advantage of native code is pronounced when the code is processor-intensive.

One of the earlier misnomers about native-code execution within Visual Basic is that you would no longer need to ship the run-time DLL (MSVBVM50.DLL or MSVBVM60.DLL) with your application or component. Whether you choose p-code or native code, the run-time DLL still needs to be deployed. Native-code programs use some of the internal resources that are contained within the run-time DLL.

Optimize for Fast Code

An advantage of a native-code application is the speed with which it executes. Marking this option will cause the compiler to convert your Visual Basic statements in the most efficient code it can, allowing your application to execute in the quickest manner possible. One caveat about this setting: what you gain in speed, you may lose in increased size. This means that even though your code may execute faster, the algorithm might be more complicated; therefore, the size of your compiled application might be larger than had you not chosen this option.

Optimize for Small Code

Marking this option will cause the compiler to examine each Visual Basic statement and determine which is the smallest algorithm to use in order to make your compiled application the smallest possible. The caveat about this setting is that you might sacrifice the speed with which your application executes, because the smallest algorithm might not be the most efficient.

No Optimization

This option will cause the compiler not to optimize your application. This will result in a straight translation of your Visual Basic statements into native code. It will make no attempt to speed up any algorithm or produce a small executable. Since no optimization is performed, your project compiles faster, and thus is more useful when testing and debugging with a third-party debugger tool.

Favor Pentium Pro

A lot of application development has moved to the 32-bit arena. With the introduction of the Intel Pentium Pro microprocessor in 1997, 32-bit performance was drastically increased. This is mostly due to the processor's built-in secondary cache internal architecture and its ability to execute 32-bit instructions in parallel.

By using this option, the compile will add an additional level of basic, but specific, compiling optimization instructions that favor the Pentium Pro or P6 line of processors. Note that you should only use this option if your application is going to run exclusively on this type of platform. Your application will still work on other Intel-based computers, but its performance will suffer significantly. For example, if you have a program that scrolls frames of images across your screen, and you compile your application with the Favor Pentium Pro switch enabled, running the application on a system other than a Pentium Pro–based system (or better) would cause the scrolling to be very jagged and unprofessional looking. It would be like watching a streaming media file on a 56Kbps modem versus over a cable modem connection.

Create Symbolic Debug Info

By selecting the Create Symbolic Debug Info option, you will be able to debug your native-code application by using Microsoft Visual C++'s debugger, or another compatible CodeView debugging utility, like CompuWare NuMega BoundsChecker. This option will increase the size of the file slightly, but it allows for enhanced debugging options and creates an accompanying PDB (program database) file, which holds debugging information. Obviously, this option does not offer a form of executable optimization, but rather a form of solution-testing optimization.

DLL Base Address

This option is only in ActiveX DLL, ActiveX Control, ActiveX Server, DHTML Application, and IIS App projects. The DLL base address is the memory address into which an ActiveX DLL (or control) will be loaded. The memory range is from 16MB (16,777,216 or &H1000000) to 2GB (2,147,483,648 or &H80000000), inclusive. The address must be a multiple of 64K. Consequently, the last four digits (in hexadecimal) will be 0000.

When Windows loads a DLL, it attempts to load it at the specified address. If the address is available, the DLL loads relatively quickly. However, if another DLL is already using that address, then Windows must relocate the DLL data and code to an available location. This is known as *rebasing*. Rebasing is time-consuming and also may complicate Windows' ability to share the DLL code with other applications. Obviously, rebasing is to be avoided as much as possible.

Visual Basic programmers who have not read *Visual Basic Annotated Archives* (Jung and Kent, Osborne/McGraw Hill, 1999) or the Microsoft

Developers Network white pages often don't bother to change the default DLL base address of &H11000000. Thus, there is a reasonably high probability that the DLL base address of &H11000000 will *not* be available. Thus, a different DLL base address will be used and the resource will be rebased.

Advanced Optimization Choices

The Advanced Optimizations button on the Compile tab of the Project Properties dialog box will display the Advanced Optimizations dialog box, which provides you with more settings for optimizing your compiled program. Figure 5-3 shows this dialog box.

Assume No Aliasing

An alias is a name that refers to a memory location that is already referred to by a different name. This occurs when variables are passed into methods by reference (**ByRef**). By marking this option, you are telling the compiler that your program does not use aliasing. Using this option allows the compiler to apply optimizations it could not otherwise use, such as storing variables in registers and performing loop optimizations. Loop optimization removes unvarying

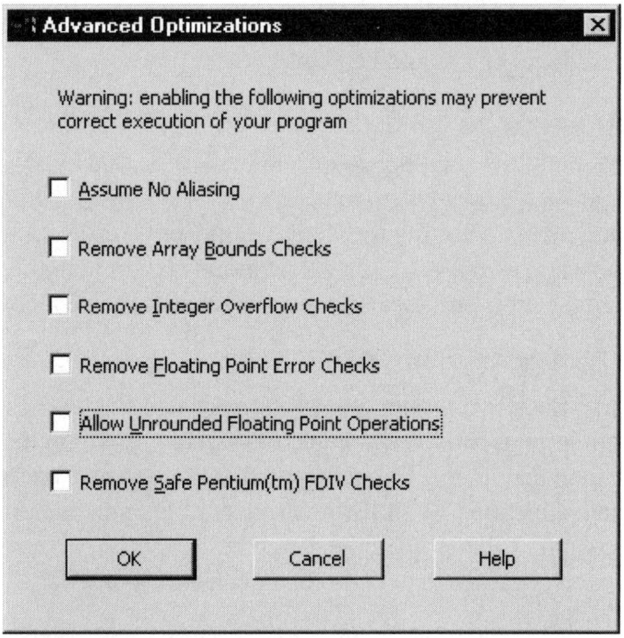

Figure 5.3 Advanced Optimizations dialog box

subexpressions from the body of a loop. One caveat, though: you should not consider using this optimization method if your project passes arguments using **ByRef**, because the optimizations could cause your project to execute incorrectly.

Remove Array Bounds Checks

By default, Visual Basic checks to make sure that a reference to an array is within the array's boundaries. By selecting this Remove Array Bounds Checks option, you are removing this fail-safe and could cause your application to crash if a reference was made to an invalid array pointer. For example, consider the following code:

```
Private Sub Form_Load()
    Dim vArray(10)
    Dim x
    For x = 0 To 10
        vArray(x) = x
    Next
    MsgBox vArray(12)
    End
End Sub
```

By default, this program will generate a "Subscript out of range" error on the line that calls the **MsgBox** statement. If you had selected the Remove Array Bounds Checks option, the program would execute, and the resulting message in the message box would be blank.

Remove Integer Overflow Checks

By default, the compiler checks to make sure that every calculation of an integer-based data type—byte, integer, and long—is within the range of that data type. By selecting the Remove Integer Overflow Checks option, you are removing this fail-safe. If a calculation is larger than the data type's capacity, no error will occur, meaning that you could receive incorrect calculated values.

Remove Floating-Point Error Checks

Visual Basic's compiler checks to make sure that every calculation of a floating-point data type—single or double—is within the range of that data type and that there will not be any division-by-zero operations. By selecting this Remove Floating-Point Error Checks option, you are removing this fail-safe. If a calculation is larger than the data type's capacity, no error will occur, meaning that you could receive incorrect calculated values.

Allow Unrounded Floating-Point Operations

Floating-point calculations are normally rounded off to the correct decimal precision before any comparisons are made. By marking the Allow Unrounded Floating Point Operations option, you are allowing the natively compiled code to compare results of floating-point calculations without first rounding the results to the correct decimal place. This can result in improved speed for some floating-point operations, but it may also result in calculations being maintained at a higher decimal precision than has been programmed for. This would result in values that might not equal one another when normally they would.

Remove Safe Pentium FDIV Checks

Remember when the Pentium processor first came out and there was a flaw found in the floating-point division (FDIV) process? By default, the compiler will implement a mathematical algorithm to produce safe code that tests for the processor bug and calls run-time routines to generate correct floating-point results. By doing this, the compiled program is relying on mathematics performed without the assistance of any built-in math coprocessing from the CPU. It's like doing all your trigonometry calculations for sine, cosine, and tangent without the assistance of a scientific calculator.

By selecting this Remove Safe Pentium FDIV Checks option, you remove the fail-safe that ensures that the calculations used by the FDIV are correct. The resulting size of your code and the speed with which it executes will increase, but your values may be slightly incorrect if your application is run on a system with a flawed Pentium processor.

Summary

Using the conditional compilation feature is really a shortcut to commenting out entire blocks of code depending on a global setting. Without it, you would literally have to comment out every line of code you wouldn't want executed. It's also a great method to help test alternative procedures and functions by setting a global constant that determines the execution path. It's a tremendous timesaving technique for coding that can help make your code more manageable, maintainable, and reusable.

The compiler properties are great methods to see how optimal your code potentially can be, but don't expect miracles. A compiler can only do a certain amount of optimization. If you distribute a lot of VB applications within your organization, you might discover that the best that optimization can do for your VB code is by compiling it as p-code rather than native code, to make your application small. Regardless how the application is compiled, it does not eliminate the need to ship the MSVBVMx0.DLL.

CHAPTER 6

Windows API

The Windows API—the very name strikes fear in the hearts of Visual Basic programmers. Well, most of us.

"He doesn't know the meaning of the word fear. He doesn't know the meaning of lots of words." —Lou Holtz, football coach talking about one of his players

The Windows API strikes the fear of the unknown in the hearts of Visual Basic programmers. The Windows API is comparatively seldom used and is shrouded in mystery. Another fear is of the consequences. There are many anecdotes, often true, about faulty use of the Windows API not only crashing the application but the operating system, too.

Yet, you can benefit greatly from being able to use the Windows API in your application. While Visual Basic itself uses the Windows API, you can also call the Windows API directly, and by doing so add functionality to your application not available through Visual Basic alone. Indeed, in more complex applications, not being able to directly call the Windows API is like programming with one hand tied behind your back.

"It's not my fault, it's General Protection's." —Ratbert, the computer consultant in Dilbert

Beginning programmers thinking of using the Windows API should bear in mind the warning often given in TV shows for children: "Don't try this at home, kids; we're trained professionals." However, as a trained professional, you should not only try, but also use the Windows API. This chapter will discuss the pitfalls and traps, so you won't have to offer any explanations or excuses to the application user whose unsaved work just got lost.

Windows API Overview

The "API" in the Windows API stands for "Application Programming Interface," which means a collection of functions that can be used in programming an application. The word "Windows" qualifies API because not only Windows has an API. Other operating systems also have APIs. Additionally, many applications have an API. Indeed, the computer-programming landscape is littered with acronyms like MAPI (Messaging Application Programming Interface), TAPI (Telephony Application Programming Interface), ISAPI (Internet Server Application Programming Interface), and so on. The word "Application" in "Application Programming Interface" means that the API functions can be accessed and used by other applications. For example, applications use MAPI for e-mail services.

Two Windows APIs

Actually there is more than one Windows API. Win16 is used by 16-bit operating systems (Windows 3.*x*). Win32 is used by 32-bit operating systems (Windows 9*x*, NT, and 2000). There also are two hybrid Windows APIs, Win32c and Win32s. Because 16-bit operating systems are going the way of the dinosaurs, this chapter will focus on the Win32 API. However, Chapter 5 discusses how, with conditional compilation, your code can include the Win16 API, as well, so your application can also run on 16-bit operating systems.

The Windows API is a collection of functions that reside in dynamic-link library (.dll) files. These dynamic-link libraries (DLLs) generally are located in the \Windows\System directory on Windows 9*x* operating systems and the \Winnt\System32 directory on Windows NT/2000 operating systems.

The Windows operating system uses the Windows API functions to do its work. For example, most Windows applications have a Help | About dialog box with a command button for System Info. Clicking that button will display, as the command button's caption suggests, system information, including the amount of available memory. This information is determined by an API function called **GlobalMemoryStatus**. Win32 API functions also retrieve system information, manage input through the keyboard and output through the screen and printer, stream data to and from files, and handle the myriad other tasks performed by Windows.

Visual Basic programs also use the Windows API. There really is no choice. No matter which programming language you choose, ultimately you have to interact with the Windows operating system to create a Windows application. The Windows API functions are necessary for creating windows and having them respond to events. However, Visual Basic hides its use of the Windows API from you. Visual Basic calls Windows API functions behind the scenes when you call a procedure or set a property.

Windows API functions can be called directly from within your Visual Basic program. You do not need to go through Visual Basic procedures and properties to access the Windows API. Indeed, the purpose of this chapter is to enable you to directly call the Windows API from your Visual Basic program safely and effectively.

However, while you can call Windows API functions directly, rather than going through Visual Basic, there are two disadvantages of doing so. The coding is more difficult, and there is a much higher risk of a crash.

When you access the Windows API functions through Visual Basic, you do so differently than you would public functions of an ActiveX DLL. You use a **Declare** statement instead of setting a reference to an ActiveX DLL through the Project | References menu item. You then call the Windows API function directly, rather than through an instance of the class in the ActiveX DLL.

Using the adage that a picture (or code example) is worth a thousand words, the difficulty of using the Windows API is illustrated by a comparison of creating a basic Windows application both with Visual Basic and with the Windows API.

To create a Windows application through Visual Basic, choose the Standard EXE project from the New Project dialog box. That's it. No code is necessary.

Life is not so easy if you use the Windows API directly to create a Windows application. The following illustrative application is written in C++ rather than Visual Basic to avoid the need of overriding Visual Basic's default Windows application. The double forward slashes (//) start a comment in C++ and are used to annotate the code.

```
#include "windows.h"

LONG WINAPI WndProc(HWND, UINT, WPARAM, LPARAM);

int WINAPI WinMain(HINSTANCE hInstance, HINSTANCE hInstance,
   WPARAM wParam, LPARAM lParam)
{
   WNDCLASS wc;  // structure to hold attributes of window
   HWND hwnd;    // handle to window
   MSG msg;      // structure to handle messages
   //start setting attributes of window
   wc.Style = NULL;              // default style
   wc.lpfnWndProc = WndProc;     // procedure to handle messages
   wc.cbClsExtra = 0;            // no extra data for class
   wc.cbWndExtra = 0;            // no extra data for window
   wc.hInstance = hInstance;     // handle to application instance
   wc.hIcon = LoadIcon(NULL, IDI_APPLICATION);        // default icon
   wc.hCursor = LoadCursor(NULL, IDC_ARROW);          // default cursor
   wc.hbrBackground = GetStockObject(WHITE_BRUSH);    // white background
   wc.lpszMenuName = NULL;                            // no menu
   wc.lpszClassName = "GoodByeWorld";                 // class name
   // finished setting attributes of window
   RegisterClass(&wc);  //register class
   //create window
   hwnd = CreateWindow {
          "GoodByeWorld",                     // class name
          "Creating windows the hard way",    // window title
          WS_OVERLAPPEDWINDOW,                // default window style
          CW_USEDEFAULT,                      // default position x
```

```
        CW_USEDEFAULT,                        // default position y
        CW_USEDEFAULT,                        // default size x
        CW_USEDEFAULT,                        // default size y
        0,                                    // no parent window
        0,                                    // no menu
        hInstance,                            // application instance handle
        NULL                                  // no window creation data
};
// window created, so show it
ShowWindow (hWnd, mCmdShow);
UpdateWindow (hWnd);
// handle messages to window
while (GetMessage (&msg, NULL, 0, 0) {
   TranslateMessage (&msg);
   DispatchMessage (&msg);
   }
return msg.wParam;
}

LONG WINAPI WndProc(HWND hWnd, UINT message,
     WPARAM wParam, LPARAM lParam)
{
switch(message)  {
   case WMDESTROY:  // user wishes to end application
      PostQuitMessage(0);
      break;
   default:  // all other messages handled by default
      return (DefWIndowProc(hWnd, message, wParam, lParam);
   }
   return NULL;
}
```

All this code just creates a functioning window. There isn't even a "Hello World" (or "Goodbye Cruel World") message. As you expand the functionality of the window, Visual Basic's ease of use, in comparison with the Windows API, becomes even more pronounced.

In addition to ease of use, Visual Basic uses the Windows API safely. Windows API functions are not easy to use. As this chapter shows, there are many pitfalls. Additionally, if you do make a mistake using the Windows API, you don't just receive a garden-variety run-time error terminating your program. Instead, your choices may be limited to a warm boot or cold.

Clearly, the Visual Basic way of creating a Windows application is preferable, unless your preference is pain and suffering, particularly your own. Thus, the question arises: If calling the Windows API directly is so difficult or dangerous, why do it?

While Visual Basic makes using the Windows API easy and safe, it only uses a subset of the myriad Windows API functions—basically the ones you are most likely to use. This limitation usually is not a problem. The Windows API functionality that you can access through Visual Basic generally is sufficient for your application, particularly for simpler applications. However, if you need functionality that Visual Basic does not give you, then you need to use the Windows API directly. Another book of ours, *Visual Basic Annotated Archives* (Osborne/McGraw-Hill, 1999), provides numerous examples of calling the Windows API directly to add functionality to your application not accessible through Visual Basic. Those examples include taking the size and position of the taskbar into account in centering your form, automatically resizing the width of a **ComboBox** control to show the entirety of the widest item, adding your own items to the system menu, and so on.

Just as you can use the Windows API to automatically resize the width of a **ComboBox** control, many third-party vendors sell custom controls that use the Windows API to enhance the ability of the standard controls packaged with Visual Basic. Rather than buy custom controls, you can use the Windows API to create your own. Creating your own custom controls removes worries about distributing the third-party controls on the users' machines, licensing, and so on. Windows API functions are guaranteed to exist on every Windows operating system, and the user has a license (or at least is supposed to) for the operating system.

You first will need to determine which of the literally hundreds of Windows API functions to use, before you can start writing your code. One solution, and perhaps the most efficient one if you do a lot of Windows API programming, is to shell out a few dollars and buy one of the several reference books on the Windows API. A good programmer must be multitalented, but rote memorization need not be one of the talents.

However, if you don't like paying for books (except this one, of course), you can get help, specifically the Platform Software Development Kit (SDK) help file. The Platform SDK help file explains the purpose, declaration, and parameters of the Windows API functions. The Platform SDK help file is in the Microsoft Developer Network (MSDN) Library. The MSDN Library, which comes on two CDs, is included in the Professional and Enterprise editions of version 6 of Visual Basic. These CDs include, in addition to the Platform SDK help file, a wealth of other information. The MSDN Library CDs are in an HTML Help format.

If you do not have the MSDN Library CDs, you can still access the Platform SDK help file online by going to http://msdn.microsoft.com, and then choosing MSDN Library Online. The Platform SDK help file on the MSDN Library Online is also in an HTML Help format.

Using the Windows API

There are two steps to using a Windows API function: declare it and call it. This may sound simple, but while there are only two steps, each has more traps than an Indiana Jones movie.

The Declare Statement

When you call a procedure in a Visual Basic project, that procedure must already be defined. The definition of a procedure includes the number, order, and data types of the function's parameters (if any), the procedure's return value (again, if any), and what the procedure does in its body. Without this information, Visual Basic would not know what to do when you call the procedure.

When you call intrinsic Visual Basic procedures, such as the string manipulation functions **Left**, **Right**, **Mid**, and **Trim**, Visual Basic knows the definitions of these procedures because they are built into Visual Basic. When you call procedures that you have defined in your Visual Basic project, Visual Basic looks in your project for the procedure's definition, and assuming the procedure is defined in your project, uses that definition to execute a procedure (otherwise an error will be raised).

Windows API functions, like intrinsic Visual Basic procedures and unlike user-defined procedures, have a preexisting definition. However, unlike intrinsic Visual Basic procedures, that definition is located outside of Visual Basic, namely in a dynamic-link library (a .dll file), usually in the \Windows\System directory on a Windows 9*x* operating system or the \Winnt\System32 directory on a Windows NT or 2000 operating system.

With dynamic-link libraries generally, there are two alternative methods of telling Visual Basic where to locate the function's definition, either by setting a reference to the DLL's type library, or by using a **Declare** statement in a module. Setting a reference to a DLL's type library usually is the easier of the two alternatives, since you then can call the DLL function as if it were part of your project. However, not all DLLs provide type libraries. In particular, the DLLs in the Windows API do not provide type libraries. Therefore, you must use a **Declare** statement to reference a function in the Windows API.

A **Declare** statement tells Visual Basic where to find a particular DLL function and how to call it. The **Declare** statement has the following syntax:

```
[Public | Private] Declare [Function | Sub] & _
  name Lib "libname" [Alias "aliasname"]
  [([arglist])] [As type]
```

Table 6-1 describes the elements of the **Declare** statement.

The **Declare** statement for the **GetTempPath** function, which returns the path to the Windows temporary folder (by default C:\Windows\Temp), is as follows:

```
Private Declare Function GetTempPath Lib "kernel32" _
   Alias "GetTempPathA" (ByVal nBufferLength As Long, _
   ByVal lpBuffer As String) As Long
```

The ***name*** element, by which the function will be called in the Visual Basic program, is **GetTempPath**. Its ***aliasname***, the actual name that it is called in the kernel32.dll DLL (the ***libname*** element), is **GetTempPathA**.

The ***libname*** element specifies, as a string, the name of the DLL that contains the Windows API function. In the **Declare** statement of **GetTempPath**, the ***libname***

Element	Required?	Description
Public | Private	No; if not included, the default access is used	**Public** is used if the API function is to be available to the entire project, or **Private** if it is to be available to only that module. This is only an option in a standard module; in a class module, a **Declare** statement must be **Private**.
Function | Sub	Yes	A DLL can be either a **Function** or a **Sub**, though it usually is a **Function**.
name	Yes	This is the DLL's name, which is case-sensitive.
Lib	Yes	The **Lib** keyword indicates that the DLL or other code resource contains the procedure being declared.
libname	Yes	This is the name of the DLL or code resource that contains the declared procedure. The DLLs containing commonly used Windows APIs are listed in Tables 6-2 and 6-3.
Alias	No, optional	This keyword indicates that the procedure has another name in the DLL. Its use is discussed later in "Use Aliases to Avoid the As Any Parameter."
aliasname	Used when the **Alias** keyword is used	This parameter is used in conjunction with the **Alias** keyword, and indicates the actual name of the procedure in the DLL or code resource.
arglist	Yes	This is a list of parameters (if any), including their corresponding data types, that is passed to the procedure when it is called.
type	No, optional (though it should be used for functions)	This is the data type returned if the DLL is a function.

Table 6.1 Elements of a **Declare** Statement

DLL	Description
Kernel32.dll	Low-level operating system functions, such as those for memory and task management and resource handling
User32.dll	Windows management functions for message handling, menus, cursors, carets, timers, communications, and other non-display functions
GDI32.dll	The Graphics Device Interface (GDI) library, which contains functions for device output, such as those for drawing, display context, metafiles, coordinates, and font management

Table 6.2 Windows Core Dynamic-Link Libraries

element omitted the *.dll* extension. This is permitted if the DLL is one of three core DLLs described in Table 6-2. Otherwise the *.dll* extension is necessary.

The ***libname*** element also may include the full path to the DLL. However, including the full path may not be a good idea, since the user may not have installed the DLL in the default location. If the full path is omitted, Windows will search for the DLL in the system directory, typically the \Windows\System directory on a Windows 9*x* operating system and the \Winnt\System32 directory on a Windows NT or 2000 operating system, or in the same directory as the application.

Microsoft adds more DLLs as the Windows operating system becomes more complex (Windows definitely is not becoming simpler). Table 6-3 lists some often-used DLLs. However, Microsoft does not change the signature (the name, parameters, and return value) of the existing DLLs. If it did, then applications that relied on prior versions of those DLLs would "break," which is a polite synonym for crash.

If the DLL specified after the **Lib** keyword is not found on the user's system, then a call to a Windows API function will raise run-time error 48, "Error in loading DLL." While you can handle this error, this should not be an issue if

DLL	Implements...
Comdlg32.dll	Common dialogs boxes, such as File Open, File Save, font and printer selection
Comctl32.dll	Common Windows controls, such as the tree view, image list, and so on
Mapi32.dll	Messaging API (MAPI), which supports e-mail
Odbc32.dll	Open Database Connectivity (ODBC)
Oleaut32.dll	OLE automation features
Ole32.dll	OLE features
Wsock32.dll	Winsock API, used for network communication

Table 6.3 Additional Windows DLLs

you're calling a function in one of the basic Windows DLLs, since these will be found on every computer with the Windows 9*x*/NT/2000 operating system.

Constants

A number of Windows API functions use constants. For example, the **SHAppBarMessage** API function sends a message to Windows to retrieve or set information concerning an *appbar* (the Windows taskbar is an appbar). The first parameter, the message being sent, is one of several constants, including **ABM_GETSTATE**, which retrieves the autohide status and the always on top status of the appbar, and **ABM_GETTASKBARPOS**, which retrieves the bounding rectangle of the appbar. These constants, like the API functions themselves, must be defined in your Visual Basic project. For example, the two constants just mentioned are declared as follows:

```
Private Const ABM_GETSTATE = &H1
Private Const ABM_GETTASKBARPOS = &H4
```

You will know which constants go with which API function the same way you know which API function to use: by looking them up in the Platform SDK help file or a reference book.

Using the API Viewer

Trying to declare Windows API functions from memory is hopeless; they all seem to have 73 parameters with weird names like **dwExStyle**. Equally hopeless is trying to memorize constants that not only have strange names but also hexadecimal values.

You can use a reference book or the Platform SDK help file to obtain the proper syntax for the **Declare** statement. However, another alternative is to use the API Viewer add-in in Visual Basic. This tool provides **Declares** and constants that you can copy and paste into your code.

You activate the API Viewer with the following steps:

1. Display the Add-In Manager dialog box by choosing Add-In Manager from the Add-Ins menu.
2. Select VB 6 API Viewer from the Add-In Manager dialog box, and check the Loaded/Unloaded check box under Load Behavior, as shown in Figure 6-1, and then click OK.
3. API Viewer is now a new choice under the Add-Ins menu. Choose it to display the API Viewer, which is shown in Figure 6-2.

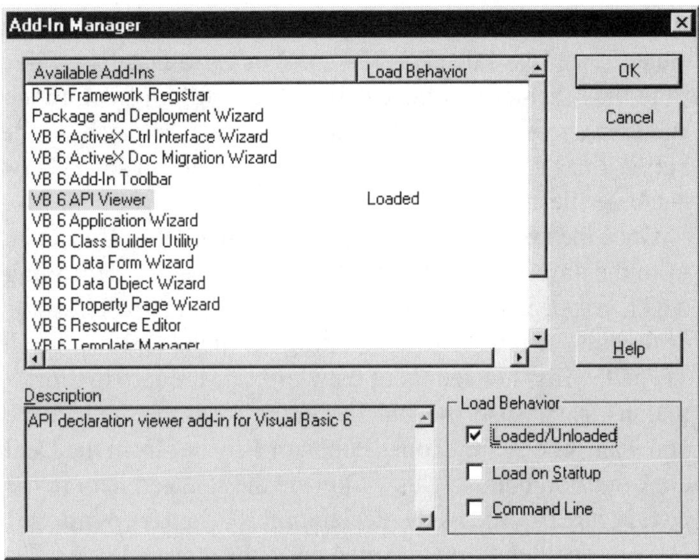

Figure 6.1 Add-In Manager dialog box

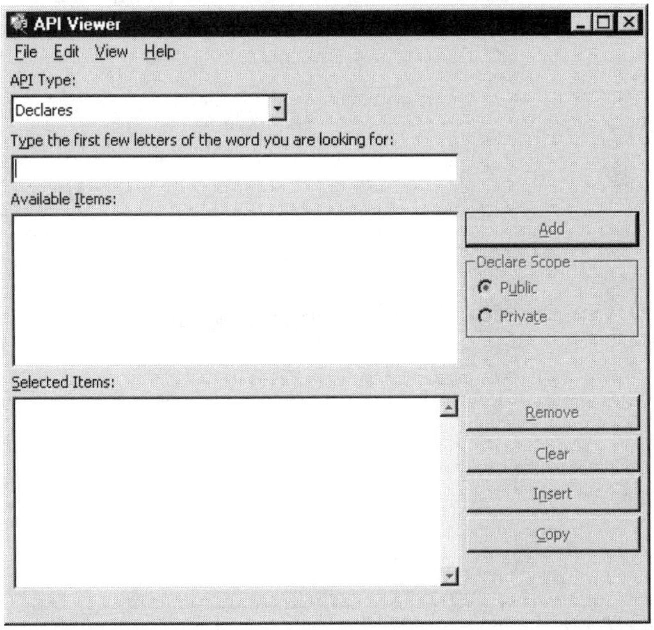

Figure 6.2 The API Viewer

Once the API Viewer is displayed, you need to load its data source. Choose either Load Text File (Win32api.txt) or Load Database File (Win32api.mdb) from the File menu. If the database file does not exist, first choose Load Text File and then choose Convert Text to Database. The database file is faster to access, but on a fast computer there is little difference in speed between the text and database files.

Once the text or database file is loaded, choose Constants, Declares, or Types from the drop-down list box labeled "API Type," depending on the item for which you need the syntax. Then type the first few letters of the constant (or the declaration or type) you are looking for in the text box labeled, naturally enough, "Type the first few letters of the word you are looking for." As you type, a "smart search" feature lists the matches in the Available Items list box. Select the item you want, choose its scope (Public or Private) from the Declare Scope group, and click the Add button. This will place the selected item in the Selected Items list box. Figure 6-3 shows the declaration for the **GetWindowRect** API function.

You can click Copy and then paste the constant or declaration into your code, or click Insert to insert the constant or declaration directly into your code.

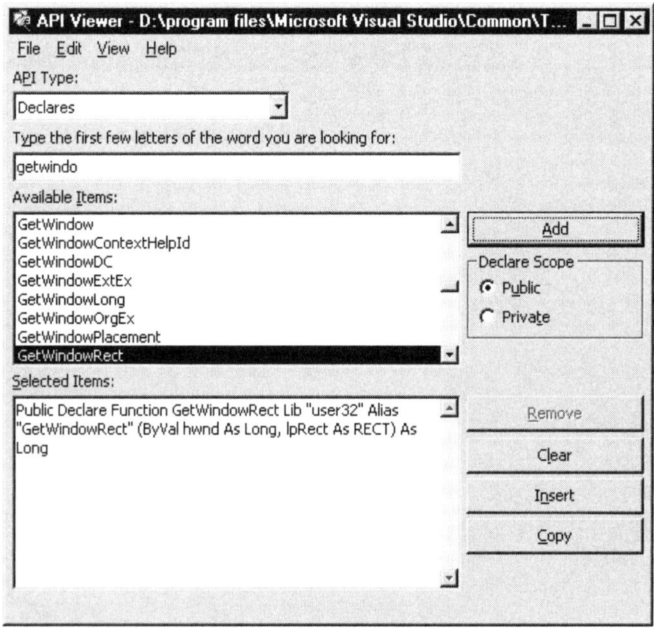

Figure 6.3 API Viewer declaration for **GetWindowRect**

Error Watch *The information in the API Viewer is not always accurate or complete. For example, the API Viewer does not include the constants SM_CXMENUCHECK and SM_CYMENUCHECK, which are used to draw checkmarks on a menu. These constants, indeed all constants used in the Windows API, are defined in one of several header (.h) files used by C and C++ programs. The values of the constants SM_CXMENUCHECK and SM_CYMENUCHECK come from the winuser.h header file. The header files used by C and C++ programs should be on your hard drive if you have installed a C or C++ program, such as Visual C++. However, if you don't have a C or C++ program on your computer because C and C++ programming is against your religious beliefs (or is perhaps too hard), there is another alternative. The C header files, which include the C function declarations, as well as the constants, are contained in the Platform SDK itself (as opposed to the help file discussed previously). The Platform SDK can be downloaded from Microsoft at the MSDN Developer site, http://msdn.microsoft.com/developer/.*

Declaration Rules

That covers the basics of the **Declare** statement. However, as you were warned, there are pitfalls. Rather than dwelling on the negative, here are some rules to follow:

- Always specify a return value.
- Use aliases to avoid the **As Any** parameter.
- Translate data types between Visual Basic and the Windows API.
- Watch the signs.
- Don't be a fool with **BOOL**.
- Explicitly pass arguments **ByVal** or **ByRef**.
- Be aware of the string exception to **ByVal** versus **ByRef**.
- Properly prepare a string being returned from a Windows API function.
- Use **Option Explicit**.

Always Specify a Return Value

Almost all Windows API procedures are functions that therefore have return values. Visual Basic permits you to declare a function without specifying a return value, in which case the return value is a variant. The penalty in a "normal" Visual Basic program for using a variant data type is that the variable unnecessarily uses more resources. The penalty when using the Windows API is more severe, an application error. Therefore, explicitly specify the data type of the return value.

Use Aliases to Avoid the As Any Parameter

The ***name*** element of the **Declare** statement is the name by which you call the function from Visual Basic. Often you can use the name of the API function within the DLL. However, sometimes you cannot, or should not. In those situations, you can use the **Alias** keyword within the **Declare** statement to indicate that you intend to call the function by a different name (an *alias*) in Visual Basic, and that different name is the ***aliasname*** element.

You *must* use the **Alias** keyword if the name of the API function begins with an underscore character (_), which is not legal in Visual Basic. However, there is another situation when you are not required to but *should* use the **Alias** keyword: if the Windows API function has one or more arguments that can take different data types.

The **SendMessage** function, which sends a message to a window or control, is an example of a Windows API function with an argument that can take different data types. **SendMessage** has four parameters: the window, the message, and the ***wParam*** and ***lParam*** accompanying the message. The ***wParam*** and ***lParam*** parameters carry additional information about the message, the nature of that information depending on the specific message being sent. While the data type of ***wParam*** is long, the data type of ***lParam*** can be, depending on the message, a number (passed **ByVal** and declared as long), a string (passed either **ByRef** or **ByVal** and declared as either string or any), or an array or a user-defined type (passed **ByRef** and declared as any). Therefore, ***lParam*** is declared **As Any** in the declaration of **SendMessage**:

```
Private Declare Function SendMessage Lib "User32" _
   Alias "SendMessageA" _
  (ByVal hWnd As Long, ByVal wMsg As Long, _
  ByVal wParam As Long, _
  lParam As Any) As Long
```

The problem is that while **SendMessage** can accept several different data types, it cannot accept *any* data type. Passing **SendMessage** a data type that it does not support will cause an application error. Nor will Visual Basic catch the wrong data type. Visual Basic normally performs type checking on the values that you pass for each argument to ensure that the data type of the value passed matches the data type of the argument in the function definition. Thus, Visual Basic type-checking will produce a compile-time error if you attempt to pass a value of type string to an argument defined as type long. However, this type checking is bypassed when you declare an argument as type any.

You can avoid this problem by using the **Alias** keyword to declare multiple versions of the same DLL procedure, each with a different ***name*** and different data type. For example, you can define multiple **SendMessage** declares, each named to reflect the type of data being passed. Thus, for passing numbers in ***lParam***, the function could be declared as follows:

```
Public Declare Function SendMessageNum Lib "user32" _
   Alias "SendMessageA" _
   (ByVal hwnd As Long, ByVal wMsg As Long, _
   ByVal wParam As Long, _
   ByVal lParam As Long) As Long
```

By contrast, for passing strings in ***lParam***, the function could be declared like this:

```
Public Declare Function SendMessageStr Lib "user32" _
   Alias "SendMessageA" _
   (ByVal hwnd As Long, ByVal wMsg As Long,
   ByVal wParam As Long, _
   ByVal lParam As String) As Long
```

Finally, to pass arrays and user-defined types, you would declare the function like this:

```
Public Declare Function SendMessage& Lib "user32" _
   Alias "SendMessageA" _
   (ByVal hwnd As Long, ByVal wMsg As Long,  _
   ByVal wParam As Long, _
   lParam As Any) As Long
```

Translate Data Types Between Visual Basic and the Windows API

"A rose is a rose." —Gertrude Stein

The Windows API DLLs are written in C/C++. While a rose is a rose, a string in C/C++ is not the same as a string in Visual Basic. There also are differences between the two languages with other data types. Blithely passing a Visual Basic data type to a Windows API function whose parameter is a data type of the same name, without taking into account the possible differences in implementation between the two languages, is the programming equivalent of crossing a busy street with your eyes closed. You might get away with it, but more likely you won't.

Table 6-4 lists C/C++ data types used in the Windows API and their Visual Basic equivalents.

The **int** data type in C/C++ is particular tricky for the unwary. In "normal" C/C++ usage, an **int** is a 16-bit integer. However, here, as in many situations in

C/C++ Data Type	Hungarian Notation Prefix	Description	Visual Basic Equivalent
BOOL	b	32-bit Boolean value—zero indicates False, nonzero indicates True	Boolean or long
BYTE, char	ch	8-bit unsigned integer	byte
HANDLE	h	32-bit unsigned integer that represents a handle to a Windows object	long
int	n	32-bit signed integer	long
Long, DWORD	l	32-bit signed integer	long
LP*	lp	(LPINT, LPCSTR, LPSTR) 32-bit long pointer to a C/C++ structure, string, function, or other data in memory	long

Table 6.4 C/C++ Data Types Used in the Windows API and Their Visual Basic Equivalents

life, context is everything. In the context of the Win32 API, an **int** is a 32-bit integer, always. The 32 in Win32 may help you remember.

Watch the Signs

"What's your sign?" —Trite pick-up line from the disco 70s

While you may not find this line effective for obtaining companionship, you may find it useful for remembering another Windows API trap. In programming, a number is signed when it can be positive or negative, unsigned when it is always positive. The range of a number depends on whether it is signed. For example, the range of an 8-bit signed number is –128 to 127, whereas the range of an 8-bit unsigned number is 0 to 255. This is because the most significant bit (the one furthest to the left) is used to indicate the sign for a signed number (1 for negative, 0 for positive), whereas in an unsigned number this bit can be used to extend the range of the positive number.

In C/C++, a number can be signed or unsigned. However, in Visual Basic, a byte variable is always unsigned, and an integer and long are always signed. Therefore, you do have to check whether the signed or unsigned nature of the C/C++ number is the same as that of the Visual Basic data type, and if not, convert the value.

Don't Be a Fool with BOOL

"True is False!" —Visual Basic programmer driven mad by the Windows API

In both programming languages, False is zero, and nonzero values are True. However, in Visual Basic, True typically is equal to –1; in C/C++, True typically is equal to 1. Therefore, avoid **If** statements like this one:

```
If APIFunction() = -1 Then
```

The reason is that a True value returned by the API function likely will be 1, so testing for equality with –1 will return False, not True. Instead, compare the return value to zero, which in both languages represents False:

```
If APIFunction() <> 0 Then
```

Explicitly Pass Arguments ByVal or ByRef

Arguments can be passed by value or by reference. This is true both in a garden variety Visual Basic program or when passing arguments from Visual Basic to a Windows API function.

Passing an argument by value passes a copy of the argument, on which the function operates. If the called procedure modifies the argument's value, it is modifying only the copy of the argument; the "original" argument back in the calling procedure is unaffected. Thus, when execution returns to the calling procedure, the variable passed as the argument has the same value it did before the procedure that passed it was called.

By contrast, passing an argument by reference passes the memory location of that argument. If the called procedure modifies that argument's value, it modifies the "original" argument, so when execution returns to the calling procedure, the value of the variable passed as the argument has been changed.

The protective cocoon that Visual Basic wraps around its programs often permits us to avoid the consequences of lazy habits. One of those lazy habits is not specifying **ByVal** or **ByRef** when declaring functions. Don't do this when declaring Windows API functions! If you pass **ByVal** (by default) when the Windows API function expects **ByRef**, or vice versa, the result will be an application error.

Be Aware of the String Exception to ByVal Versus ByRef

Texts on the Windows API often contain two seemingly contradictory statements. One is that Visual Basic strings must be passed to Windows API functions with the **ByVal** keyword. The other is that Visual Basic strings are always passed to Windows API functions by reference, and therefore can be modified by the Windows API function. These seemingly inconsistent statements are both true, and in fact consistent.

In the C programming language, strings are referred to, in Hungarian notation, as LPSTR, which means a pointer to a string that is terminated by a null character (an ASCII value of zero). By contrast, in Visual Basic, strings are stored in a different format called BSTR. BSTR strings, like C strings, are null-terminated.

BSTR strings need to be converted to C strings in order for Visual Basic programs to use the Windows API. A programmer reasonably could assume that since C requires a pointer to a string, Visual Basic should pass strings **ByRef** to Windows API functions. This assumption, while reasonable, is wrong, and it would result in the usual illegal exception penalty for passing an API function a bad parameter.

Visual Basic handles the conversion of BSTR strings to C strings by overloading the **ByVal** attribute. Passing a BSTR string **ByVal** does not pass the string by value. Rather, it passes by value a pointer to the string. In other words, passing a BSTR string **ByVal** passes the address of the string. This is the value expected by the API function.

By contrast, passing a BSTR string **ByRef** would pass the address of the pointer to the string. In other words, what would be passed is the address of the address of the string. This is not the value expected by the API function, and the result of ignorance of the string exception to **ByVal** versus **ByRef** will be another exception—an illegal exception.

Properly Prepare a String Being Returned from a Windows API Function

If you are passing a string that simply provides information to a Windows API function, and that string will not be changed, then you simply pass a normal Visual Basic string variable. However, matters become more complicated if you want to return a string from a Windows API function.

In the first place, you don't return a string from a Windows API function as you would from a Visual Basic function. Since strings, notwithstanding the **ByVal** keyword, are passed by reference to Windows API functions, as just discussed, the Windows API function can modify the value of the string argument. The return value of the Windows API function usually is a long integer specifying the number of bytes that were written into the string argument.

The string variable must be a *null-terminated string*. While BSTRs often are null-terminated, it doesn't hurt to be sure by adding a null character (represented by the ASCII value zero) to the end of the string:

```
StrValue = strValue & chr$(0)
```

Additionally, while a Windows API function can change the value of a string passed to it as an argument, it can't change the size of the string. Therefore, you need to ensure that the string that you pass to a Windows API function is large enough to hold the entire return value. The **Space** or **String** functions can be used to create a string of a specified size that is filled with a given character (the space character with the **Space** function, or a specified character with the **String** function).

Use Option Explicit

Using **Option Explicit** is a good idea in any event, but it is especially prudent when using the Windows API. Otherwise, the inadvertently created variable will be a variant, which almost invariably will be the wrong data type for the Windows API function.

Calling Windows API Functions

Once you've declared a Windows API function, the next step is to call it. You can call Windows API functions as you would any other function. However, calling Windows API functions directly can be difficult, given the number of arguments Windows API functions can have, and the differences between Visual Basic and C/C++ in how the arguments are handled.

Wrapping the Windows API

An alternative to calling Windows API functions directly is to call them from inside a Visual Basic function, which provides the parameters needed by the Windows API function called inside of it. This is known as *wrapping* Windows API functions, because the Windows API function is "wrapped" inside of the Visual Basic function. Wrapping API functions is common in advanced programming. Indeed, Microsoft Foundation Classes (MFC), used extensively in Microsoft Visual C++, essentially wrap Windows API functions in classes for better object-oriented access to the API functions.

Wrapping Windows API functions has several advantages. Since the arguments passed to the Windows API function come from the parameters of the containing Visual Basic function, the Visual Basic function, once tested, guarantees that the parameters will be of the correct data type and, in the case of strings to be returned, properly initialized. Additionally, you can reuse the Visual Basic function (or, more accurately, the class module containing it) in other applications, saving you the problem of relearning how to directly call the Windows API function. Still another advantage is, as explained next, you will be able to work with Windows API functions in an object-oriented manner.

For example, the Windows API **GetWindowRect** function stores in its second parameter the coordinates of the window whose handle is passed as its first parameter:

```
Private Declare Function GetWindowRect Lib "user32" _
   (ByVal hwnd As Long, lpRect As Rect) As Long
```

The following user-defined Visual Basic **GetWinHeight** function wraps **GetWindowRect** to obtain the height of the window whose handle is the first (and only) parameter to the Visual Basic function:

```
Public Function GetWinHeight(ByVal hwnd As Long) As Long
    Dim temp As Rect
    Call GetWindowRect(hwnd, temp)
    GetWinHeight = temp.bottom - temp.top
End Function
```

Obtaining the width, the *x*-coordinate of the top-left corner, and the *y*-coordinate of the top-left corner of the window is done by other user-defined Visual Basic functions:

```
Public Function GetWinWidth(ByVal hwnd As Long) As Long
    Dim temp As Rect
    Call GetWindowRect(hwnd, temp)
    GetWinWidth = (temp.right - temp.left)
End Function

Public Function GetWinLeft(ByVal hwnd As Long) As Long
    Dim temp As Rect
    Call GetWindowRect(hwnd, temp)
    GetWinLeft = temp.left
End Function

Public Function GetWinTop(ByVal hwnd As Long) As Long
    Dim temp As Rect
    Call GetWindowRect(hwnd, temp)
    GetWinTop = temp.top
End Function
```

The reason for wrapping API functions is rooted in one of the philosophies underlying object-oriented programming (OOP), which is that your object should show "what it does" without having to show "how it does it." This way, the complexity of accessing the API functions can be hidden from someone accessing the public methods of your application. This makes your application easier and more understandable for other programmers to use, and therefore more attractive and presumably more successful commercially.

The wrapper functions used in this example do make life easier for anyone using this code. For example, the API functions do not return the height, width, etc., of the window. Rather, they change values in a structure that is one of their parameters, and that structure has to be mirrored by a user-defined type. By contrast, the wrapper functions and the class that contains them have done all the hard work, and all that is necessary is to obtain their return values.

Additionally, wrapping the API functions in functions that address specific practical problems (such as determining a window's height) also saves the user the trouble of figuring out a solution to those practical problems. For example, if there is a need to determine a window's height, there is no need to determine the algorithm. All that is necessary is to make a call to **GetWinHeight**.

Using the LastDLLError Property

As mentioned in Chapter 4, you cannot use standard Visual Basic error-handling techniques for run-time errors that occur in Windows API functions. However, Windows API functions usually return a value that indicates success or failure. If the code indicates failure, then you can use the **LastDLLError** property of the **Err** object to determine which error occurred.

The value that indicates success or failure varies with the particular Windows API function. For example, the **GetWindowRect** API function, discussed previously, returns either a nonzero value indicating success or a zero value indicating failure.

The API Viewer tool will not tell you which error numbers correspond with which errors. You can use the winerror.h file to determine this information. You should have this file if you have Visual C++ on your computer. If you do not have this file, you still can obtain the error numbers and corresponding descriptions from the Microsoft Platform SDK, available on the Microsoft Developer Network site at http://msdn.microsoft.com/developer/.

The user-defined Visual Basic procedure **GetWinHeight**, discussed previously, retrieved the height in pixels of a window whose handle was its one parameter. The procedure calls the **GetWindowRect** function, passing to **GetWindowRect** the window handle. However, if the window handle is invalid, an error will occur. The previous implementation of **GetWinHeight** did not handle this error. **GetWinHeight** should handle this error, and it can through the **LastDLLError** property:

```
'create user-defined type to store window rectangle coordinates
Type RECT
   Left As Long
   Top As Long
   Right As Long
```

```
   Bottom As Long

End Type
Declare Function GetWindowRect Lib "user32" _
   (ByVal hwnd As Long, lpRect As RECT) As Long

'define error constant obtained from winerror.h
Const ERROR_INVALID_WINDOW_HANDLE As Long = 1400
Public Function GetWinHeight(ByVal hwnd As Long) As Long
    Dim temp As Rect
    'Pass in window handle. If function returns 0, error occurred.
    If GetWindowRect(hwnd, temp) = 0 Then
    'Check LastDLLError. Return zero if invalid handle was passed.
       If Err.LastDllError = ERROR_INVALID_WINDOW_HANDLE Then
           GetWinHeight = 0
       End If
   Else
       GetWinHeight = temp.bottom - temp.top
   End If
End Function
```

Summary

You will at times need to access the Windows API directly, to go beyond the limitations of accessing the Windows API through Visual Basic procedures and properties. You can safely access the Windows API directly by using properly constructed **Declare** statements and wrapping your calls of Windows API functions in Visual Basic procedures. You also can use the **LastDLLError** property of the **Err** object to handle errors that occur in Windows API functions called from your Visual Basic program.

One final word (actually two) of advice: Save yourself! Despite your best efforts, your program will crash when you use the Windows API. Not might, *will.* Unless you like typing code all over again, save your work just like they used to vote in Chicago: early and often!

CHAPTER 7

ActiveX Data Objects

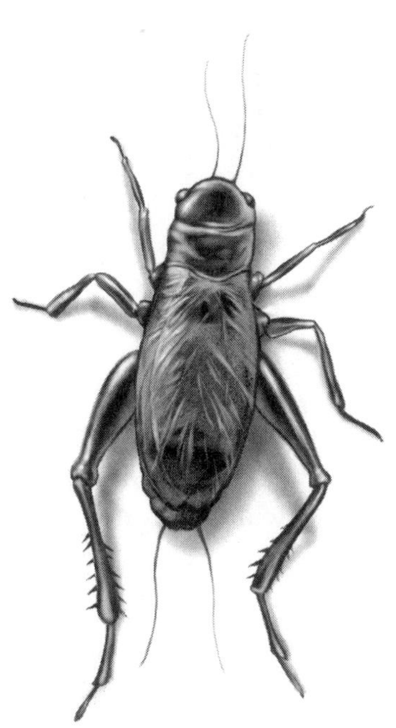

While games and graphics may be more fun, the purpose of most Visual Basic applications, certainly most business applications, is data access. Visual Basic programmers who cannot develop data access applications will suffer the same fate as fish without fins; they won't get anywhere.

Microsoft did not get to be Microsoft by ignoring important areas like data access. Indeed, Microsoft offers a host of data access strategies under an umbrella ambitiously named "Universal Data Access." Like everything else in computer programming, these data access strategies are referred to by a blizzard of acronyms, such as DAO, RDO, MDAC, UDA, and ADO.

The good news is that you don't need to learn all of these data access strategies; many have been superseded by others. The bad news is that as soon as you learn a data access strategy, it is replaced by another that you then have to learn. The good news is that, as with programming languages, data access strategies are more alike than different, so once you learn one it is easier to learn another. The bad news is that, as with programming languages, data access strategies are different, so there is still much to learn when you have to learn another one.

Microsoft's latest and greatest data access strategy is ActiveX Data Objects, which is referred to as ADO. Since ADO promises to be Microsoft's premier data access strategy for the foreseeable future—which these days is not very long at all—that data access strategy will be the one featured in this chapter.

While ADO is an improvement over previous data access strategies, it is no more immune from errors than its predecessors. Additionally, ADO does not access data directly, but rather does so through *providers*. These providers have their own properties that supplement those of the ADO objects you are using. Additionally, these providers are quite capable of generating their own errors in addition to those that might be generated by ADO. This additional layer of objects with their own properties and errors adds an additional level of complexity to data access and to handling the inevitable errors. Therefore, understanding the interplay between ADO and its providers is necessary to trapping and handling errors generated by one or both of them.

What Is ADO?

The formal definition of ADO is that it is a high-level programming interface with lower-level providers for accessing data in different formats and locations. However, this definition, while technically accurate, is not very informative.

Not so long ago, data access was focused primarily on relational database management systems (RDBMSs). SQL Server, Access, Oracle, and Btrieve are widely used RDBMSs.

Each RDBMS was accessed by a "driver" that handled communication with the RDBMS. This driver was akin to a device driver that handles communications between the computer and a peripheral device. There was a different driver for each RDBMS.

Microsoft developed an API named Open Database Connectivity (ODBC) to utilize these drivers. However, the ODBC API is not "programmer-friendly." In fact, it is quite difficult to use.

More recently there has been a trend to store data in non-relational databases, in which data is stored in a relatively unstructured format. Exchange Server is a prime example of a non-relational database. ODBC does not work well, or at all, with these non-structured databases.

In 1996 Microsoft announced a new strategy, ambitiously named Universal Data Access (UDA). Component Object Model (COM) interfaces named OLE DB are at the heart of UDA. Unlike ODBC, OLE DB works with non-relational databases.

Whereas ODBC uses *drivers* to access different data formats, OLE DB uses *providers*. OLE DB providers exist for Microsoft SQL Server, Oracle, and so on. While OLE DB is the successor to ODBC, ODBC is not dead. In fact, OLE DB includes a data provider that allows you to use it with ODBC data sources.

Thus, OLE DB went beyond ODBC's limitation to RDBMSs and has the promise of relatively universal access to data, no matter how or where it is stored. However, from the programmer's perspective, OLE DB, like ODBC, is still difficult to use.

ADO, itself, does not access data. The OLE DB provider still does that. Rather, ADO provides a programmer-friendly interface through which the programmer can access the provider, which in turn accesses the data.

ADO is programmer-friendly mostly because its interface is consistent no matter which OLE DB provider it is using. However, while ADO's interface is consistent, its actual data access capabilities will vary among OLE DB providers because the respective data sources the providers are accessing are, after all, different. Similarly, there are major differences among the providers, reflective of the differences among data sources that they access. Errors can be avoided, or at least properly handled, by understanding these differences among providers and how to take these differences into account when you are using ADO.

Providers

Applications that use ADO to access data through providers are called *consumers*. ADO then accesses data through *providers*, which expose OLE DB interfaces. Since providers are COM components with standard interfaces, consumers can access them using any COM-compliant programming language. There are providers for most forms of data, hence the promise of "universal data access."

There are two types of providers: those that provide data (data providers) and those that provide services (service providers). The promise of UDA is that your application, through ADO, which in turn uses data and service providers with OLE DB interfaces, can access disparate forms of data, both non-relational and relational. Figure 7-1 shows the architecture of Universal Data Access:

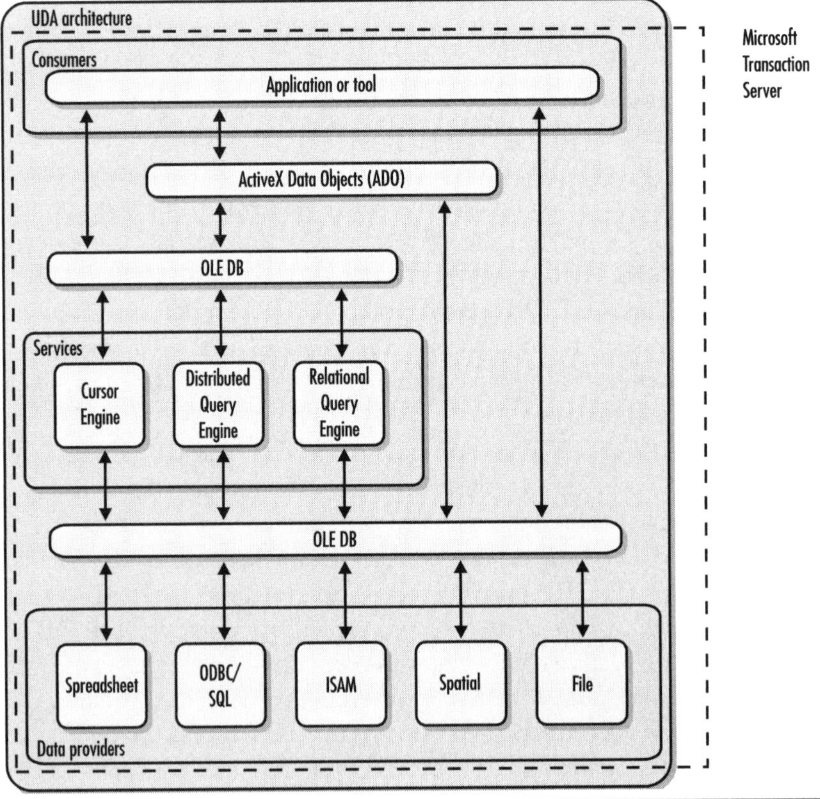

Figure 7.1 UDA architecture

Data Providers

A *data provider* owns its own data and exposes it in tabular form to your application. It is not dependent on other providers—service or data—to provide data to the consumer. Table 7-1 lists three of the most commonly used data providers.

Design Tip *If your data source is Access, then Jet will be your choice of data provider. However, if your data source is SQL Server, then you can choose between the OLE DB providers for SQL Server and ODBC. While both providers access SQL Server data, they do so differently. The OLE DB Provider for SQL Server (SQLOLEDB) directly maps OLE DB interfaces and methods to SQL Server data sources. By contrast, the OLE DB Provider for ODBC (MSDASQL) maps OLE DB interfaces and methods to ODBC APIs, and OLE DB consumers connect to a SQL Server database through an existing SQL Server ODBC driver. Microsoft recommends, and we agree, that you use SQLOLEDB as your OLE DB provider to access SQL Server data, since SQLOLEDB maps OLE DB interfaces and methods directly to SQL Server data sources without using the ODBC API or the SQL Server ODBC driver as intermediaries.*

Service Providers

A *service provider* encapsulates a particular service, which augments the functionality of your ADO applications. A service provider does not own its own data and, in reality, serves a dual role of consumer and provider. Table 7-2 lists service providers.

A *service component* is a service provider that cannot stand alone but instead must work in conjunction with other service providers or components. The Cursor Service for OLE DB service component supplements the cursor support functions of data providers. A cursor controls record navigation, updating of data, and the visibility of changes made to the database by other users. This service

Data Provider	Source Data
Microsoft OLE DB Provider for ODBC	Data traditionally accessed using ODBC
Microsoft OLE DB Provider for Jet	Access, Paradox, dBASE, Excel, and FoxPro, among others
Microsoft OLE DB Provider for SQL Server	SQL Server

Table 7.1 OLE DB Data Providers for ODBC, Jet, and SQL Server

Service Provider	Functionality
Microsoft Data Shaping Service for OLE DB	Supports the construction of hierarchical (shaped) Recordset objects from a data provider.
Microsoft OLE DB Persistence Provider	Enables the saving of a Recordset object to a file (Extensible Markup Language, XML, format is supported) from which it later can be restored.
Microsoft OLE DB Remoting Provider	Enables a local user on a client machine to invoke data providers on a remote machine, the effect being that you will access the remote machine as if you were a local user.

Table 7.2 Service Providers

component is used to make the differences among the data providers transparent to users.

As of the writing of this book, a list of Microsoft OLE DB providers is available from the OLE DB section of the Microsoft Universal Data Access Web site at http://www.microsoft.com/data/oledb/.

Dynamic Properties

ADO has a number of objects. The ADO objects that are particularly affected by the differences among providers, and which are therefore a focus of this chapter, are the following:

- **Connection** This object represents the connection between your application and the data source.
- **Command** This object represents a request to manipulate data, usually the retrieval of a subset of data, with the ability, depending on circumstances, to view, add, edit, or delete it.
- **Recordset** This object represents the data retrieved, such as through the request made by the **Command** object.

Each of these objects has a number of built-in properties, that is, properties implemented in ADO. For example, as discussed later in this chapter, the **Connection** object has a **ConnectionString** property that is used to make the connection from ADO through the data provider to the data source. The **Command** object has a **CommandText** property that holds the text of the command and a

CommandType property that determines whether the command's text represents a table name, SQL statement, or name of a stored procedure. The **Recordset** object has a **CursorType** property that determines, among other things, whether records can be edited or just viewed.

These ADO objects have these built-in properties no matter which data provider is being used. They also may have additional properties, referred to as *dynamic* properties. Dynamic properties are properties specific to a data or service provider. For example, a property specific to the provider may indicate whether a Recordset object supports transactions or editing. Since dynamic properties are provider-specific, an ADO **Connection**, **Command**, or **Recordset** object's dynamic properties will vary as it uses different providers.

You will need to view and, if necessary, change the property values for these ADO objects to avoid errors. For example, trying to move to previous records in a **Recordset** will cause an error if the value of the **CursorType** property permits only forward navigation.

You can easily read the values of built-in properties through the usual *object.property* syntax, and change them if the property is writable. For example, assuming that you have an instantiated **Recordset** object **rs**, the **CursorType** property could be set to a static cursor with this statement:

```
rs.CursorType = adOpenStatic
```

However, you cannot view or change dynamic properties through the *object.property* syntax because the dynamic properties are not standard (built-in properties) of the ADO object. Instead, the **Connection**, **Command**, and **Recordset** objects each has a **Properties** collection. This collection contains **Property** objects, each of which is a dynamic property specific to the provider being used. You can read and, if writable, change one of the dynamic properties through the **Properties** collection.

Note *Only dynamic properties appear as **Property** objects in **Connection**, **Command**, or **Recordset** objects' **Properties** collections; the built-in properties do not. However, as discussed previously, you can use the object.property syntax to view and change the built-in properties.*

Property Object

In what seems to be a case of infinite regression, the **Property** object has properties! Table 7-3 lists these properties.

Property	Data Type	Description
Name	String	Identifies the property.
Type	Integer	Specifies the property data type.
Value	Variant	Default. Contains the property setting.
Attributes	Long	Indicates characteristics of the property specific to the provider.

Table 7.3 Properties of the ADO **Property** Object

The **Name** property is, as its name suggests, the name of the property. Each dynamic property's name is unique among the dynamic properties of the particular provider.

The **Type** property indicates the data type of a property. The data type is identified by one of the **DataTypeEnum** values listed in Table 7-4.

Constant	Value	Data Type
adArray	0x2000	A flag value instead of a data type. This constant is always combined with another data type constant that indicates an array of that other data type.
adBigInt	20	An eight-byte signed integer.
adBinary	128	A binary value.
adBoolean	11	A Boolean value.
adBSTR	8	A null-terminated character string.
adChapter	136	A four-byte chapter value that identifies rows in a child rowset.
adChar	129	A string value.
adCurrency	6	A currency value.
adDate	7	A date value stored as the number of days since December 30, 1899, plus a fraction of a day.
adDBDate	133	A date value in yyyymmdd format.
adDBTime	134	A time value in hhmmss format.
adDBTimeStamp	135	A date/time stamp in yyyymmddhhmmss format, plus a fraction in billionths.
adDecimal	14	An exact numeric value with a fixed precision and scale.

Table 7.4 **DataTypeEnum** Values for the **Property** Object's **Type** Property

Constant	Value	Data Type
adDouble	5	A double-precision floating-point value.
adEmpty	0	Specifies no value.
adError	10	A 32-bit error code.
adFileTime	64	A 64-bit value representing the number of 100-nanosecond intervals since January 1, 1601.
adGUID	72	A globally unique identifier (GUID).
adIDispatch	9	A pointer to an **IDispatch** interface on a COM object (not currently supported by ADO).
adInteger	3	A four-byte signed integer.
adIUnknown	13	A pointer to an **IUnknown** interface on a COM object (not currently supported by ADO).
adLongVarBinary	205	A long binary value (**Parameter** object only).
adLongVarChar	201	A long string value (**Parameter** object only).
adLongVarWChar	203	A long null-terminated Unicode string value (**Parameter** object only).
adNumeric	131	An exact numeric value with a fixed precision and scale.
adPropVariant	138	An Automation PROPVARIANT.
adSingle	4	A single-precision floating-point value.
adSmallInt	2	A two-byte signed integer.
adTinyInt	16	A one-byte signed integer.
adUnsignedBigInt	21	An eight-byte unsigned integer.
adUnsignedInt	19	A four-byte unsigned integer.
adUnsignedSmallInt	18	A two-byte unsigned integer.
adUnsignedTinyInt	17	A one-byte unsigned integer.
adUserDefined	132	A user-defined variable.
adVarBinary	204	A binary value (**Parameter** object only).
adVarChar	200	A string value (**Parameter** object only).
adVariant	12	An Automation **Variant** (not currently supported by ADO).
adVarNumeric	139	A numeric value (**Parameter** object only).
adVarWChar	202	A null-terminated Unicode character string (**Parameter** object only).
adWChar	130	A null-terminated Unicode character string (DBTYPE_WSTR).

Table 7.4 **DataTypeEnum** Values for the **Property** Object's **Type** Property *(continued)*

The **Value** property lists the setting of the property. This data type necessarily is a Variant since the data type corresponding to a property varies with the property.

The read-only **Attributes** property lists information about a property that is quite helpful for error avoidance, such as whether the property is supported at all, whether it is read/write, read only, or write only, and whether the user must specify a value for this property before the data source is initialized. Each of these characteristics is represented by one of the **PropertyAttributesEnum** values listed in Table 7-5. The value of the **Attributes** property is the sum of the applicable **PropertyAttributesEnum** values.

Properties Collection

The **Properties** collection is automatically populated with the dynamic properties, each a **Property** object. This population does not occur until the ADO object is connected to a data source through a particular data provider. This timing is logical, since the nature of the object's dynamic properties is provider-dependent.

The **Properties** collection has two properties: **Count** and **Item**. **Count**, as usual, indicates the number of items in the collection, and is zero-based as it is for other intrinsic collections. The **Item** property returns from the collection the **Property** object, specified either by its zero-based position or by its name, which necessarily is unique.

You usually will use the **Count** property to loop through the **Properties** collection using a **For-Next** loop. This code snippet, which assumes an instantiated **Recordset** object **rs**, prints the name of each dynamic property in the collection to the Immediate window using **Debug.Print**:

```
Dim colADOProps As Properties
Set colADOProps = New rs.Properties
Dim counter As Integer
For counter = 0 to colADOProps - 1
   Debug.Print colADOProps.Item(counter).Name
Next counter
```

Constant	Value	Description
adPropNotSupported	0	The property is not supported by the provider.
adPropRequired	1	The user must specify a value for this property before the data source is initialized.
adPropOptional	2	The user does not need to specify a value for this property before the data source is initialized.
adPropRead	512	The user can read the property.
adPropWrite	1024	The user can set the property.

Table 7.5 **PropertyAttributesEnum** Values for the **Property** Object's **Attributes** Property

You also can use the **For Each ... Next** syntax to enumerate the collection without using the **Count** and **Item** properties:

```
Dim colADOProps As Properties
Set colADOProps = New rs.Properties
Dim prpADOProp As Property
For Each prpADOProp In colADOProps
   Debug.Print prpADOProp.Name
Next
```

The **Item** property can be used to access a specific **Property** object in the **Properties** collection and, if the property is writable, change its value:

```
Dim colADOProps As Properties
Set colADOProps = New rs.Properties
colADOProps.Item("propertyName").Value = newValue
```

The **Properties** collection has one method, **Refresh**. This method updates the **Property** objects in the **Properties** collection to reflect the objects available from, and specific to, the then applicable provider. You will need to use the **Refresh** method when your code changes from one provider to another.

Next, the dynamic properties represented by the **Property** object and contained in the **Properties** collection will be used by the ADO **Connection**, **Command**, and **Recordset** objects to access data.

Accessing and Using Providers

As discussed earlier in this chapter, ADO's object model remains the same regardless of which data provider ADO is connected to, but since each data provider is different, the way you access the various data providers through ADO varies. Failing to properly account for these differences is a common cause of errors.

The portions of the ADO object model particularly affected by the differences among data providers are as follows:

- Parameters in the **ConnectionString** property of the **Connection** object
- **Command** arguments
- **Recordset** arguments

Connection Parameters

Your application must connect to a data source in order to view and manipulate the data. Consistent with object-oriented programming, ADO represents your application's connection to a data source with the aptly named ADO **Connection** object.

You create the **Connection** object with syntax common to the creation of other objects:

```
Dim cnnSample As Connection
Set cnnSample = New Connection
```

The **Connection** object has a number of built-in properties. Table 7-6 lists the more commonly used ones.

By default, the OLE DB Provider for Microsoft Jet opens Microsoft Jet databases in read/write mode. To open a database in read-only mode, set the **Mode** property on the ADO **Connection** object to **adModeRead**.

The **ConnectionString** property has five arguments supported by ADO. Table 7-7 describes the ADO-supported arguments.

Property	Description
CommandTimeout	Specifies how long to wait while executing a command before terminating the attempt and generating an error.
ConnectionString	Information used to establish a connection to a data store.
ConnectionTimeout	Specifies how long to wait while establishing a connection before terminating the attempt and generating an error.
CursorLocation	Sets or returns a value determining whether cursor services are provided by the provider, the client, or not at all.
Mode	Indicates available permissions for modifying data.
Provider	Specifies the name of the provider used by the connection.
State	Indicates whether a connection is currently open, closed, or connecting.

Table 7.6 Properties of the **Connection** Object

Argument	Description
Provider	Specifies the name of a provider to use for the connection.
File Name	Specifies the name of a provider-specific file (for example, a persisted data source object) containing preset connection information.
Remote Provider	Specifies the name of a provider to use when opening a client-side connection. (Remote Data Service only.)
Remote Server	Specifies the path name of the server to use when opening a client-side connection. (Remote Data Service only.)
URL	Specifies the connection string as an absolute URL identifying a resource, such as a file or directory.

Table 7.7 ADO-Supported Arguments of the **ConnectionString** Property

The **Provider** argument is an acronym, and a rather long one at that, for the provider. Table 7-8 summarizes the provider argument values for three commonly used data providers.

ConnectionString for Jet Provider

You pass the **ConnectionString** arguments by a series of *argument = value* statements separated by semicolons. For example, the following could serve as a connection string for the OLE DB Provider for Microsoft Jet:

```
"Provider=Microsoft.Jet.OLEDB.4.0;Data Source=databaseName; " &
   "User ID=userName;Password=userPassword;"
```

Table 7-9 describes the keywords in the connection string.

Data Provider	Provider Argument
Microsoft OLE DB Provider for ODBC	MSDASQL
Microsoft OLE DB Provider for Jet	Microsoft.Jet.OLEDB.4.0
Microsoft OLE DB Provider for SQL Server	SQLOLEDB

Table 7.8 **Provider** Arguments for Commonly Used Data Providers

Keyword	Description
Provider	Specifies the OLE DB Provider for Microsoft Jet.
Data Source	Specifies the database path and filename.
User ID	Specifies the user name. The default is "admin."
Password	Specifies the user password. The default is an empty string (" ").

Table 7.9 Keywords for the **ConnectionString** for Jet Provider

You also can add additional parameters to the connection string. Table 7-10 lists those that are specific to the OLE DB provider for Microsoft Jet.

Parameter	Description
Jet OLEDB:Compact Reclaimed Space Amount	Gives an estimate of the amount of space, in bytes, that can be reclaimed by compacting the database. This value is only valid after a database connection has been established.
Jet OLEDB:Connection Control	Indicates whether users can connect to the database.
Jet OLEDB:Create System Database	Indicates whether a system database should be created when creating a new data source.
Jet OLEDB:Database Locking Mode	Indicates the locking mode for this database. The first user to open the database determines the mode used while the database is open.
Jet OLEDB:Database Password	Indicates the database password.
Jet OLEDB:Don't Copy Locale on Compact	Indicates whether Jet should copy locale information when compacting a database.
Jet OLEDB:Encrypt Database	Indicates whether a compacted database should be encrypted. If this property is not set, the compacted database will be encrypted if the original database was also encrypted.
Jet OLEDB:Engine Type	Indicates the storage engine used to access the current data store.
Jet OLEDB:Exclusive Async Delay	Indicates the maximum length of time, in milliseconds, that Jet can delay asynchronous writes to disk when the database is opened exclusively. This property is ignored unless Jet OLEDB:Flush Transaction Timeout is set to 0.
Jet OLEDB:Flush Transaction Timeout	Indicates the amount of time to wait before data stored in a cache for asynchronous writing is actually written to disk. This setting overrides the values for Jet OLEDB:Shared Async Delay and Jet OLEDB:Exclusive Async Delay.

Table 7.10 Additional **ConnectionString** Parameters for Jet Provider

Parameter	Description
Jet OLEDB:Global Bulk Transactions	Indicates whether SQL bulk transactions are transacted.
Jet OLEDB:Global Partial Bulk Ops	Indicates the password used to open the database.
Jet OLEDB:Implicit Commit Sync	Indicates whether changes made in internal implicit transactions are written in synchronous or asynchronous mode.
Jet OLEDB:Lock Delay	Indicates the number of milliseconds to wait before attempting to acquire a lock after a previous attempt has failed.
Jet OLEDB:Lock Retry	Indicates how many times an attempt to access a locked page is repeated.
Jet OLEDB:Max Buffer Size	Indicates the maximum amount of memory, in kilobytes, Jet can use before it starts flushing changes to disk.
Jet OLEDB:Max Locks Per File	Indicates the maximum number of locks Jet can place on a database. The default value is 9500.
Jet OLEDB:New Database Password	Indicates the new password to be set for this database. The old password is stored in Jet OLEDB:Database Password.
Jet OLEDB:ODBC Command Time Out	Indicates the number of milliseconds before a remote ODBC query from Jet will timeout.
Jet OLEDB:Page Locks to Table Lock	Indicates how many pages need to be locked within a transaction before Jet attempts to promote the lock to a table lock. If this value is 0, then the lock is never promoted.
Jet OLEDB:Page Timeout	Indicates the number of milliseconds Jet will wait before checking to see if its cache is out-of-date with the database file.
Jet OLEDB:Recycle Long-Valued Pages	Indicates whether Jet should aggressively try to reclaim BLOB pages when they are freed.
Jet OLEDB:Registry Path	Indicates the Windows Registry key that contains values for the Jet database engine.
Jet OLEDB:Reset ISAM Stats	Indicates whether the schema Recordset DBSCHEMA_JETOLEDB_ISAMSTATS should reset its performance counters after returning performance information.
Jet OLEDB:Shared Async Delay	Indicates the maximum amount of time, in milliseconds, Jet can delay asynchronous writes to disk when the database is opened in multiuser mode.
Jet OLEDB:System Database	Indicates the path and filename for the workgroup information file (system database).
Jet OLEDB:Transaction Commit Mode	Indicates whether Jet writes data to disk synchronously or asynchronously when a transaction is committed.
Jet OLEDB:User Commit Sync	Indicates whether changes made in transactions are written in synchronous or asynchronous mode.

Table 7.10 Additional **ConnectionString** Parameters for Jet Provider *(continued)*

You can set only those dynamic properties that are read/write. Dynamic properties that are read-only can only be used to check the value of a property at run time.

Error Watch *Usually if a dynamic property is read/write, it can be set only before opening or executing the ADO object to whose **Properties** collection the dynamic property belongs. For example, the **Jet OLEDB:System database** dynamic property can be used to specify the workgroup information file (system database) that defines the user and group accounts to use when working with a Microsoft Access database (.mdb) that has been secured with user-level security. This property can only be set before using the **Open** method to open the **Connection** object. After a **Connection** object is opened, the **Jet OLEDB:System database** property becomes read-only.*

You can set dynamic properties either through the **Properties** collection or as additional arguments to the **ConnectionString** property. The following code snippet uses the **Properties** collection to set the **Jet OLEDB:System database** property in a **Connection** object before opening a database.

```
Dim cnnSample As Connection
Set cnnSample = New Connection
With cnnSample
   .Provider = "Microsoft.Jet.OLEDB.4.0"
   .Properties("Jet OLE DB:System Database") =
"\\Godzilla\MyShare\EnemiesList.mdw"
   .Open "\\Godzilla\MyShare\EnemiesList.mdb"
End With
```

Alternatively, you can set the **Jet OLEDB:System database** property as an additional argument before opening a database:

```
Dim cnnSample As ADODB.Connection
Set cnnSample = New ADODB.Connection
cnnSample.Open "Provider= Microsoft.Jet.OLEDB.4.0;" _
               & "Data Source\\Godzilla\MyShare\EnemiesList.mdb;" _
               & "Jet OLE DB:System Database =
\\Godzilla\MyShare\EnemiesList.mdw"
End Sub
```

ConnectionString for ODBC Provider

The following would serve as a connection string for the OLE DB Provider for ODBC:

```
"Provider=MSDASQL;DSN=dsnName;UID=userName;PWD=userPassword;"
```

Table 7-11 describes the keywords in the connection string.

Keyword	Description
Provider	Specifies the OLE DB Provider for ODBC.
DSN	Specifies the data source name.
UID	Specifies the user name.
PWD	Specifies the user password.

Table 7.11 Connection String for ODBC Provider

The Microsoft OLE DB Provider for ODBC is the default provider for ADO. Therefore, if you omit the **Provider=** parameter from the connection string, ADO will attempt to establish a connection to this provider.

The OLE DB Provider for ODBC does not support any connection parameters in addition to those supported by ADO. However, it does add the dynamic properties that are listed in Table 7-12 to the **Connection** object. You can access these additional properties through the **Properties** collection.

Property Name	Description
Accessible Procedures	Specifies whether the user has access to stored procedures.
Accessible Tables	Specifies whether the user has permission to execute SELECT statements against the database tables.
Active Statements	Specifies the number of handles an ODBC driver can support on a connection.
Driver Name	Indicates the filename of the ODBC driver.
Driver ODBC Version	Indicates the version of ODBC that this driver supports.
File Usage	Specifies whether the driver treats a file in a data source as a table or as a catalog.
Like Escape Clause	Specifies whether the driver supports the definition and use of an escape character for the percent character (%) and the underline character (_) in the LIKE predicate of a WHERE clause.
Max Columns in Group By	Indicates the maximum number of columns that can be listed in the GROUP BY clause of a SELECT statement.
Max Columns in Index	Indicates the maximum number of columns that can be included in an index.
Max Columns in Order By	Indicates the maximum number of columns that can be listed in the ORDER BY clause of a SELECT statement.

Table 7.12 Dynamic Properties That the OLE DB Provider for ODBC Adds to the **Connection** Object

Property Name	Description
Max Columns in Select	Indicates the maximum number of columns that can be listed in the SELECT portion of a SELECT statement.
Max Columns in Table	Indicates the maximum number of columns allowed in a table.
Numeric Functions	Specifies which numeric functions are supported by the ODBC driver.
Outer Join Capabilities	Indicates the types of OUTER JOINs supported by the provider.
Outer Joins	Specifies whether the provider supports OUTER JOINs.
Special Characters	Specifies which characters have special meaning for the ODBC driver.
Stored Procedures	Specifies whether stored procedures are available for use with this ODBC driver.
String Functions	Specifies which string functions are supported by the ODBC driver.
System Functions	Specifies which system functions are supported by the ODBC driver.
Time/Date Functions	Specifies which time and date functions are supported by the ODBC driver.
SQL Grammar Support	Indicates the SQL grammar that the ODBC driver supports.

Table 7.12 Dynamic Properties That the OLE DB Provider for ODBC Adds to the **Connection** Object *(continued)*

ConnectionString for SQL Server Provider

The following would serve as a connection string for the OLE DB Provider for SQL Server:

```
"Provider=SQLOLEDB;Data Source=serverName;" & _
   "Initial Catalog=databaseName;" & _
   "User ID=userName;Password=userPassword;"
```

Table 7-13 describes the keywords in the connection string.

Keyword	Description
Provider	Specifies the OLE DB Provider for SQL Server.
Data Source or **Server**	Specifies the name of a server.
Initial Catalog or **Database**	Specifies the name of a database on the server.
User ID or **uid**	Specifies the user name (for SQL Server Authentication).
Password or **pwd**	Specifies the user password (for SQL Server Authentication).

Table 7.13 Connection String Parameters for SQL Server Provider

You can also add to the additional parameters to the connection string. Table 7-14 lists additional parameters that are specific to the OLE DB provider for SQL Server. As with Jet, you can set these additional parameters either through the **Properties** collection or as additional arguments through the **ConnectionString** property.

Parameter	Description
Trusted_Connection	Indicates the user authentication mode. This can be set to Yes or No. The default value is No. If this property is set to Yes, then SQLOLEDB uses Microsoft Windows NT Authentication Mode to authorize user access to the SQL Server database specified by the **Location** and **Datasource** property values. If this property is set to No, then SQLOLEDB uses Mixed Mode to authorize user access to the SQL Server database. The SQL Server login and password are specified in the **User Id** and **Password** properties.
Current Language	Indicates a SQL Server language name. Identifies the language used for system message selection and formatting. The language must be installed on the SQL Server; otherwise, opening the connection will fail.
Network Address	Indicates the network address of the SQL Server specified by the **Location** property.
Network Library	Indicates the name of the network library (DLL) used to communicate with the SQL Server. The name should not include the path or the .dll filename extension. The default is provided by the SQL Server client configuration.
Use Procedure for Prepare	Determines whether SQL Server creates temporary stored procedures when commands are prepared (by the **Prepared** property).
Auto Translate	Indicates whether OEM/ANSI characters are converted. This property can be set to True or False. The default value is True. If this property is set to True, then SQLOLEDB performs OEM/ANSI character conversion when multi-byte character strings are retrieved from, or sent to, the SQL Server. If this property is set to False, then SQLOLEDB does not perform OEM/ANSI character conversion on multi-byte character string data.
Packet Size	Indicates a network packet size in bytes. The packet size property value must be between 512 and 32767. The default SQLOLEDB network packet size is 4096.
Application Name	Indicates the client application name.
Workstation ID	A string identifying the workstation.

Table 7.14 Additional Connection String Parameters for SQL Server Provider

The OLE DB Provider for SQL Server also adds other dynamic properties to the Connection object. The list is rather long, and it appears in the article "Microsoft OLE DB Provider for SQL Server" in the chapter titled "Using Providers with ADO" of the *Microsoft ADO Programmer's Reference*, which is available at Microsoft's MSDN Library Online site (http://msdn.microsoft.com/library).

Command Arguments

Once you have a connection to your data source, your next step is to execute commands to retrieve or manipulate data. Each command, like the connection, is represented by an object. This object is named, as you probably have guessed, the **Command** object. This object is most commonly used to query a database and return records in a **Recordset** object, though it also has other uses.

The **Command** object's **CommandText** property holds the text of a command to be issued against a provider. This text could be the name of a table, a SQL statement, or the name of a stored procedure. A stored procedure is a procedure that executes SQL statements and is stored on the server. Like other procedures, a stored procedure has a name by which it is called, and it may contain control statements and variables. Stored procedures execute quickly because they are precompiled, avoiding the need to parse SQL statements.

The **Command** object's **CommandType** property determines whether the text of a command is the name of a table, a SQL statement, or the name of a stored procedure. This property's value is one of the **CommandTypeEnum** constants listed in Table 7-15.

Constant	Value	Description
adCmdUnspecified	-1	Does not specify the command type argument.
adCmdText	1	Evaluates **CommandText** as a textual definition of a command or stored procedure call.
adCmdTable	2	Evaluates **CommandText** as a table name whose columns are all returned by an internally generated SQL query.
adCmdStoredProc	4	Evaluates **CommandText** as a stored procedure name.
adCmdUnknown	8	Default. Indicates that the type of command in the **CommandText** property is not known.
adCmdFile	256	Evaluates **CommandText** as the filename of a persistently stored Recordset.
adCmdTableDirect	512	Evaluates **CommandText** as a table name whose columns are all returned.

Table 7.15 Values of the **CommandType** Property of the ADO **Command** Object

24x7

Although using the **CommandType** property optimizes performance, you need to ensure that you are giving ADO the right information. If the **CommandType** property does not match the type of command in the **CommandText** property, an error will occur when you call the **Command** object's **Execute** method. While the error of calling a table a stored procedure, or vice versa, appears easily avoidable, it actually is easy to make this mistake simply by relying on whatever then happens to be the value of the **CommandType** property based on other and unrelated code in your application. While that value may as happenstance work for your invocation of the Execute method, that value could easily change later if you, or someone else on your programming team, changes that value in a portion of your code that is seemingly unrelated to your invocation of the Execute method. Therefore, always explicitly set the value of the **CommandType** property.

You do not *need* to specify a value for the **CommandType** property. If you do not, the value of that property will be the default, **adCmdUnknown**. However, using this default value will slow performance, because ADO then has to determine, through calls to the provider, whether the **CommandText** property is a table name, an SQL statement, or a stored procedure. The **CommandType** property tells ADO this information.

The primary difference among the data providers in their support of commands is that the OLE DB Provider for Microsoft Jet does not support stored procedures. If your data provider is the OLE DB Provider for Microsoft Jet, mistakenly retaining a previous value of **adCmdStoredProc** for the **CommandType** property will cause an error. This is another reason why you should always explicitly set the value of the **CommandType** property.

While the OLE DB Providers for ODBC and SQL Server do support stored procedures, the syntax that they use to call stored procedures is not the same. You should check MSDN help for the syntax particular to the provider you are using.

The OLE DB Providers for Jet, ODBC, and SQL Server all support SQL statements. However, SQL, like spoken languages, has dialects. Therefore, an SQL statement must be of the particular dialect or version supported by the provider's query processor.

Each of these providers adds a number of dynamic properties to the **Connection** object. The lengthy list for each provider can be viewed under the provider's name (such as "OLE DB Provider for Microsoft Jet") in the chapter titled "Using Providers with ADO" of the *Microsoft ADO Programmer's Reference*, available online at the Microsoft's MSDN Library Online site (http://msdn.microsoft.com/library).

Recordset Arguments

Command objects always are executed. That may seem like harsh treatment, but **Command** objects don't seem to mind. Execution in this case means the processing of the table query, SQL statement, or stored procedure represented by the **Command** object. The end result of that processing is a **Recordset** object, which represents the set of records requested by the table query, SQL statement, or stored procedure.

The **Recordset** object can be used to view, add, edit, or delete records. Whether a **Recordset** object can be used to edit records, or only to view them, depends on several of its properties.

The **CursorType** property indicates the type of cursor used by a **Recordset** object. As discussed earlier in connection with service components, a cursor is a database element that controls record navigation, the updateability of data, and the visibility of changes made to the database by other users. The value of the **CursorType** property is one of the **CursorTypeEnum** constants described in Table 7-16. However, the data providers do not universally support all available cursor types.

Constant	Value	Description
adOpenDynamic	2	Uses a dynamic cursor. Additions, changes, and deletions by other users are visible, and all types of movement through the **Recordset** are allowed, except for bookmarks, if the provider doesn't support them.
adOpenForwardOnly	0	Default. Uses a forward-only cursor. Identical to a static cursor, except that you can only scroll forward through records. This improves performance when you need to make only one pass through a **Recordset**.
adOpenKeyset	1	Uses a keyset cursor. Similar to a dynamic cursor, except that you can't see records that other users add, although records that other users delete are inaccessible from your **Recordset**. Data changes by other users are still visible.
adOpenStatic	3	Uses a static cursor. This is a static copy of a set of records that you can use to find data or generate reports. Additions, changes, or deletions by other users are not visible.
adOpenUnspecified	-1	Does not specify the type of cursor.

Table 7.16 **CursorTypeEnum** Values for the **CursorType** Property of the ADO **Recordset** Object

If a provider does not support the requested cursor type, it may return another cursor type. In the case of Jet, if the unsupported **adLockDynamic** cursor is used, the OLE DB Provider for Microsoft Jet will return a keyset cursor and reset the **CursorType** property accordingly to match the actual cursor type in use when the **Recordset** object is open. After you close the **Recordset**, the **CursorType** property reverts to its original setting.

Additionally, the **CursorType** setting can affect whether another **Recordset** property is available for a given provider. For example, if the data provider is the OLE DB Provider for ODBC, and the **CursorType** is **ForwardOnly** or **Dynamic**, properties such as **AbsolutePage**, **AbsolutePosition**, and **Bookmark** are not available and **EditMode** is read-only.

Similarly, the **CursorType** setting can affect whether a particular **Recordset** method is available for a given provider. For example, if the data provider is the OLE DB Provider for ODBC, and the **CursorType** is **ForwardOnly**, methods such as **MoveLast** and **MovePrevious** are not available.

The **Recordset** object's **Supports** method determines whether a particular **Recordset** supports a particular property or method. The following example (which assumes **rs** is an instantiated **Recordset**) illustrates the syntax of this method:

```
Dim blnSupported
blnSupported = rs.Supports(CursorOptions)
```

The **CursorOptions** argument is one of the **CursorOptionEnum** values listed in Table 7-17.

Constant	Value	Description
adAddNew	0x1000400	Supports the **AddNew** method to add new records.
adApproxPosition	0x4000	Supports the **AbsolutePosition** and **AbsolutePage** properties.
adBookmark	0x2000	Supports the **Bookmark** property to gain access to specific records.
adDelete	0x1000800	Supports the **Delete** method to delete records.
adFind	0x80000	Supports the Find method to locate a row in a **Recordset**.
adHoldRecords	0x100	Retrieves more records or changes the next position without committing all pending changes.
adIndex	0x100000	Supports the **Index** property to name an index.
adMovePrevious	0x200	Supports the **MoveFirst** and **MovePrevious** methods, and **Move** or **GetRows** methods to move the current record position backward without requiring bookmarks.

Table 7.17 Arguments for the **Recordset** Object's **Supports** Method

Constant	Value	Description
adNotify	0x40000	Indicates that the underlying data provider supports notifications (which determines whether **Recordset** events are supported).
adResync	0x20000	Supports the **Resync** method to update the cursor with the data that is visible in the underlying database.
adSeek	0x200000	Supports the **Seek** method to locate a row in a **Recordset**.
adUpdate	0x1008000	Supports the Update method to modify existing data.
adUpdateBatch	0x10000	Supports batch updating (**UpdateBatch** and **CancelBatch** methods) to transmit groups of changes to the provider.

Table 7.17 Arguments for the **Recordset** Object's **Supports** Method *(continued)*

Error Watch *Although the **Supports** method may return True for a given functionality, it does not guarantee that the provider can make the feature available under all circumstances. The **Supports** method simply returns whether the provider can support the specified functionality, assuming certain conditions are met. For example, the **Supports** method may indicate that a **Recordset** object supports updates even though the cursor is based on a multiple-table join, some columns of which are not updateable.*

Each of these providers adds a number of dynamic properties to the **Recordset** object. The lengthy list for each provider can be viewed under the provider's name (such as "OLE DB Provider for Microsoft Jet") in the chapter titled "Using Providers with ADO" of the *Microsoft ADO Programmer's Reference*, available online at the Microsoft's MSDN Library Online site (http://msdn.microsoft.com/library).

ADO Errors

There are three guarantees in life: death, taxes, and errors when accessing data using ADO. For example, the possibilities for errors abound in editing a record:

- The new value for the record may be the wrong data type.
- The new value for the record may be a non-unique value that violates referential integrity.
- The new value for the record may fail a validation rule.

- The new value for the record may be blank and the field doesn't accept null values.
- The new value is fine but you don't have permission to edit the record.

Your task of handling errors in your data access application is further complicated by the fact that the error may come from the provider, a service the provider is using, or ADO itself.

However, ADO does not trap errors. Nor does ADO have an error handler. Rather, ADO reports errors to the consumer, in this case your Visual Basic application that is using ADO's services. If the error does not originate from ADO itself, but instead from the provider or a service the provider is using, then the provider reports the error to ADO, which in turn reports the error to your application. Your application has the responsibility to trap and handle the error.

Chapter 4 discussed trapping and handling errors. The concepts discussed there concerning how to trap and handle errors also apply to ADO data access applications. Thus, you may use the **On Error** statement to trap errors, the **Err** object to obtain information about the error, and statements such as **Resume** and **Resume Next** to control the flow of error handling.

However, to properly handle errors, you may need information beyond what the **Err** object provides. For example, if the error originates from a provider, you may need to know the provider's error code in order to handle the error effectively. The **Err** object will not provide this information.

ADO, in addition to reporting errors, records them in an ADO **Error** object. This object has, in addition to **Number**, **Description**, and other properties akin to those in the **Err** object, additional properties, such as **NativeError**, which reports the provider-specific error code. The ADO **Error** object, because of its additional properties, provides you with richer error information than the **Err** object.

Additionally, more than one error may occur when ADO accesses a provider. ADO, consistent with the goal of supporting richer error information, enables the return by a provider of multiple errors resulting from a single ADO operation. While this does provide richer information on the error, it also exposes a limitation of the **Err** object—it can hold information about only one error at a time. Therefore, the **Err** object will hold information about whichever error was "first." The **Err** object will provide no information about the other errors or even indicate their existence.

The ADO **Error** object would seemingly have the same limitation as the **Err** object, since the **Error** object holds information about a single error. ADO's solution is to permit the creation of multiple **Error** objects, one for each error, and to store these multiple **Error** objects in an **Errors** collection.

24x7

While the reporting to ADO of errors from the provider is *supposed* to populate the **Errors** collection with **Error** objects, this does not always happen, depending on the source of the error, or (gasp) a bug in the provider or within ADO itself. Therefore, it is prudent to check the Visual Basic **Err** object as well as the ADO **Errors** collection.

Error Object

An ADO **Error** object is created for each error raised by an underlying provider (data or service) used by ADO. In addition, components underlying the provider may raise errors back to the provider, which the provider then passes to ADO. For example, each error encountered by ODBC is raised to the OLE DB Provider for ODBC, and from there to ADO, where the error is represented by an ADO **Error** object.

All **Error** objects reported by the provider to ADO are contained in the ADO **Errors** collection, which is discussed in the next section. These **Error** objects persist and are available from the **Errors** collection until another statement in your application results in further errors being raised by the provider. The occurrence of these further errors clears the **Errors** collection of the existing **Error** objects and replaces them with **Error** objects representing the new errors.

Errors that do not occur in the provider, but rather in ADO itself, such as an invalid use of ADO properties or methods, generally are captured by the exception-handling mechanism of the run-time programming environment. Thus, in Microsoft Visual Basic, the occurrence of an ADO-specific error will trigger an **On Error** event and appear in the **Err** object.

Error Watch *You should preserve the values of the* ***Err*** *object before examining and displaying the* ***Errors*** *collection. In the process of handling errors in the* ***Errors*** *collection, you may reset and thus change the values of the* ***Err*** *object.*

24x7

Again, there are occasions that an ADO error will be represented by an **Error** object in the **Errors** collection but not be accurately reflected by the Visual Basic **Err** object because the value of the Err object was overwritten by a subsequent error. Therefore, once again the advice applies that your error handling should check the ADO **Errors** collection as well as the Visual Basic **Err** object.

An **Error** object's properties contain specific details about each error. Table 7-18 describes the properties of the ADO **Error** object.

The **Description** property is a short textual description of the error. The string will come from either ADO or a provider. Providers are responsible for passing specific error text to ADO.

The **Number** property returns a long integer that uniquely identifies the error. The error number can be displayed in one of three ways:

- **Positive decimal** The low two bytes of the full number in decimal format. This number is displayed in the default Visual Basic error message dialog box. For example, "Run-time error '3707'."
- **Negative decimal** The decimal translation of the full error number.
- **Hexadecimal** The hexadecimal representation of the full error number. The Windows facility code is in the fourth digit. The facility code for ADO error numbers is *A*. For example: 0x800*A*0E7B.

For example, the error message "No current record" may have the value 3021, 0x80040BCD or –2147218483. 0x0BCD is simply the hexadecimal conversion of the value 3021. The value shows up as 0x80040BCD because all ADO errors have 8004 prepended to them. The long negative value, –2147218483, is simply a Long conversion of 80040BCD.

As with the Visual Basic **Err** object, the **Number** and **Description** properties of the ADO **Error** object are paired.

The value of the **Number** property also can be expressed by an **ErrorValEnum** constant. Table 7-19 lists these constants.

Property	Description
Description	String describing the error.
Number	Long integer value of the error constant.
Source	String identifying by name the object or application that originally generated the error.
NativeError	Long value representing the provider-specific error code.
SQLState	The **SQLState** and **NativeError** properties provide information from SQL data sources.
HelpContext	String containing the context ID for a topic in a Help file identified by the **HelpFile** property.
HelpFile	String containing the path to a Help file.

Table 7.18 Properties of the ADO **Error** Object

Constant	Value	Description
adErrBoundToCommand	3707 -2146824581 0x800A0E7B	Cannot change the **ActiveConnection** property of a **Recordset** object that has a **Command** object as its source.
adErrCannotComplete	3732 -2146824556 0x800A0E94	Server cannot complete the operation.
adErrCantChangeConnection	3748 -2146824540 0x800A0EA4	Connection was denied. New connection you requested has different characteristics than the one already in use.
adErrCantChangeProvider	3220 -2146825068 0X800A0C94	Supplied provider is different from the one already in use.
adErrCantConvertValue	3724 -2146824564 0x800A0E8C	Data value cannot be converted for reasons other than sign mismatch or data overflow. For example, conversion would have truncated data.
adErrCantCreate	3725 -2146824563 0x800A0E8D	Data value cannot be set or retrieved because the field data type was unknown or the provider had insufficient resources to perform the operation.
adErrCatalogNotSet	3747 -2146824541 0x800A0EA3	Operation requires a valid **ParentCatalog**.
adErrColumnNotOnThisRow	3726 -2146824562 0x800A0E8E	Record does not contain this field.
adErrDataConversion	3421 -2146824867 0x800A0D5D	Application uses a value of the wrong type for the current operation.
adErrDataOverflow	3721 -2146824567 0x800A0E89	Data value is too large to be represented by the field data type.
adErrDelResOutOfScope	3738 -2146824550 0x800A0E9A	URL of the object to be deleted is outside the scope of the current record.

Table 7.19 **ErrorValEnum** Constants for the **Error** Object's **Number** Property

Constant	Value	Description
adErrDenyNotSupported	3750 -2146824538 0x800A0EA6	Provider does not support sharing restrictions.
adErrDenyTypeNotSupported	3751 -2146824537 0x800A0EA7	Provider does not support the requested kind of sharing restriction.
adErrFeatureNotAvailable	3251 -2146825037 0x800A0CB3	Object or provider is not capable of performing requested operation.
adErrFieldsUpdateFailed	3749 -2146824539 0x800A0EA5	Fields update failed. For further information, examine the **Status** property of individual field objects.
adErrIllegalOperation	3219 -2146825069 0x800A0C93	Operation is not allowed in this context.
adErrIntegrityViolation	3719 -2146824569 0x800A0E87	Data value conflicts with the integrity constraints of the field.
adErrInTransaction	3246 -2146825042 0x800A0CAE	**Connection** object cannot be explicitly closed while in a transaction.
adErrInvalidArgument	3001 -2146825287 0x800A0BB9	Arguments are of the wrong type, are out of acceptable range, or are in conflict with one another.
adErrInvalidConnection	3709 -2146824579 0x800A0E7D	Operation is not allowed on an object referencing a closed or invalid connection.
adErrInvalidParamInfo	3708 -2146824580 0x800A0E7C	**Parameter** object is improperly defined. Inconsistent or incomplete information was provided.
adErrInvalidTransaction	3714 -2146824574 0x800A0E82	Coordinating transaction is invalid or has not started.
adErrInvalidURL	3729 -2146824559 0x800A0E91	URL contains invalid characters. Make sure the URL is typed correctly.
adErrItemNotFound	3265 -2146825023 0x800A0CC1	Item cannot be found in the collection corresponding to the requested name or ordinal.

Table 7.19 **ErrorValEnum** Constants for the **Error** Object's **Number** Property *(continued)*

Constant	Value	Description
adErrNoCurrentRecord	3021 -2146825267 0x800A0BCD	Either **BOF** or **EOF** is True, or the current record has been deleted. Requested operation requires a current record.
adErrNotExecuting	3715 -2146824573 0x800A0E83	Operation cannot be performed while not executing.
adErrNotReentrant	3710 -2146824578 0x800A0E7E	Operation cannot be performed while processing event.
adErrObjectClosed	3704 -2146824584 0x800A0E78	Operation is not allowed when the object is closed.
adErrObjectInCollection	3367 -2146824921 0x800A0D27	Object is already in collection. Cannot append.
adErrObjectNotSet	3420 -2146824868 0x800A0D5C	Object is no longer valid.
adErrObjectOpen	3705 -2146824583 0x800A0E79	Operation is not allowed when the object is open.
adErrOpeningFile	3002 -2146825286 0x800A0BBA	File could not be opened.
adErrOperationCancelled	3712 -2146824576 0x800A0E80	Operation has been canceled by the user.
adErrOutOfSpace	3734 -2146824554 0x800A0E96	Operation cannot be performed. Provider cannot obtain enough storage space.
adErrPermissionDenied	3720 -2146824568 0x800A0E88	Insufficient permission prevents writing to the field.
adErrPropConflicting	3742 -2146824546 0x800A0E9E	Property value conflicts with a related property.
adErrPropInvalidColumn	3739 -2146824549 0x800A0E9B	Property cannot apply to the specified field.

Table 7.19 **ErrorValEnum** Constants for the **Error** Object's **Number** Property *(continued)*

Constant	Value	Description
adErrPropInvalidOption	3740 -2146824548 0x800A0E9C	Property attribute is invalid.
adErrPropInvalidValue	3741 -2146824547 0x800A0E9D	Property value is invalid. Make sure the value is typed correctly.
adErrPropNotAllSettable	3743 -2146824545 0x800A0E9F	Property is read-only or cannot be set.
adErrPropNotSet	3744 -2146824544 0x800A0EA0	Optional property value was not set.
adErrPropNotSettable	3745 -2146824543 0x800A0EA1	Read-only property value was not set.
adErrPropNotSupported	3746 -2146824542 0x800A0EA2	Provider does not support the property.
adErrProviderFailed	3000 -2146825288 0x800A0BB8	Provider failed to perform the requested operation.
adErrProviderNotFound	3706 -2146824582 0x800A0E7A	Provider cannot be found. It may not be properly installed.
adErrReadFile	3003 -2146825285 0x800A0BBB	File could not be read.
adErrResourceExists	3731 -2146824557 0x800A0E93	Copy operation cannot be performed. Object named by destination URL already exists. Specify **adCopyOverwrite** to replace the object.
adErrResourceLocked	3730 -2146824558 0x800A0E92	Object represented by the specified URL is locked by one or more other processes. Wait until the process has finished and attempt the operation again.
adErrResourceOutOfScope	3735 -2146824553 0x800A0E97	Source or destination URL is outside the scope of the current record.

Table 7.19 **ErrorValEnum** Constants for the **Error** Object's **Number** Property *(continued)*

Constant	Value	Description
adErrSchemaViolation	3722 -2146824566 0x800A0E8A	Data value conflicts with the data type or constraints of the field.
adErrSignMismatch	3723 -2146824565 0x800A0E8B	Conversion failed because the data value was signed and the field data type used by the provider was unsigned.
adErrStillConnecting	3713 -2146824575 0x800A0E81	Operation cannot be performed while connecting asynchronously.
adErrStillExecuting	3711 -2146824577 0x800A0E7F	Operation cannot be performed while executing asynchronously.
adErrTreePermissionDenied	3728 -2146824560 0x800A0E90	Permissions are insufficient to access tree or subtree.
adErrUnavailable	3736 -2146824552 0x800A0E98	Operation failed to complete and the status is unavailable. The field may be unavailable or the operation was not attempted.
adErrUnsafeOperation	3716 -2146824572 0x800A0E84	Safety settings on this computer prohibit accessing a data source on another domain.
adErrURLDoesNotExist	3727 -2146824561 0x800A0E8F	Either the source URL or the parent of the destination URL does not exist.
adErrURLNamedRowDoesNotExist	3737 -2146824551 0x800A0E99	Record named by this URL does not exist.
adErrVolumeNotFound	3733 -2146824555 0x800A0E95	Provider cannot locate the storage device indicated by the URL. Make sure the URL is typed correctly.
adErrWriteFile	3004 -2146825284 0x800A0BBC	Write to file failed.
adWrnSecurityDialog	3717 -2146824571 0x800A0E85	For internal use only. Don't use.
adWrnSecurityDialogHeader	3718 -2146824570 0x800A0E86	For internal use only. Don't use.

Table 7.19 **ErrorValEnum** Constants for the **Error** Object's **Number** Property *(continued)*

Some properties and methods return warnings that appear as **Error** objects in the **Errors** collection but do not halt a program's execution. A warning has a positive number value, which differentiates it from an error.

Note *Critical warning or status messages (such as calls made with unsupported or conflicting properties) may be ignored by ADO and not saved to the* ***Errors*** *collection if the operation succeeded.*

The **Source** property identifies the name of the object or application that originally generated the error. The **Source** property returns the project name for errors that occur in a standard or form module, and *projectname.classname* for errors that occur in a class module. The **Source** property is useful for errors that occur outside your application. This is particularly useful when you have several **Error** objects in the **Errors** collection following a request to a data source. For example, if your application uses OLE automation to access Microsoft Word, and an error occurs in Word, the value of the **Source** property would be **Word.Application**.

The **NativeError** and **SQLState** properties provide information from SQL data sources.

The **NativeError** property indicates the provider-specific error code for a given **Error** object. For example, when using the Microsoft ODBC Provider for OLE DB with a Microsoft SQL Server database, native error codes that originate from SQL Server pass through ODBC and the ODBC Provider to the ADO **NativeError** property.

The **SQLState** property indicates the SQL state for a given **Error** object. Its value is a five-character string value that follows the ANSI SQL standard and indicates the error code. You use the **SQLState** property to read the five-character error code that the provider returns when an error occurs during the processing of an SQL statement. For example, when using the Microsoft OLE DB Provider for ODBC with a Microsoft SQL Server database, SQL state error codes originate from ODBC, based either on errors specific to ODBC or on errors that originate from Microsoft SQL Server, and are then mapped to ODBC errors. These error codes are documented in the ANSI SQL standard but may be implemented differently by different data sources.

The **HelpContext** property is used to automatically display a particular topic in the Help file designated by the **HelpFile** property. The **HelpContext** property is similar to a bookmark in Microsoft Word.

Errors Collection

The **Errors** collection is a collection of the **Connection** object. Therefore, you need to instantiate a **Connection** object to access the **Errors** collection. You query the properties of the **Error** object to obtain information about a provider-generated error. You use the **Errors** collection to obtain, through a loop, all the errors generated by the provider.

The **Errors** collection has two properties: **Count** and **Item**. **Count**, as usually is the case, returns the number of items, in this case the number of **Error** objects, in the **Errors** collection. **Item** returns a specific **Error** object in the collection by its position, which is zero-based as is usually the case for intrinsic Visual Basic objects.

Count and **Item** often are used in a **For-Next** loop to iterate through the **Errors** collection to retrieve errors. This code snippet uses these properties to retrieve and print the number and description of each error in the **Errors** collection to the Immediate Window (using Debug.Print):

```
Public Sub CauseError()
On Error GoTo Handler
Dim cnnSample As Connection
Dim counter As Integer

Set cnnSample = New Connection
' Intentionally cause error
cnnSample.Open "I goofed"
Exit Sub
Handler:
For counter = 0 To cnnSample.Errors.count
   Debug.Print cnnSample.Errors(counter).Description & vbCrLf
Next counter
```

You also can use the **For Each … Next** syntax to accomplish the same purpose. This code snippet enumerates all of the properties of the **Error** object:

```
Public Sub CauseError()
      On Error GoTo Handler
Dim cnnSample As Connection
Dim errSample As Error
Dim strError As String

' Intentionally cause error
cnnSample.Open "I goofed"
Exit Sub
Handler:
For Each errSample In cnnSample.Errors
   strError = "Error #" & cnnSample.Errors.count & vbCrLf & _
   "    " & errSample.Description & vbCrLf & _
   "    (Source: " & errSample.Source & ")" & vbCrLf & _
```

```
      "   (SQL State: " & errSample.SQLState & ")" & vbCrLf & _
      "   (NativeError: " & errSample.NativeError & ")" & vbCrLf
   If errSample.HelpFile = "" Then
      strError = strError & _
      "   There is no Help for you" & vbCrLf
   Else
      strError = strError & _
      "   (HelpFile: " & errSample.HelpFile & ")" & vbCrLf & _
      "   (HelpContext: " & errSample.HelpContext & ")" & vbCrLf
   End If
   Debug.Print strError
Next
```

The **Errors** collection also has two methods: **Refresh** and **Clear**. The **Refresh** method updates the objects in a collection to reflect objects available from, and specific to, the provider. The **Clear** method removes all **Error** objects from the **Error** collection.

When another ADO operation generates an error, the **Errors** collection is cleared, and the new set of **Error** objects is placed in the **Errors** collection. However, the **Errors** collection on the **Connection** object is cleared and populated only when the provider generates a new error, or when the **Clear** method is called.

As mentioned previously, some properties and methods return warnings that appear as **Error** objects in the **Errors** collection but do not halt a program's execution. Before you call the **Resync**, **UpdateBatch**, or **CancelBatch** methods on a **Recordset** object, the **Open** method on a **Connection** object, or set the **Filter** property on a **Recordset** object, call the **Clear** method on the **Errors** collection. You then can use the **Count** property of the **Errors** collection to test for returned warnings.

Summary

ADO does not access data directly, but rather does so through providers. ADO is programmer friendly because its interface is consistent no matter which provider it is using. The differences among providers do not change ADO's interface. Rather, each provider adds properties, referred to as dynamic properties, to the intrinsic or built-in properties of ADO objects. These dynamic properties are **Property** objects, and they can be accessed through the **Properties** collection of the ADO **Connection** object.

ADO does not trap or handle errors. The application that uses ADO has that responsibility, and it can use the **On Error** statement to trap errors, the **Err** object to obtain information about the errors, and the **Resume** and **Resume Next** statements to control the flow of error handling. However, more than one error may occur when ADO accesses data through a provider. The **Err** object can hold information about only one error at a time, and it will not provide information such as the provider-specific error code. ADO provides an **Error** object to provide richer error information, and it supports the creation of multiple **Error** objects that are contained in and accessible from an **Errors** collection.

CHAPTER 8
ActiveX Controls

Building blocks are common childhood toys. A child can use a block of a certain size as part of a car one day, and reuse the same block another day as part of a space ship. All the child has to do is snap the block in place and the block performs its purpose.

ActiveX controls are a programmer's building blocks. If you need a combo box, you simply drag the **ComboBox** from the toolbox and drop it in a container, usually a Visual Basic form. If you later need a combo box for another application, you again drag the **ComboBox** control from the toolbox and drop it to a form. The combo box (or list box, text box, command button, and so on) then performs as that control is designed to perform.

ActiveX controls are an example of *reusable software components*. Software is "reusable" when it can be used in many different applications. For example, a Visual Basic **ComboBox** control can be reused in application after application simply by adding it to different forms.

However, a **ComboBox** control would be of little use, reusable or not, if you, as the programmer, could not control its features (properties), actions (methods), and reactions (events). For example, a **ComboBox** control includes a **ListIndex** property by which the index of the selected item can be accessed, an **AddItem** method by which an item can be added to the combo box, and a **Click** event that fires when a mouse clicks on the combo box or an item in it. Having properties, methods, and events is the hallmark of a software "component."

These controls are easy to customize. The standard controls each have a Properties window, and often property pages, through which properties such as background color can be changed.

However, programmers are never satisfied, nor should they be, and they try to improve on or add to the controls in the Visual Basic toolbox. You can create your own custom control that improves on a standard control. One example is a "smart search" **ComboBox** control in which, as the user enters text in the edit box, the first matching item in the list box portion is highlighted. This "smart search" combo box, once created, could be reused effectively in many different types of applications simply by dropping it into a form.

Visual Basic eases your task of creating custom controls. You start a new ActiveX control project, drop a **ComboBox** control (for example) in a **UserForm**, which is the functional equivalent of a form in an ActiveX control project, write the code necessary for the logic of the smart search feature, compile the control, and you're ready to add it to your applications. Visual Basic also provides an ActiveX Control Interface Wizard to further ease your task.

It wasn't always so easy. In the dark old days of control development (a few years ago), writing your own controls was no simple matter. Controls could not be written in Visual Basic. Instead, they had to be written in C or C++, and they also required you to have a thorough knowledge of the Component Object Model (COM).

Version 5 of Visual Basic, and the accompanying Visual Basic CCE (Control Creation Edition), was a breakthrough in control development. Visual Basic developers now could write their own controls without having to know C/C++ or COM. The controls still have to comply with COM, but the control will comply with COM if you create it using (correctly, of course) the Visual Basic IDE. This is just another example of how Visual Basic makes your life easier by enabling Windows programming without the complexity of C or C++.

Although creating an ActiveX control has become a much easier task, the interplay between the control and the container in which it is sited is far less understood and documented.

ActiveX Controls are a hybrid. Like a Standard EXE project, they have the functional equivalent of a form, a **UserControl**, that, like a form in a Standard EXE project, may contain its own constituent controls. However, unlike a Standard EXE project, an ActiveX Control project is not a stand-alone object. Rather, it exists inside of a container, which usually is a form in a separate Standard EXE project, but may also be, for example, Internet Explorer. Thus, the control cannot be viewed in isolation from the container in which it is sited, and the container cannot be viewed in isolation from the control sited in it.

The connection between the control and its container goes even further. The container adds properties to the control through the **Extender** object, and the control may view so-called ambient properties of the container through the **AmbientProperties** object. These objects, which are rarely discussed but which

ActiveX: What's in a Name?

When 32-bit Windows replaced 16-bit Windows, OCX controls replaced VBX controls. Windows is still 32-bit, but the controls are no longer referred to as OCX. Instead, the controls are referred to as ActiveX. What happened to OCX controls? The answer is: Nothing. Indeed, ActiveX controls often have the extension .ocx. Microsoft just changed the name of OCX controls to ActiveX controls. Why? Marketing! "ActiveX" sounds "sexier" than "OCX."

are quite important to the creation and use of ActiveX controls, will be the focus of this chapter.

Before turning to the **Extender** and **AmbientProperties** objects, there is an additional issue, the perspective through which you are dealing with ActiveX controls—author, developer, or user.

Developers, Authors, and Users

Usually there are two roles in application development: developer and user. The developer develops the application, and the user, or end user, uses it. For example, Microsoft is the developer of Microsoft Word, and the authors of this book used Word to write it.

By contrast, in the context of ActiveX controls, there are three roles: author, developer, and user. The author of a control creates an ActiveX control that is compiled, usually as an .ocx file. The developer purchases the control and incorporates it into the developer's application, the .ocx file being included in the application's setup program. The user (the end user) purchases, installs, and uses the application. Thus, in the context of ActiveX controls, the author's customer is the developer, the developer's customer being the end user.

You likely will find yourself in the role of developer, and therefore you will be a customer of ActiveX controls. The relative ease of building ActiveX controls created a new industry, third-party independent software vendors (ISVs) who make custom controls. The success of, and competition among, the ISVs has made it possible for you to purchase a professionally written, royalty-free control for a few hundred dollars, or less.

However, even as a developer you may find yourself authoring ActiveX controls. This may seem curious because notwithstanding the relative ease of using Visual Basic as compared with, for example, Visual C++, developing your own ActiveX controls still entails thousands of dollars (or more) in development time. Why spend all this time when you could purchase a professionally written, royalty-free control for a few hundred dollars?

There are some circumstances in which building makes more sense than buying:

- The control can be customized to meet your needs. ISV-built controls have to meet the needs of a wide range of customers. Being "one size fits all" controls, they are necessarily generic.
- Even if the ISV-built control currently meets your needs, business needs change, and these changes may require modifications or enhancements to

the control. You can make these changes without having to put them on the vendor's "wish list" and hope they are adopted in the next release.

- Another consequence of the ISV-built controls being "one size fits all" is that the control contains more features than you can possibly use. A control may offer over 200 methods, properties, and events, but you may only need to use 20. These additional features might be desirable to someone else with different needs, but for you they are only flab that makes the control unnecessarily large and slow.
- By writing your own control, you will be able to limit the number of resources that need to be shipped with the control. Yet another consequence of the ISV-built controls being "one size fits all" is their reliance on a plethora of DLLs which would need to be shipped with your application. Alternatively, by tailoring your control to your needs, you can limit the number of DLLs.
- What if something goes wrong? For example, it is not unusual for OCXs to have memory leaks. Since you have access to and control over the source code, you can fix the problem rather than call the ISV and rely on the uncertainties of their technical support.

Regardless of whether you are an author, a developer, or both, it is important to analyze ActiveX controls from both perspectives because the distinction between developer and author is not merely that of buyer and seller. Authors and developers have different programming tasks. The author writes code in connection with the creation of the ActiveX control and has to anticipate the containers in which the control may be sited. By contrast, the developer writes code in the container to utilize the features of the control. However, in an application, an ActiveX control does not exist in isolation from the container, but rather the two form a cohesive whole. Similarly, the respective programming tasks of the author and developer should not be performed in isolation of the other, but rather in anticipation and consideration of the other's task.

When a developer sites an ActiveX control in a container, more is happening than just the addition of a control to a form. The container also adds properties to the ActiveX control that the ActiveX control did not have before it was sited in the container. These extended properties that the container adds to the ActiveX control are accessed through the logically named **Extender** object. Developers usually are the ones to access extended properties, though authors on occasion may as well.

Additionally, an author of an ActiveX control needs to be able to access the properties of the container in which the control will be sited. The author may want certain properties of the ActiveX control to be synchronized with corresponding properties of the container. For example, if the background color of the container changes, the ActiveX control is notified of the change and the new background color, and can change its own background color to match that of the container. The difficulty is that the author has to write the code for the ActiveX control without knowing the container in which the ActiveX control may later be sited by a developer. Nevertheless, the author may access the properties of the as yet nonexistent container through the **AmbientProperties** object.

Extender Object

As discussed previously, when a developer sites an ActiveX control in a container, the container adds to the control properties, as well as to the methods and events. The reason for these additional properties is that the control is not on its own but is living inside a container. Therefore, the container supplies **Height** and **Width** properties for the size of the control, **Left** and **Top** properties for the position of the control, a **Visible** property for the visibility of the control, and so on.

From the perspective of the developer viewing the properties of the control, the joining of the "original" properties of the control and those added by the container is seamless. Both appear to be part of a single interface.

The **UserControl** object, which is the base object used to create an ActiveX control, has an **Extender** property. This property returns the **Extender** object for the control. The **Extender** object holds not only the original properties of the control but also those added by the container.

When a developer references an ActiveX control, the developer is not accessing the ActiveX control itself, but instead the **Extender** object returned from the **UserControl**'s **Extender** property. Thus, the developer sees, as properties of the ActiveX control, both the original properties of the control and those added by the container in a single, seamless interface.

Developers use the **Extender** object more often than authors. One reason is that the developer, not the author, usually should control properties added by the container. For example, the developer, not the author, should decide the location of the control in the application form, as determined by the extended **Left** and **Top** properties. Indeed, some properties added by the container cannot be implemented by a control because the container must provide the prerequisites of these properties.

Nevertheless, authors can also use the **Extender** object to give the control access to the properties added by the container so that the control can determine the value of a property added by the container or whether the container added the property at all. Additionally, there are instances in which an author may want to change the value of one of the properties added by the container.

24x7 Extender Properties Are Late Bound

When you compile your ActiveX control, Visual Basic has no way of knowing the type of container in which your control may be placed. Consequently, a reference to the **Extender** object returned by the **Extender** property is always late bound. Therefore, an object variable to which the **Extender** object is assigned should be declared as **Object**.

Error Watch *The **Extender** object is not yet available when the **UserControl** object's Initialize event is raised, but becomes available when the **InitProperties** event or **ReadProperties** event is raised. The Initialize event is raised when a **UserControl** object is created and any constituent controls are sited on it. The **InitProperties** event is raised when a new ActiveX control is sited on a form in a Standard EXE project. The **ReadProperties** event occurs when the form is thereafter opened. This is only an issue for authors. The **InitProperties** (or **ReadProperties**) event necessarily will have occurred before the developer interacts with the ActiveX control.*

A **UserControl** object can access **Extender** properties through its **Extender** property. For example, an ActiveX control could use the following code to initialize its **Caption** property:

```
Private Sub UserControl_InitProperties()
     Caption = Extender.Name
End Sub
```

The **Extender** object has a number of properties. Some of these properties are referred to as "standard" because the ActiveX control specification lists them as properties that all containers should provide. However, this listing is a recommendation, not a requirement. Containers do not have to implement any of them. Thus, you should always use error trapping when referring to properties of the **Extender** object in your code, even standard properties.

Table 8-1 lists the standard properties of the **Extender** object. Table 8-2 lists additional **Extender** properties.

As discussed previously, when a developer references an ActiveX control, the developer is not accessing the ActiveX control itself, but instead the **Extender** object returned from the ActiveX control's **Extender** property. By contrast, when an author references an ActiveX control, the author is accessing the ActiveX control itself, not the **Extender** object. Nevertheless, it is possible both for the developer to reference the ActiveX control, itself, and for the author to reference the **Extender** object.

Property	Data Type	Read/Write	Meaning
Name	String	R	The name the developer assigns to the control instance.
Visible	Boolean	RW	Indicates whether the control is visible.
Parent	Object	R	Returns the object that is the container of the control, such as a Visual Basic form. Only accessible at run time.
Cancel	Boolean	R	True if the control is the default Cancel button for the container. Cancel will only be a property if the control's **DefaultCancel** property is True.
Default	Boolean	R	True if the control is the default button for the container. Default will only be a property if the control's **DefaultCancel** property is True.

Table 8.1 Standard Properties of the **Extender** Object

Property	Data Type	Read/Write	Meaning
Container	Object	R	Object that represents the container (usually a form) of the control. Only accessible at run time.
DataBinding, DataChanged, DataField, DataSource	Various	R	Not present unless the control has a property that is bound to a database.
DragIcon	String	RW	Specifies the file of the icon to use when the control is dragged.
DragMode	Integer	RW	Specifies whether the control will automatically drag, or if the user of the control must call the Drag method.
Enabled	Boolean	R	Specifies whether the control is enabled. This **Extender** property is not present unless the control also has an **Enabled** property with the correct procedure ID.
Height	Integer	RW	Specifies the height of the control in the container's scale units.
HelpContextID	Integer	RW	Specifies the context ID to use when the F1 key is pressed and the control has the focus.
Index	Integer	R	Specifies the position in a control array that this instance of the control occupies.
Left	Integer	RW	Specifies the distance from the left edge of the control to the left edge of the container, measured in the container's scale units.

Table 8.2 Additional **Extender** Object Properties

Property	Data Type	Read/Write	Meaning
Negotiate	Boolean	R	Specifies whether a control that can be aligned is displayed when an active object on the form displays one or more toolbars. Not present unless the control's **Alignable** property is True.
Object	Object	R	References the underlying object (usually the control), not the **Extender**. Only accessible at run time.
TabIndex	Integer	RW	Specifies the position of the control in the tab order of the controls in the container. Not present unless the control's **CanGetFocus** property is True.
TabStop	Boolean	RW	Specifies whether TAB will stop on the control. Not present unless the control's **CanGetFocus** property is True.
Tag	String	RW	Contains a user-defined value.
ToolTipText	String	RW	Specifies the text to be displayed when the cursor hovers over the control for more than a second.
Top	Integer	RW	Specifies the distance from the top edge of the control to the top edge of the container, measured in the container's scale units.
WhatThisHelpID	Integer	RW	Specifies the context ID to use when the What's This pop-up is used on the control.
Width	Integer	RW	Specifies the width of the control in the container's scale units.

Table 8.2 Additional **Extender** Object Properties *(continued)*

The developer can reference the ActiveX control by using the **Object** property of the **Extender** object. For example, in the following code the developer accesses the **Tag** property of the **Extender** object, not the ActiveX control

24x7 Always Check

Just as life holds no guarantees, there likewise is no guarantee that a given container will support a given property of the **Extender** object. Accessing a property that the container does not support will cause an error unless your control happens to have a property of the same name. Therefore, a control author must either check the **Properties** collection of the **Extender** object to determine if the given property is supported, or trap the error that results from accessing an unsupported property.

named **ctlSample**, because a developer's reference to an ActiveX control is to the **Extender** object:

```
ctlSample.Tag
```

If the developer wishes to access the **Tag** property of the ActiveX control, as opposed to the **Tag** property of the **Extender** object, then the developer uses the **Object** property of the **Extender** object returned by the reference to **ctlSample**:

```
ctlSample.Object.Tag
```

In contrast, the author would access the **Tag** property of the ActiveX control simply by referring to the control, again named **ctlSample** in this example:

```
ctlSample.Tag
```

If the author instead wanted to access the **Tag** property of the **Extender** object, then the author would use the control's **Extender** property:

```
ctlSample.Extender.Tag
```

Design Tip *As the preceding discussion suggests, the control can implement a property with the same name as a property of the* ***Extender*** *object, such as with the* ***Tag*** *property. Such "collisions" between control and* ***Extender*** *object properties are permissible and do not cause a run-time error. However, they may create a logical error, since a developer's and author's respective references to* ***ctlSample.Tag*** *would refer to two separate* ***Tag*** *properties. As shown previously, the developer can refer to the control's* ***Tag*** *property through the* ***Object*** *property and the author can refer to the Extender's* ***Tag*** *property through the* ***Extender*** *property.*

Why risk the confusion that can result from a collision? The reason is that there is no guarantee that an ***Extender*** *object will support a given property. While in the preceding examples both the control and the* ***Extender*** *object had a* ***Tag*** *property, differences among containers make it impossible to guarantee that any given* ***Extender*** *object will have a* ***Tag*** *property. Even so, a developer's reference to* ***ctlSample.Tag = someValue*** *would not cause an error, so long as the control itself had a* ***Tag*** *property. Instead, the value would be assigned to the* ***Tag*** *property of the control.*

The container does not just add properties to the ActiveX control. It also adds methods and events, which are listed and described in Tables 8-3 and 8-4, respectively.

Method	Meaning
Drag	Begins, ends, or cancels a drag operation of the control.
Move	Moves the position of the control.
SetFocus	Sets the focus to the control.
ShowWhatsThis	Displays a selected topic in a Help file using the What's This pop-up provided by Help.
ZOrder	Places the control at the front or back of the z-order.

Table 8.3 Methods of the **Extender** Object

While the developer usually uses the **Extender** object, the author also can use it to access and, if warranted, change the extended properties. However, before changing extended properties, an author should keep in mind the advice often given by parents to their children: "Just because you can do something doesn't mean you should do it." Normally the container should control the control, not the other way around.

Ambient Properties

While **Extender** properties are properties added by a container to a control, ambient properties are information that a container provides to a control about the container's properties. A control can use these ambient properties to tailor its appearance to the particular container in which it is sited. For example, ambient properties may disclose information about a container's background color and

Event	Raised When
DragDrop	Another control on the form is dropped on the control.
DragOver	Another control on the form is dragged over the control.
GotFocus	Control gets the focus.
LostFocus	Control loses the focus.
ObjectEvent	Generic event that allows you to handle events of a control and return values through the control's event parameters.
Validate	Focus is about to shift to another control that has its **CausesValidation** property set to True. The purpose is to prevent the first control from losing the focus until the validation criteria are met.

Table 8.4 Events of the **Extender** Object

font that the control then can use to keep its own background color and font consistent with that of the container. However, ambient properties are not limited to visual appearance. The **UserMode** ambient property, for example, indicates whether the container is in run or design mode.

Just as the **Extender** property of the **UserControl** returns a reference to an **Extender** object through which the properties added by the container to the control can be accessed, the **Ambient** property of the **UserControl** returns a reference to an **AmbientProperties** object through which the ambient properties of the container can be accessed.

The **AmbientProperties** object, like the **Extender** object, provides properties defined by the ActiveX Controls Standard. As is the case with the **Extender** object, not all properties provided by the **AmbientProperties** object will necessarily be supported by a particular container. Containers generally support only a subset of ambient properties, just as containers only support a subset of **Extender** object properties. Indeed, some containers may not support any ambient properties. However, while attempting to access an **Extender** object property that is not supported by a container will raise an error if the underlying control does not happen to support the property, the consequence of attempting to access an unsupported ambient property is far less drastic—a default value is returned. Therefore, a call to standard ambient properties is early bound.

Control containers can define their own additional ambient properties. These container-specific ambient properties can be accessed as if they were properties of the **AmbientProperties** object. However, since they are not standard ambient properties, they are not in Visual Basic's type library, so Visual Basic cannot verify their existence at compile time. Therefore, you should always use error handling when working with ambient properties.

Table 8-5 lists the standard ambient properties.

UserMode is the most important property of the **AmbientProperties** object. The **UserMode** property allows an instance of your control to determine whether it's executing at design time, when **UserMode** is False, or at run time, when **UserMode** is True. That **UserMode** is False at design time and True at run time is not intuitive. The logic is that the "user" in **UserMode** is the end user, not the developer. During design time, it is the developer who is interacting with your control. The end user is not, so **UserMode** is False. By contrast, during run time it is the end user who is interacting with your control, so **UserMode** is True.

Property	Description	Default Value
BackColor	Background color of the container.	&H80000005
DisplayAsDefault	Whether the control's **DefaultCancel** property is True and the developer specifies this as the default control.	False
DisplayName	The name of the control assigned by the developer.	Empty string (" ")
Font	The default font used or recommended by the container.	MS Sans Serif 8
ForeColor	The foreground color of the container.	&H80000008
LocaleID	A Long that specifies the language and country of the user.	System default
Palette	The palette used or recommended by the container.	Not applicable
RightToLeft	True if the control should draw text from right to left, as in the Hebrew language.	False
ScaleUnits	String representing type of coordinates, such as twips, pixels, inches, etc.	Twips
TextAlign	Text alignment used or recommended by the container.	Zero
UserMode	True if control is at run time, False if at design time.	True

Table 8.5 Standard Ambient Properties

The **UserMode** property often is used in conjunction with properties that can only be written to at design time and read only at run time, or written to only once at run time.

The **ScaleUnits** property is used to determine the type of coordinate units used by the container. Possible values can include twip, pixel, point, inch, millimeter, and centimeter. When the container is supplied by Visual Basic, the **ScaleUnits** property also can be accessed through the **Container** property of the **Extender** object.

The **DisplayName** property is useful for identifying your control. A developer can use the **DisplayName** property to identify the control instance that is the source of a design-time error raised by a control.

Design Tip *The **ForeColor**, **BackColor**, **Font**, and **TextAlign** properties can be used by your control to make its appearance match that of the container. For example, in the **InitProperties** event, which each instance of your **UserControl** receives when it is first placed on a container, you can set your control's **ForeColor**, **BackColor**, **Font**, and **TextAlign** properties to the values provided by the ambient properties.*

If a control can serve as a default button, then the **DisplayAsDefault** property tells you whether your control is the default button for the container, so you can supply the extra-heavy border that identifies the default button for the end user. This property will be discussed in connection with the **AmbientChanged** event.

Table 8-6 lists additional standard ambient properties. These properties are important, but you do not need to deal with them because they are managed by Visual Basic's implementation of ActiveX controls.

Sometimes one of the properties of the **AmbientProperties** object changes. For example, the container's background color may change during an instance of an application. Such a change fires the **AmbientChanged** event of the **UserControl** object. This is the syntax of the event procedure:

```
Private Sub ControlName_AmbientChanged (strPropName As String)
```

ControlName is the name of the **UserControl** and *strPropName* is a string containing the name of the property that changed.

The **AmbientChanged** event can be used to keep a control instance in sync with the container. The following code keeps the control's **BackColor** property synchronized with that of the container:

```
Private Sub ControlName_AmbientChanged (strPropName As String)
   If strPropName = "BackColor" Then _
      BackColor = Ambient.BackColor
```

Property	Description
MessageReflect	Indicates whether the container should reflect certain window messages back to the control.
ShowGrabHandles	Indicates whether the container can display grab handles for resizing the control.
ShowHatching	Indicates that the container can display a hatching pattern over an inactive control.
SupportsMnemonics	Indicates that the container can support access keys for a control.
UIDead	Indicates that the container should ignore all user input.

Table 8.6 Standard Ambient Properties Implemented by Visual Basic

Design Tip *As discussed earlier, if the* ***DefaultCancel*** *property of the ActiveX control is True, the* ***Extender*** *object will have* ***Default*** *and* ***Cancel*** *properties. These properties then can be used to determine whether the control is the* ***Default*** *or* ***Cancel*** *button for the container. (The default button can be clicked by pressing the* ENTER *key and the Cancel button can be clicked by pressing the* ESC *key). A default button customarily shows a different appearance (such as a raised and darker border around a command button) than a standard button. You could view the* ***Extender*** *property to determine whether a control should be displayed as default. However, it is preferable to use the* ***DisplayAsDefault*** *ambient property because (1) the ambient property is early bound, whereas the* ***Extender*** *property is late bound, and (2) the* ***AmbientChanged*** *event will notify you of any change in the status of the button as a default button, whereas the* ***Extender*** *object has no corresponding event that notifies you of a change in the status.*

Summary

ActiveX controls are a hybrid. Like a Standard EXE project, they have the functional equivalent of a form—a **UserControl**—that, like a form in a Standard EXE project, may contain controls. However, unlike a Standard EXE project, an ActiveX control project is not a stand-alone project. Rather, it exists inside of a container, which usually is a form in a separate Standard EXE project, but may also be, for example, Internet Explorer.

Consistent with this duality of ActiveX controls, you may be approaching them from two roles. You may be the author who writes the ActiveX control or the developer who uses the ActiveX control in your application.

This duality of ActiveX controls also results in dual sets of properties. The control itself specifies one set of properties, and the container in which the control is sited specifies the other set of properties. These extended properties supplied by the container are accessed through the **Extender** object.

Finally, the control may need to know about properties of its container in order to keep its own properties synchronized with those of the container. The container exposes its ambient properties that the control can access through the **AmbientProperties** object.

CHAPTER 9

User Interface

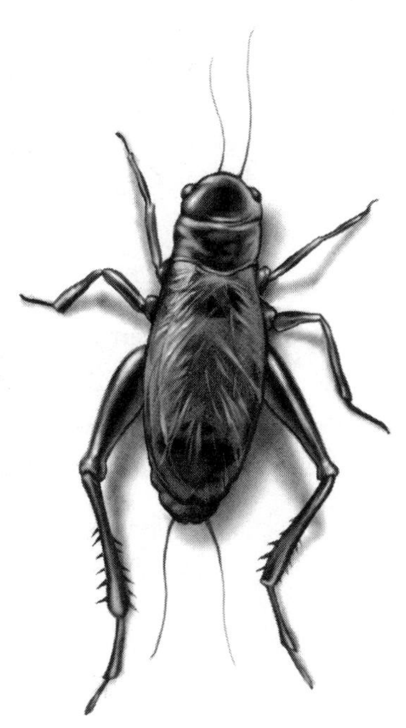

While programmers quite properly focus tremendous effort and care on their code, too often they give short shrift to designing the user interface, viewing that task as "not real programming." This view may be misguided. Buyers of software cannot see the code "under the hood" and may not know how to benchmark performance. However, they can see and interact with the user interface. Consequently, they often base their purchasing decision on the appearance and ease of use of the user interface.

Appearance is important. No further proof is needed than the millions of dollars spent every year on personal appearance and the packaging of products. Indeed, unattractive programs may not receive a second look.

However, a good appearance, while important, can only make a favorable first impression. You may be attracted to a product because of its lovely packaging, but if the product does not do what you want it to, you likely will return it, and certainly will not buy it again.

Software buyers' perceptions of how well your application meets their needs will be based primarily on their interaction with the user interface. A user will perceive an application to not be working well if its interface is difficult to understand or use, even if the application in reality would meet their needs.

Additionally, programmers frequently are blamed for errors that really are not errors at all, but instead are the user's misunderstanding of how to use the application. As partial revenge, programmers often regale each other with comical tales of ignorant users. However, far too often the reason for the user's mistake was a poorly designed user interface that confused or misled the user. While the programmer may contend that a more intelligent user would have known better, this argument misses the point. Misleading or confusing an *average* user with a poor user interface is an error by the *programmer*.

There are three hallmarks of an application that has a well-designed user interface:

- The menu items and toolbar buttons through which the user issues commands to your application are easy to locate.
- The menus and controls of the application are easy to navigate, particularly with a keyboard.
- The application provides visual cues, messages, and other information to assist the user, particularly when problems arise.

Consistency

Windows programs have a consistent interface. Even a novice user quickly learns that to print from *any* Windows program, they can click the Print menu item under the File menu, use the shortcut key CTRL-P, or click the toolbar icon of a printer.

Consistency often is disparaged:

"Consistency is the hobgoblin of little minds."—Common misquote of Ralph Waldo Emerson

While this adage may be correct in other contexts, keeping the interface of your application consistent with other Windows applications shortens and flattens the learning curve for the users of your application because they can reuse the knowledge they have gained from using other Windows applications. Making the interface of your application inconsistent with other Windows applications will simply confuse the users of your application. Of course, you can blame the confused users for not reading the manual or Help file, but a user should not have to read a manual (few users do anyway) or Help file to perform common Windows tasks, such as opening a file. They should be able to open a file in your application the same way as they open a file in other Windows applications.

Keeping the interface of your application consistent with other Windows applications makes it easy for the user to locate the menu items, toolbar buttons, and controls that the user needs to access. Consistency will be a recurrent theme in this chapter.

Keyboard Accessibility

Your application's user should be able to access your application with the keyboard as well as with the mouse. The mouse may be the more heavily used input device of the two, and it certainly is becoming more capable, with scrolling and wireless functionality. Nevertheless, the keyboard has its uses. For example, data entry operators, being keyboarding experts, generally prefer the keyboard to a mouse.

Sometimes using a keyboard instead of a mouse is not a preference but a necessity. Try using a mouse when sitting in the middle seat of a commuter airplane between two sumo wrestlers! Additionally, some disabilities make it difficult, if not impossible, for the user to work with a mouse. For these users, the ability to use a keyboard determines whether they can use your application at all.

The bottom line is that, to the extent possible, your application should be accessible through *both* the mouse and the keyboard. In particular, two components of your application that should be keyboard-accessible are menus and those controls, such as command buttons, list boxes, and text boxes, that require clicking, typing, or other user interaction.

Menus

Menus are an integral element of the GUI of a Windows application in that they enable your users to issue commands to your application. Indeed, it is hard to imagine a Windows application without a menu.

Consistency is the first rule. The structure of your top-level menu items should be consistent with other Windows applications. For example, the File menu should be on the left, with Help on the right. Moving the top-level menus from their usual order simply confuses users.

The placement and order of menu sub-items also should be consistent with other Windows applications. The user should be able to open a file by clicking on the Open item under the File menu. Placing the open-file menu command under the Tools menu is confusing to users because the menu command is not where they expect it to be. Similarly, the internal order of menu sub-items should be consistent with other Windows applications. For example, the Print command should be below the Open command because that is the arrangement that users expect.

Assuming your menu is "Windows standard," the next step is to enable your application's users to access the various menu items via the keyboard. The tools you will use to accomplish this are access keys and shortcut keys. You also should be aware of the new Windows and Application keys.

Access Keys

You should give both top-level menu and submenu items access keys so that the menu commands are accessible from the keyboard as well as with a mouse. An access key is a combination of ALT and a key that corresponds to the letter underlined in the menu item. For example, the access key for the Edit menu is ALT-E. Pressing ALT-E will display the submenu items of the Edit menu.

The letter underlined in the menu item is preferably, but not necessarily, the first letter in the text label of the control. The other alternatives, in order of preference, are a distinctive consonant in the label (such as the "x" in Exit) or a vowel in the label (such as the first "e" in Replace). The main point is to use a mnemonic that is easy for the user to associate with the menu command.

Submenu items similarly have access keys. As Figure 9-1 shows, the access key for the Copy submenu item is C. The submenu item is accessed by a combination of the access key for the top-level menu item and the access key for the submenu item. Thus, the access key for the Edit | Copy menu command is ALT-E-C.

Figure 9-2 shows how you create access keys in the menu editor by prefacing the desired access letter with an ampersand (&). Specifically, Figure 9-2 shows the Save menu command under the File menu. The Save menu command is given the access key "S" by typing **&Save** in the Caption text box.

The use of the "Caption" label for the text box in the Menu Editor is not random. A menu item's text label is determined by its **Caption** property. You can use the **Caption** property, which is read/write, to create an access key through code. This is the syntax of writing to the **Caption** property:

```
object.Caption [= string]
```

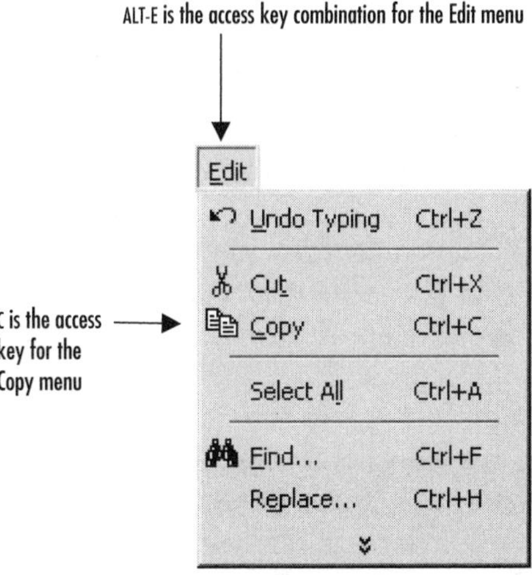

Figure 9.1 Access key for the Copy menu command under the Edit menu

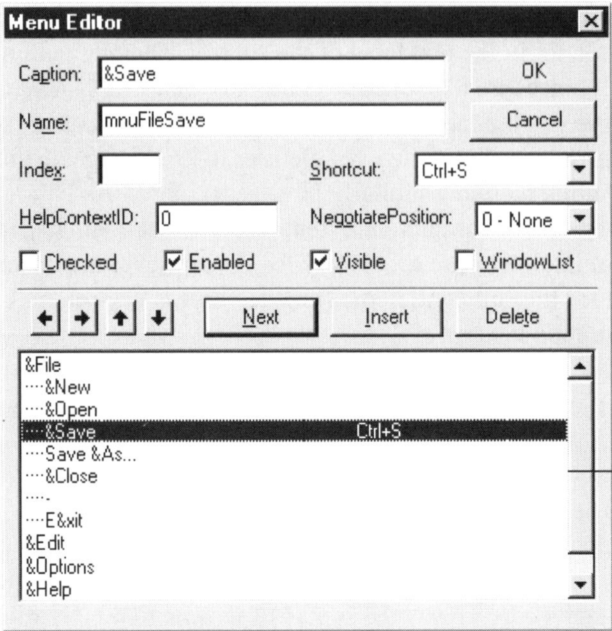

Figure 9.2 Creating access keys in the Menu Editor

You create the access key by embedding an ampersand (&) in the string. For example, you could create the access key of ALT-V-G for a hypothetical GoTo menu sub-item under the View menu with this code:

```
mnuViewGoTo.Caption = &GoTo
```

Error Watch *Do not use duplicate access keys on menus. If you use the same access key for more than one menu item, the key will not work for the second menu item, and may not work for either one.*

Shortcut Keys

In addition to assigning access keys to *all* menu items, you should assign shortcut keys to *frequently used* menu items. A shortcut key (also referred to as an accelerator key or a hot key) is a key or combination of keys that causes a menu command to be invoked without the user having to access the menu. For example, as Figure 9-1 shows, the Copy menu command can be accessed with the shortcut key CTRL-C as well as with the access key ALT-E-C.

24x7

A shortcut key is, as its name implies, a shortcut, which means it is a faster *alternative*. A shortcut key should not be the *only* way to access a particular command.

Choosing a Shortcut Key The shortcut key may be a single key. An example is the shortcut key F7 in Microsoft Word that runs the spell checker. The shortcut key may also be a combination of keys, usually consisting of a CTRL, SHIFT, or ALT key combined with a letter or function key.

The advantage of using function keys is that only one key is involved. However, the function key has no mnemonic relationship with the menu command, making it more difficult for the user to remember.

If you will be using a combination of keys, then the CTRL and SHIFT keys may be preferable to the ALT key because the ALT key is used for access keys and also for system use (ALT-TAB, ALT-ESC, and ALT-SPACEBAR).

In choosing between the CTRL and SHIFT keys, you should use SHIFT-*key* combinations for actions that extend or complement the actions of the key or key combination used without the SHIFT key. For example, ALT-TAB switches windows in a top-to-bottom order, so SHIFT-ALT-TAB switches windows in reverse order. However, SHIFT-*text* keys should be avoided, since in that context the SHIFT key is used for capitalization. By contrast, you should use the CTRL-*key* combination for actions that enlarge the effect of an action. For example, in Microsoft Word and other word processing programs, HOME moves to the beginning of a line, so CTRL-HOME moves to the beginning of the document.

Design Tip *Since you should avoid* ALT-*text and* SHIFT-*text combinations, as stated previously, you will be using* CTRL-*text combinations. However, keep in mind who in this wide world will be using your application.* CTRL-O *may be a meaningful mnemonic for File | Open for English-speaking users; it won't be meaningful to a Spanish-speaking user for whom "open" is "abir."*

Once you have chosen a shortcut key, you define it in the Menu Editor. As Figure 9-2 shows, you define a shortcut key using the Shortcut drop-down list box.

Basic and Extended Shortcut Keys There are two types of shortcut keys: basic and extended. Basic shortcut keys are shortcut keys commonly used in Windows applications. Table 9-1 lists examples of often-used basic shortcut keys.

Shortcut Key	Menu Command
CTRL-C	Copy
CTRL-O	Open
CTRL-P	Print
CTRL-S	Save
CTRL-V	Paste
CTRL-X	Cut
CTRL-Z	Undo
F1	Display contextual Help window
SHIFT-F1	Activate context-sensitive Help mode (What's This?)
SHIFT-F10	Display pop-up menu
SPACEBAR	Select (same as a mouse click)
ESC	Cancel
ALT-TAB	Display next primary window (or application)
ALT-ESC	Display next window
ALT-SPACEBAR	Display System menu for the window
ALT-F4	Close active window
ALT-PRINT SCREEN	Capture active window image to the Clipboard
PRINT SCREEN	Capture desktop image to the Clipboard
CTRL-ESC	Access Start button in taskbar
CTRL-ALT-DEL	Reserved for system use

Table 9.1 Basic Shortcut Keys

You should implement basic shortcut keys in your application as much as possible. Users are accustomed to using shortcut keys, so not implementing a shortcut key could confuse users who don't understand, for example, why the Print dialog box does not appear when they press CTRL-P.

If there is a reason for you not to implement a particular basic shortcut key, then by all means you should not use that shortcut key for some other purpose. Users will be legitimately confused if they press CTRL-P and, instead of seeing a Print dialog box, a Help screen appears.

Extended shortcut keys are shortcut keys that are not predefined in standard Windows applications, as are basic shortcut keys. An example of an extended shortcut key is SHIFT-F7 for the thesaurus in Microsoft Word or ALT-F11 for the Visual Basic Editor, in all Microsoft Office applications. Ideally, the extended shortcut keys should match those used in other Windows applications. If there is no such match, then the extended shortcut key should be a logical key combination, provided, of course, that the combination is not one already "reserved" for a basic shortcut key. For example, CTRL-Q is a more intuitive extended shortcut key than CTRL-T for Quit.

Windows and Application Keys

Some newer keyboards also support two new keys, the Application key and the Windows key. The primary use for the Application key is to display the pop-up menu for the current selection (same as SHIFT-F10). Pressing either of the Windows keys—left or right—displays the Start menu. These keys are also used by the system as modifiers for system-specific functions. Table 9-2 lists and describes the shortcuts that use the Application and Windows keys.

Toolbars

Windows applications usually do, and should, have toolbars. The toolbar items permit quick accessibility to the most frequently used commands. While the functionality of toolbar buttons usually are (and should be) duplicated by menu items, toolbar buttons have two advantages over menu items. First, toolbar buttons always are visible and immediately accessible. By contrast, menu items may be nested several levels deep and may be accessed only by several mouse

Shortcut Key	**Menu Command**
APPLICATION key	Display the pop-up menu for the selected object.
WINDOWS key	Display the Start button menu.
WINDOWS-F1	Display the Help Topics browser dialog box for the main Windows Help file.
WINDOWS-TAB	Activate the next application window.
WINDOWS-E	Explore My Computer.
WINDOWS-F	Find a file.
WINDOWS-CTRL-F	Find a computer.
WINDOWS-M	Minimize All.
SHIFT-WINDOWS-M	Undo Minimize All.
WINDOWS-R	Display the Run dialog box.
WINDOWS-BREAK	Reserved system function.
WINDOWS-NUMBER	Reserved for computer manufacturer use.

Table 9.2 Shortcuts Using the Windows and Application Keys

clicks or keystrokes. Second, toolbars are visual and graphical, far more attractive to the user than the plain text of menu items.

While toolbars have advantages over menu items, one disadvantage is that they usually are not accessible via the keyboard. Therefore, you should have a menu item for every toolbar button. This is a corollary of the rule that features of your application should be accessible via the keyboard as well as the mouse. The fact that toolbar buttons usually are not accessible via the keyboard is not a problem so long as your application has a corresponding keyboard-accessible menu item.

Additionally, as with menu items, the order of the toolbar items should be consistent with other Windows applications. The New File and Open File toolbar items should precede the cut, copy, and paste toolbar items.

Controls

Applications, particularly those involving data access, use controls such as text boxes, list boxes, and combo boxes to enable the user to view or change data. The user needs to interact with these controls, such as by clicking or typing in them. The user needs to be able to access the control in order to interact with it and should be able to access these controls with the keyboard as well as the mouse. Accessing controls via the keyboard usually involves moving the focus from one control to another until the desired control is reached, a process often referred to as *navigation*.

TabIndex Property

The TAB key is the Microsoft Windows standard key for moving the focus forward through the controls on a form. Similarly, the SHIFT-TAB key is the Microsoft Windows standard key for moving the focus backward through the controls on a form. Your application should enable the user to navigate both forward and backward through all appropriate controls with the TAB and SHIFT-TAB keys.

The order in which control focus progresses as the user presses the TAB key is known as the *tab order*. The tab order is determined by the **TabIndex** and **TabStop** properties of the controls on the form.

All controls that can receive the focus (as well as a few that cannot) have a **TabIndex** property. The **TabIndex** property is read/write, and its data type is integer. However, it represents a zero-based index, so its value will not be negative.

Visual Basic assigns a tab order to most controls as you draw them on a form. There are certain controls, such as the **Menu**, **Timer**, **Data**, **Image**, **Line**, and

Shape controls, that are not included in the tab order. The first control you draw has a **TabIndex** value of 0, the next 1, and so on.

TabStop Property

The **TabStop** property is related to but different than the **TabIndex** property. The **TabStop** property also is read/write, and its data type is Boolean. The **TabStop** property returns or sets a value indicating whether a user can use the TAB key to give the focus to an object.

As with the **TabIndex** property, you can change the value of the **TabStop** property order in design mode by changing the **TabStop** value in the Properties window or at run time through code having the following syntax:

```
object.TabStop [= Boolean value]
```

with *object* evaluating to any control that supports a **TabStop** property.

You set the **TabStop** property to False to prevent the user from tabbing to a control with a **TabIndex** property. You don't need to worry about invisible or disabled controls. At run time, tabbing skips invisible or disabled controls, as well as controls that cannot receive focus, such as the **Frame** and **Label** controls. However, if, for example, your application is using a **PictureBox** control to draw a graphic, you should set its **TabStop** property to False so the user can't tab to the **PictureBox**.

Setting a control's **TabStop** property to False does not remove it from the tab order. The control retains its **TabIndex** property. Instead, the control simply is bypassed when the user is tabbing.

Thus, when a user presses the TAB key, the focus is moved from the control that currently has the focus to the control that has the next highest **TabIndex** property value, unless that control is not visible, is disabled, or has its **TabStop** property set to False. In that case, the search continues, one **TabIndex** at a time, until it reaches the next visible, enabled control with its **TabStop** property set to True.

Setting the Tab Order

As just discussed, Visual Basic assigns a tab order to controls as you draw them on a form, the first control you draw having a **TabIndex** value of 0, the next 1, and so on. Since the order in which you draw controls on a form does not necessarily have any relation to the order in which you intend the user to navigate through controls, you very likely will want to change the **TabIndex** properties of the controls.

24x7

Even after you change the **TabIndex** properties of the controls to the desired order, you can make last minute changes. Therefore, you should verify tab order.

The **TabIndex** property is read/write, and you can change the default tab order either in design mode by changing the **TabIndex** value in the Properties window or at run time through code having the following syntax:

```
object.TabIndex [= index]
```

with *object* evaluating to any control that supports a **TabIndex** property and *index* being an integer between 0 and one less than the number of controls that support a **TabIndex** property.

When you change a control's **TabIndex** property, whether in design or run mode, the **TabIndex** properties of the other controls are necessarily affected. However, you don't have to adjust the **TabIndex** properties of the other controls. Instead, Visual Basic automatically renumbers them. But, while Visual Basic does help you out by automatically renumbering the **TabIndex** properties of the other controls, the renumbering likely will not fit your intentions. Indeed, you have to renumber the **TabIndex** properties one at a time. If this sounds like a lot of grunt work, you're right.

One approach is to select the control you want to be the first control in the tab order and assign it a **TabIndex** of 0, then select the next control in the intended tab order and assign it a **TabIndex** of 1, and so on, until you have assigned values to all the controls or have been driven insane in the process.

Another, preferable, approach is to work from the last control in the tab order backward instead of from the first control in the tab order forward, and assign each control a **TabIndex** of 0. What makes this work is that when you assign a control a **TabIndex** value, any control with the same value, as well as every control with a higher value, is automatically incremented to preserve its place in the tab order. Thus, when you assign the second-to-last control a **TabIndex** of 0, the last control's **TabIndex** is automatically incremented from 0 to 1. When the third-to-last control has its **TabIndex** property set to 0, the **TabIndex** of the second-to-last control is incremented from 0 to 1 and the **TabIndex** of the last control is incremented from 1 to 2. You still have to visit each control, but at least you can automatically enter 0 instead of having to remember the next value in order.

Command Buttons

The preceding section discussed controls used for data access. However, you also can use controls, particularly command buttons, as you use menu items, to enable the user to issue commands to your application. These command buttons also should be keyboard accessible.

Access Keys

You can, and should, assign access keys to command buttons, just as you do to menu items. The access keys enable the user to access the command button through the keyboard as well as via the mouse.

You assign access keys to command buttons by prefixing a character in the command button's **Caption** property with an ampersand (&). When Visual Basic displays a command button's caption, it looks for an ampersand. If one is found, the ampersand is not displayed. Instead, the character immediately following the ampersand is shown with an underscore, and that character becomes the access key for the command button. Pressing ALT in conjunction with a command button's access key triggers the command button's **Click** event just as though the user had clicked the button with a mouse.

24x7

This section later discusses setting some command buttons' **Default** or **Cancel** properties to True. You should not assign an access key for those command buttons. The reason is that when a command button has its **Default** or **Cancel** property set to True, it can be "clicked" by pressing ENTER or ESC, so an access key would be superfluous.

Error Watch *Don't assign access keys that conflict with the access keys of menu items. For instance, if a form has a File menu, the "F" in "File" should be designated as the access key for the menu in order to be consistent with other programs. Don't assign the letter "F" as a button access key on a form that already has "F" as the access key of a menu. The access key* ALT-F *will access the File menu, never the command button.*

Default and Cancel Properties

You should create a default command button and a Cancel command button in dialog boxes. Dialog boxes usually contain at least two command buttons: OK and Cancel. Clicking the OK button commits the user's settings and closes the dialog box; clicking the Cancel button closes the dialog box and discards the user's settings.

In most Windows applications, pressing the ENTER key has the same effect as clicking the OK button. Similarly, pressing the ESC key has the same effect as clicking the Cancel button. Since users are used to this behavior, you should duplicate it in your application.

You can assign the ENTER key to a command button by setting the button's **Default** property to True. Doing so has the effect of triggering the button's **Click** event when the user presses ENTER while any control on the form has focus. Only one command button per form can have its **Default** property set to True. Therefore, if you set one command button's **Default** property to True and then set the **Default** property of a second command button to True, the first button's **Default** property will be automatically set to False.

You can assign the ESC key to a command button by setting the command button's **Cancel** property to True. Doing so has the effect of triggering the button's **Click** event when the user presses ESC while any control on the form has focus. As is the case with the **Default** property, only one command button per form can have its **Cancel** property set to True. Thus, if you set one command button's **Cancel** property to True and then set the **Cancel** property of a second command button to True, the first button's **Cancel** property will be automatically set to False.

You should set the **Cancel** property of every dialog box's Cancel button to True. However, depending on the nature of the dialog box, you may not want to assign a default command button by setting a command button's **Default** property to True. For example, if the dialog box includes a multiline text box, the user would expect that pressing ENTER would result in a new line of text. However, if a command button's **Default** property is set to True, Visual Basic would interpret the user's pressing ENTER as a clicking of the default button.

Mouse

While your application should be accessible through the keyboard, the mouse usually is the primary device for interacting with the computer. However, the mouse, in addition to being a tool for taking action, also can be used to provide context-specific menus, known as pop-up menus, and to provide visual cues via the mouse pointer.

Pop-Up Menus

Figure 9-3 shows a pop-up menu. A pop-up menu pops up (hence its name) when the user right-clicks an object that supports pop-up menus. Pop-up menus started with Microsoft Windows 95, and they are becoming more, not less, prevalent. Users expect pop-up menus, so your application should have them. Windows displays standard pop-up menus for certain controls, but you will need to add a pop-up menu for most controls.

Pop-up menus are also referred to as *context menus*. The term context menu may be more accurate, since the items that appear on the menu depend on the context. For example, as Figure 9-3 shows, clicking on text brings up a context menu with options such as Cut, Copy, and Paste, all of which are common operations in word-processing. By contrast, if you click on a folder in Windows Explorer, the pop-up menu items will include Open and Explore, common operations in file management.

While the items on these two pop-up menus are different because of the differing context, the number of items on both is relatively small. A pop-up menu with 73 items would not be particularly useful. Therefore, the items that appear should be the ones most commonly used.

You use the **PopupMenu** method of a **Form** object to display a pop-up menu. The **PopupMenu** method has the following syntax:

```
object.PopupMenu menuname, flags, x, y, boldcommand
```

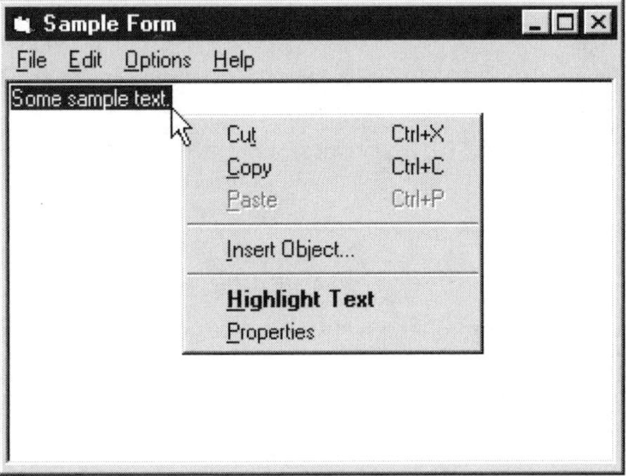

Figure 9.3 A pop-up menu

The object usually is a **Form**, though it may also be a **MDIForm**, **PropertyPage**, **UserControl**, or **UserDocument**. Table 9-3 describes the parameters of the **PopupMenu** method.

You may not need to use any of the optional parameters. Often the defaults are sufficient. However, the optional parameters are helpful if you want to fine-tune the location or behavior of the pop-up menu.

The optional *flags* parameter combines the values of two constants. Table 9-4 lists the constants pertaining to the location of the menu, and Table 9-5 lists the constants pertaining to the behavior of the menu.

Error Watch *Pop-up menus must be displayed programmatically, by calling the **PopupMenu** method. A common mistake is to call the **PopupMenu** method from the **MouseDown** event. However, as you can confirm by displaying a pop-up menu, the menu displays when the mouse button is released. Therefore, the **PopupMenu** method should be called from the **MouseUp** event, not the **MouseDown** event.*

Mouse Pointer

Few users, or developers for that matter, enjoy watching the hourglass mouse pointer when an application appears to hang. On the bright side, however, the

Parameter	Required?	Description
object	No	The form that displays the pop-up menu. If *object* is omitted, the form with the focus is used.
menuname	Yes	The name of the pop-up menu to display. The specified menu must have at least one submenu or else the pop-up menu would have no items to display.
flags	No	One of the constants listed in Tables 9-4 and 9-5 below that specifies the location and behavior of the pop-up menu being displayed.
x	No	Specifies the x-coordinate where the pop-up menu is displayed. If omitted, the x-coordinate of the mouse is used.
y	No	Specifies the y-coordinate where the pop-up menu is displayed. If omitted, the y-coordinate of the mouse is used.
boldcommand	No	Specifies the name of a menu item in the pop-up menu that will be displayed in bold text. If omitted, no items in the pop-up menu will be bold.

Table 9.3 Parameters of the **PopupMenu** Method

Constant	Value	Description
vbPopupMenuLeftAlign	0	The left side of the pop-up menu is located at *x*. (Default)
vbPopupMenuCenterAlign	4	The pop-up menu is centered at *x*.
vbPopupMenuRightAlign	8	The right side of the pop-up menu is located at *x*.

Table 9.4 Location Constants for the *flags* Parameter

hourglass is providing a visual cue to the status of the application, much as a progress bar provides a visual cue to the progress of an operation. While no one likes to see an application hang, at least the hourglass cues the user to the fact that that the application may be hanging. This is a better alternative than no cue at all.

The mouse pointer also can give visual cues under less adverse circumstances than a hanging application. For example, when you are moving selected text in Microsoft Word by dragging your mouse, a square appears below the mouse pointer (to signify the text being dragged) and a vertical line appears above the mouse pointer (to signify where the text is being dragged to).

You change the icon of the mouse pointer by changing the **MousePointer** property of an object. The syntax for using the **MousePointer** property is this:

```
object.MousePointer = value
```

The *object* is often the **Screen** object, but many types of controls also support the **MousePointer** property. The *value* is one of the constants listed in Table 9-6.

Note *North, south, east, and west are really up, down, right, and left on the computer screen, rather than being the actual directions.*

The two most commonly used icons are **vbDefault** and **vbHourglass**. You can notify your user that your program is busy processing and cannot accept input

Constant	Value	Description
vbPopupMenuLeftButton	0	An item on the pop-up menu reacts to a mouse click only when clicked with the left mouse button. (Default)
vbPopupMenuRightButton	2	An item on the pop-up menu reacts to a mouse click when clicked with either the right or the left mouse button.

Table 9.5 Behavior Constants for the *flags* Parameter

Constant	Value	Description
vbDefault	0	Shape determined by the object (default)
vbArrow	1	Arrow
vbCrosshair	2	Cross (crosshair pointer)
vbIbeam	3	I-beam (often used for positioning within text)
vbIconPointer	4	Icon (small square within a square)
vbSizePointer	5	Size (four-pointed arrow pointing north, south, east, and west)
vbSizeNESW	6	Size NE SW (double arrow pointing northeast and southwest)
vbSizeNS	7	Size N S (double arrow pointing north and south)
vbSizeNWSE	8	Size NW SE (double arrow pointing northwest and southeast)
vbSizeWE	9	Size W E (double arrow pointing west and east)
vbUpArrow	10	Up arrow
vbHourglass	11	Hourglass (wait)
vbNoDrop	12	No drop
vbArrowHourglass	13	Arrow and hourglass
vbArrowQuestion	14	Arrow and question mark
vbSizeAll	15	Size all
vbCustom	99	Custom icon specified by the **MouseIcon** property

Table 9.6 Constants for the **MousePointer** Property

by displaying the hourglass—just set the **Screen** object's **MousePointer** property to **vbHourglass**:

```
Screen.MousePointer = vbHourglass
```

Providing the visual cue of the hourglass prevents the user from thinking that a delay means that the program is not working and thus giving the program the three-fingered salute (CTRL-ALT-DELETE). Of course, when your application is finished processing and is ready for input, you need to set the **Screen** object's **MousePointer** property back to **vbDefault**.

Error Watch *While visual cues are good, false visual cues are bad. A common mistake is to forget to set the mouse pointer back to the default. For instance, leaving the pointer as an hourglass when the application is ready for new input fools the user into thinking that they can't interact with the program even though they can. The result would be a stalemate. The user would just sit and wait while the program sits and waits for the user's input.*

```
Private Sub  cmdFillListBox_Click()
'Fills a list box with numerous items
'Set the pointer to hourglass to cue user application busy
Screen.MousePointer = vbHourglass
'Populate the list box
Dim counter As Integer
For counter = 0 To 1000
   lstSample.AddItem counter
Next counter
'Restore mouse pointer to default
Screen.MousePointer = vbDefault
End Sub
```

The changes you make to the **Screen** object's **MousePointer** property affect the pointer only when it is over a window of your application. This is different than in earlier versions of Visual Basic, in which setting the **Screen** object's **MousePointer** property to **vbHourglass** changed the pointer to an hourglass regardless of the location of the pointer on the screen. The reason for the change relates to multi-tasking. Just because your program is busy should not prevent the user from switching to a different program.

Error Watch *While the **Screen** is the usual object from which you access the **MousePointer** property, as discussed above, other objects, including the **ListBox** control, also support this property. When displaying pop-up menus that perform actions on selected list items, always select the item that is clicked before displaying the pop-up menu. The issue with the **ListBox** control is that although the right mouse button is used to display pop-up menus, the **ListBox** control does not recognize the right click as a way to select an item. When you display a pop-up menu with commands that operate on the selected item in a **ListBox** control, you must write code to ensure that the item under the mouse when the right click occurred is the item that is selected when the menu appears.*

Notifications

Notifications are the mechanism by which your application communicates with the user. Notifications can be active or passive. Message boxes are an example of active notification. A message box appears, displays a message, and requires the user to dismiss it by clicking a command button before the user can proceed with the application.

By contrast, an example of passive notification is disabling a menu item or other control, such as disabling the Cut and Copy commands if nothing is selected. The user doesn't need to do anything and may not even notice anything. Instead, the menu item or control simply is grayed out.

Message Boxes

Message boxes are often used to notify the user. The notification may be purely informational, may be asking for an answer to a question, or may be a warning of a potential or actual problem.

You use the **MsgBox** function to create a message box. Using the **MsgBox** function to create a message box is a relatively easy task compared to other programming chores. Perhaps because creating message boxes is comparatively simple, this task is taken for granted, but it shouldn't be. Message boxes are very important to the user because they are one of the few ways your application communicates with the user, particularly when something has gone wrong. Additionally, creating an effective message box requires you to resolve several not-so-simple issues, some of which involve programming skills and others which involve writing skills. These issues include:

- Communicating effectively
- Providing the user with an effective response
- Enabling keyboard navigation

The syntax of the **MsgBox** function is as follows:

```
MsgBox(prompt[, buttons] [, title] [, helpfile, context])
```

Table 9-7 explains these parameters.

The required *prompt* argument may not require programming skills, but it does require good language skills. The message should meet the following common-sense criteria:

- **Informative** The very purpose of the message box is to convey information to the user. Messages such as "Data connection error, Error code 76432, Program Terminating" leaves the user with little information. A message such as "Program could not find specified data source; check database name and path specified in Tools | Options | Data" at least gives the user a fighting chance to correct the problem.
- **Simple** Avoid large words when small ones will do. Not all your users will be skilled in the English language. Also, avoid technical jargon. Using jargon

Parameter	Required?	Description
prompt	Yes	String expression displayed as the message in the dialog box. The maximum length of *prompt* is approximately 1,024 characters, depending on the width of the characters used. If *prompt* consists of more than one line, you can separate the lines using the carriage return (Chr(13)) and linefeed (Chr(10)) character combination.
buttons	No	Numeric expression that is the sum of values specifying the number and type of buttons to display, the icon style to use, the identity of the default button, and the modality of the message box. If omitted, the default value for *buttons* is 0.
title	No	String expression displayed in the title bar of the dialog box. If you omit *title*, the application name is placed in the title bar.
helpfile	No	String expression that identifies the Help file to be used to provide context-sensitive Help for the dialog box. If *helpfile* is provided, *context* must also be provided.
context	No	Numeric expression that is the Help context number assigned to the appropriate Help topic by the Help author. If *context* is provided, *helpfile* must also be provided.

Table 9.7 Parameters of the **MsgBox** Function

is an easy mistake to make if you are used to talking to your coworkers all day in computer-speak. However, to an average user, OLE is what you shout at bullfights. Of course, if the user will be in a technical profession, then technical words used in that profession would be appropriate.

- **Polite** The tone should be formal, consistent with the professional nature of your application. However, the tone also should be polite and helpful. The user feels bad enough when a mistake occurs; don't make the user feel even worse.
- **Short** The Gettysburg Address is famous, but the message box is not the place for it. Although you are permitted approximately 1,024 characters, you should try to restrict the length of the messages to no more than two short sentences.

The *buttons* argument is a combination of constants that represent the following:

- The icon to be displayed
- The button or buttons to be displayed
- Which button (if any) is the default

Five different groups of constants may be combined. Table 9-8 describes these constants.

Description	Range of Values
Icon style	16, 32, 48, 64
The number and type of buttons displayed in the dialog box	0–5
Which button is the default	0, 256, 512
Modality of the message box	0, 4096
Miscellaneous	See Table 9-13

Table 9.8 Groups of Constants for *buttons* Parameter of **MsgBox** Function

The icon is a visual cue to the type of message. There are four types of messages, each with a different icon style:

- **Information** The information icon indicates that the message is informational; there is no problem.

- **Question** The question icon indicates that the message asks the user a question.

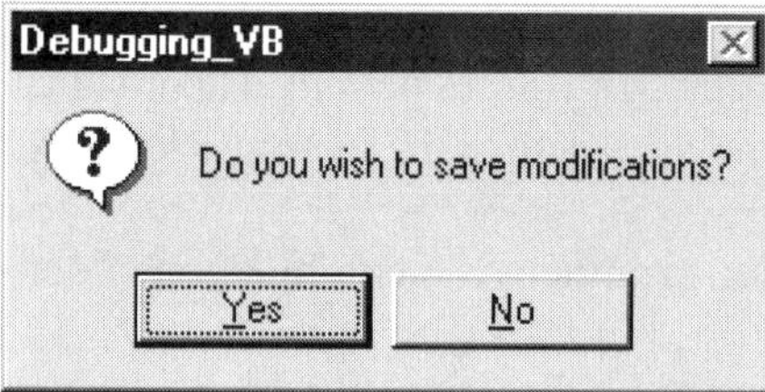

- **Warning** The warning icon indicates that the message warns of a possible, but not critical, problem.

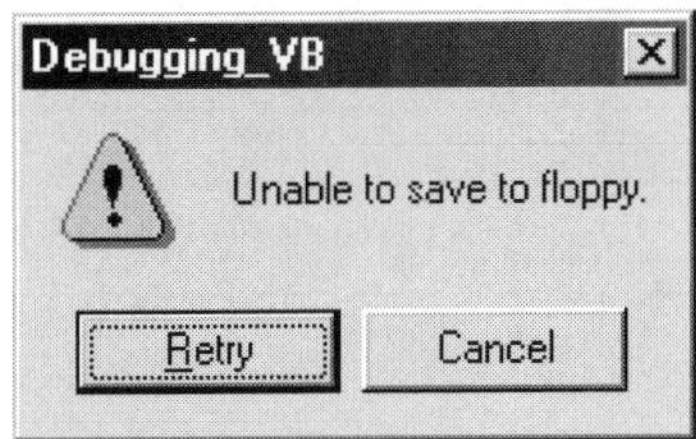

- **Critical** The critical icon (red with an X) indicates that the message warns of a serious problem that needs to be resolved.

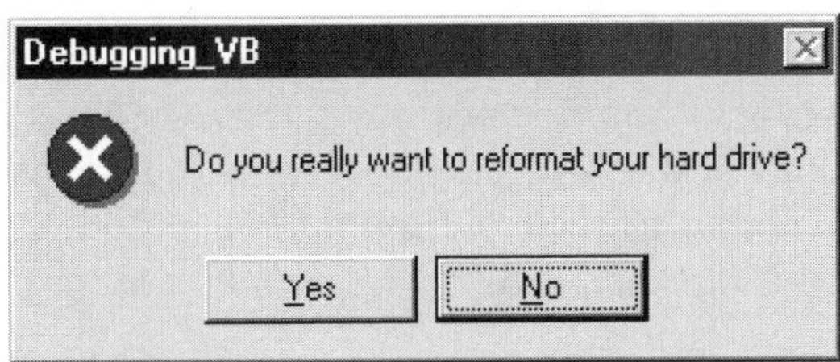

Each of these four icons is represented by one of the constants listed in Table 9-9.

The message box also displays buttons. Table 9-10 lists these buttons and their corresponding constants.

Design Tip *You need to coordinate the icon and the button(s). Your user will be truly confused if you ask a yes/no question, displaying a question-mark icon, but instead of Yes and No buttons, the only button is OK.*

You also can designate a specific button as the default button (the button that is "clicked" when the user presses ENTER) by using one of the constants listed and described in Table 9-11.

Constant	Value	Icon
vbInformation	64	Information
vbQuestion	32	Question
vbExclamation	48	Exclamation, also often referred to as warning.
vbCritical	16	Critical

Table 9.9 Constants for Icons in the *buttons* Parameter of the **MsgBox** Function

Constant	Value	Button(s)
vbOKOnly	0	OK
vbOKCancel	1	OK and Cancel
vbAbortRetryIgnore	2	Abort, Retry, and Ignore
vbYesNoCancel	3	Yes, No, and Cancel
vbYesNo	4	Yes and No
vbRetryCancel	5	Retry and Cancel

Table 9.10 Constants for Buttons in the *buttons* Parameter of the **MsgBox** Function

Design Tip *Make the default button of every message box a deliberate choice. For example, if you're displaying a message box with a Yes button and a No button, and you're asking the user if he or she wants to format the hard drive, set No as the default button, as shown earlier in the illustration for the critical icon.*

Table 9-12 lists and describes the modality constants. The default is application modal, which means that the user must respond to the message box before continuing work in the current application. System modal means that all applications are suspended until the user responds to the message box. Rarely will system modal be appropriate, as the hanging of your application could hang the operating system.

Table 9-13 lists and describes the remaining, miscellaneous constants.

You usually will be specifying more than one constant for the *buttons* parameter, and you use the **Or** operator to do so. For instance, the following code displays an OK button along with an information icon:

```
MsgBox "Processing completed.", vbOKOnly Or vbInformation
```

Constant	Value	Description
vbDefaultButton1	0	The first button is the default.
vbDefaultButton2	256	The second button is the default.
vbDefaultButton3	512	The third button is the default.
vbDefaultButton4	768	The fourth button is the default.

Table 9.11 Constants for the Default Button in the *buttons* Parameter of the **MsgBox** Function

Constant	Value	Description
vbApplicationModal	0	Application modal
vbSystemModal	4096	System modal

Table 9.12 Modality Constants for Buttons in the *buttons* Parameter of the **MsgBox** Function

The order of the buttons on a message box is always the same as the order listed in the *buttons* parameter. For example, the following code sets the No button as the default in a Yes/No message box, as shown earlier in the illustration of the critical icon:

```
If MsgBox("Do you really want to format your hard drive?", _
   vbYesNo Or vbCritical Or vbDefaultButton2) Then ...
```

The *title* parameter is used to specify the text that will appear in the title bar of a message box. Often, however, you will omit the *title* parameter. If you do, Visual Basic uses the application title specified in the Project Name field on the General tab of the Project Properties dialog box, shown in Figure 9-4. The advantage of using the default title is that your message boxes will have a consistent title, which gives your program a more consistent appearance.

Design Tip *The **Help** and **HelpContext** arguments are used, as in other Visual Basic functions, to identify the Help file to use for providing context-sensitive help. If the subject of the message box is too complex for a one or two sentence message, then you should associate a Help file with the message box.*

Finally, the **MsgBox** function, in addition to its parameters, has a return value. This return value is a constant that represents the button the user clicked. These constants are listed and described in Table 9-14.

Constant	Value	Description
vbMsgBoxHelpButton	16384	Adds Help button to the message box
VbMsgBoxSetForeground	65536	Specifies the message box window as the foreground window
vbMsgBoxRight	524288	Specifies that text is right aligned
vbMsgBoxRtlReading	1048576	Specifies that text should appear as right-to-left reading on Hebrew and Arabic systems

Table 9.13 Miscellaneous Constants for Buttons in the *buttons* Parameter of the **MsgBox** Function

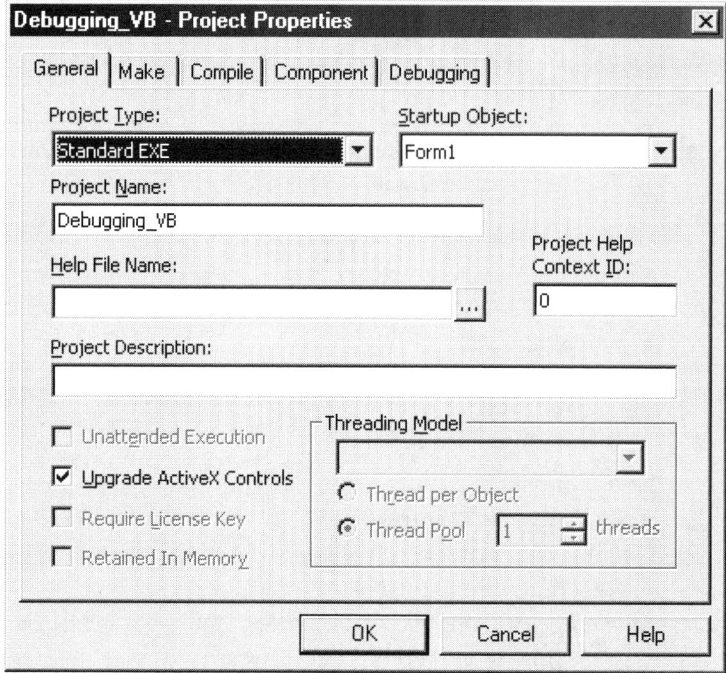

Figure 9.4 Using the Project Name for the title parameter

Constant	Button Caption	Value
vbOk	OK	1
vbCancel	Cancel	2
vbAbort	Abort	3
vbRetry	Retry	4
vbIgnore	Ignore	5
vbYes	Yes	6
vbNo	No	7

Table 9.14 Constants Representing the Return Value of the **MsgBox** Function

Error Watch *The constants used for displaying the buttons are quite similar to the constants used for the return values. For example, the constant for displaying just an OK button is* ***vbOKOnly****, which has a value of 0. If you mistakenly specify the button as* ***vbOK*** *(the constant for the return value of the OK button being clicked), then your message box will have both an OK button and a Cancel button, since the value of* ***vbOKCancel*** *and* ***vbOK*** *is 1.*

Enabling

Menu items and other controls have an **Enabled** property, whose data type is Boolean. This property determines whether the control can respond to user-generated events, such as a mouse click. If the value of the **Enabled** property is True, then a mouse click (or other event) will run the code in the event procedure of the control. However, if the value of the **Enabled** property is False, then the mouse click will have no effect at all.

There are many occasions when a control should not respond to an event (such as a click) that runs its underlying code. For example, in a word processing program, the Cut and Copy items on the Edit menu should not be enabled unless text has been selected.

Windows applications customarily provide users with a visual cue that a control is not enabled. That visual cue is that the control is grayed out. Figure 9-3, earlier in the chapter, shows that the Paste item on the Edit menu is grayed out because no text has yet been copied to the Clipboard.

The alternative to setting the **Enabled** property of a control to False (when appropriate) is to provide notification via a message box. For example, assume the purpose of a command button named "cmdDelete" and labeled "Delete" is to delete the selected item in a **ListBox** control named "lstPersons." The code would have to check first if any item was selected before removing the selected item. If no item was selected, then the user would be notified via a message box that an item must first be selected:

```
Private Sub cmdDelete_Click()
'check to see if item selected
If lstPersons.ListIndex = -1 Then
   MsgBox "Need to select item"
Else
```

```
    'Following statement would raise error if ListIndex was -1
    lstPersons.RemoveItem lstPersons.ListIndex
End If
End Sub
```

Of course, if instead you wrote code disabling the Delete command button until an item was selected, then you would not need to check if an item was selected.

Design Tip *Disabling a control usually is preferable to presenting the user with a message box telling the user that they should not have clicked the control. The user may question, quite legitimately, why your application permitted them to take an action that they should not have taken. Disabling controls is common in Windows applications, so the user should know that a grayed-out control means that a precondition to the use of the control has not occurred. One possible exception is if the reason why the control is grayed out is not intuitive. Under those circumstances a message-box warning may be preferable because the message box, and possibly a Help file associated with the message box, can provide a fuller explanation.*

Data Entry

The **Text** setting for a **TextBox** control is limited to 2,048 characters unless the **MultiLine** property is True, in which case the limit is about 32K. However, often you will need to restrict the length of the text entered by the user to far fewer characters. For example, if the text entry is to be saved to a database, the length of the text should not exceed the number of characters that can be stored in that field.

One solution is to have the user complete the data entry and then advise the user that the input is too long. Bonus points are awarded if the user's input is erased and if the user is not told the number of characters allowed. Only sadistic, user-hating programmers would prefer this solution.

A more humane solution is to use the **MaxLength** property to limit the number of characters that can be entered in the **TextBox** control. The default value for the **MaxLength** property is 0, which means the only limit on the number of characters the text box can contain is 2,048 characters or 32K if the **MultiLine** property is True. Setting the **MaxLength** property to a value greater than 0 causes the text box to limit the number of characters it accepts to the value of the **MaxLength** property. If the user then attempts to enter more characters than the amount allowed by **MaxLength**, Visual Basic prevents the characters from being entered in the text box and alerts the user with a beep.

Error Watch

*Binding a **TextBox** to a data control does not automatically set the **MaxLength** property to the length of the field to which the control is bound. You have to set the **MaxLength** property manually, either at design time or at run time, through code that determines the maximum number of characters allowed by a field in the **Recordset** and that sets the **MaxLength** property accordingly.*

Summary

The user interface, while often ignored by programmers, is quite important. Users evaluate your application primarily on its user interface. Furthermore, a user may, because of an interface that is difficult to understand or use, make errors that they will blame on the application.

A user interface should be consistent with the Windows standard. This enables the user to easily locate the menu items and toolbar buttons through which the user issues commands to your application.

The menus and controls of your application should be easy to navigate, particularly with a keyboard. Your primary tools for accomplishing this are access and shortcut keys.

Finally, your application should provide visual cues, messages, and other information to assist the user, particularly when problems arise. Your tools for accomplishing this include pop-up menus, the mouse pointer, message boxes, and disabling controls when they should not be accessed.

CHAPTER 10

Optimization and Tuning

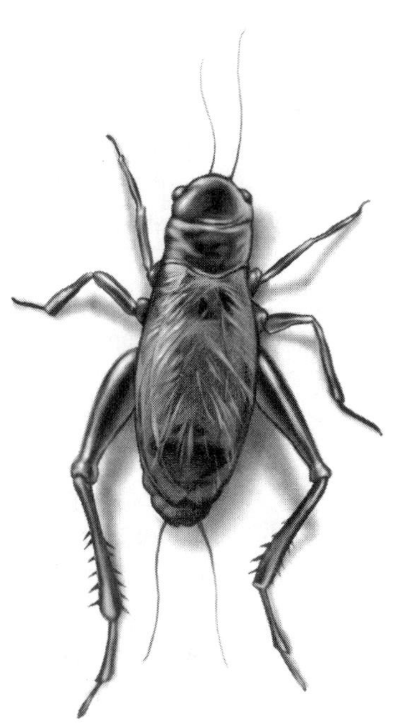

If we took a time machine back to the late 1980s, we'd discover it was a commandment of all programmers to make sure that their programs would run within a 640K memory footprint. At the time, Bill Gates even said that 640K should be all the memory that anyone would ever need. When Lotus Corporation released version 3.0 of their flagship product, Lotus 1-2-3, they claimed that the PC systems needed a minimum of 1MB of memory to run the program. This was considered an outrageous request, and customers started to look for alternative products to handle all their number crunching.

Nowadays, it's rare to find a system that has less than 64MB of memory onboard. A lot of this has to do with the type of operating systems people are running now. Linux/Unix, OS/2, Mac OS, and all flavors of Windows are operating systems that require a lot of memory to run, so any applications that run within the operating system require additional memory.

Many times during the development cycle, project managers and technical leaders are so caught up in the bottom line—the delivery date—that they forget about optimizing the code or even fine-tuning it. In days long past, the delivery schedule was important, but what was more important was producing tight, well-written code. This is an art that has been lost, except for a few dedicated programmers who still believe that you can write good, clean code and still meet your delivery dates.

The reason why this is such a lost art is due to the fact that developers quite often have the latest and greatest computer configurations. These systems have as much physical memory and storage as money can buy, so developers with unlimited resources don't tend to think about how many lines of code it takes to get the program to run. They are told that they have a deadline and to do whatever it takes to meet it. In the past, developers would have to get approval from their managers if they felt that they had to write a function or feature that would push up the system requirements of the program. Nowadays, managers don't care if the system requirements increase.

Another reason why coding optimization and tuning is something of a lost art is because schools are educating new developers in languages that are moving further and further away from native-code development. During a keynote presentation, Alan Cooper—who is known throughout the Visual Basic community as the "Father of Visual Basic"—talked about the development community being inundated with a bunch of lightweight programmers. "Bring in the Lightweights" was the title of his talk, and the gist was that as developers move further and further away from machine language, the more lightweight they become as programmers. The further your code moves from machine language, the slower your code executes.

Optimization

Optimization is the process of examining an application's performance once it has been moved into production. You should wait until after the program is in production before you consider optimization. Otherwise your projects may never get done. In many cases, the slowness of an application might not be due to the code at all. It could be that your target audience is using a slower PC or that their PC doesn't meet the recommended minimum system configuration. In other words, the problem may be a hardware issue rather than a software issue.

Question: How many software engineers does it take to screw in a light bulb?
Answer: None. It's a hardware problem.

It's almost impossible to optimize an application to satisfy everyone's speed requirements. When it comes to optimizing your application, you and your team need to look at three basic issues:

- Where to optimize
- What to optimize
- How much to optimize

Where to Optimize

The issue of where to optimize involves finding out what procedures and functions seem to be having a performance problem. Once you find the procedures and functions that appear to be slow, analyze the algorithms they use to determine if there is a way to improve efficiency. If a procedure or function needs to manage a large amount of data, you might need to design efficient data structures for it to use. You might find out that your algorithms are designed properly and that the perceived system degradation is due to system or network resources.

When determining where to optimize, you also need to consider what end result you wish to achieve after optimization. Is the end result to reduce the overall size of the program, to increase the execution speed, or something else? It could be that a program is oversized due to redundant code. Historically, it has been taught that your code will execute faster if you reduce the number of procedure calls for short, commonly used code. For example, a routine to center a form on the screen is the most commonly found routine.

```
Me.Move ((Screen.Width - Me.Width) / 2), ((Screen.Height - Me.Height) / 2)
```

If this code is in every form, the program will execute faster, but you are increasing the size of the application and adding a maintenance nightmare for yourself. If you find that the algorithm used for the centering routine is incorrect, you will need to find every instance of the code and change it. In a small- or medium-size application, this might not be a problem. In a large application, a change like this can waste a lot of precious development time. To reduce the size of your code, you're better off putting this redundant routine within a procedure.

What to Optimize

The issue of what to optimize involves focusing your efforts on predefined performance expectations. For example, suppose you have a program that searches a system's hard drive(s) for files, based on user input. If you used the Windows Explorer's Find function, it would scan three hard drives and return a result set in about two minutes. A predefined performance expectation should be that your program will return its result set back, using the same criteria, within a similar timeframe. If your program takes five minutes to complete that task, you've just determined where you need to look for optimization.

How Much to Optimize

The question of how much you should optimize involves knowing when to stop optimizing your code. Often during the optimization phase of a program's life cycle, you will find that enough is enough. When you run your benchmark tests, you will probably find yourself at a point where you can't optimize your design any more because you're not adding any real value. If you find that by changing an algorithm you're only gaining a fraction of a second on response time, it's probably not worth implementing the change. Remember that most of the time an application is running, it's sitting idle waiting for user input.

Often the best form of optimization is providing user feedback while a process is working. As a developer, you have control over how the user's mouse button looks by using the **Screen.MousePointer** property from within your program. You might be surprised how your users perceive changes to the mouse pointer. For example, to test how people perceive the mouse pointer's change from a pointer to an hourglass, write a small application that changes the pointer to an hourglass when a process begins, and don't change it back to a pointer until a minute after the process finishes. Even though the screen changed to display the end result within a fraction of a second, they will think that your program is still processing because they see the hourglass. Then change the application to handle the mouse pointer properly and give the program back to the user to test. They will believe that you actually increased the performance of the application.

> **24x7**
>
> Provide user feedback to the user during long processes. If the process takes longer than a few seconds, you might want to consider a progress bar.

Performance Tuning

Now that you know how to approach optimization, there are some tips and techniques you can use as general development rules in order to avoid some areas of code deficiency. The rest of the chapter points out some programming and tuning tips. These aren't the be-all, end-all techniques that will give your application cat-like reflexes. These are just some general suggestions for you to consider.

Programming Tips

One aspect of performance tuning is how you program your routines. You can reduce the number of bugs and other application problems by keeping in mind some of the following:

- Determine when to handle data validation on your form
- Ensure uppercase versus lowercase input
- Validate numeric versus alphabetic character entry
- Making data fields read-only to prevent users from trying to change read-only information
- Ensuring that a data field only allows the maximum number of characters in a field to prevent database errors

Data Validation

Often during development, you need to consider where it is appropriate to place your code. Should the routine go in the **Unload** event or the **QueryUnload** event? Does this validation routine go in the **LostFocus** event or with the Commit button? Depending on the type of solution you are developing, placement of your data validation routines is key.

Let's look at two different examples. The first would be an application for a high transaction–based commerce company like the Home Shopping Network. You will want to provide immediate feedback to your users when they enter a value into a data entry cell on the form incorrectly. This means that you program in data validation routines on important data entry cells so that when the user tabs from field to field, the validation routine is executed. Having data validation occur interactively while the data is entered will slow down your users, but it offers data validity at the time it's entered.

The next example is a scenario where "heads down" data entry is preferred, like in a clinical study department of a pharmaceutical company. In this situation, the data entry associates are supposed to enter the data into the system as it appears on the paper forms. Since field validation isn't needed, you would put the data validation as part of the commit process.

Talking to your users about how they think the program should operate can give you some insight as to where the more appropriate place is for the code. By talking with them, you will also find out how strict the validation needs to be. For example, you have a business rule that a certain value can't be greater than 25: you could enforce a rule where the user can't enter a value greater than that, or you could allow the user to enter values greater than 25 and then use a data discrepancy report to show that data does not match the business rule. This is something only the users of the systems can answer. As the developer, don't assume anything. It will only get you into trouble.

Uppercase and Lowercase Input

There are times when your program specifications require that the user input be either in all uppercase or all lowercase characters. If this is a requirement in your design specifications, you will find that there are two different ways you can implement this. Either by using the **KeyPress** event within the **TextBox** control or by using the control's **LostFocus** event. The **KeyPress** event is triggered every time a keystroke occurs, and it passes the ASCII character value of the key that was pressed. In order to convert the value to uppercase, you need to first convert ASCII value to its character equivalent by using the **Chr$** function. Once you get the letter, the **UCase$** function converts the letter to uppercase. Finally, you need to convert the character back to the ASCII code using the **ASC$** function so that you can pass it back to the **KeyAscii** argument.

```
Private Sub txtTextBox_KeyPress(KeyAscii As Integer)
    KeyAscii = Asc$(UCase$(Chr$(KeyAscii)))
End Sub
```

At first glance, you might think there's nothing wrong with the code, and you would be absolutely correct. The problem is that the **KeyPress** event is triggered each time a key is pressed. This might slow down the input process a bit. The question you need to ask yourself and your users is whether it is important that the characters convert into uppercase (or lowercase) immediately as they type into a field. If the answer is yes, then you'll have to use the code just described. If they can wait until after they finish typing and move to the next field, then you can use the **LostFocus** event to handle the task.

The **LostFocus** event triggers when the user tabs out of the text box. By using the **LostFocus** event, you only need to use the **UCase$** function to convert the entire text box value to uppercase. The user has to wait until they tab out of the text box or click on another field to see their text converted, but the result is the same, and this method is a bit more efficient.

```
Private Sub txtTextBox_LostFocus()
    txtTextbox = UCase$(txtTextbox)
End Sub
```

When converting your text input to lowercase, change the **UCase$** function to the **LCase$** function in the preceding code snippets.

Input Numbers Only

When you need to test whether a character entered in a field is a number, there are two ways to do it. You can use a **Select ... Case** method or you can use the **IsNumeric** function.

Using the **Select ... Case** statement, you should first check to see if the DELETE or BACKSPACE keys have been pressed. This will allow the user to correct what they type into the text box. In order to determine if alphabetic characters have been entered, use the ASCII values for numeric characters, which are 48 through 57.

```
Private Sub txtTextBox_KeyPress(KeyAscii As Integer)
    Select Case KeyAscii
        Case vbKeyDelete          ' Delete Key
        Case vbKeyBack            ' Backspace
        Case 48 To 57             ' Number 0 thru 9
        Case Else
            Beep
            KeyAscii = 0          ' Cancels the keystroke
    End Select
End Sub
```

When using the **IsNumeric** function, you will use an **If-Then** statement rather than the **Select ... Case** statement. If the function returns a 0 value, then it means that a non-numeric character was typed. Since the **KeyAscii** value is an integer, the value is always a number, so you need to use the **Chr$** function to return the string value of the **KeyAscii** value.

```
Private Sub txtTextBox_KeyPress(KeyAscii As Integer)
    If KeyAscii = vbKeyDelete Or _
       KeyAscii = vbKeyBack Then              ' Backspace
       Exit Sub
    End If
    If IsNumeric(Chr$(KeyAscii)) = 0 Then
        Beep
        KeyAscii = 0
    End If
End Sub
```

Input Alphabetic Characters Only

When you need to test whether a character is alphabetic, there are two ways to do it. You can use a **Select ... Case** statement or you can use the Windows **IsCharAlpha** API function. Both will accomplish the same task, but if you're developing an international application, the **IsCharAlpha** API function provides an added bonus of using the language characters defined within the Control Panel, whereas in Visual Basic, you must do that yourself.

Using the **Select ... Case** statement, you should first check to see if the DELETE or BACKSPACE keys have been pressed. This will allow the user to correct what they type into the text box. In order to determine if alphabetic characters have been entered, use the ASCII values for both uppercase and lowercase alphabetic characters, which are 65 to 90 and 97 to 122, respectively.

```
Private Sub txtTextBox_KeyPress(KeyAscii As Integer)
    Select Case KeyAscii
        Case vbKeyDelete        ' Delete Key
        Case vbKeyBack          ' Backspace
        Case 65 To 90, 97 To 122 ' Uppercase/Lowercase
                                ' A thru Z
        Case Else
            Beep
            KeyAscii = 0        ' Cancels Keystroke
    End Select
End Sub
```

When using the **IsCharAlpha** function, you first need to declare the function within a Standard module. Then, in order to use it, you will use an **If-Then** statement rather than the **Select ... Case** statement. If the function returns a 0 value, it means that a non-alphabetic character was typed.

```
Public Declare Function IsCharAlpha Lib "user32" _
    Alias "IsCharAlphaA" (ByVal cChar As Byte) As Long
```

```
Private Sub txtTextBox_KeyPress(KeyAscii As Integer)
    ' KeyAscii = vbKeyDelete checks for Delete Key
    ' KeyAscii = vbKeyBack checks for Backspace
    If KeyAscii = vbKeyDelete Or KeyAscii = vbKeyBack Then
       Exit Sub
    End If
    If IsCharAlpha(KeyAscii) = 0 Then
        Beep
        KeyAscii = 0
    End If
End Sub
```

Input Characters and Numbers

There may be times when your data entry field can accept only alphabetic and numeric characters. You can use the **Select ... Case** statement as before, but it's more efficient to use the Windows **IsCharAlphaNumeric** API function. Like its **IsCharAlpha** function counterpart, it uses the language selected by the user in the Control Panel.

```
Public Declare Function IsCharAlphaNumeric Lib "user32" _
    Alias "IsCharAlphaNumericA" (ByVal cChar As Byte) As Long
Private Sub txtTextBox_KeyPress(KeyAscii As Integer)
    ' KeyAscii = vbKeyDelete checks for Delete Key
    ' KeyAscii = vbKeyBack checks for Backspace
    If KeyAscii = vbKeyDelete Or KeyAscii = vbKeyBack Then
       Exit Sub
    End If
    If IsCharAlphaNumeric(KeyAscii) = 0 Then
        Beep
        KeyAscii = 0
    End If
End Sub
```

Locking a TextBox

There are occasions when you might want to use a **TextBox** control to display information as well as allow users to enter data. It might be based on user privileges, where some users are allowed to enter and view data, while other users can only view data. Historically, the way to "lock" a **TextBox** control to prevent a user from entering or changing data is to use the Windows **SendMessage** API function. Since version 4.0 of Visual Basic, you can use the **Locked** property of the **TextBox**. You might be surprised that a lot of developers still use the **SendMessage** technique for locking the control.

In order to use the **SendMessage** function, you need to add it to a Standard module within your project. In addition, you will need to add two constants. To turn the **Text1 TextBox** control into a read-only control, use the **SendMessage** function referencing the Windows handle of the **Text1 TextBox** control, as shown here:

```
Public Declare Function SendMessage Lib "user32" Alias _
    "SendMessageA" (ByVal hwnd As Long, ByVal wMsg As Long, _
    ByVal wParam As Long, lParam As Any) As Long
Public Const WM_USER = &H400
Public Const EM_SETREADONLY = (WM_USER + 31)
Sub Form_Load ()
Dim rc As Long
    rc = SendMessage(Text1.hwnd, EM_SETREADONLY, _
        True, ByVal 0&)
End Sub
```

A faster, more efficient way to set a **TextBox** control to read-only in version 4.0 or greater of Visual Basic is to use the **TextBox**'s **Locked** property. If the property is set to True, the **TextBox** is a read-only control. The user cannot modify any information displayed in it.

```
Text1.Locked = True
```

Error Watch *It's well documented, but the technique of using the **SendMessage** function to lock a text box from allowing input might not work on computers that use Windows NT or 2000. Since the **TextBox** control now includes the **Locked** property, it would be best to avoid any confusion as to whether or not it works on NT by using the **Locked** property.*

Design Tip *If you have a text box or several text box controls with their **Locked** property set to True, it's helpful to provide a visual cue to your users that that information can't be changed. Changing the **BackColor** property to a color other than **White** provides adequate feedback. It's common for developers to change the color to a shade of gray.*

Limiting Characters

There are times when you want to limit the number of characters the user can enter into a **TextBox** control. The best way to limit this is to set the **MaxLength** property of the control. You can either set this property at design time or at run time. The following code illustrates setting the **MaxLength** property at run time, and the value is based on the size of a database field. To find the length of the database field, and if you're using ADO, use the **Recordset** object's **DefineSize** property.

```
Public Sub Form_Load()
    Dim rsFieldInfo As ADODB.RecordSet
    Set rsFieldInfo = oConn.Execution("CustInfo")

    If not rsFieldInfo.EOF Then
        Dim x As Integer
        For x = 0 To rsFieldInfo.Fields.Count - 1
            txtData(x).MaxLength = rsFieldInfo(x).DefinedSize
        Next
        rsFieldInfo.MoveNext
    End If

    rsFieldInfo.Close
End Sub
```

Speed and Size Tuning

Making a program run faster and reducing the size of the application don't seem to be very important nowadays, because computers are faster and system resources are not as expensive as they used to be. For a lot of in-house development, this goal isn't often considered. If you're part of an independent software vendor (ISV), this should be a concern. After all, you and your organization's reputations are on the line. You don't want to be known for producing slow and bloated code.

This section describes some tips to improve the speed and reduce the size of your application.

The Move Method Is Faster than Setting Left and Top Properties

The **Move** method is faster than setting a control's **Left** and **Top** properties. Each call to the **Left** or **Top** property results in a series of related calls and a screen-paint call. By using the **Move** method, the method sets both **Left** and **Top** properties and moves the control or object all at once, instead of one property at a time.

Watch Out for Dead Code

When you delete a control or rename it, Visual Basic automatically moves all non-empty procedures to the General section of the form. This code that remains in the project is present in the compiled EXEs. Before you compile your applications for distribution or during optimization, you should examine the General section of every form in the project and delete any unused procedures.

Another source of dead code is unused **Declare** statements. If you routinely add Windows API declarations to your projects, but only use a few of them, you may have a lot of excess baggage in your compiled program. Also, if you use **Declare** statements from resources other than the standard Windows resources—Kernel32, GDI, and User32—you will make your application distribution larger. For example, if you leave in the reference to the Windows API **timeBeginPeriod** function, which helped you specify procedure time, not only will it make the size of your application larger, but you will need to deploy the WinMM.dll file with your application.

```
Public Declare Function timeBeginPeriod Lib "winmm.dll" _
    Alias "timeBeginPeriod" (ByVal uPeriod As Long) As Long
```

You can determine what resource file a Windows API function or statement uses by referring to the filename specified after the **Lib** keyword within the **Declare** statement.

Testing for Non-Null Strings

In many applications where working with data is involved, you will have to determine if the recordset field returns a valid value or a Null value. Many developers use the following comparative statement to check for null values:

```
If A$ <> "" or A$ > "" Then
    ' A$ contains a valid string value
End If
```

A more efficient way to determine whether the value is valid is by using the **Len** function. By using the **Len** function, a valid value will return a value greater than 0. In an **If-Then** statement, when a value is greater than 0, the statement reacts in the affirmative. To use the **Len** function, your code would look like this:

```
If Len(A$) Then
    ' A$ contains a valid string value
End If
```

This technique is more efficient, because you are now performing a mathematical comparison between string values. Using the **Len** function, you're basically determining if the variable is greater than 0 or not.

Testing for Zero

When developers are testing a variable to determine whether it contains zero or not, they will use a "not equal to" (< >) operator.

```
If nbr <> 0 Then
    ' nbr something other than 0
End If
```

As when testing for non-Null values, it's more efficient to simply check the value itself within an **If-Then** statement. A zero value within an **If-Then** statement means that the statement is False. This is more efficient because you're using the native function of the **If-Then** statement to determine which path to execute. By using the "not equal to" operator, Visual Basic first has to execute the comparison, then execute the **If-Then** check.

```
If nbr Then
    ' nbr something other than 0
End If
```

Determining Performance Bottlenecks

Unless you use a third-party tool, such as NuMega TrueTime, which can determine how long each procedure took to execute, you will have to use your own technique to determine how long a procedure takes to execute or to return a value from a data query.

The most commonly taught technique for determining procedure timing is to use the Windows **GetTickCount** API function. The **GetTickCount** function retrieves the number of milliseconds that have elapsed since the operating system was started. The only caveat is that the tick count resets itself after 49.7 days. To use the **GetTickCount** function, include the **Declare** statement in a Standard module file.

```
Public Declare Function GetTickCount Lib "KERNEL32" () As Long
```

To determine how long a procedure took to execute, get the tick count before and after a procedure or function is called. Subtract the end time from the start time and, optionally, convert milliseconds to seconds. Once you've determined how long it took the procedure to execute, you have a benchmark time to improve upon, if possible.

```
Dim StartTime as long
Dim EndTime As Long
Dim TotalTime As Long

StartTime = GetTickCount()
Call ProcedureX
EndTime = GetTickCount()
TotalTime = ((EndTime - StartTime) / 1000)
Debug.Print "ProcedureX took " & TotalTime & " to execute."
```

Use Third-Party Controls Sparingly

This is probably one of the most controversial topics among developers and technical leads: When is it appropriate to use third-party controls? Since version 1.0, custom controls have helped make Visual Basic what it is today—the most popular Windows development tool on the market, because of its rapid application development environment and its ability to use third-party controls to extend the development environment.

Many of the third-party controls are good, robust controls; however, there are distinct advantages and disadvantages to using them.

The advantages include the following:

- Almost all of them are easy to use.
- You don't need to learn a complicated programming model.
- The controls fill a niche feature that you would otherwise have to develop yourself.
- Many controls are reasonably priced when compared to the time and cost of building it yourself.

On the other side, the disadvantages are as follows:

- Most of the time, you don't own the source code—a lot of the third-party control vendors offer their source code, but it's usually for a substantial fee.
- Some controls aren't as optimized for speed as other controls.
- You need to rely on the third-party technical support if something goes wrong.
- If an error is found in your program, and it's due to the control, you are at the mercy of the vendor to resolve the issue. Then you will have to revalidate your application against the new build of their control.
- Not all third-party controls work with every build of Visual Basic. You might have to wait for the vendor to release a new version.

The advantages of third-party controls are fairly straightforward. Their purpose is to help you add features to your program that you might not have the time or experience to build yourself. Assuming you do have the in-house talent to build the control yourself, the question you need to ask yourself is "what is the return on investment (ROI) for building it ourselves, versus buying the control?"

This is where the disadvantages come in. When you purchase a third-party control to use with your application, you are at the mercy of the vendor if anything goes wrong with that control. Most of the ISVs try to build small, optimized controls. They know that you are going to be shipping their control with your application and they want their control to be as "lean and mean" as possible. The problem is that often they build "one size fits all" controls, or "lets include everything and the kitchen sink" controls. The problem is that no matter how optimized the control is, you might be shipping it with your application but end up using only 10 percent of its functionality.

You also need to consider your business needs. If changes in the business require changes in or additions to the control, can you make these changes without having to put them on the vendor's wish list and hoping they are adopted in the next release?

Working with third-party controls is a double-edged sword. On one side, they can help you add features and functionality that you might not have been able to do yourself. On the other side, you're at the mercy of the vendor to develop any future enhancements or bug fixes.

Summary

Often, optimization and tuning is overemphasized once an application is deployed. It may be that there is nothing you can do programmatically to improve the performance of your application. You might be able to make some minor speed improvements in one area or another, but on the whole, it's rare that you can increase your application performance enough to warrant a lot of development time trying to optimize every algorithm.

In many cases, the best optimization is by providing more feedback to be sure that something is actually happening while a process is executing. Windows Explorer is a great example of providing user feedback. When you copy a file from one folder to another, or from one drive to another, you see a dialog box that provides how much progress the task has completed. Now, it's questionable on how accurate the progress bar really is, but at least you know its doing something. Subtle cues like this go a long way toward offering "perceived" speed.

CHAPTER 11

COM, DCOM, and COM+

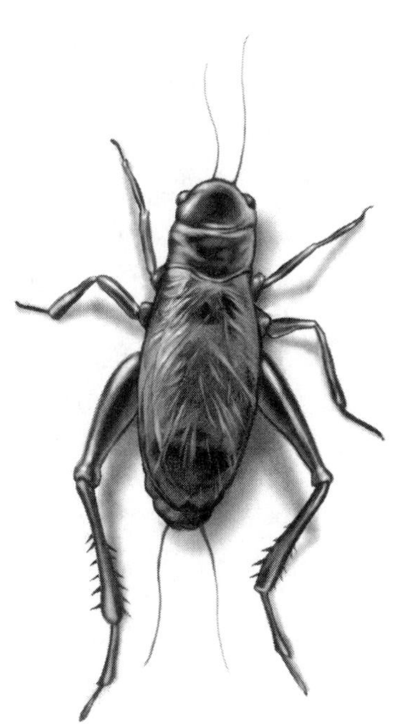

Despite what Microsoft wants you to think, the notion of reusable code did not originate from the Redmond campus; they simply promoted the concept and made it a mainstream ideal. Since the dawn of the computer industry, developers have been doing their best to make their code reusable. The last thing a developer wants to do is rewrite in another program the same code that has already been written, tested, and implemented in a previous one. It's a lot more efficient when procedures are written into reusable objects or components that programs can simply call upon when needed. For example, you might need a procedure to verify the accuracy and validity of credit card numbers. By not placing this procedure in an object that can be reused by other programs, you would have to enter this procedure into every program that needed it. If the procedure changed, you would have to find every program that used the code and modify it accordingly. If the procedure is part of an object or component, you would only need to make the changes to the object or component—the programs that use it don't need to be modified at all.

Microsoft's component strategy of COM, DCOM, and COM+ are the focus of this chapter, including strategies on writing error handling routines to properly track and trap errors within them.

A Brief History of COM

An important feature of the Microsoft Windows operating system is the way it allows applications to share information. Prior to Microsoft Windows, in order to share information among applications, you had to save the data to a file and then import it into the target application. This technique was very time consuming and not very efficient.

As the Windows operating system matured, so did its application data-interchange. Microsoft introduced *dynamic data exchange* (DDE), which was the means of communication between Microsoft Windows applications. This link acts as a conduit for the exchange of data between connected applications. The data exchanged may either be information copied from one application to another or commands or keystrokes from one application for the other to process.

As with all technology, there was room for improvement. Microsoft later introduced *object linking and embedding* (OLE). OLE gives your application the power to directly use and manipulate another Windows application's data in its native format. If the other application supports OLE automation, you may also be able to use its objects, properties, and methods just as you would with a Visual Basic control. *OLE automation*, later to be known as just *Automation*, introduced in Visual Basic 3.0, is one of the most important additions to Windows and serves as the basis for creating a true object-oriented environment. Applications like spreadsheets and word processors have a lot of features that can be useful to other applications, such as mail-merge and spell-checking.

In 1996, in Microsoft's rush to establish their Internet presence, they introduced a new term to the world of developers: *ActiveX*. When the term was first introduced, it was believed to be a variation of OLE, and that its technology was for the Internet and Internet-based applications. As the technology became more defined and the dust started to settle, however, the development world realized that ActiveX wasn't just a variation of OLE, but was OLE redefined. ActiveX included the OLE implementation but also improved on it by extending its capabilities to take advantage of the Internet, something that OLE didn't have in its specifications.

After all the hoops and learning curves that Microsoft put developers through, they decided that OLE and ActiveX were two different sets of technology after all. OLE remained the technology that referred to working with compound documents. ActiveX became the reference name for custom controls as well as in-process and out-of-process servers.

When it comes to Microsoft technology, Microsoft writes Microsoft history. They will claim that no matter what technology was introduced first, building component-based applications has always been their goal. OLE and ActiveX were just introduced first because the technology was mature enough. The component-based architecture that they have always been trying to promote has been COM, which stands for Component Object Model. It is a general architecture that lays the foundation on which OLE and ActiveX are based. It establishes a common model for interaction among software, including applications, library modules, system software, and more. Therefore, COM can be implemented with almost any kind of software technology that follows the COM guidelines.

For example, a COM object that deals with customers may implement a Customer interface. The interface itself is made up of methods and properties that define the functions of the interface and store its data. Methods for the Customer interface may include **CreditCheck** to check the customer's credit and **GetBalance** to calculate and retrieve the customer's current balance. Properties of the Customer interface might include name, address, and phone number. The interfaces are each assigned a *globally unique identifier*, more commonly known as a GUID (pronounced GOO'id) at the time the component is compiled, and it is a method of differentiating one interface from another.

By using GUIDs, a calling program can be certain that the interface it is communicating with is the correct one. Once an interface has been defined and published, any program that uses the interface is relying on this consistency. If the interface is changed, a new GUID must be generated. For this reason, COM interfaces are often referred to as *self-versioning*. A developer who makes changes to the interface is essentially creating a new version that cannot be used by calling programs that used the previous version without causing an error. To prevent a new GUID from being generated and causing errors, when you compile your COM component within Visual Basic, make sure you have Version Compatibility enabled. By having it enabled, the original GUID will be used when you recompile the component, ensuring your component will be compatible with your existing client applications that use the components. Version Compatibility is set on the Component tab of the Project Properties dialog box, as shown in Figure 11-1.

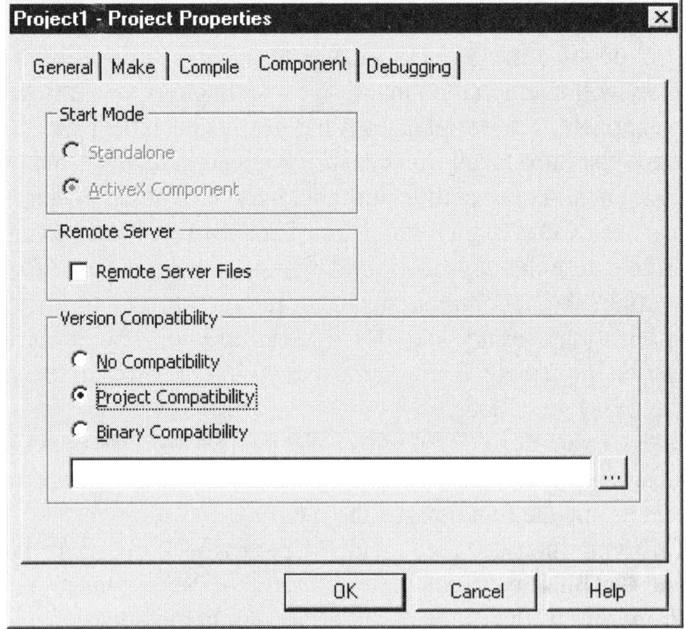

Figure 11.1 Version Compatibility has three possible choices for component projects

24x7

Project Compatibility should always be set on to ensure that the COM object is compatible with previous versions.

DCOM allows you to take your COM components and access them across a network. Many people refer to DCOM, which stands for Distributed COM, as COM on a very long string. To an application loaded locally on a client's system, the remote component appears the same as if it were local as well. To create and use DCOM components, there is nothing you, as the developer, must do differently. The programming model is the same.

Just as Windows applications allow developers to concentrate on the application itself, DCOM allows developers to concentrate on the business rules and functionality rather than worry about where the component will be accessed from. The only thing that must change is the component's registration process. COM components put some basic information about themselves in the Windows Registry, such as where they are located on the client's machine. With DCOM components, everything is the same except that the Registry will hold information telling the application where on the network the component is located.

Allowing remote execution of components can be a great boost in a number of situations. Processor-intensive operations can be moved off slow client systems onto fast servers. Components that need to shuffle large amounts of data can run right on the server instead of moving the data back and forth across the network. Code that changes often can be kept running on one centralized site, reducing administration costs.

Design Tip *Starting with version 6.0 of Visual Basic, you don't need to use DCOM to access COM components across the network. If you know where the COM component is installed on the network, you can access it directly by using the* ***CreateObject*** *function to specify the component's network location.*

In 1998, Microsoft started talking about a new set of COM features, and it was referred to as COM+. Microsoft would nebulously talk about how great the technology was but never fully defined it until the specifications for Windows 2000 were officially released to the public. COM+ is based on COM, the

Microsoft Transaction Server (MTS), and the Microsoft Messaging Queue (MSMQ), and it is the foundation that Windows 2000 is based upon. With improvements to both MTS and MSMQ, it also includes new features, such as an In-Memory Database (IMDB) and queued components. The tighter integration between COM+ and the transaction server means less work for the developer; however, that means that if you haven't considered using the MTS style of application development, you'd better start. The COM+/MTS model is a mandate from Microsoft. Until you've upgraded your servers to Windows 2000, you should make sure that you're building MTS-compliant components, because a good MTS component is a good COM+ component.

Most of the COM+ facilities will work in Visual Basic 6.0, but full integration won't be available until version 7.0.

Referencing COM Objects

Before you can use the events, methods, and properties of a COM component, you must first instantiate, or create an instance, of the component in memory. To do this, you must first declare a local object variable to hold a reference to the component, and then assign a reference to the component to the local object variable. There are two ways to do this: *early binding* and *late binding*.

Early Binding

Early binding is the most efficient method of accessing a COM component, or *object*. Early binding is more efficient because it directly references the type library of the object before the project is compiled. This gives you access to all the object's events, methods, and properties, and it allows memory to be allocated based on the type library. To provide early binding for an object, you must use the References dialog box, shown in Figure 11-2, to add a reference to the object to your project. Once the object is referenced, you can instantiate the object by one of two methods:

```
Dim oObjBinding As New ObjectName.Class
```

or

```
Dim oObjBinding as ObjectName.Class
Set oObjBinding = New ObjectName.Class
```

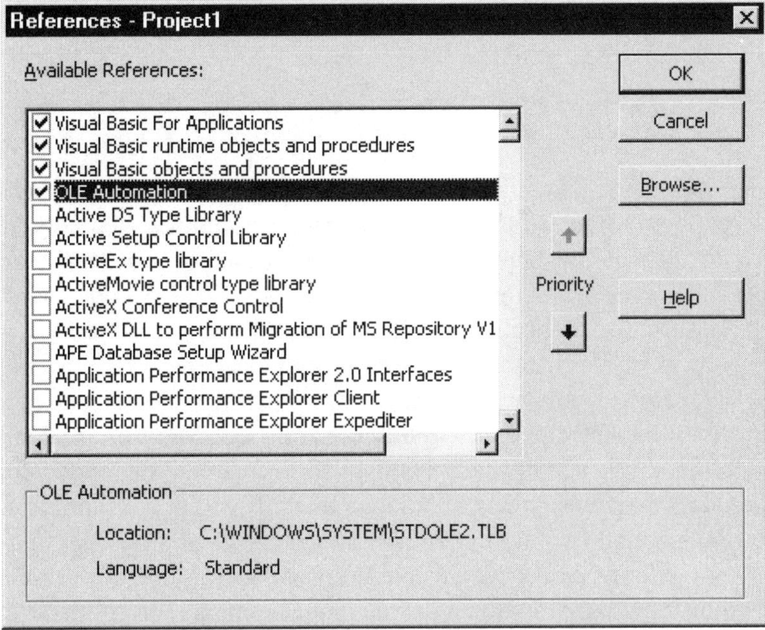

Figure 11.2 References dialog box used for early binding

Either method is acceptable but the latter method is preferred. The purpose of binding is to instantiate an object and declare an object variable. By using the first method, you create an instance of the object as soon as the object variable is declared. The problem is that the object remains in memory the entire time the host application is running. If the user never chooses the option or function that uses the object, you've wasted resources that could have been used by other processes or programs.

The latter method declares the object to an object variable, and then the Set statement instantiates the object when the object is needed. This also provides you with a method of controlling when an object is loaded into memory, thus maintaining control over the object and the resources it may use.

Late Binding

In cases where the object you are trying to reference doesn't provide a type library, or when you're not sure at design time precisely which object you might need to reference, you can simply declare an object variable as **Object**, rather than the name of the object. The **CreateObject** function is used to instantiate the object for use, as shown here:

```
Dim oObjBinding As Object
Set oObjBinding = CreateObject("ObjectName.Class")
```

Visually, you might think there is no difference except whether or not you explicitly state which object you plan to instantiate. In reality, that is a big difference. The method of late binding causes your code to execute more slowly, and it makes your development process slower. The code executes more slowly because the application does not bind to the object's interface until after it executes. This means that the object's events, methods, and properties aren't available to you during development. The Integrated Development Environment's (IDE's) IntelliSense Auto List Member and Statement Completion features won't assist you in creating your application because it doesn't know anything about the object. If you're not familiar with the Auto List Member, it's a feature that lists the methods and properties that relate to an object or the list of objects you can reference in a drop-down list box. Figure 11-3 illustrates the drop-down list box after typing just five letters. The Statement Completion feature completes your code statement for you. Once you have found the method or property you are looking for in the drop-down list box by typing the first few letters, press CTRL-SPACE to complete the text.

By utilizing the Auto List Member during development, you get immediate feedback on the objects you can reference and the properties and methods they have available to them. There are developers out there who remember all the properties and methods of an object, but for those who don't, this feature saves time that would be spent looking them up in the online help file or manual. With so many controls and objects available to a developer, you might get confused as to the properties and methods available in each control or object. For example, you might want to use a particular control and use the **MouseOver** method to change the Mouse property when a user places the mouse over the control. This method is in a lot of controls, but the control you chose to use doesn't have that method. Since the method is not part of the control, the method will not appear in the Auto List Member drop-down list box. You then have one of two choices, write some elaborate code that emulates the **MouseOver** method for the control or use another control.

Object Browser

Each COM application provides a list of objects, methods, and properties that are available to other developers. This list is known as the object model, and it is

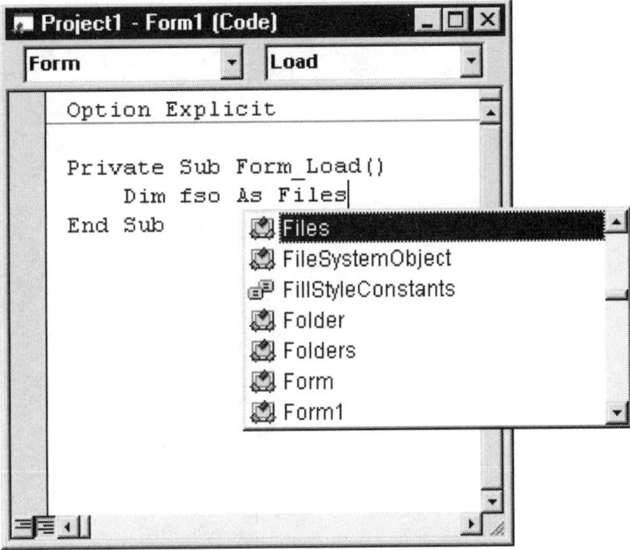

Figure 11.3 Auto List Member showing referenced objects starting with "files"

stored in either an object library (.olb) or type library (.tlb) file. Visual Basic provides you with a facility that allows you to look at the object model in a hierarchical manner. This facility is called the *Object Browser*, shown in Figure 11-4, which is accessed by pressing F2.The Object Browser has several windows for displaying an object's properties and methods. It only displays the object libraries that are referenced in the project, so if you don't see the object reference you're looking for, then you haven't referenced it yet in the project.

CreateObject vs. GetObject

There are two different functions that instantiate a COM object: **CreateObject** and **GetObject**. They both use the same syntax to reference an object:

```
Set oObjBinding = CreateObject("Outlook.Application")
```

or

```
Set oObjBinding = GetObject("Outlook.Application")
```

However, when they should be used differs. If there is no instance of the component running, use the **CreateObject** function. It will create an instance of the object and return a reference to it. The **GetObject** function is used when an

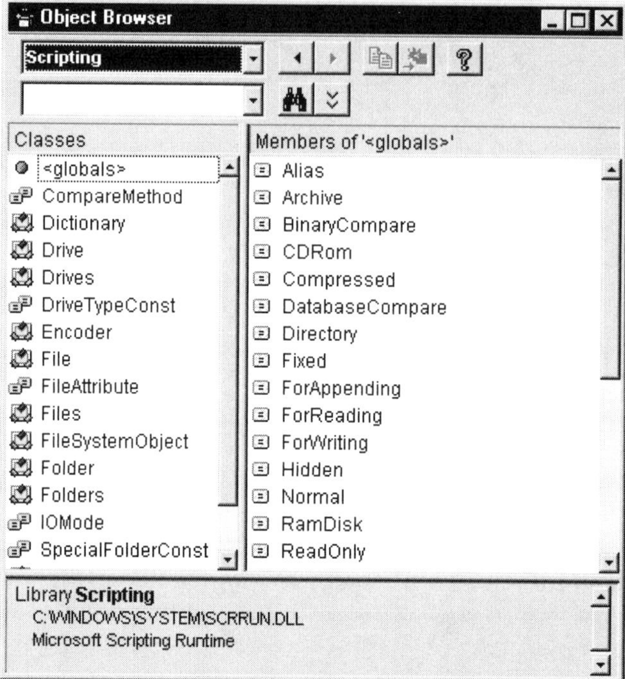

Figure 11.4 The Object Browser displaying some elements of the Microsoft Scripting Runtime object model

instance of an object is already running and you want to get its reference for Automation. The following code shows an example:

```
Public Function MSWord_Open() As Boolean

    On Error Resume Next

    ' Check to see if Word is already loaded
    Set oWord = GetObject(, "Word.Application")

    If oWord Is Nothing Then
        ' Create a new Instance of it
        Set oWord = CreateObject("Word.Application")

        ' check to make sure instantiating it worked
        If oWord Is Nothing Then
            MsgBox ErrCreatingWord, vbCritical, _
                "Word Automation Problem"
            GoTo Err_MSWord_Open
```

```
        End If
    End If

    MSWord_Open = True

Exit_MSWord_Open:
    Exit Function

Err_MSWord_Open:
    MSWord_Open = False
    GoTo Exit_MSWord_Open

End Function
```

The **GetObject** method is used to determine whether an instance of Microsoft Word is loaded in memory. The argument, **Word.Application**, is the class name of the object, consisting of the application's name and the object type. If the value of the **oWord** object variable is Nothing, then an instance of Microsoft Word isn't instantiated yet; otherwise, the object variable will be a reference to the instance of Word. If an instance isn't loaded, the **CreateObject** function is used to launch a new instance of it and assign it to the **oWord** object variable. In order to ensure that the object was instantiated, the **If ... Then** statement checks the status of the **oWord** variable to ensure that it's not still set to Nothing. If it is, that means that the **CreateObject** function failed to instantiate the object and the overall function is a failure.

Messages from a COM Object to Developers

When it comes to COM development, a lot of developers overlook one important feature: providing helpful comments to their fellow developers. In this case, we aren't referring to providing comments within the source code; we're referring to adding helpful comments in the class and member elements.

To add a comment to a class or member, you need to use the Object Browser. To add or change a comment, select the class or member with the right mouse button to display the context menu and select Properties, as shown in Figure 11-5. If you're changing a class description, the Member Options dialog box will appear. The description you type will show up in the Object Browser's description window, as shown in Figure 11-6. If you're changing the member description, a Procedure Attribute dialog box will appear. As with the Member Options dialog box, whatever you type in the Description field will appear in the Object Browser's description window.

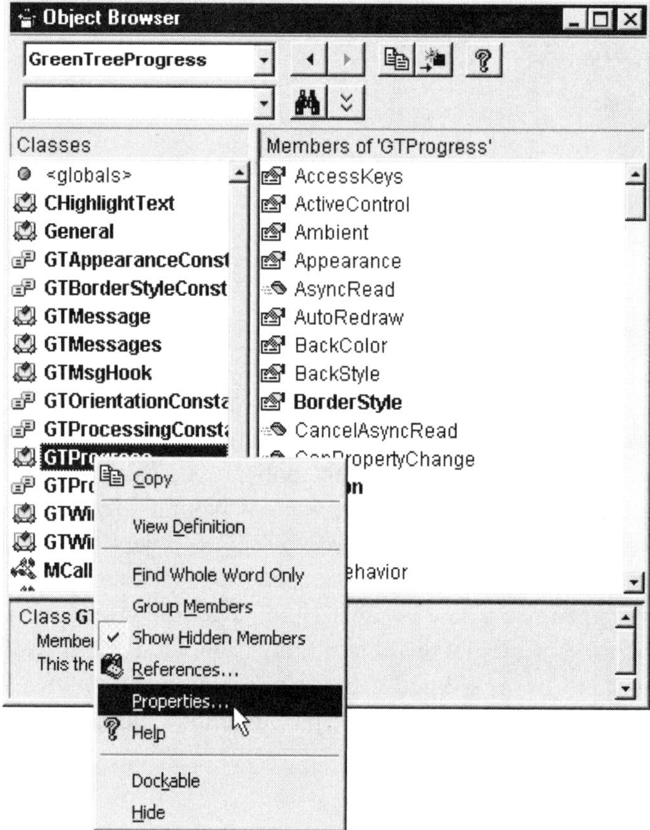

Figure 11.5 Selecting the Properties item from the context menu

If you develop an online help file for your COM component, you can also assign context-sensitive help to each property and method. In both the Member Options and Procedure Attribute dialog boxes there is a Help File field. That field is linked to the Help File field in the Project Properties setting. If you create a help file for your COM component, a Help Context ID is used to reference each topic in the help file, much like how the index of a book references the page number where the item is located. The Help Context ID field in the Member Options dialog box references the ID value you assigned the topic in your help file. When a developer is looking at your component in the Object Browser, they can select one of the attributes of your component and press F1 to receive whatever context-sensitive help you've provided for them.

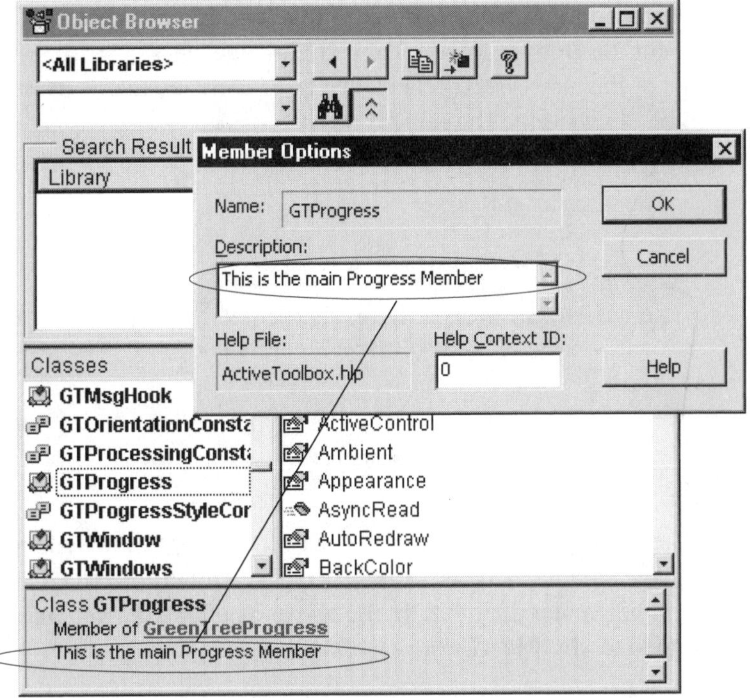

Figure 11.6 The description in the Member Options dialog box is displayed in the Object Browser

Error Handling in COM Components

When you begin working with errors in COM components, you might think there is a certain level of mysticism to error handling. The reality of it is that handling errors within COM components really isn't any different than handling errors in stand-alone programs. You still need to trap and manage errors internally by using the **On Error** statement. What you need to consider are two other approaches: passing back errors to the client program that calls it, and handling errors from other components that reference your component.

Passing Back Errors to a Client Program

In order to pass errors back to a client program, you can use the **Raise** method of the **Err** object. For the error to be raised in the client, you must call **Raise** from your procedure's error-handling routine within your component. In the following code for the **Item** property of a **V2JMessage** class, an error will be raised if the range of the index is exceeded. The error message that is passed back to the client will be "Index out of bounds."

```
Public Property Get Item(Index) As V2JMessage
    Dim lIndex As Long

    lIndex = ConvertIndex(Index)

    If lIndex < 1 Or lIndex > m_colMessages.Count Then
        Err.Raise vbObjectError + 1053, , "Index out of bounds."
        Exit Property
    End If

    Set Item = m_colMessages(lIndex)
End Property
```

The **vbObjectError** constant is assigned to a predefined value in the VBA language, and its value is –2,147,221,504. Any user-defined error numbers should be greater than that. In the above example, the generated error number is assigned to **vbObjectError** + 1053.

Handling Errors from Another Component

There may be instances when your component is going to reference another component, so you will need to develop procedures to handle errors resulting from methods within the other components. You should be able to obtain a list of these errors from the other component.

In cases where your component is called from another component, it's particularly important that you handle these errors within your component and not return them to the client application. The client application is written to use your component and is designed to respond to your component's error code and messages, not to the errors of any methods your component subsequently calls.

Working with DCOM

Before an application implementing DCOM can be used on a client or server system, you must first set up certain application properties. If you are running a server application, security settings need to be set. On a client application, the location of the server needs to be set. If DCOM isn't configured on the client and server computers, the application won't function.

Installing and Configuring DCOM

In order for a client application to call a remote server using DCOM or a component running in MTS, the DCOM client files must be installed on the client's computer. On most Windows 98/Me and Windows NT 4.0/2000 systems, the files for configuring DCOM are included as part of the base installation. However, on Windows 95 systems, the DCOM files must be installed manually. The DCOM98 version 1.0 installation comes with Visual Studio and can be installed using the DCOM98.EXE program. This version will install DCOM on all Windows 9*x* systems.

When you're troubleshooting or implementing increased security, you'll need to use the DCOM Configuration (DCOMCNFG.EXE) utility to configure the way a client or server computer uses DCOM. A shortcut is not placed in the Start menu; instead, you need to execute it using either the command line or the Run menu item.

In order for DCOM to work, the network security access-control level needs to be set to User-level. The access-control level is set using the Network applet found in the Control Panel. By default, the access-control level is set to Share-level access control. To change it, simply select the User-level access control radio button and then enter the name of the computer or network domain where the master list of users is stored in the text box, as shown in Figure 11-7.

24x7

If you don't see your component on the list, it may be listed by its CLSID (class identifier) and not by its ProgID (programmatic identifier). The CLSID is a 128-bit number and is considered a GUID, while the ProgID is the character string that describes the DCOM component like DCOMComponent.Object. To display the component by its ProgID, change the Registry key HKEY_CLASSES_ROOT\AppID*your CLSID* and change the Default key that reads "value not set" to the ProgID. For DCOMCNFG to recognize the change, you need to close and reopen the program.

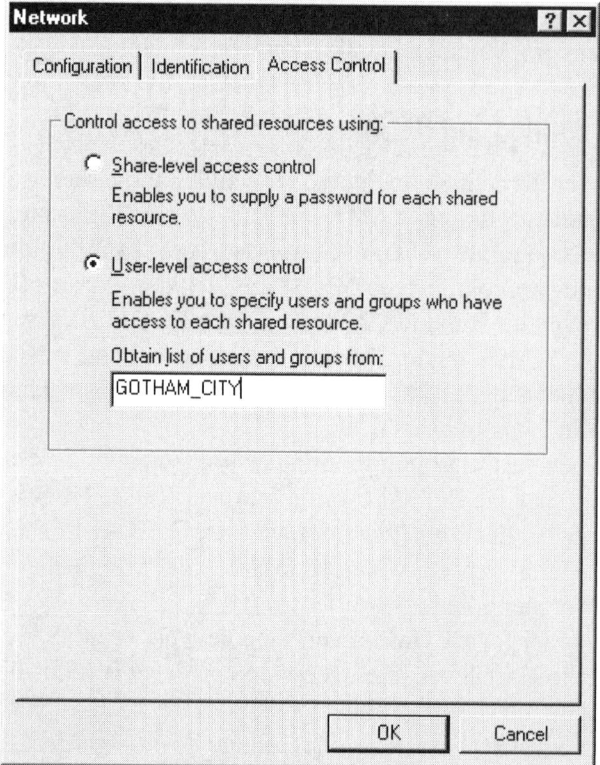

Figure 11.7 Configuring the network access-control level

Three Common DCOM Errors

Assuming you tested your components thoroughly before deploying them, the most common errors you will encounter when you use them in a DCOM setting are related to security. The simplest way to troubleshoot security problems is by changing the combination of security settings on both the client and server systems. Most people usually start by removing all security from the object and then re-enabling settings one at a time until they encounter the error. This way, you will know what is causing the error and hopefully will understand why the error is occurring.

Error 70: Permission Denied

This error is obviously a permissions issue—the question is where there is a permission deficiency. You should first verify that DCOM is enabled on both the client and server computers. If they are, then check to see if the user name associated with the local computer has permission to access the remote system and its objects.

If you are still having problems and your client system is Windows 9*x*, try granting the user access to everything possible on the system through the Default Security tab of the DCOM Configuration utility. If that works, then start eliminating access until you find out where it stops working.

Error 429: ActiveX Component Can't Create Object

If you encounter this error, it usually means that the object is not installed or registered correctly, either on the client system, the server, or both. It is very probable that at one point during the development process the DCOM component worked perfectly, but when the component was moved to the production environment, it stopped worked. The first thing you should do is to make sure that the component installed on the test server is the same one as on the production server. The way to do this is by scanning the Registry on both systems for the component's GUID. If the component is installed on the system but there isn't a Registry entry, then simply reregister the component. To do this, use the REGSVR32.EXE. If you register a lot of components, it might be a good idea to make a shortcut on the desktop to REGSVR32.EXE so you can just drag and drop the component onto the shortcut to register it.

24x7

REGSVR32.EXE is usually found in the Windows\System directory. It's a good idea to create a desktop shortcut to it so you can drag and drop components on it to register them for a system.

Error 462: The Remote Server Machine Does Not Exist or Is Unavailable

This error is usually related to two possible causes. The first is that the name of the remote computer is not spelled correctly. The second is that the remote server system is down or has become unavailable due to network problems.

Developing for COM+

In order to understand how to develop and debug COM+ components, we need to have a good understanding of what COM+ is made up of. COM+ was developed as a standard for designing distributed n-tier applications. It builds upon standard COM specifications and incorporates technology found in the Microsoft Transaction Server (MTS) and Microsoft Messaging Queue (MSMQ).

Transaction Processing

In business solutions, each task takes the form of a transaction. A *transaction* is a collection of database actions and processes that represent a unit of work. A transaction must be completed in its entirety or the information it processed needs to roll back to its original state. *Rollback* is a term in transaction processing that refers to a transaction being returned to its original state before the transaction occurred. ADO (ActiveX Data Objects) can be used for transactions via their **BeginTrans**, **CommitTrans**, and **RollbackTrans** methods. Most DBMS environments also provide a way to handle transactions within their stored procedures.

ADO and other data access models offer methods for handling a single transaction. Using a stored procedure is also a good way to perform single transaction processing. But in either case, there doesn't seem to be an easy way to coordinate nested transactions, which is when a transaction executes another transaction before the first one is completed. For example, transferring money from one account to another would be a nested transaction. The unit of work for this transaction would involve validating that the account does have the money to transfer, withdrawing the money from one account, and then depositing the money in the new account. If something goes wrong in the middle of the transaction, you need to know how to set all the records back to the way things were before the transaction began. As a developer, you would have to program the proper steps to roll back each transaction within the unit of work in order to roll the transaction back successfully.

Mainframe environments use transaction monitors, such as IBM's CICS, to manage large numbers of simultaneous transactions against a DBMS. The Microsoft Transaction Server (MTS), Microsoft's transaction monitor, is designed for robustness and scalability in the client/server arena. It comes with database support for Microsoft SQL Server and Oracle and will be extended to support DBMS environments in the future.

A transaction should function as a consistent and reliable unit of work for the database system and must pass a so-called "ACID" test—it must have the following four key properties:

- **Atomic** All of the work gets done, or none of the work gets done.
- **Consistent** The operation being performed is legal and does not endanger the system's integrity.
- **Isolated** The behavior of a transaction is independent of the actions of any other transaction.
- **Durable** Once a transaction has been completed, the work is committed to storage before reporting a success.

Essentially, a transaction forms a binding contract between a client application and the components running on the server. Once the server's components signal the client that a transaction has succeeded, it has effectively guaranteed to the client that it has committed the transaction to storage. Conversely, if the server's components signal the client that the transaction was aborted, the client application assumes that an attempt was made to perform the transaction, but it failed, and the server will be in the state it would have been if the transaction were never attempted in the first place.

Using the analogy of the bank transfer again, what would happen if an error occurred between the process of transferring the money from one account to another? Without a transaction monitor, you would have to know how to roll back each process in order to restore the system to the way it was prior to the beginning of the transaction. With a transaction monitor, the entire unit of work is monitored so that nothing is completely committed to storage until the entire transaction is validated as having been processed correctly. Not only does the transaction monitor oversee that one transaction, it monitors all the transactions that are occurring.

As you can see, transactions greatly simplify the code that you have to write to recover from error conditions. A transaction will either commit in its entirety or roll back in its entirety; therefore, your error-recovery code doesn't have to struggle with undoing partially completed work.

MTS Services

MTS provides your distributed application with a number of services that you would normally take into account, such as session management, server resource management, data contention, network roundtrips, and security, but it also allows you to manage the application on a large scale. Without MTS to assist you, you would have to manage all this information yourself within each component that you develop. You want to develop your components so they are independent of one another, but you also want them to be able to interoperate with one another. Using the money transfer transaction mentioned earlier, the process of validating available funds in an account can be built into one component, the process for withdrawing funds is another component, and the process of depositing the funds is another component. Each one is its own component because it can be used within one transaction or used separately. By not programming these components as MTS services, you would have to program the session management information, data contentions handling, and security authentication into each component. If one of the components failed to execute properly within a transaction, each component would have to know how to roll back its information to its previous state and return to its original values. By using MTS services within your component, MTS manages the entire transaction from start to finish. If any part of the transaction fails, MTS knows how the information looked before the transaction started and simply returns everything back to the way it was before the transaction began. You will find that MTS is a valuable ally in the development of your distributed applications.

Session Management Maintaining each connection between the client and the server involves establishing some form of session between them. A *session* requires memory resources to store its state and processing resources to maintain and update its state. By *state*, we're referring to information about which clients are logged in and connected at all times. This information is passed on to the applications running on the server, so it can provide data caching and other services to the clients as required. If you've done any work with Web-based applications, you've probably discovered that the Internet technology is more or less a stateless environment. This means that each time a user navigates through your Web site, the server doesn't know if the user has made a previous request or if a new person has jumped to the page. By using session information and cookies, you can produce a quasi-state environment.

There are typically far more clients than there are servers. In a traditional two-tiered client/server environment, you might have a situation where there are *x* number of clients connected to *y* number of servers. This means that the total number of connections is *x* times *y*. In other words, if you have 10,000 users connecting to 10 servers, the servers would need to maintain 100,000 separate sessions.

By adding a transaction monitoring service like MTS, you can reduce the number of sessions required to maintain state throughout your distributed environment from *x* times *y* to *x* plus *y*. If you have the same 10,000 users, and you introduce a transaction monitor service onto a server, it links to each session the 10,000 users and the transaction monitor service links to the 10 servers, distributing and effectively managing an equal percentage of the total workload across all servers; therefore each one maintains 1,000 sessions with its clients. The total number of sessions works out to 1,000 + 10, or 1,010 sessions, versus the 100,000 separate sessions in the scenario without transaction monitors. The transaction monitor service acts as a traffic cop managing all communication and traffic to and from the servers.

By reducing the number of sessions, we reduce the amount of system resources needed to manage the sessions. This translates into the system being able to handle more users, which brings us to our next point: server resource management.

Server Resource Management Even by adding transaction monitors into the architecture, it's still possible to exceed the threshold of any server. Too many users can take a toll on both memory and processing time for any given transaction. If you go beyond the limits of your system, your processor might end up spending too much time juggling all the active sessions instead of dedicating some of its time to processing the work that it is supposed to be doing.

Earlier, we discussed how a transaction monitor could coordinate the activities of one or more servers. More importantly, you can place logic within the transaction monitor that allows for efficient sharing of database connections in a scheme known as *connection pooling*. Connection pooling is not a new concept in the Microsoft development environment. It has been available through DCOM since its introduction in version 4.0 of VB.

MTS ships with a component called the ODBC resource dispenser, which automatically pools ODBC connections to ODBC-compliant databases. Pooling can yield significant performance gains, because it eliminates the overhead of constructing and tearing down an ODBC connection each time a user submits work to an ODBC database. Instead, the ODBC resource dispenser maintains a pool of preexisting ODBC connections and assigns incoming work to the next available connection, much like a bank assigns incoming customers to the next available teller.

Data Contention In distributed database applications, the biggest barrier to scalability is contention for database records. Database manufacturers like Microsoft and Oracle spend hundreds of thousands of hours and dollars optimizing their database-locking technology to ensure maximum performance without a database administrator's intervention. However, the burden of database optimization doesn't lie solely on the DBMS. The application developer has a responsibility, as well, to ensure that the application doesn't cause any more database contention than is necessary for the task at hand. In other words, if a developer only needs to return information from a table for a report, it would be inconsiderate for him or her to issue a database lock on the entire table. You might laugh, but it's been known to happen.

The developer can control two elements: the number of database locks held by an application, and the amount of time the application holds on to those locks. Redesigning the application code can minimize the number of locks held by the application. Placing code that manipulates the data closer to the database can help minimize the amount of time that an application holds onto a database lock, as well.

In a traditional two-tier client/server environment, a lot of the database activity is done through the use of SQL stored procedures. Unfortunately, the language used to implement stored procedures is, on the whole, not based on any object-oriented programming language. Also, database administrators (DBAs) usually develop stored procedures, because most developers don't have authority to create them on the database server.

MTS objects can be written using virtually any programming language, such as VB, C/C++, Delphi, and even Assembler. An MTS object, like any business object, resides on the middle tier of a three-tier client/server environment. These middle-tier components let you centralize the application logic that accesses your databases. More importantly, by centralizing your data access in components that can take advantage of connection pooling and higher-speed connections to the database servers, the total time that database locks are held by these components is minimized. The amount of contention for data in the database services tier is also minimized.

Network Round Trips Another factor that can limit the scalability of your application is the total number of network round trips required to do a unit of work on your server. In today's object-oriented client/server applications, we typically perform three atomic operations, each requiring at least one network round trip to perform a given logical operation: creating an instance of an object on the server computer, invoking one or more methods on the object, and destroying the object on the server computer.

Middle-tier objects usually acquire resources to do their work—typically database connections and database locks. For your application to scale well, it is essential that we conserve these resources. Therefore, application programmers have traditionally created the objects just when they need to use them and destroyed them immediately after. Thus, we pay the price of at least three network round trips to invoke a method on a server-side object, which introduces another potential limit on the scalability of the application. Additional remote procedure call (RPC) run-time resources are required to handle the overhead of processing three distinct messages where only one does meaningful work. In theory, the operations required to create and destroy the object could be optimized out of existence.

MTS reduces the number of network round trips required for transactions to perform a single operation to *almost* one. It optimizes the creation and destruction operations by using a *context wrapper*. The context wrapper—which is an object itself—is a transparent layer that MTS places between the application and the MTS object. It allows MTS to monitor all inbound method calls and destroy the object without dropping its connection to the application. To an application, it appears as if it's interacting directly with the MTS object itself when in fact it's really interacting with the context wrapper.

For MTS to eliminate the need for a client application to create and destroy MTS objects, the client application must follow a completely different set of rules, acquiring a reference to the MTS object as early as possible and releasing it as late as possible. This lets MTS create an instance of the MTS object whenever a procedure call comes in. When the object signals to MTS that it has finished doing what it was doing, MTS destroys the object but keeps the context wrapper alive to service the next incoming request. This effectively allows MTS to leverage an object's creation and destruction overhead across the total number of times that you invoke methods of the object.

The MTS network round-trip optimization is called *just-in-time* activation, and the key is the MTS context wrapper object, which implements the methods for the interfaces implemented by the actual object. It is created dynamically at run time by MTS and is inserted transparently between the client application and the real MTS object. The context wrapper creates an instance of the MTS object at the moment it receives an incoming call from a client application, hence the term just-in-time activation.

For MTS to create a context wrapper object for *any* MTS object dynamically, it must know the details of the object's interface. That requires that an MTS object meet a certain set of requirements. An MTS object must be created as a 32-bit ActiveX DLL, which means that it must meet the general requirements for COM objects. These requirements are that it must be a self-registering DLL that exports the DLLRegisterServer and DLLUnregisterServer function, and it must implement the entry points DLLGetClassObject and DLLCanUnloadNow. Additionally, the MTS object must be created through a standard class factory object that implements the IClassFactory interface. Most development tools like Delphi, Visual Basic, and Visual C++ can create ActiveX DLLs that fit these requirements.

Security Programmers who have implemented server-side security have had to deal with a plethora of Windows NT/2000 data structures and API functions. To eliminate many of the details associated with security programming, MTS introduced the concept of *role-based security*. To use role-based security, you must group your MTS components into *packages* and assign *roles* to those packages during development. For example, you could create Manager and Teller roles. At deployment time, a Windows NT/2000 administrator would assign actual users to the roles defined during development. At run time, users will be allowed or denied access to different pieces of functionality within the MTS package, based on their roles.

Role-based security allows MTS to make security checks automatically. When a client application attempts to make a call into an MTS object, MTS performs a security check on the client. The security check is concerned with *authentication* and *access control*. Authentication involves ensuring that users are who they say they are. MTS takes advantage of Windows NT/2000's existing security infrastructure to perform the authentication. Access control is concerned with whether a user is permitted to perform the operation he or she is requesting. MTS checks whether a user has been assigned to a particular role to determine whether or not the request will succeed.

Message Queues

Message queuing is essentially application-to-application communication, but unlike e-mail, information that is sent from one application to another is data, not a message, so the terminology might seem misleading. In any case, the term "message queuing" is an established term in the industry, so you can't blame Microsoft for this one. One of the best-known message-queuing applications is IBM's MQ (Message Queue) Series, which probably had an influence on Microsoft's name for its own product, the Microsoft Message Queue Server (MSMQ).

To understand message queues, we first need to discuss the types of messaging that can occur. There are essentially two forms of communication pathways: synchronous and asynchronous. In a *synchronous* environment, the sending application has to establish a connection with the receiving application before a message or data is sent. Once the data is sent, the sending application must wait for a response from the receiving application before any further processing can be performed. Synchronous communication is like a telephone call. In order for any communication to take place, you first need to contact the person you want to communicate with. Once you make the connection, you provide the receiver with information and wait for the receiver to respond.

In an *asynchronous* environment, the sender sends a request to a receiver application, but rather than waiting for a response, the sender can continue processing information. It's up to the sender to determine when to process a response from the receiver, if it does at all. In some cases, a response might not be required. Asynchronous communication is like an e-mail environment. You can send out dozens of messages to various people while online with your network or Internet service provider, or offline while you're traveling with your mobile computer. When the message is sent, you're not concerned with whether the receiver is available or not. There are times when you don't expect an immediate response back from the receiver because some work might have to be done on the receiver's end. You're only concerned about whether or not the message got through.

Message queuing provides a way of implementing asynchronous communication in your environment. Messages are stored in a message queue on the sending system before being transmitted to a message queue server. Storing messages in a queue is important for providing disaster recovery. If a transaction sent via a queue is lost or damaged, you can just resubmit the queue from the sending system to continue processing. On a message queue server, there is a service called the *queue manager*, whose purpose is to determine whether a message in the queue is supposed to be delivered to an application on its server or forwarded on to a different server. Again, using the analogy of e-mail, when you send a message to your e-mail server, it first determines whether the message you sent is to be delivered to a local user or forwarded to a different e-mail server.

Message queuing also provides a way to process transactions based on priority. Using the e-mail analogy, you can have messages sent with three different priority levels. The higher the message priority, the higher the message is placed in the queue. Unlike the messages you hear when you're on hold with technical support that "your call will be answered in the order in which it was received," the message queue processes based on priority.

When it comes to receiving a message from the message queue that your message was received and processed or that it was not completed, your application will need to periodically check the message queue for a return message. If we weren't using a message queue and we tried to receive a message from an empty queue, our application would stall and appear to be unresponsive. One of the core concepts of a message queue is that it guarantees delivery of messages on slow and unreliable networks, or from disconnected clients. Rather than the application constantly checking the message queue for a return message, the application waits for the message to arrive from the message queue. It's the message queue's responsibility to ensure that the return message is sent to the client application.

We've explained what message queuing is, but why is it important? There are several reasons:

- **Availability** Your organization might have a lot of systems and networks to interact with. We can't always assume that an application is going to be 24×7 (24 hours a day, 7 days a week). There are some systems that only process information nightly, and if you were processing information against a system that only worked on a nightly basis in a synchronous environment, you wouldn't get much work accomplished. By using message queues, you can send your requests to the queue to be processed at a later time, and you would receive an acknowledgement that your request had been processed. Also, as much as we'd like to think that our computers and network environment are bulletproof, the reality is that this isn't always the case. There will be times when the network connection is down, a server fails, and so on. With message queues, you can store all the transaction requests and process them when the system or network becomes available. With the increasing number of distributed environments, the failure rate of an entire environment multiplies. Using message queues gets around these problems.

- **Cost of system failure** As systems multiply and environments become more distributed, the cost of system failure and transaction recovery becomes more significant. Imagine how much the Home Shopping Network or stockbrokers would lose if their customers' transactions were lost due to a "hiccup" in the system? Also, when system failures occur, human intervention is often needed to resolve the failure and restart the system.
- **Mobile users** As the term "mobile" implies, these computer users are probably not connected to their networks at all times; therefore, they need to be able to process information in a disconnected manner in order to get their work completed. An example of a mobile user would be a traveling salesperson. Imagine how long it would take to enter orders if the salesperson needed to be connected at all times to enter orders—he or she would have to find a phone line to make a connection, put up with busy signals, and wait if the system was down or if network traffic was being drained because a department had engaged in a Quake II death-match.
- **Workload priorities** If a lot of low-priority transactions, like address changes, are being processed before higher-priority changes, like a transfer of funds from a client's holdings account to purchase stock in the IPO (initial public offering) of the next hot Internet stock, your clients will be very upset. In a traditional environment, most transactions are processed in a FIFO (first-in, first-out) manner. In the banking community, this is not always acceptable, because a lot of processing, such as payroll and mortgage payments, is now done electronically. For example, you may have direct-deposit with your employer and get paid the same day your mortgage payment is due. In a FIFO environment, the transaction that comes in first gets processed first. That means that if the mortgage-payment transaction comes in before your paycheck, your account might be overdrawn, which would subject you to late fees, overdraft charges, and so on. By adjusting message queue priorities, you can ensure that all credits to your customers' accounts occur before any debits.
- **Concurrency** As more and more systems become distributed, the number of users increases, and as the number of system connections increases, there will be increased concern that all the transactions occur in a timely and orderly manner. Another concern is that system response time and data be available when needed. A message queue can be used as an intermediary buffer for transactions. For example, in the case of trading stocks, there is a high need for systems to be available at all times and for the transactions to be committed to the system in real time (or its closest equivalent). If for some reason a server crashes or isn't processing fast enough, a message

queue will work as an intermediary buffer for transactions—open transactions aren't lost because they haven't been cleared out of the buffer, and new transactions can still be accepted. When the server comes back online, or when another server is freed up to handle the buffer, the transactions start processing again with no loss of information.

MTS, MSMQ, and Windows 2000

COM+ was built upon the blocks that COM started with, which includes MTS and MSMQ, which came on the NT Option Pack. COM+ combines all those elements into a single programming model that is integrated into Windows 2000. If you have applications that need to execute on Windows NT systems, or have clients that don't have access to Windows 2000 servers, many of the same development principles will apply.

COM+ and Visual Basic

When it comes to writing COM+ applications in Visual Basic, you will be surprised that you really don't have to learn a lot of new programming techniques, assuming you've already had experience programming MTS components. If you haven't built MTS components before, that's all right—you will when you build COM+ components. There are a few special objects that you will need to reference within your component to take advantage of COM+, but after that, the code between an MTS component and a COM+ component is essentially the same.

Creating a COM+ Component

A COM+ component isn't anything more than an ActiveX DLL with transaction facilities within it. The requirements are that it must be a self-registering DLL that exports the **DLLRegisterServer** and **DLLUnregisterServer** functions, and it must implement the entry points **DLLGetClassObject** and **DLLCanUnloadNow**. Additionally, the COM+ component must be created through a standard class factory object that implements the **IClassFactory** interface. Most development tools, such as Delphi, Visual Basic, and Visual C++, can create ActiveX DLLs that meet these requirements.

COM+ components also need to know the function names and parameter types for all interfaces implemented by a COM+ component. There are some restrictions with respect to the properties of the interfaces that are implemented by a COM+ component. The interface definition information must be provided in some kind of machine-readable form, so that COM+ can dynamically create the context wrapper object. The context wrapper object is what external clients see as the actual COM+ object.

A COM+ component's interfaces must be either Automation-compatible, in which case the COM+ object's type library provides the interface definition, or they must be standard-marshaled interfaces that use the fully interpreted marshaler, in which case the proxy/stub DLL provides the interface definition. Marshaling allows interfaces exposed by an object in one process to be used in another process.

This may sound like a lot of steps, but when you look at the code and read the comments in the code, you'll probably find that it's simpler than you think.

```
Public Sub Login(sID As String, sPassword As String, _
    vRecNames As Variant, vRecValues As Variant)

    Dim objContext As ObjectContext
    Set objContext = GetObjectContext()

    On Error GoTo err_Login

    Dim sSelect As String
    Dim sWhere As String

    sSelect = "fname, lname"
    sWhere = "StudentPIN = '" & PadStringWZeros(sID, 10) & "' "
    sWhere = sWhere & "AND Password = '" & sPassword & "' "

    GenericRead "DSN=dsnUVB;UID=admin;PWD=;", "tblStudent", _
        sSelect, sWhere, vRecNames, vRecValues

    objContext.SetComplete
    Exit Sub

err_Login:

    objContext.SetAbort

End Sub
```

You're probably looking at the code and thinking, "How is this any different from what I've normally done?" For the most part, your suspicions are correct—the code listed above is like any other transaction that you've done before, with one exception—it references the **ObjectContext** object model.

The sample code itself is a simple login procedure that verifies a user's access to a system. The routine starts by declaring the **objContext** to the **ObjectContext** object model. The **Set** statement obtains a reference to the **ObjectContext** object model that's associated with the current MTS object. The **ObjectContext** object model provides access to a single COM+ object, sometimes referred to as the *root object*. Once the root object has been instantiated, you can create additional objects, known as *enlisted objects*, which will run within the same context as the root object. By tying these objects together under a single **ObjectContext**, COM+ allows you to manage multiple transactions with multiple data sources through a single object interface. If a transaction fails within any enlisted object, the error is reported back to you via the **ObjectContext** interface. This interface triggers COM+ so if one part of the transaction fails, the entire transaction fails.

If the procedure executes without an error, the **ObjectContext** object variable, **objContext**, needs to be told that the transaction has completed successfully. Having **objContext** call the **SetComplete** method does this. This tells COM+ that the current enlisted object has completed its work, and that it should be deactivated when the currently executing method returns to the client application. For objects that are executing within the scope of a transaction, this is also an indication that the object's transactional updates can be committed to the database server.

In case an error occurs within this procedure, the flow of logic will go to the **err_Login** label. Within this subroutine, the **objContext** object variable calls the **SetAbort** method. You call the method within the error handler to ensure that the transaction aborts when the error occurs. If this is the root of the transaction, COM+ aborts the transaction. If this object is part of a unit of work, then the entire unit of work will be aborted, even if the previous components executed successfully.

COM+ Component Deployment

After you've created a COM+ component, it needs to be deployed to your Component Services console. The console is found under Component Services within the Administration Tools. Select the COM+ Applications tree item to review all the COM+ applications installed on your system, as shown in Figure 11-8.

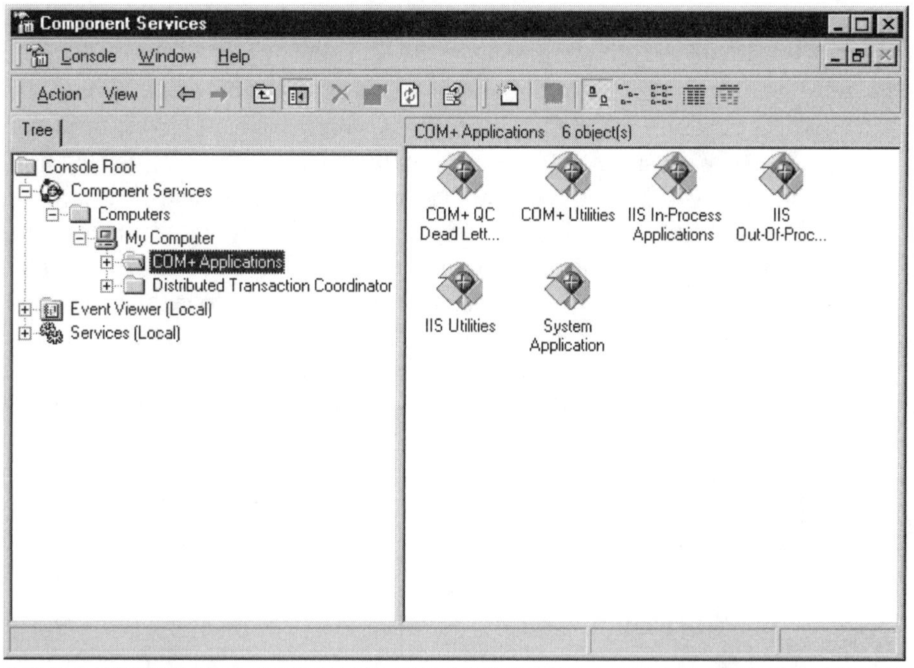

Figure 11.8 Component Services console displaying the COM+ Applications on the server

Note *If you're developing in Windows 9*x*, the console is called the Transaction Server Explorer, and in Windows NT it's the MTS Explorer contained with the Microsoft Management Console.*

A *package* in COM+ is a collection of one or more ActiveX DLL components. Each component can contain one or more classes, which are referred to as COM+ objects. A package can be defined as either a Server Package, which means its components will be activated in a dedicated server process, or a Library Package, which means they will be activated in the client's process. Putting these terms into VB perspective, a Server Package would be equivalent to an out-of-process server, and a Library Package would be equivalent to an in-process server.

Before you can use COM+ components within Component Services, you must first build and register the components as ActiveX DLLs. When you build an

ActiveX DLL from within the VB IDE, the components are automatically registered as COM components. This means that all of the Registry entries that identify the VB class modules as COM components are automatically created. This is why Version Compatibility is so important—it helps maintain COM Registry consistency. After the components have been registered as COM objects, you need to register them within the Component Services console.

When you register the package, it can be incorporated either through an empty application container or imported into an existing one. To either create a new entry or import an existing one, right-click on Component Services in the left-hand pane of the Component Services console, and then select New | Application from the context menu. Click the Next button to begin the creation process. Unfortunately, there isn't a way to deactivate the initial screen, so you'll always see the Welcome Wizard screen.

From the COM Application Installation Wizard, you can choose either Install Prebuilt Application(s), which is used to install COM+ applications into the Console, or Create an Empty Application, to create a new COM+ application into which you can install components. When installing packaged COM+ components, the wizard imports files that were created by the Windows Installer (.MSI) or MTS Package files (.PAK). If you choose Create an Empty Application, you are prompted for the COM+ application name, which is the name for the object container that will contain the COM+ components and roles.

Once the COM+ Application has been defined, you can add new components to the container, import ones that are already registered on the system, or install new event classes from an ActiveX DLL or type library. Add a New Component is used when you wish to install components that have not been installed and registered on the server. If you already have components registered on the server and encapsulated in other COM+ applications, you can import them into other COM+ applications for reusability.

Accessing a COM+ Component

Once you have a COM+ component installed in the Component Services console, you will want to reference the COM+ application. You instantiate the reference to the COM+ component the same way you would any other component on a remote server. Starting with version 6.0 of Visual Basic, the **CreateObject** function has the optional ability to accept arguments for the location of a remote server. Rather than having a stub of the component installed on the client system, you can specify the name of the server in which the COM+ component resides:

```
Dim objEnroll as Enrollment
Set objEnroll = CreateObject("COMApp.Enrollment", "ECTO1")
```

In this sample code, the **CreateObject** function references the **Enrollment** object within the **COMApp** component, but instead of referencing the object on the client's computer, the function references the object on the server called "ECTO1". Obviously, the names of your servers will vary.

Summary

Using a transaction server offers big advantages for developers building complex, distributed applications regardless of the application's user interface. Transactions allow you to build relatively complex procedures without having to worry about every detail of the transaction executing successfully or failing at one point.

COM+ is the next level of COM and MTS. In some ways, because MTS is now incorporated in the operating system, starting with Windows 2000, MTS doesn't really exist anymore. You no longer have to program components for the COM object model and the MTS object model. You just have to program for the COM+ object model. Remember, if you aren't using Windows 2000, but you are developing transaction-based applications, you should build your components using the COM+ object model specifications. COM+ is compatible with MTS and Windows NT.

CHAPTER 12

Package and Deploy

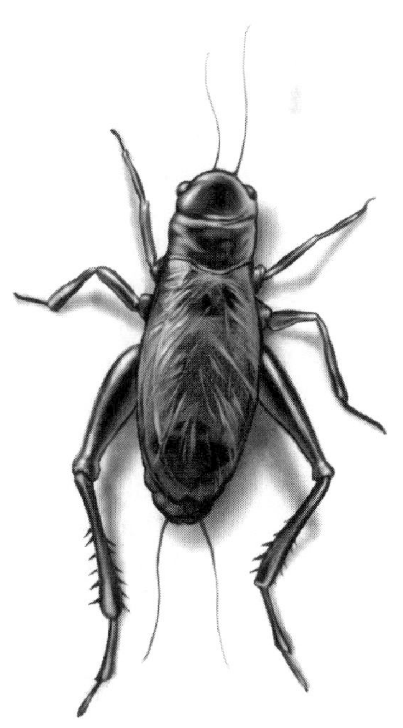

When it comes to distributing your application, creating a setup file and distributable media come to mind. In the early days of Visual Basic, there was the Setup Wizard, which was good for creating simple installation packages. There was also the Setup Toolkit that provided you with VB source code. You could customize the setup to specify where resources were to be installed and could identify whether additional resources needed to be installed, such as ODBC, and more.

The major drawbacks were that for each modification you did, you would have to save your modified setup source code into its own folder. Whenever you wanted to create a new "build" of the setup file, you would have to remember to copy the project into the Setup folder found within the folder that Visual Basic was installed to. Also, there wasn't any built-in version checking for components being installed, which meant you could install older versions of DLLs (dynamic-link libraries) and OCXs (ActiveX controls) onto your client's system. In addition, whenever Microsoft released a new service pack for Visual Basic and the Visual Studio suite, they often neglected to update the *dependency file* for the setup application, SETUP.DEP. A dependency file lists all the files and version numbers of all the resources that need to be distributed with a particular resource.

This became a problem when Microsoft modified their base DLLs for Windows. For example, when version 5.0 of Visual Basic was released, the MSVCRT40.DLL relied on only the Windows resource libraries (Kernel32, GDI, and User32). When Microsoft released the first Windows 95 service pack, the MSVCRT40.DLL relied on an additional resource, MSVCRT.DLL. Therefore, prior to the Windows 95 service pack, developers only needed to ship their applications with MSVCRT40.DLL. If the developer installed the Windows 95 service pack and created a setup file, the creation of the setup file would be successful, but when the application got installed on a client's system, they would have received an error that the MSVCRT.DLL is missing. You might think that Microsoft or you could just update the dependency file and everything would be all right, but prior to version 6.0, this file was a binary file, so developers could not modify it. Dependency files are now stored as ASCII files that developers can modify if necessary.

Due to all these problems, a number of third-party installation tools, such as InstallShield and Wise InstallMaster, were created. They allowed developers to create setup scripts for each application and to include other installation programs with the main application to ensure that all dependent components were distributed, and, most importantly, they also had component version control capability. Component version control capability ensures that when your program is installed on a client's computer, it does not overwrite a newer DLL with an older one. This is what the software industry calls "DLL Hell" and this topic is discussed in greater detail later in this chapter. Today, with the Package and Deployment Wizard, many developers still rely on these third-party tools to distribute their software.

Microsoft Package and Deployment Wizard

A tool that comes with version 6.0 of Visual Basic is the Package and Deployment Wizard. If it is installed, it can be found under the Visual Studio 6.0 Tools item in the Start folder. It's a tool that helps you create setup packages for your Visual Basic applications, replacing the old Setup Wizard and Setup Toolkit. The Setup Toolkit still shops with Visual Basic, but they've made the Setup Wizard more intelligent, so you don't have to modify the source VB code contained within the Setup1 subfolder of the PDWizard folder. In addition, it allows you to create deployment packages for applications that are to be distributed via the Internet or a company's intranet. Lastly, it allows you to create dependency files for your ActiveX components.

Unlike the previous setup tools that came with VB, the Package and Deployment Wizard allows you to create a single setup executable or it can create a Setup executable that relies on multiple compressed cabinet (.CAB) files that can be copied onto floppies. In previous versions of the Setup Wizard, you could not save any of the changes you made during the setup process. You would have to remember what you did to ensure that each distribution script was the same from build to build. With the Package and Deployment Wizard, you can save your settings as scripts that you can reuse if you need to package or deploy the same application again.

In case you were wondering why the wizard is called the Package and Deployment Wizard, rather than the traditional Setup Wizard and Setup Toolkit, it is to get developers to start thinking of their Visual Basic programs as not just applications but as components of a complete solution. A complete solution is built upon packages of objects—thus the use of the term "package." Also, distribution of an application is only a facet of a solution—you are now "deploying" applications and components across the enterprise in the form of business components, applications with a graphical user interface, or components to be deployed in the Microsoft Transaction Server (MTS).

Creating a Package

To create a setup package, use the Package and Deployment Wizard by either selecting it from the Windows Start menu or by selecting it from the Add-ins menu found in the VB IDE. If you select it from the Windows Start menu, choose the project you want to distribute and click the Package button. If you select it from the Add-ins menu, the project you are creating the package for needs to be the active project in the IDE. The wizard checks to make sure that the project has been compiled into an EXE or DLL. If the compiled file's date and time stamp is different from the date and time stamps of any file within the project, you will receive a warning message like the one shown in Figure 12-1. You will be asked if you want to recompile your application or continue.

The wizard performs a quick scan of the project for any VB run-time modules, components, and their dependencies that need to be distributed with the application. After the scan, you will be prompted for the type of package to create, which can be either a *standard setup package* or a *dependency file*. A standard setup package is a package that can be used to create a single SETUP.EXE program to install an application, rather than have it building a small SETUP.EXE stub that is downloaded through a browser with the content of the application residing on a Web or FTP server. A dependency file lists information about the run-time components required by your application. When prompted to select a package type, select Standard Setup Package.

Setting Up a Standard Setup Package

When you build a standard setup package, you might encounter some problems during the process. For the most part, these are merely warnings that the wizard couldn't find everything it was expecting to find. The first rule to remember is

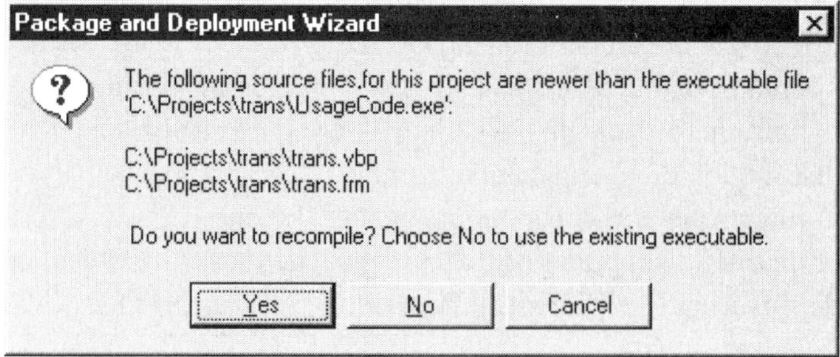

Figure 12.1 Sample error indicating that some files within the project are more current than the compiled program

not to panic. It is still possible that the package will be built correctly. However, there are some potential problems and warning messages you should be aware of, such as missing files, missing dependency information, and out-of-date dependency information. Once those potential problems have been dealt with, you can continue on with the wizard and finish creating the setup package.

Missing Files A common warning message is the Missing Files dialog box, shown in Figure 12-2. You will receive this warning message if the wizard can't find a file on your system that it determined was necessary for the package. You can try to find the file by using the Browse button on the dialog box. Or, if you determine that the file isn't necessary, you can proceed to the next step by clicking OK. Otherwise, you will need to find the file to ensure that your package will install correctly and the application will execute.

Missing Dependency Information When you encounter the Missing Dependency Information dialog box, shown in Figure 12-3, the dialog box will display the components that are missing DEP files. This occurs when the wizard cannot find the dependency files for the ActiveX components used by the project. There are occasions when independent software vendors (ISVs) don't include DEP files with their components. If you have the source code for the ActiveX component, you can use the Package and Deployment Wizard to create the dependency information file yourself. Otherwise, you will need to make sure that you're distributing the correct dependency files with your application.

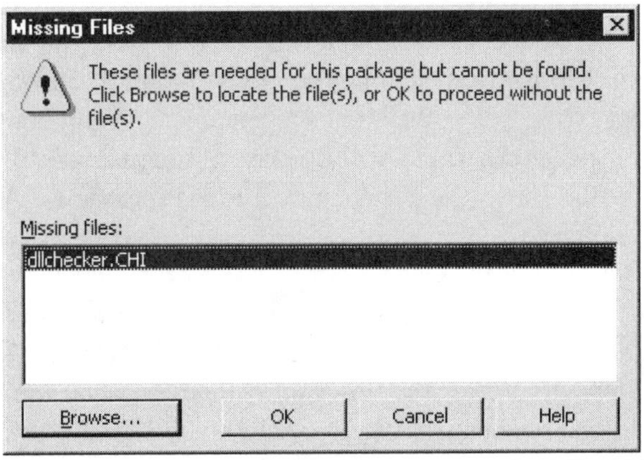

Figure 12.2 Missing Files dialog box

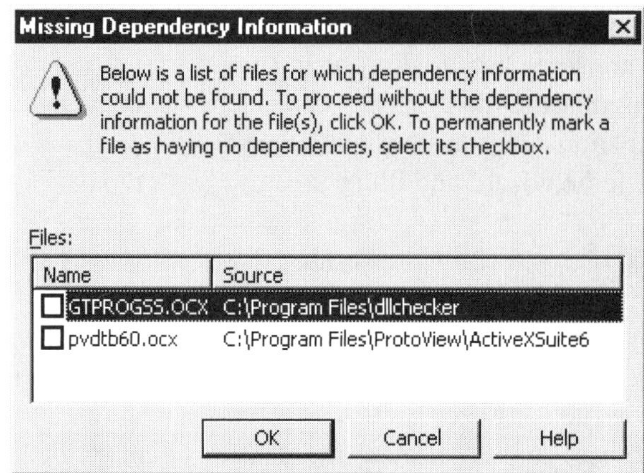

Figure 12.3 Missing Dependency Information dialog box

With the Professional and Enterprise editions of Visual Basic and Visual Studio, there is a tool called Dependency Walker that displays the files that a selected program or resource relies on. It is found under the COMMON\TOOLS folder on the CD that you used to install Visual Basic. There are three files that you need:

- DEPENDS.EXE, the executable
- DEPENDS.HLP, the online help file
- DEPENDS.CNT, the help files index

To use the Dependency Walker, select the file you want to find the dependency information for from within Windows Explorer, and right-click to bring up the context menu. Select the View Dependencies menu item to launch the Dependency Walker program, which will display all the resource files the chosen file uses. Figure 12-4 shows the dependency list for ProtoView's ActiveX DataTable control.

Design Tip *Steve Miller of Microsoft has updated the Dependency Walker, and it includes a feature that allows you to profile your program as it executes. This means you can execute a program and watch how it interacts with its run-time dependency files. That version of the program can be found on the Dependency Walker Web site, http://www.dependencywalker.com.*

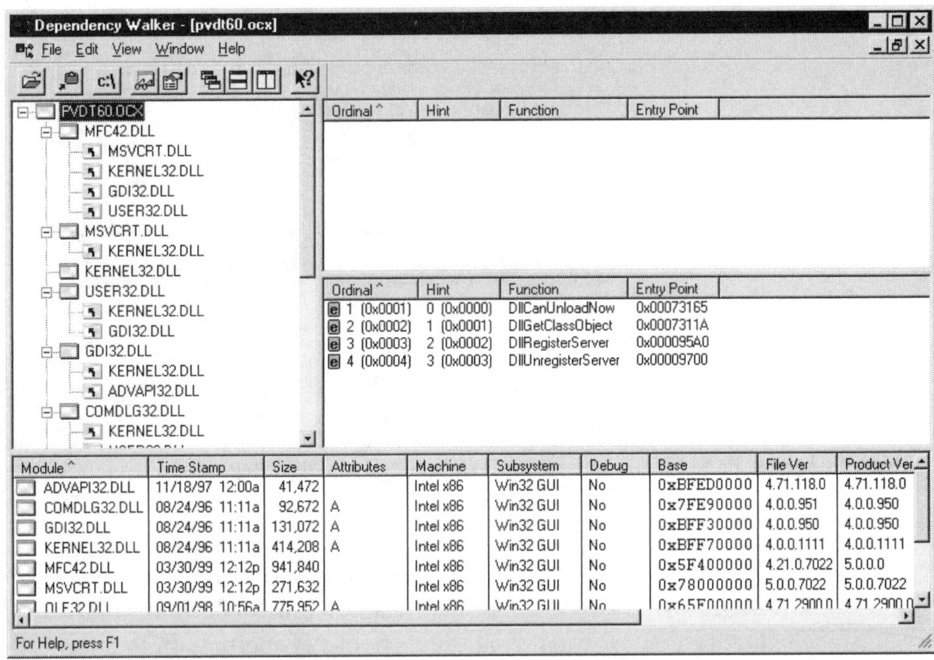

Figure 12.4 Dependency Walker information for ProtoView's ActiveX DataTable control

Design Tip *Another tool that can help you view the file dependencies is a freeware utility called PESX. When you view the properties of a DLL, EXE, or OCX, you will see a Dependencies tab that displays the dependencies of the file. If you want to download the program, it can be found on Johannes Plachy's Win32 Tools Page at http://www.jps.at/win32tools.html.*

Out-of-Date Dependency Information Every so often an ISV will update a resource file and the files it is dependent on and will forget to update the dependency information file. When this occurs, you will see an Out-of-Date Dependency Information dialog box, like the one shown in Figure 12-5. Most dependency information files (.DEP) are standard text files, and they can be edited with a line editor like Windows Notepad.

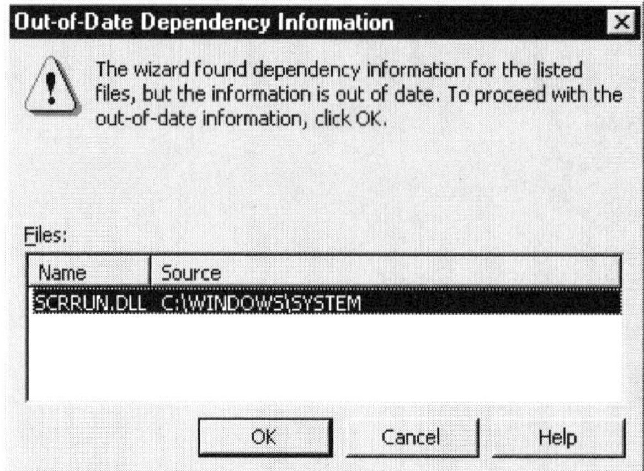

Figure 12.5 Out-of-Date Dependency Information dialog box

As an example, we will use the filename shown in Figure 12-5, which is SCRRUN.DLL. To view the file's version information, right-click the file to display the context menu, and then choose Properties. In the Properties dialog box, select the Version tab to display the version information of the file. In this example, the version of the SCRRUN.DLL is 5.0.0.3715, as shown in Figure 12-6. According to the SCRRUN.DEP file, listed next, it is expecting to use version 4.0.0.2926:

```
; Dependency file for setup wizards.
[Version]
Version=4.0.0.2926
; Dependencies for ScrRun.DLL
; Default Dependencies
----------------------------------------------
[scrrun.dll]
Dest=$(WinSysPath)
Register=$(DLLSelfRegister)
Version=4.0.0.2926
Uses1=MSVCRT.dll
CABFileName=ScrRun.cab
CABDefaultURL=http://activex.microsoft.com/controls/vb6
CABINFFile=ScrRun.inf
```

This listing was taken from the SCRRUN.DEP file. It contains the version information for the control, any files that it is dependent on (under the Uses1 line item), and where an updated copy of the file can be downloaded from, either on a shared network server or a Web server.

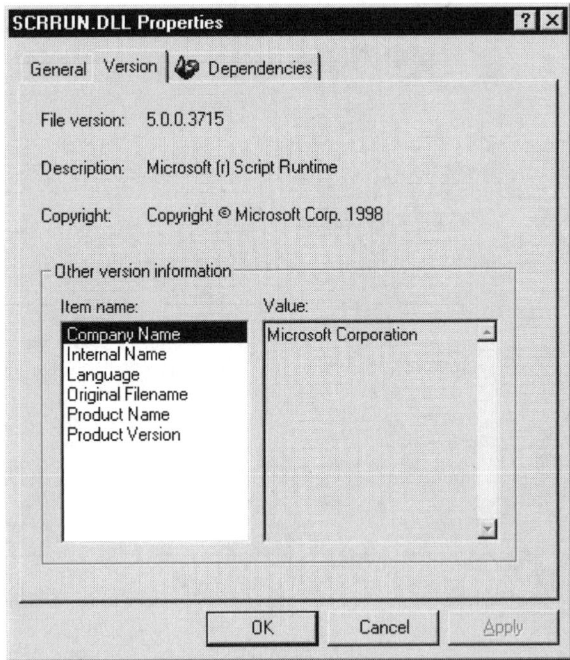

Figure 12.6 Properties window displaying the version information for SCRRUN.DLL

Included Files When the Included Files dialog box appears, as shown in Figure 12-7, the listed files are to be included in the setup package. The list is generated from files listed in the Visual Basic project (VBP) file, resources that are referenced within the project itself, and run-time modules that are to be distributed with every program.

You can check or uncheck any file at this point. Files that should always be checkmarked to be included are listed in Table 12-1. If a file fails to appear in the list, you can always add it by clicking the Add button and browsing for it on your system.

24x7

Make sure that all your component's dependency information is up-to-date. Otherwise, your application will not work correctly when installed on your client's computers.

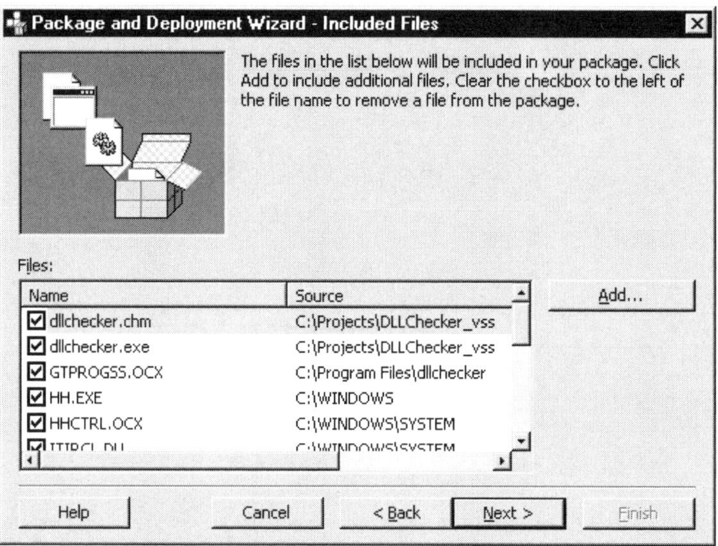

Figure 12.7 Included files for the package

Install Locations In the Install Locations dialog box, shown in Figure 12-8, you can choose the folder into which you will install your files. The descriptions of the locations are explained in Table 12-2.

Filename	File Description
SETUP.EXE	Main program to pre-install files that are needed for an application to be installed on the user's machine, like the SETUP1.EXE and VB Run-time DLL
SETUP1.EXE	The setup program that installs the VB application
ST6UNST.EXE	Uninstall program
VB6 Runtime and OLE Automation	VB run-time and OLE resources
VB6STKIT.DLL	The resource that contains functions used by SETUP1.EXE

Table 12.1 Files That Should Always Be Included Within a Setup Package

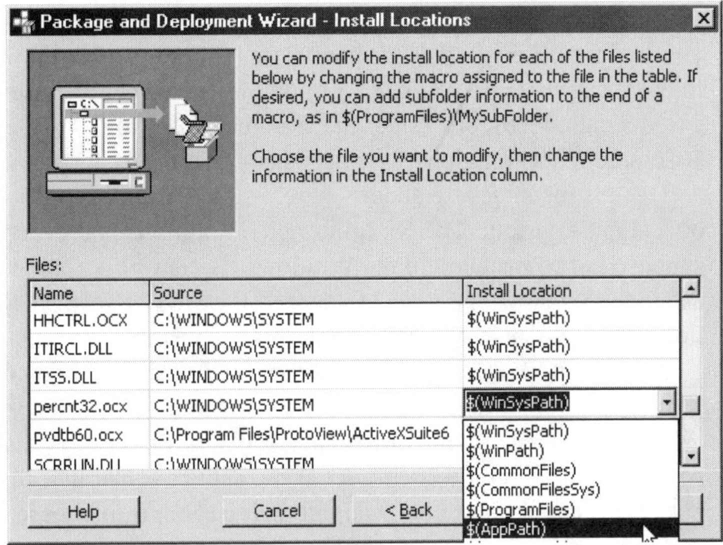

Figure 12.8 Installation Locations dialog box

Location	Description
$(AppPath)	The folder where the application is to be installed
$(ProgramFiles)	The Program Files folder
$(CommonFiles)	The Program Files\Common Files folder
$(CommonFilesSys)	The Program Files\Common Files\System folder
$(WinPath)	The Windows folder (WinNT folder for Windows NT and 2000 systems)
$(WinSysPath)	The Windows\System folder
$(MSDAOPath)	The folder where the Microsoft Data Access Object components were installed
$(Font)	The Windows\Fonts folder (WinNT folder for Windows NT and 2000 systems)

Table 12.2 Descriptions of the Installation Locations

You are not limited to the locations shown in the drop-down list box. You can use the Install Location drop-down items as a starting point and enter additional folder locations. For example, you might want to put all your resource files in a folder called Sandbox under the Common Files folder. To do this, select the $(CommonFiles) location, place the cursor after the location, and type in **\Sandbox**.

There is much debate about where resource files are supposed to be installed on a client's system. The common rule of thumb is that every resource file is supposed to be installed in the Windows\System folder for Windows 9*x* systems and in the Windows\System32 folder on Windows NT and 2000 systems. However, this philosophy has been rethought over the years.

Prior to Windows 2000 and Windows Millennium Edition (Me), developers placed only Windows system resources or commonly used resource files in the Windows\System folder. If a resource file didn't fall under this category, it was to be placed either in the same folder as the application or in a common folder for the ISV. For example, Adobe would put their custom resources in an Adobe folder under \Program Files\Common Files. All Adobe products that required resources other than system resources would know to find them in the Adobe folder.

With Windows 2000 and Windows Millennium (Me), Microsoft is recommending that only resource files that pertain to the operating system belong in the Windows\System folder. They are doing this to protect the core resource files so an older version doesn't overwrite them, which is one of the most common reasons for system crashes. Starting with Office 2000, Microsoft started to adopt this policy and put all resource files specific to Office 2000 in a Microsoft shared folder in the \Program Files\Common Files folder.

Note *The Windows\System folder on Windows NT and 2000 systems is for 16-bit resource files.*

Shared Files In the Shared Files dialog box, shown in Figure 12-9, you can check resource and executable files that you want to install as shared files. Shared files are files that can be used by more than one program. For example, SCRRUN.DLL is a resource file that can be used by a lot of programs, so it is marked as a shared file. Files that are marked as shared can only be removed if every program that uses them is removed.

Setting Up a Dependency Package

When you develop applications and resource files within Visual Basic, you will want to build a dependency package for them. This way, you can avoid encountering the Missing Dependency Information dialog box when you build a standard setup package. The Package and Deployment Wizard can create a

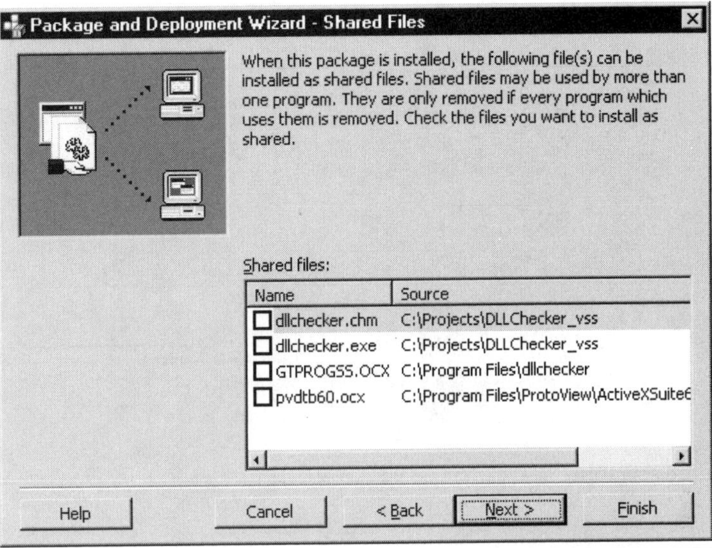

Figure 12.9 Shared Files dialog box

dependency package for any VB project. If you want to create a dependency package for a program or resource file you don't have the project for, you will need to use a third-party installation program, such as InstallShield or Wise InstallMaster.

To create a dependency package, you go through a lot of the same steps as creating a standard setup package. When the wizard's dialog window prompts you for the package type you wish to make, select Dependency file. For the dependency package you will need to add the Cab information. In the Cab Information Screen dialog box, shown in Figure 12-10, you can indicate that you want to include the dependency file in a cab for dependency on the Web. To include the dependency file in a cab, you must provide its name and a URL from which it can be retrieved. In the File to Execute field, the file indicated must be either an EXE or INF file.

24x7

Components your application relies upon need to be installed only once. If the setup program detects a newer version of the component on the user's computer than identified in the dependency package, it will not install the older version.

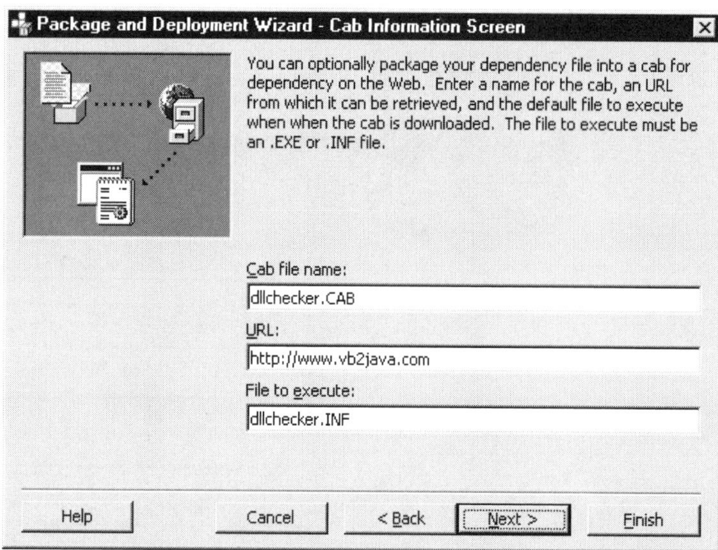

Figure 12.10 Cab Information Screen dialog box

Deploying the Application

The Package and Deployment Wizard can use three methods to deploy an application after it has been packaged. They can either be deployed on removable media, such as floppy disks or a CD-ROM, on a folder (local or network), or through a Web site.

The last question the wizard asks you when creating a setup package is whether you want to build your setup files into a single cab file or multiple cab files. The name *cab* is short for cabinet and it's a Microsoft compression method to package multiple files into a single file. When deploying the application through floppy disks, you must select Multiple Cabs in the Cabs option when building your standard package. You can choose 720KB, 1.2MB, 1.44MB or 2.88MB. With all the dependent files that a VB application relies on, an application that is going to be deployed on floppy disks will never fit onto a single diskette. To deploy the cab on a CD-ROM, you should select the Single Cab option.

Select the Deploy button on the Package and Deployment Wizard to copy the setup files to a particular destination. You are prompted to choose the package

24x7

When deploying an application via floppy disks, you should always format them before using them. Even if the manufacturer has preformatted them, you should reformat them to ensure that the media is good. The last thing you want is to ship your application and have it not install due to corrupted media.

name you wish to deploy. The names it lists come from the package names you provided when creating a package. If you choose to create the package using multiple cab files, you can choose to deploy your files on floppy disks, local or network folders, or to a Web server. If your package was set for deployment in a single cab file, you can only distribute it through a folder or Web server.

Distributing your application on floppies is a bit passé, but there are some software developers that would rather ship their program on a few floppies than copy a 2MB file on a CD-ROM. The wizard gives you the option of formatting each disk before you copy your cab files to it. If you don't format the disk, you need to make sure that the disk is empty; therefore, it's a good idea to format the disk regardless of whether it's empty or not.

Folder deployment basically copies the contents of the Package folder to any location on an accessible hard drive or network server. This method is typically used when you're copying an application to a shared resource, or if you want to copy the contents to a CD-ROM. After all, CD-ROMs are easier to duplicate than floppy disks.

Web-based deployment provides you with the ability to upload the contents of the package to a URL on a Web server. This method makes it easy for components to be accessed by IIS and DHTML applications that depend on them.

24x7

Make sure that when you deploy your program to a network server, the target audience has access to the server. Developers often have access to more network resources than clients do.

24x7

In order to upload your package to the Microsoft Internet Information Server (IIS), you need to have the Posting Acceptor installed on the server, which is included in the NT Option Pack. For more information, check out the Microsoft Knowledgebase articles Q192116 and Q192639.

Troubleshooting Installed Components

With an intranet or Internet application, if an installed component has become corrupted and is causing application problems, it should be removed from the system and either updated or reinstalled. To update the component, go to the client's Windows\Downloaded Program Files folder (or the Windows\OCCache folder on some systems). This folder lists all the components installed by intranet and Internet applications. To update the component, right-click it to display the context menu and select the Update menu item. Windows will use the CodeBase property of the component to check to see if an updated component is available. If one is not available, no action will be performed; otherwise the newer version will be installed.

When a component is corrupted and a newer version is not available, Windows will not install a "clean" version of the component because it only checks the version information of the component to see if it is out of date. It doesn't check to see if the component is working correctly or not. In this case, you should remove and reinstall the component. To remove the component, right-click the file and select Remove from the context menu. When you launch the intranet or Internet application and it finds that the component is missing, Windows will download the missing component and reinstall it.

Design Tip *When deploying intranet or Internet applications, provide an accessible site on the network where run-time and support files can be stored. This gives you more control over the file versions that get installed on your customers' systems.*

Error Watch *If errors in an intranet or Internet application occur as the result of a corrupted installed component, go to the Windows\Downloaded Program Files folder (or Windows\OCCache folder) and use the context menu to either remove or update the component.*

"DLL Hell"

In the beginning, programs were self-contained within one executable file. As applications became more complex, they might consist of several executable files that were chained one to another. One thing, however, was certain. The executables that accompanied a particular application could be used only by that application. For most programs, software vendors would distribute all of the files used by that program without being concerned that other products might interfere with theirs.

As years passed, the size of application files grew dramatically. The Windows operating system took advantage of a capability called dynamic linking to allow code modules to be shared by applications. The most important demonstration of the use of this capability is Windows itself—the code modules that contain the functions that make Windows work (the Windows API) are shared by all Windows applications. A code module that can be shared in this way is called a *dynamic link library* and it normally has the .DLL extension.

Initially, the sharing of such files was not a problem. Most applications only used the Windows system DLLs, or "private" DLLs. As the Windows operating system evolved, Microsoft began to create additional DLLs that were designed to be shared amongst their own applications, and to design others that were to be used by all Windows programs. These DLLs contain groups of functions that provide a standard functionality, eliminating the need for each application to implement that functionality independently.

One of the best examples of these DLLs is COMMDLG.DLL, the common dialog library. This DLL contains a group of common dialog boxes that can be used by any Windows application to perform standard operations, such as obtaining a filename, choosing a font, or customizing a printer.

This made it easier for developers to concentrate on their applications and its features, rather than worrying about how their program would work on their client's computers. By making reusable resource libraries, applications would have a common look and feel.

Through the years, as application developers started to understand how to properly use DLLs as a source of reusable code, the sheer number of DLLs deployed with applications increased. As the number of DLLs increased, so did application problems. These problems came about due to the following reasons:

- Older DLLs overwriting newer ones
- Duplicate DLLs on a system
- Same name, different purpose

Older DLLs Overwriting Newer Ones

One of Microsoft's standards for DLLs was that developers needed to ship all DLLs used with their applications because you couldn't be sure whether the client would have the ones your application needs on their system. Another Microsoft standard was that all DLLs should reside in the System folder where Windows is installed. Unfortunately, Microsoft never enforced good versioning standards in their operating system, which meant that every software company would distribute the DLLs with their distribution diskettes, but the installation would and did overwrite any existing DLLs that were already on the customer's system, regardless of whose version was the most current.

If the versions of the DLLs were the same, there wouldn't be a problem because it would be replaced with the exact same version. Problems would occur when older DLLs overwrote newer ones. DLLs contain a library of reusable code, and a newer version usually has more functions than the previous one. When a program references a DLL function, and that function isn't there because the DLL has been replaced with an older version, you get an error. That's what 99 percent of the Windows errors relate to.

To resolve the problem of older DLLs overwriting newer ones, applications that had their setup packages made with the Package and Deployment Wizard had component version control built in. Component version control prevents older DLLs from overwriting newer ones because it checks the DLL version number that is embedded in the DLL.

Starting with Windows 2000 and Windows Millennium Edition (Me), Microsoft no longer wants developers to place any DLLs in the System folder. They want to reserve the System folder for resource files that pertain only to the operating system. Regardless of the Windows operating system you're using, if you develop your own DLLs or reusable components, Microsoft wants developers to start placing them in their own directory under the Common Files folder within the Program Files folder.

Duplicate DLL Problems

A technique a lot of independent software vendors (ISVs) use for deploying DLLs and reusable components with their applications is to place the files within the folder the application is installed into. They did this whether the file existed on the system or not; it was their way to avoid overwriting an existing DLL. This causes a new problem—duplicate DLLs. With duplicate DLLs, it's difficult to know what version of the DLL is being used. Is the latest version being used or an outdated one? Because all ISVs didn't adhere to the same installation process, your computer can contain a large amount of duplicate DLL files and this could be the cause of many unexplained errors.

The primary areas to check for duplicate DLLs are in the \Windows\System folder and the program's own local folder. Some DLLs may also be duplicated in \Windows\Sysbckup—this is for safety purposes, and because they are usually the same versions as those in the \Windows\System folder, they can be ignored.

The most common causes of DLL conflicts are in the six groups of DLLs that begin with the letters identified in Table 12-3.

Begins with	Example Files	Description
BW	BWCC.DLL	Borland Windows Custom Control
COM	COMCAT.DLL	Microsoft Component Category Manager Library
	COMCT232.OCX	Microsoft Custom Control 2 ActiveX Control DLL
	COMCT332.OCX	Microsoft Custom Control 3 ActiveX Control DLL
	COMCTL16.DLL, COMCTL32.DLL, COMCTL32.OCX	Microsoft Custom Control Library
	COMDLG16.DLL, COMDLG32.DLL, COMDLG16,OCX, COMDLG32.OCX,	Common Dialogs DLL
	COMPOBJ.DLL	OLE Interoperability Library
CTL	CTL3D.DLL, CTL3D32.DLL, CTL3D321.DLL, CTL3D95.DLL, CTL3DNT.DLL, CTL3DV2.DLL	3D Windows Control
MFC	MFC30.DLL, MFC40.DLL, MFC42.DLL	Microsoft Foundation Class Shared Library
MSV	MSVBVM50.DLL, MSVBVM60.DLL	Visual Basic Virtual Machine
	MSVCIRT.DLL, MSVCRT.DLL, MSVCRT10.DLL, MSVCRT20.DLL, MSVCRT40.DLL	Microsoft Visual C++ Runtime Library
OLE	OLE2.DLL, OLE2DISP.DLL, OLE32.DLL, OLEAUT32.DLL, OLEPRO32.DLL	Microsoft OLE for Windows and Windows NT
	OLEDB32.DLL	OLE DB Core DLL

Table 12.3 The Six Most Common Groups of Duplicate DLLs

For the most part, none of the other DLLs really cause much of a problem because the ones listed are the most commonly used by developers.

To find the duplicate DLLs, you can use the Find feature of Windows Explorer, VB2Java.Com's DLL Checker, or a similar program. After the search is complete, look at the alphabetized list of DLLs. The most recent version belongs in the \Windows\System folder (or Windows\System32 folder, if you're using Windows NT or 2000), where it will be available to any program that needs it. You don't need to be too concerned with duplicates in local program folders if there isn't a copy in \Windows\System. The only time these duplicates might possibly cause a problem is if two different programs tried to use their respective DLLs at the same time. If this is the case, first determine whether they are in fact the same DLL from the same company. If so, you should copy the most current version into the \Windows\System folder and rename the older version. The situation of the two DLLs not really being the same is discussed in the "Same Name, Different Purpose" section, a little later in this chapter.

One DLL in Memory at a Time

With all the different versions of DLLs out there, how does Windows know which one to use? When a program loads, all the DLLs it uses get loaded into memory. Here are the steps that Windows goes through when loading a program that requires DLL files:

1. Check to see if the DLLs the program needs are already loaded in memory
2. Check the folder the program is launched from for any DLLs it needs
3. Check the Windows\System folder for any DLLs it needs
4. Check the PATH statement for any DLLs it needs

Once a DLL is loaded in memory, it stays in memory until it is no longer needed. If another program requires the same DLL, it goes through the same steps, regardless of whether the second program requires a newer version or not. When Windows loads a DLL into memory, it loads the first one it can find, based on the steps above. A good majority of your Windows problems will be due to the fact that the DLL loaded in memory does not have all the features and functions that the program that is calling it requires.

To resolve this problem, it's best to only have one copy of the DLL on your system and to keep it in the System folder in the Windows folder. To find the duplicate files, use the Find feature of Windows Explorer and search for any of the six groups of DLLs described earlier in Table 12-3. Once you have found them, determine the latest version by checking the file's property page. To access the file's property page, right-click the file and select Properties from the context menu. In the Properties dialog window, select the Version tab to display the file's version number. Once you've determined the newest version, make sure it's in the System folder. If the version in the System folder is older, you should rename the file to something like *filename.D_L*, where *filename* is the name of the file, and use an underscore as the middle letter of "DLL". This will prevent Windows from using that file. After renaming it, copy the latest file into the System folder.

If Windows does not allow you to rename the file or copy the file, it's possible that the file is being used by the operating system. When this happens, you will have to rename and copy the files from a DOS prompt. It should be a real DOS prompt, not a DOS window from within Windows.

It's recommended that you rename and copy the files rather than delete and move them. This is for safety reasons—yours in particular. If you've never dealt with DLL Hell in this manner, or if this is completely new to you, you really want to tread lightly. By renaming and copying, you can always go back to the way your system was by undoing what you did. If you deleted a file, you might not be able to restore your system properly. Programs like VB2Java.Com's DLL Checker make this process a lot more straightforward.

Same Name, Different Purpose

As improbable as it may seem, there might be an occasion when you encounter multiple DLLs with the same name, but that are not really the same DLL. Any of the following situations might be the case:

- The DLLs are developed by one company but they serve two different functions altogether.
- The DLLs are developed by two different companies.
- The DLLs belong to two different operating systems.

24x7

When dealing with duplicate DLLs, it's best to rename and copy files instead of deleting and moving them. You can always undo a rename and copy. It's difficult to undelete a file once data has been moved.

Same Company, Different Function

Sometimes when independent software vendors (ISVs) write programs for international distribution, they may use the same DLL name for their components for each language they are writing for. For example, Microsoft (who else would we identify?) develops their Windows operating system for different countries in different languages. Instead of writing their entire operating system for each language, they use a DLL to contain all the language resources. The SHDOCLC.DLL file is the Shell Doc Object and Control Library DLL, and different versions of it will exist in different languages.

Same Name, Different Company

As improbable as it may seem, occasionally an ISV will name their DLL with the same name as someone else's DLL. This is rare, but it does happen. If the ISV is good, they will have loaded their DLL in their application's folder, and not the Windows System folder. Only DLLs that are to be shared by other applications should be placed in the Windows System folder.

Belongs to Two Different Operating Systems

A lot of developers write their software on Windows NT and now Windows 2000, even if their target audience's operating system is Windows 9*x*. They do this because Windows NT and 2000 are a bit more stable due to their subsystem architectures. Windows NT and 2000 aren't crash-proof, but each application runs in its own memory space as a subsystem, and if the application crashes, only the subsystem is affected, and not the entire operating system.

Since development is done on Windows NT and 2000, the distribution files are also built on that system. The problem with this scenario is that a DLL may be specific to an operating system. For example, Microsoft's CTL3D.DLL (and its cousins CTL3DV2.DLL and CTL3D32.DLL) seems to fall in this category. It's used by older applications to display screen elements in 3-D, where the controls in some windows look "carved" out. The problem is that some versions were developed specifically for Windows 95 and others for Windows NT. The kicker is that the version numbers, descriptions, and dates are all identical. The only obvious difference is that one file is 1K bigger than the other. The application will still work, but every time the application launches, your client will receive an error that the DLL does not belong to the operating system and that it may affect your application's performance. InstallShield and Wise InstallMaster have included script switches to prevent these problems from happening.

24x7

Microsoft has compiled a database accessible through the Web that contains version information on the most popular DLL files. This site is called the Microsoft DLL Help database and it can be reached at http://support.microsoft.com/servicedesks/fileversion/dllinfo.asp.

Windows Installer

The Windows Installer is a software deployment process that was first introduced with Microsoft Office 2000. It's an installation process that uses a custom database you build for each application. Rather than building a Setup executable, you distribute a .MSI database file. This file contains all the application settings, files, and conditions that have to be met in order to install the application. If you've used Microsoft's System Management Server (SMS), you will be somewhat familiar with this software deployment technique. As a matter of fact, the MSI database file that the Windows Installer creates can be used with an SMS script to deploy the program.

The best part of this installation technology is that the applications become self-healing. If any file relevant to the application gets corrupted or deleted, Windows will automatically reinstall the file when you attempt to launch the program, thereby eliminating the common "Problem with Shortcut" error or the problem when the file needed to run the program is not where it is expected to be.

The Windows Installer allows you to perform just-in-time (JIT) installations. This allows you to install components for an application when the user first executes it. For example, when you install Microsoft Office 2000, you may have only installed just the basic applications, such as Word, Excel, and PowerPoint. You probably didn't install any of the applets, because the average user doesn't use them. If you want to use an applet like Org Chart or Formula Writer, you would have to rerun Office Setup, select the missing features, and reboot the system. With the JIT installation, the options are available for the user to select, but they aren't installed—Installer will install the components onto the client's system when they are needed. As soon as it has completed that task, the component is ready for use. The caveat is that the image MSI file needs to be accessible. The Office CD needs to be in the CD drive, on the network, or on a partition of the hard drive.

With the Windows Installer becoming part of the operating system, it allows you, as a developer, to focus on the custom elements of your application rather than how to deploy your application. The Windows Installer can be downloaded from the Microsoft MSDN Web site at http://msdn.microsoft.com/vstudio/downloads/vsi/default.asp.

Summary

The Package and Deployment Wizard is a great tool for building distribution packages for your application. It is superior to previous versions of the Setup Wizard and Setup Toolkit. It makes packages for distribution and takes into consideration that you need a way to deploy the packages as well. Despite the fact that it's a good tool, if you want to distribute your application on a commercial level, you might want to consider using one of the two leading third-party installation programs. After all, even Microsoft uses them to install their applications.

With that said, the new Windows Installer that has been released is definitely something to look into. It has definitely taken software installation to the next level by helping reduce the total cost of ownership for clients by enabling them to efficiently install, configure, and maintain the applications you develop. If you plan to deploy applications that are going to be Windows 2000–logo products, using the Windows Installer is one of the criteria you need to adhere to. If you use third-party installation programs, such as InstallShield or Wise InstallMaster, they offer versions that are compatible with Microsoft's Window Installer.

PART III

VBA and Automation

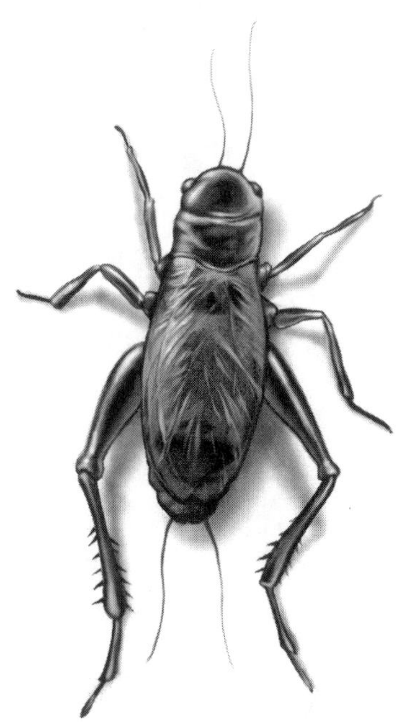

CHAPTER 13

Microsoft Office Integration

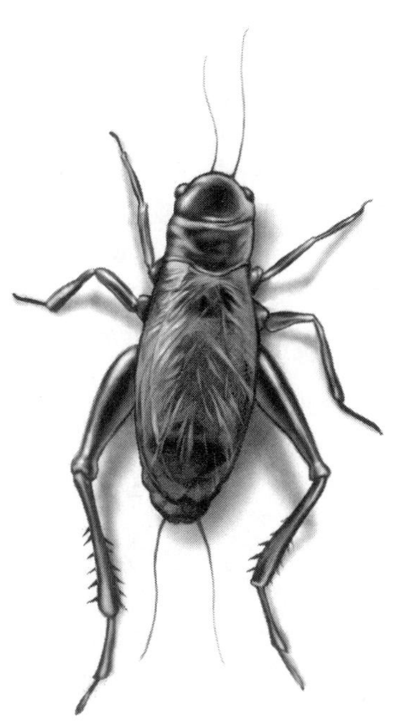

Automation has been formally defined as a data communication protocol for applications meeting the Component Object Model (COM) specification. In plainer English, Automation allows one application to access another application's information and functionality.

Of course, just having applications purposelessly talk to each other would be no more than the computer-programming equivalent of the biblical Tower of Babel. The promise of Automation is that you can enable your applications to access databases, calculate formulas, write reports, and send e-mail without having to reinvent the wheel and write code for accessing databases, calculating formulas, writing reports, and sending e-mail. Instead, through Automation, you can access existing applications that already have that functionality. For example, using Automation, a book publisher's Visual Basic application can direct Microsoft Access to retrieve the authors' book sales from information stored in a database, command Microsoft Excel to apply a formula to this sales information to calculate royalties, order Microsoft Word to put the sales and royalty figures in a report, and finally instruct Microsoft Outlook to e-mail the report to the authors.

Automation enables you to extend the functionality of your custom applications by using the preexisting and powerful functionality of other applications, such as those in the Microsoft Office suite. Not surprisingly, much has been written on how to manipulate the rich functionality of the Office applications. However, comparatively cursory and at times incorrect treatment is given on how to access these applications.

Accessing an Office application is an important topic because you cannot begin to utilize the functionality of an Office application until you access it. The possibility of generating errors in accessing an Office application is not trivial. To take just one example, the Office application may not be installed on the user's machine, and may be accessible only on a remote computer on the network, and there is no guarantee that the network will be accessible. In these scenarios, blithely assuming that your program will access the Office application will result in your user witnessing your program's abrupt termination.

Other important issues arise when you are finished using the Office application. Memory that was committed so that your application could access the Office application needs to be released to avoid memory leaks. You also need to determine whether to close the Office application, which depends on whether the Office application was running already when your application accessed it.

All of these issues are discussed in this chapter.

A (Brief) History of Automation

These days the hypothetical Visual Basic book-royalty application described above would be routine. But for a long time it was an unrealized dream. Integrating applications was difficult and often impossible because programs were closed environments that, if they "talked" to any other programs at all, only talked to programs made by the same company. The reason was that one application could access another only if it understood completely how the other application worked. Since software developers understandably did not give away their application's source code, each company's programs were virtual islands.

During the time of Windows 3.0, Microsoft introduced a technology called Dynamic Data Exchange (DDE). This technology was imperfect and it is now only used for backwards compatibility. However, DDE was the first step in enabling one application to talk to another without having to completely understand how the other worked.

Microsoft next introduced Object Linking and Embedding (OLE). Version 1.0 of OLE supported compound documents. In this context, a "document" was not limited to a standard word processing document, but extended to any file containing data, such as a Microsoft Excel spreadsheet. Compound documents enabled one application to contain data from a different application, such as the insertion of a Microsoft Excel spreadsheet into a Microsoft Word document. Indeed, starting with Version 3.0, Visual Basic provided an **OLE Container** control that not only facilitated the insertion of one document into another, but also permitted *visual editing* within the placeholder. For example, after you embedded an Excel worksheet in your VB application, the user did not need to go outside of your application to Excel to update the worksheet. Instead, the user could click on the embedded worksheet and use Excel's functionality and features to update the worksheet without leaving your application. When the user was finished editing, the interface returned to being a placeholder for the worksheet and Excel was removed from your interface.

The ability to insert and edit one document within another, while useful, did not fulfill the promise of Automation. Automation also enables one application to use the functionality of another application. This ability was provided in Version 2.0 of OLE. OLE 2.0 was based on COM, and is the direct ancestor of Automation. Indeed, Automation previously was referred to as OLE Automation.

Microsoft Office 2000 Automation Features

The applications in the Microsoft Office 2000 suite are excellent candidates for Automation, as the book-royalty application example demonstrates. One reason is the functionality they provide: Access for database services, Excel for calculations, Word as a report writer, and, of course, Outlook for e-mail services. Another reason is that with these applications being part of an application suite, they integrate well with each other.

The integration of Office 2000 applications goes beyond menu items that, for example, permit an Excel worksheet to be exported as a table to an Access database. Office 2000 applications now share a common macro programming language, Visual Basic for Applications (VBA). In previous versions of Office, you used WordBasic for creating Word macros, AccessBasic for Access, and so on. Now you need to know only one language. Better yet, as a Visual Basic programmer, you are already familiar with VBA even if you are using VBA for the first time, because VBA is a subset of Visual Basic.

VBA can be used to write and edit macros. A *macro* is a sequence of menu commands and keystrokes. A macro may accomplish a simple task, such as replacing a phrase such as "closing paragraph" with the actual text of a closing paragraph. However, macros can do much more than act as typing shortcuts; they can query and export data. Also, VBA is not limited to macros. VBA, like Visual Basic, can be used to automate one Office application from another.

The Microsoft Office 2000 applications can be either Automation *clients* or *servers*. At the risk of offering a circular definition, a client uses the services of a server, and a server provides the requested service to a client. For example, Excel, as a client, could request Word, as a server, to create a report based on data in a worksheet. Conversely, Word, as a client, could request Excel, as a server, to determine the standard deviation of table data in a Word document. In the book-royalty example, the book-royalty application is an Automation client and the Microsoft Office applications it uses for database services, calculations, reports, and e-mail are the servers.

Automation arises in several contexts. As just mentioned, you can write a program that runs within an Office application using VBA. The book-royalty application represents another choice, a stand-alone application that is an Automation client utilizing the services of Office applications. Such applications generally are written in Visual Basic, though other COM-compliant programming languages, like Visual C++, also will do the job.

A code component, such as an ActiveX DLL, can also be an Automation server. Once again, such code components are often written in Visual Basic, though other COM-compliant programming languages will suffice. Additionally, Office applications can utilize a specialized ActiveX DLL called a COM add-in, which is a specialized dynamic-link library (DLL) that is registered specifically to be loaded by Office 2000 applications.

Objects and Collections

Using Automation requires an understanding of *objects* and *collections*. Automation clients and servers consist of objects that represent different parts of an application. For example, Outlook has an **Application** object that represents the Outlook application itself, a **NameSpace** object that represents the root of the Outlook folders, a **Folder** object that represents particular Outlook folders, such as the Inbox, and **Item** objects that represent, depending on the type of item, mail messages, task requests, appointments, or contact information.

The book-royalty application would access Outlook through Outlook's **Application** object. However, accessing Outlook is not enough. The book-royalty application also needs to create an Outlook mail item, add a message to the item, and direct the message to recipients. It does so through the *properties*, *methods*, and *events* of objects.

A property is a characteristic of an object. For example, a **MailItem** object has a **Body** property whose value is the text of the mail message, such as "No royalties, you owe us." This property can be used to *return* the value of the text in the subject line so you can programmatically read this value. The ability to return the value of the **Body** property could be used to find, among all mail messages in the Inbox, those containing particular text, such as the word "royalties."

The **Body** property also can be *set*, which means that you can programmatically assign the text of the message. The ability to set the value of the **Body** property would be useful in, for example, automated mass e-mailings. However, some properties are *read-only*, which means they can return but not set a value. For example, a **MailItem** object's **ReceivedTime** property, which indicates when a mail message was received, is read-only because the time at which an item was received is an objective fact that should not be altered through code.

A method is an action that the object may take. For example, a **MailItem** object has a **Send** method that sends the mail message. This method accomplishes programmatically what the user usually does by clicking the Send button of an e-mail message.

A method may have one or more parameters. A parameter is information that the method needs to perform its action. Some methods do not require parameters. For example, the **Send** method sends the **MailItem** object that calls that method; no further information is required. Other methods do require parameters. For example, the **Move** method moves a **MailItem** object to a different folder. This method requires as a parameter the **Folder** object to which the **MailItem** object is to be moved.

An event tells an object that something is happening to it. Perhaps the most commonly used event is a **CommandButton** object's **Click** event. You can write code in the **CommandButton** object's **Click** event procedure, and this code will run when the button is clicked.

Objects in Microsoft Office 2000 applications also have events. For example, a **MailItem** object has a **Send** event, which occurs when the item is sent, either by the user clicking the Send button or by code in which the item's **Send** method is called. This relationship between the **Send** method and the **Send** event is not unusual between methods and events. Often a method will cause a corresponding event to occur, or *fire*. While a method enables an object to do something, an event tells the object that something is happening to it. Events also can be used to prevent a method from completing. For example, you can write code in the **Send** event procedure to cancel the sending of a message if the user did not fill out certain required fields.

Applications often contain more than one of a given object. For example, Outlook has several **Folder** objects, for the Inbox, Outbox, Contacts, Tasks, and so on. These **Folder** objects are part of a **Folders** collection. Similarly, the Inbox may contain numerous **MailItem** objects. These objects are part of the **Items** collection belonging to the **Inbox** folder, which belongs to the **Folders** collection.

A collection is a container for objects, usually the same kind of object. The **MailItem** object just discussed may be one of many mail messages in an Inbox or other folder. Each **Folder** object has an **Items** collection, which contains all of the **MailItem** objects and any other **Item** objects in the folder. Additionally, the mail message about book royalties has three recipients: the two co-authors and their literary agent. Each is a **Recipient** object, and these three **Recipient** objects are contained in the **Recipients** collection of the **MailItem** object. Further, the mail message may have attachments, such as an Excel spreadsheet showing the royalty calculation. Each attachment is an **Attachment** object, and the attachments are contained in the **Attachments** collection of the **MailItem** object.

A collection may have its own properties, methods, and events. For example, the **Items** collection has a **Count** property whose value is the number of objects in the collection, an **Add** method to add items to the collection, a **Remove** method to remove objects from the collection, and an **ItemRemove** event which fires when an item is removed from the collection.

Object Models

The objects and collections of an Office application are contained in its *object model*. Whether you use Visual Basic to write an application that automates Office applications, or use VBA to automate an Office application from inside another Office application, or create a COM add-in, you will need to access the object models of the Office applications.

Each Microsoft Office application has an object model. That object model consists of the public collections, objects, properties, methods, and events. Each Office application may also have private collections, objects, properties, methods, and events. However, since these cannot be accessed programmatically, except perhaps by Microsoft, they are not considered part of the object model.

The object models of Microsoft Office applications have a hierarchical structure typical of applications that support Automation. This hierarchy of objects is comparable to Windows Explorer, in which the first level is the computer, the second level is the drives, the third level consists of the top-level directories of a drive, the fourth level is the subdirectories, and so on, until the files of a directory or subdirectory are reached.

Using Outlook as an example, the top-level object in the Outlook object model is the **Application** object. A next level object is the **NameSpace** object, which is the root of the Outlook folders. The **NameSpace** object contains **Folders** collections, such as Personal Folders and Public Folders, which themselves usually contain other folders. These top-level folders can be used to access the **MAPIFolder** objects they contain, such as the Inbox and Outbox. Finally, **MAPIFolder** objects contain **Items** collections, which contain the individual **Item** objects, which may be mail messages, task requests, appointments, or contact information.

In Windows Explorer, one method of accessing a file is "drilling down" through drives, directories, and subdirectories until you reach the file. Similarly, in Outlook the top-level **Application** object is used to access the second-level **NameSpace** object, which is used to access the **Folders** collection, which in turned is used to access individual **MAPIFolder** objects, each of which has an **Items** collection, which contains the folder's items, whether they are mail messages, contacts, appointments, or other item types.

Consistent with the different functionality of the Microsoft Office applications, there are differences among their respective object models. However, the object models are quite similar, so the Outlook example is not very different from the others.

Referencing the Office Application

The first step in automating an Office application is to *reference* the application you want to automate. This reference makes the objects exposed by the Office application visible to your application.

You reference an Office application by setting a reference to the application's type library in the References dialog box. A type library is a file, usually with a .tlb extension, though sometimes it will have a .dll or .exe extension, and it provides information about a code component. The purpose of a type library is to be accessed by other applications seeking information about the object that is the subject of the type library, such as the object's properties and methods. Not all applications have a type library. Microsoft Schedule+ 95 is an example of an application without a type library. However, the Microsoft Office applications all have type libraries.

You open the References dialog box by selecting Tools | References from the menu in the Visual Basic Editor. Figure 13-1 shows the References dialog box.

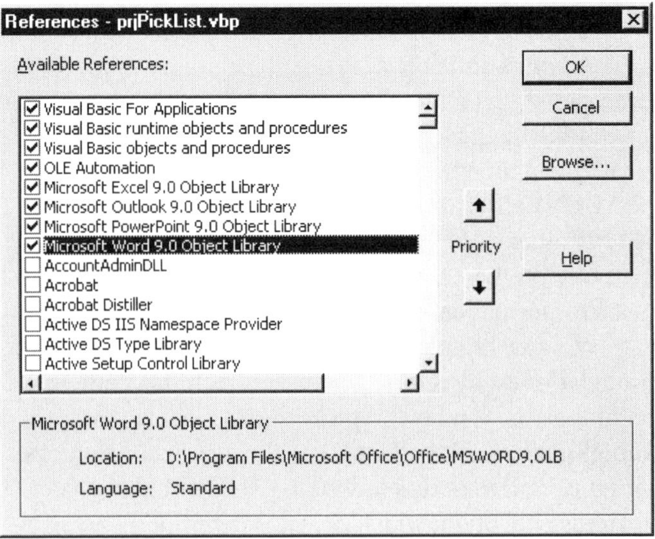

Figure 13.1 The References dialog box

Several libraries pertaining to Visual Basic are checked automatically. You simply need to check the check box pertaining to the Microsoft Office application you wish to automate. For example, if you want to automate Outlook 2000, you need to set a reference to the Microsoft Outlook 9.0 Object Library. References have been set to several Office applications in Figure 13-1.

Design Tip *You can check as many boxes as you want. However, including unnecessary references will increase both the time it takes for your application to load and the amount of memory used by your application.*

Visual Basic determines the type of object to which you are referring by searching the type libraries selected in the References dialog box. However, different type libraries may contain objects of the same name. For example, ActiveX Data Objects (ADO), discussed in Chapter 7, and its predecessor, Data Access Objects (DAO), each have a **Recordset** object. If you reference both the DAO and ADO type libraries and refer in code to a **Recordset** object, like this:

```
Dim rs As Recordset
```

Visual Basic will need to resolve whether you are referring to the ADO **Recordset** object or the DAO **Recordset** object. It does so by the order in which the type libraries are listed in the Available References list. You can use the Priority buttons to move the type libraries (except for the Visual Basic for Applications and the host application's type library) up or down the list.

Adding a reference also eases your job of writing code. First, you obtain the benefit of Visual Basic's IntelliSense feature. Figure 13-2 shows the Auto List Member feature, which lists an object's properties and methods when you type a dot after an object variable name.

24x7

Assuming that the type libraries are in the correct order of priority is asking for errors. A better practice is to eliminate ambiguous object references with fully qualified type declarations—simply include the programmatic identifier in front of the object name:

```
Dim rs As ADODB.Recordset
```

This reference makes it clear that the **Recordset** object is an ADO **Recordset**, not a DAO **Recordset**.

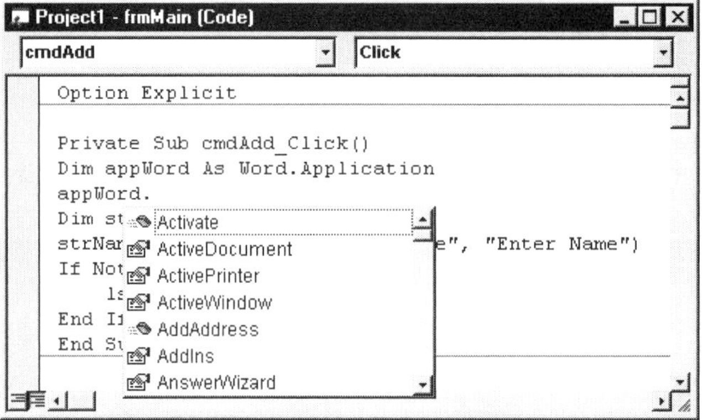

Figure 13.2 The Visual Basic IntelliSense feature

This list saves you from having to memorize or look up the available properties and methods. The ability to insert properties and methods directly from the list also prevents typographical errors from typing the property and method names manually.

You also obtain the benefit of the Object Browser, shown in Figure 13-3, which likewise provides you with information on an object's properties and methods.

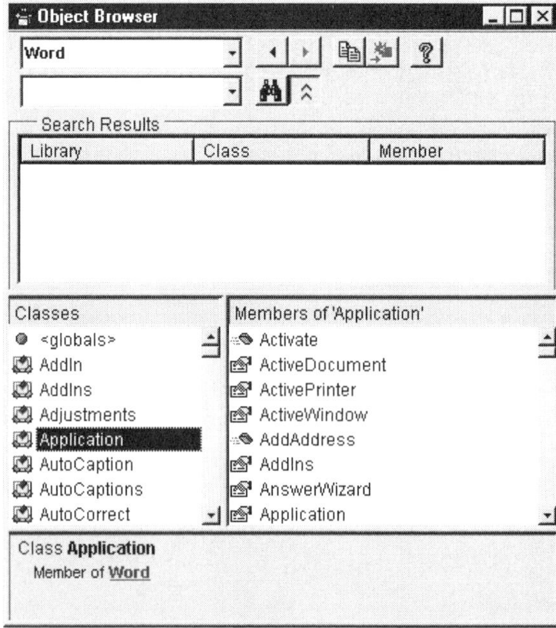

Figure 13.3 The Visual Basic Object Browser

Finally, all of the object's constants are accessible, so you don't have to define them.

Creating an Object

Before you use the events, methods, and properties of the object, you must first instantiate, or create an instance, of the object. This is a two-step process:

1. Declare an object variable to hold a reference to the object.
2. Instantiate the object by assigning to the object variable a reference to the object.

You then can access the properties, methods, and events of the object through the object variable.

Declaring the Object Variable: Early vs. Late Binding

The first decision you need to make is whether to declare the object variable as a generic object or as a specific object. The following code snippet declares the object variable as a generic object:

```
Dim objBinding As Object
```

You also can declare the object variable as a specific object, in this case the **Application** object of Outlook:

```
Dim objBinding As Outlook.Application
```

The decision of which of the two methods you should use to declare the object variable depends on *when* you wish to connect, or *bind*, the object variable to the object it is to represent. Since not all objects support the same properties and methods, your application must verify that the object represented by the object variable supports the particular property or method that your external application is calling. This verification process is known as *binding*, and can be done either when the project is compiled or when the project is running.

Verification at compile time is referred to as "early binding." To verify at compile time, you need to declare the object variable as a specific object. Verification at run time is referred to as "late binding." With late binding, you declare the object variable as a generic object.

One form of binding is not necessarily better than the other. The choice between the two forms of bindings, as with other choices in life, involves trade-offs. In this case, the trade-off basically is between speed and flexibility. The differences between early and late binding are discussed in more detail in Chapter 11.

Instantiating an Object

You have three ways of instantiating an object:

- Use the **New** keyword.
- Use the **CreateObject** function.
- Use the **GetObject** function.

Which method you choose depends on whether you choose early or late binding, what type of object you are trying to instantiate, and whether the object is on the local machine or a remote computer. As a general rule, you will use the **New** keyword if you are using early binding to create an object that you know exists on the local machine. However, you will use the **CreateObject** or **GetObject** function if you are using late binding, if you are not sure the object you are creating exists on the local machine, or if the object will be created on a remote computer.

Office applications have many objects. However, most of these objects can be instantiated only from other objects of that Office application. For example, in Outlook, the **MailItem** object, which represents an Outlook mail message, cannot be instantiated from an external application. Instead, a **MailItem** object can only be instantiated from another Outlook object, such as through the Outlook **Application** object's **CreateItem** method. This is consistent with the drill-down, hierarchical nature of the object models of the Office applications, in which child objects, such as the **MailItem** object, can be accessed only through top-level, externally creatable objects, such as the **Application** object.

All Office applications do have a top-level, externally creatable **Application** object. Additionally, Word and Excel have other top-level objects. Table 13-1 lists the top-level Office objects you can reference and their class names.

Usually you will access an Office application through its **Application** object. An **Application** object can be instantiated with the **New** keyword or the **CreateObject** or **GetObject** functions. However, you must use the **CreateObject** (or **GetObject**)

Object Type	Class Name
Access Application	Access.Application
Office Binder	OfficeBinder.Binder
Excel Application	Excel.Application
Excel Workbook	Excel.Sheet Excel.Chart
FrontPage Application	FrontPage.Application
Outlook Application	Outlook.Application
PowerPoint Application	PowerPoint.Application
Word Application	Word.Application
Word Document	Word.Document

Table 13.1 Top-Level Office Objects

function to create a **Workbook** object through either **Excel.Sheet** or **Excel.Chart**, because **Excel.Sheet** and **Excel.Chart** cannot be instantiated by the **New** keyword.

The New Keyword

The following code snippet uses the **New** keyword to instantiate the object variable **objBinding** as an **Outlook.Application** object:

```
Dim objBinding As Outlook.Application
Set objBinding = New Outlook.Application
```

Error Watch *This code is dependent on your previously having set a reference to the Outlook type library. Without that reference, the compiler would have no idea what **Outlook.Application** is, much less whether **Outlook.Application** supports a particular property or method.*

With primitive (built-in) Visual Basic variables, such as integers, declaring a variable would be sufficient to allocate memory for the variable. However, **Outlook.Application** is not a primitive variable; it is an object. Therefore it is necessary to use the **Set** statement with the **New** keyword to allocate memory for the object variable, otherwise known as *instantiating* the object variable.

An alternative syntax is to declare the object variable and use the **New** keyword in one statement instead of two:

```
Dim objBinding As New Outlook.Application
```

With this alternative syntax, an instance of the object that the object variable refers to is created when the object variable first calls a property or method of the object—in this case the **Name** property:

```
Debug.Print objBinding.Name
```

Design Tip *The one-statement syntax is often used in code examples, including the Microsoft Visual Basic Reference help files for various Office applications. However, the two-statement method, which dimensions the object variable without the* ***New*** *keyword and then uses the* ***Set*** *statement, is preferable to declaring the object variable with the* ***New*** *keyword in one statement. This is because with the two-statement method you know exactly where in the code the object is instantiated—at the* ***Set*** *statement. By contrast, if you declare the object variable with the* ***New*** *keyword, exactly where the object is instantiated depends on where your application first calls a property or method of the object through the object variable, and this could change as you change your code. This could present a problem if you are relying on the instantiation event of the object variable (such as the* ***Startup*** *event of the* ***Application*** *object) to perform other tasks in your program— when these tasks will be performed depends on the somewhat arbitrary point at which your application first invokes a property or method through the object variable.*

CreateObject and GetObject Functions

The **CreateObject** function creates and returns a reference to an Automation object. The syntax of the **CreateObject** function is this:

```
CreateObject(class,[servername])
```

Table 13-2 describes the parameters of the **CreateObject** function.

Name	Required?	Data Type	Description
class	Yes	String or Variant	The application name and class of the object to be created.
servername	No (optional)	String or Variant	The name of the computer where the object will be created. The default, an empty string (" "), means the object will be created on the local machine.

Table 13.2 Parameters of the **CreateObject** Function

The *class* argument uses the syntax *appname.objecttype*. Table 13-3 describes these parts of the class argument:

The following code snippet uses the **CreateObject** function to instantiate an Excel **Application** object:

```
Dim xlApp As Excel.Application
Set xlApp = CreateObject("Excel.Application")
```

One circumstance in which the **CreateObject** function is preferable to the **New** keyword is if you are uncertain whether the Office application you intend to automate is installed on the computer that will run your code. The following example illustrates how to use the **CreateObject** function to make sure an application is available for Automation:

```
Dim objOutlook As Object
Const ERR_APP_NOTFOUND As Long = 429
On Error Resume Next
Set objOutlook = CreateObject("Outlook.Application")
If Err = ERR_APP_NOTFOUND Then
   MsgBox "Outlook not installed on this computer."
   Exit Sub
End If
```

Error Watch *In this example, the object variable **objOutlook** was declared as a generic object rather than as **Outlook.Application**. In other words, late binding was used. This is necessary because the code would break if the object variable **objOutlook** were declared as **Outlook.Application** and that application were not present.*

Name	Required?	Data Type	Description
appname	Yes	String or Variant	The name of the application providing the object.
objecttype	Yes	String or Variant	The type or class of object to be created.

Table 13.3 Parts of the *class* Argument of the **CreateObject** Function

An alternative error-handling method uses the **Nothing** keyword. If the object could not be created, then the object variable does not reference an actual object. Instead, the **Is Nothing** test returns True:

```
Dim objOutlook As Object
On Error Resume Next
Set objOutlook = CreateObject("Outlook.Application")
If objOutlook Is Nothing Then
   MsgBox "Outlook not installed on this computer."
   Exit Sub
End If
```

Another advantage of the **CreateObject** function over the **New** keyword is that you can use the **CreateObject** function to create an object on a remote computer in the network. You do so by passing the name of the remote computer as the *servername* argument of the **CreateObject** function. That name is the same as the Machine Name portion of a share name: for a share named "\\NTServer\Pub", *servername* is "NTServer". Thus, if the Excel application object is to be created on the server named NTServer, you could use this code:

```
Dim xlApp As Excel.Application
Set xlApp = CreateObject("Excel.Application", "NTServer")
```

GetObject Function

The **GetObject** function usually is used to assign a reference to an existing object. However, the **GetObject** function, like the **CreateObject** function, can be used to create, as well as to assign, a reference to a new object.

The syntax of the **GetObject** function is this:

```
GetObject([pathname] [, class])
```

24x7

Once again, error-checking is necessary even if you are certain that Excel is installed on the remote server, because a run-time error will result if the remote server is unavailable or Excel is otherwise inaccessible.

While neither of the arguments of the **GetObject** function is required, at least one of the two arguments must be supplied.

The *pathname* argument is the full path and name of the file containing the object to be retrieved. The following code snippet opens a Word document with the filename "sample.doc" in the "C:\document" directory:

```
Dim wdDoc As Word.Document
Set wdDoc = GetObject("C:\document\sample.doc")
```

Note *The document will open in Word, assuming Word is the application associated with the .doc extension.*

If the *class* argument is supplied, then the *pathname* argument can be an empty string or omitted entirely. Using an empty string for the first argument causes **GetObject** to act like **CreateObject**—it will create a new object of the class specified in the *class* argument:

```
Dim xlApp As Excel.Application
Set xlApp = GetObject("", "Excel.Application")
```

If the *pathname* argument is omitted entirely, then the **GetObject** function will reference an existing object, assuming one exists. For example, this code will reference an existing Excel object:

```
Dim appOutlook As Outlook.Application
Set appOutlook = GetObject( , "Outlook.Application")
```

However, if no object of the specified type is currently running, an error occurs. As discussed shortly, this error can be used to determine if the Office application is already running.

Single-Use vs. Multi-Use Applications

The principal difference between the **CreateObject** and **GetObject** functions is that **CreateObject** usually is used to create a new instance of an Office object (usually an application), whereas **GetObject** usually is used to reference an existing instance. However, the significance of this distinction depends on whether the Office application in question is a *single-use* application or a *multi-use* application. Table 13-4 lists the various Office applications and whether they are single-use or multi-use.

Application	Use Type
Access	Single-use
Binder	Single-use
Excel	Single-use
FrontPage	Single-use
Outlook	Multi-use
PowerPoint	Multi-use
Word	Single-use

Table 13.4 Single-Use vs. Multi-Use

With a single-use application, a new instance of the application is created whenever an object variable is instantiated. Since Microsoft Word is a single-use application, the following code creates a new instance of Microsoft Word, regardless of how many instances of Word are already running:

```
Dim appWord As Word.Application
Set appWord = New Word.Application
```

With a multi-use Office application, host applications share the same instance of the Office application. Since Microsoft Outlook is a multi-use application, the following code creates a new instance of Outlook only if Outlook is not running when the code is executed. If Outlook is already running when this code is run, the object variable points to the currently running instance.

```
Dim appOutlook As Outlook.Application
Set appOutlook = New Outlook.Application
```

Indeed, creating an object variable that references a multi-use application, such as Outlook, that is already running will return a reference to the running instance no matter which method you use to create the object variable. For example, if Outlook is already running, the final three lines of code all return a reference to the same instance of Outlook:

```
Dim appOutlook As Outlook.Application
Dim appOutlook As Outlook.Application
Dim appOutlook As Outlook.Application

Set appOutlook = New Outlook.Application
```

```
Set appOutlook = CreateObject("Outlook.Application")
Set appOutlook = GetObject(, "Outlook.Application")
```

Thus, the common advice that **CreateObject** should only be used when there is no current instance of the object is far more significant for single-use Office applications, such as Word, than for multi-use applications, such as Outlook.

With multi-use applications, it still is a good technique to determine if an instance is currently running. If an instance currently is running, then you don't want to terminate the application when your code is finished with the application because the user previously had the application open for another purpose. You can determine if an instance currently is running by first calling the **GetObject** function without the first argument. This will cause an error if an instance of Outlook is not currently running. In that event, you then can use the **CreateObject** function to create a running instance of Outlook:

```
Dim objOutlook As Object
Const ERR_APP_NOTFOUND As Long = 429
On Error Resume Next
Set objOutlook = GetObject( , "Outlook.Application")
If Err Then _
   Set objOutlook = CreateObject("Outlook.Application")
If Err = ERR_APP_NOTFOUND Then _
   MsgBox "Outlook not installed on this computer."
   Exit Sub
End If
```

As discussed in the preceding section, another approach is to use the **Nothing** keyword:

```
Dim objOutlook As Object
On Error Resume Next
Set objOutlook = GetObject( , "Outlook.Application")
If objOutlook Is Nothing Then _
   Set objOutlook = CreateObject("Outlook.Application")
   If objOutlook Is Nothing Then _
      MsgBox "Outlook not installed on this computer."
   Exit Sub
End If
```

The other significant difference between the **CreateObject** and **GetObject** functions is that the **GetObject** function can be used to open an Office file and return a reference to the host application object at the same time. The **CreateObject** function has no corresponding ability.

24x7

Don't assume the Office application is visible. Many applications, such as Word, are by default not visible when started through Automation. You can test the visibility of the application-level variable's **Visible** property, which is a Boolean type whose value is True if the application is visible and False if it is not.

Cleaning Up

Just as a well-behaved child cleans up after playing, a well-behaved application cleans up when it is closed. In the context of an application, cleaning up means releasing the memory it has obtained from the operating system, such as when it sets an object variable to an Office application's **Application** object. Failing to release allocated memory may result in a memory leak. Users of your application may not be pleased as they watch available RAM drop like a stone with repeated use of your application.

A local variable is normally destroyed when it goes out of scope at the end of the procedure or application in which it was declared. However, it is good programming practice to explicitly destroy an application-level object variable used to automate another application by setting it equal to the **Nothing** keyword. The following code snippet does this:

```
Set objOutlook = Nothing
```

It is often recommended, including by Microsoft Help, that you use an **Application** object's **Quit** method. This is the syntax:

```
objOutlook.Quit
Set objOutlook = Nothing
```

The **Quit** method is used before setting the object variable equal to **Nothing**. Reversing these steps would not work because after setting the object variable equal to **Nothing** the object variable would no longer point to an Outlook **Application** object so the **Quit** method would make no sense to the compiler.

However, using the **Quit** method, which ends the running of the Office application, is not very polite if the Office application was already running when the object variable was created. Therefore, you should first check whether the Office application was previously running before you invoke the **Quit** method. You can do this by using an application-level (global) Boolean variable, as illustrated in the following code:

```
Option Explicit
Public objOutlook As Object
Public bOutlookRunning As Boolean

Public Function Outlook_Open() As Boolean
   On Error Resume Next
   bOutlookRunning = False
   Set objOutlook = GetObject( , "Outlook.Application")
   If objOutlook Is Nothing Then _
      Set objOutlook = CreateObject("Outlook.Application")
   If objOutlook Is Nothing Then _
      MsgBox "Outlook not installed on this computer."
      OutlookOpen = False
      Exit Function
   End If
   bOutlookRunning = True
   Outlook_Open = True
End Function

Public Sub Outlook_Close()
   On Error Resume Next
   If objOutlook Is Nothing Then _
      objOutlook.Close
   If Not bOutlookRunning Then _
      objOutlook.Quit
   Set objOutlook = Nothing
End Sub
```

The global Boolean variable **bOutlookRunning** is set in the **Outlook_Open** function to True or False depending on whether Outlook was previously running. The **Outlook_Close** subroutine occurs when the external application finishes. In that procedure, the Outlook **Application** object's **Close** method is used to terminate this particular instance of Outlook, and the object variable is set to **Nothing**. However, whether or not the Outlook **Application** object's **Quit** method is used depends on the value of **bOutlookRunning**.

Summary

The ability to automate Office applications greatly extends the reach of the applications you write. You have several alternative ways to instantiate the Office application: the **New** keyword, the **CreateObject** function and the **GetObject** function. Which one you use depends on circumstances such as whether the Office application is on a local or remote computer or whether you want to use the Office application to open a particular file. However, regardless of the method you use, you should use error handling in the event that the Office application cannot be instantiated. Finally, when closing the Office application, you should release the memory you requested when instantiating the Office application, but not close the Office application if it was running before your application started.

CHAPTER 14

Database Programming

In Visual Basic version 3.0, VB programmers were introduced to the world of database development through the wonders of DAO (Data Access Objects). DAO made it easy for developers to access information on PC-based relational database systems like dBASE, Paradox, and of course, Microsoft Access because it was an object model that provided easy-to-use methods and properties to the ODBC API (application programming interface). Before DAO, developers had to write their database applications using the ODBC API itself or DB-LIB. DB-LIB is SQL Server's API library, often referred to as the native drivers, and DB-LIB only worked with the SQL Server. If you changed from SQL Server to a different database management system, say Oracle, after your application was deployed, you would have to rewrite all your database access routines.

Since version 3.0, Microsoft has constantly improved their methods of database connectivity. The latest and greatest incarnation of database connectivity is called ActiveX Data Objects, which is commonly referred to as ADO. The history of ADO is covered in greater detail in Chapter 7. What's not covered in that chapter are a lot of the common mistakes developers might make during the coding process, as well as techniques on handling large amounts of data.

Coding Tips

No matter how long you've been developing, coding mistakes are very common. Developers hate to admit they made a mistake when coding, which is why many of them prefer using an integrated development environment like VB, because they can test their code immediately and fix any errors before they ship their component off to the test lab.

24x7

As this book goes to press, the latest version of ADO available is version 2.5, and it ships with Windows 2000, unlike previous versions of the Windows operating system. If you haven't upgraded to Windows 2000, fear not! You can always download the latest version of ADO by visiting the Microsoft Data Access Center Web site at http://www.Microsoft.com/data.

Bang (!) vs. Dot (.)

One of the greatest debates Access and VB developers get into is the difference between the exclamation mark and the dot syntax. For the uninformed, the exclamation points within an expression are called "bangs." The bang character is a way to save at least three keystrokes when referring to a member of a collection by its literal name. Instead of using ***Collection("MemberName")***, or ***Collection.Item("MemberName")***, you can use ***Collection!MemberName***. This also works when referring to a member of a collection you create. For example:

```
Dim col As New Collection
col.Add "Item1", "Item1KeyVal"
Debug.Print col!Item1KeyVal
```

The most common myth about using bangs is the notion that they are used before objects that you name, and dots are used before objects that VB or Access names. This is an old wives' tale, urban myth, or otherwise unsubstantiated rumor. Use bangs because the objects are being identified as members of a collection, not because you or another developer named them. ***FormName!ControlName*** is actually shorthand for ***FormName.Controls!ControlName***. The **Controls** collection can be left out, because it's the default property of a form.

One big advantage of using the dot in your code is that unless there's a bang earlier in the expression, you get the handy IntelliSense drop-down list showing all the properties you can choose from. Your form's controls, properties, and methods will be in the list, saving you memorization time and preventing typing errors. When you use a bang, you won't get the drop-down list, since IntelliSense doesn't have the good sense to look beyond the bang. Microsoft doesn't guarantee future compatibility with the bang in future releases.

When you compile or run your code for the first time, the IDE checks the calls for the property or method, matching any names you use after a dot, and it alerts you with a compile error if one isn't found. If you use a bang before the control name, your code will compile even if the control name is misspelled. You will only know if there is an error when you, your testers, or your users happen across the code at run time. You might say that the use of the dot is like Automation early binding, and using the bang is like Automation late binding.

Using dots rather than bangs also makes your code run a bit faster. Your users are unlikely to notice the difference, but every little bit of performance helps, right? The downside of using the dot is that you might run into trouble if your control or **Recordset** field has the same name as that of the built-in properties of a form. You know what that means? Don't give them the same names.

The main reason for discussing this argument of bang versus dot is the use of them when dealing with **Recordsets**. Access developers have used bangs with **Recordsets** since version 1.0. Once you've opened a **Recordset**, you can reference the fields within it as recordsetObjectVariableName-bang-fieldName (that is, ***rsObjectName!FieldName***). VB developers who have followed the database-access object models through their various stages wax and wane between using bangs and dots. To use the dot with **Recordsets**, you would use the format recordsetObjectVariableName-dot-property(fieldName), like this:

rsObjectName.Fields("ColumnName")

The following code example shows the difference between using a bang and dot when working with ADO **Recordsets**.

```
Dim rsFieldData As ADODB.Recordset
Dim sConn As String
Dim sSQL As String

sConn = "Provider=Microsoft.Jet.OLEDB.4.0;" _
   & "Data Source=C:\Progra~1\Micros~2\vb98\Nwind.mdb;"
sSQL = "SELECT * FROM Customers"

Set rsFieldData = New ADODB.Recordset
With rsFieldData
   .Open sSQL, sConn, , , adCmdText
End With
Do While Not rsFieldData.EOF
    Debug.Print "! = " & rsFieldData!CustomerID
    Debug.Print ". = " & rsFieldData.Fields("CustomerID")
rsFieldData.MoveNext
Loop
```

In the preceding description, the use of the bang seems a lot more straightforward than the use of the dot. However, you should not be using bangs within Active Server Pages (ASP) server-side scripting. The following code is very similar to the previous code, but it's formatted to be executed within an ASP file accessed through Internet Information Server (IIS) or Personal Web Server. Although the code specifies that ADO is supposed to be used, ISAPI (Internet Server Application Programming Interface), which processes the VBScript with the ASP file on the Web server, doesn't know how to interpret the bang, so it results in the error displayed in Figure 14-1.

```
<%
Dim rsFieldData
Dim sConn
Dim sSQL

sConn = "Provider=Microsoft.Jet.OLEDB.4.0;" _
   & "Data Source=C:\Progra~1\Micros~2\vb98\Nwind.mdb;"
sSQL = "SELECT * FROM Customers WHERE Region = 'WA'"

Set rsFieldData = server.createobject("ADODB.Recordset")
With rsFieldData
   .Open sSQL, sConn, , , adCmdText
End With
Do While Not rsFieldData.EOF
    Response.Write "! = " & rsFieldData!customerid
    Response.Write ". = " & rsFieldData.Fields("customerid")
    rsFieldData.MoveNext
Loop
%>
```

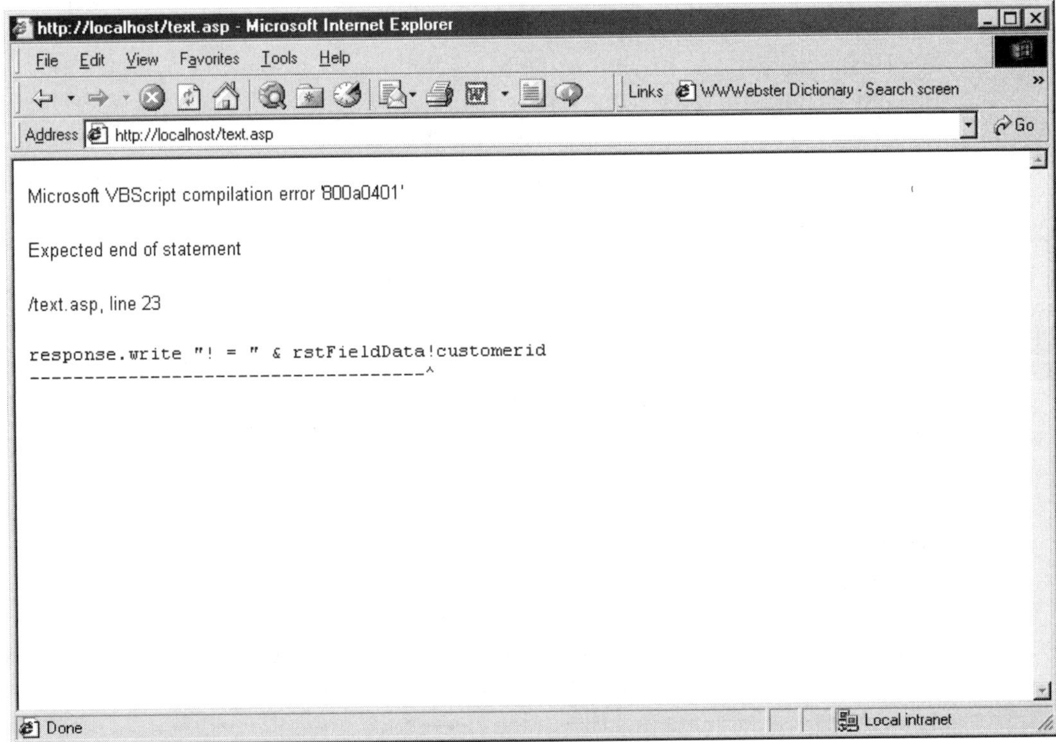

Figure 14.1 Error using the bang in VBScript for an ASP file

To avoid such an error, the bang needs to be replaced with a dot. You can still continue using bangs in your VB applications if that's what you are familiar and most comfortable with. However, as you move forward with new development or develop Web-based applications through ASP files, you will want to start using dots rather than bangs. Software development has moved from building applications in a client/server environment within an enterprise to building applications that are accessible through the Internet. This means more server-side scripting, which means that if you move any of your VBA code over to a VBScript model, any references to **Recordsets** with bangs will have to be rewritten. Save yourself some time and start incorporating dots into your development.

Forgetting to MoveNext

The **Recordset** object's **MoveNext** method repositions the row pointer to the next record within the **Recordset** you've generated. As simple as the **MoveNext** method is, you will be surprised how many developers in their haste forget to put it into their code. No matter how many notes you write for yourself, you will probably do this at least once or twice during a project.

What's the harm of forgetting the **MoveNext** method within your code? The result is an endless loop. Sounds like a recurring theme for a Star Trek episode, doesn't it? By forgetting to use the method, the row pointer will stay on the first row of the entire **Recordset** and never move. This is probably one of the most frustrating and embarrassing errors you can find yourself trying to resolve. Figure 14-2 illustrates what happens when a **Recordset** object is opened and how information is processed.

During development, if you notice that your queries are taking a long time and you're expecting only a few rows to be returned, you might have forgotten to include the ***MoveNext*** *method within your loop.*

Checking for BOF and EOF

Since the beginning of data access from within VB, developers have looked at the **BOF** (beginning of file) and **EOF** (end of file) properties when determining if the beginning or end of the **Recordset** has been reached. When you first open a **Recordset** and there is data to be retrieved, the entire table or subset of the table's contents is loaded into the recordset object variable. The recordset object variable is then set to point to the first row of the **Recordset**. If the **Recordset** does not contain any information, both the **BOF** and **EOF** properties are set to True.

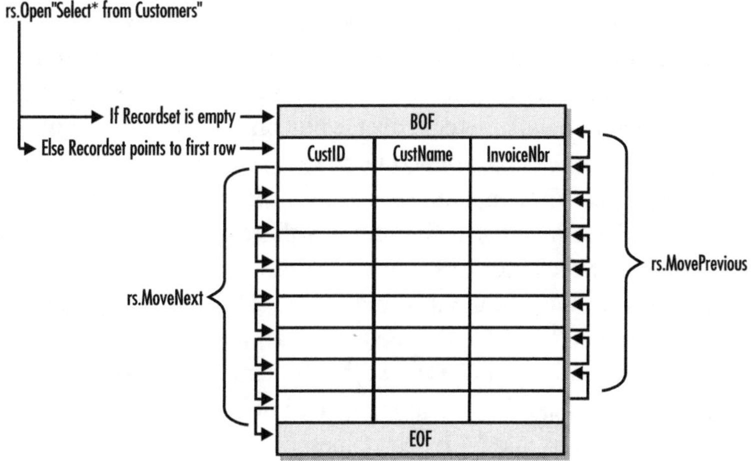

Figure 14.2 What happens when a **Recordset** object is opened, and how information is processed through the use of **MoveNext** and **MovePrevious** commands

When Microsoft started publishing examples on how to use the Microsoft data-access object models, they would show code similar to the following:

```
Dim rs As ADODB.Recordset
Dim sConn As String
Dim sSQL   As String

sConn = "Provider=Microsoft.Jet.OLEDB.4.0;" _
   & "Data Source=C:\Progra~1\Micros~2\vb98\Nwind.mdb;"
sSQL = "SELECT * FROM Customers"

Set rs = New ADODB.Recordset
rs.Open sSQL, sConn

If Not rs.BOF then
    Do Until rs.EOF
        Debug.Print rs.Fields("CustomerID")
        rs.MoveNext
    Loop
End If
```

If you follow the logic, after the **Recordset** is open, the **BOF** property is checked. If the **BOF** property is True, then the **Recordset** does not contain any data; otherwise **BOF** would be set to False and the **Do-Loop** would be executed until the **EOF** property is set to True. There is nothing wrong with coding like this, but it really is a bit more coding than is needed. When a **Recordset** is open and no data is returned from the query to populate it, both the **BOF** and **EOF** properties are set to True. In functions and procedures where you expect the set of data to populate a **Recordset**, you can use the **Do-Loop** using the **EOF** property as the condition to check for.

With that said, checking the **BOF** or **EOF** properties can determine whether the data that is going to be entered will generate either a new record or a data update. If either property is set to True when you open the **Recordset**, it will give you a clue that the information might not exist in the database and will need to be added as a new record, as opposed to being a record update.

Another use of the **BOF** and **EOF** properties is to determine whether your user has reached the beginning or end of the **Recordset** rows when using the **MovePrevious** and **MoveNext** methods. As the pointer scrolls through the **Recordset**, it moves from row to row. Once the pointer goes beyond the first row or the last row, the **BOF** or **EOF** property gets set to True. Once that has happened and you continue to allow your users to scroll through the **Recordset**, an error will be produced. Figure 14-3 helps illustrate this point a bit more clearly.

The following code shows how you could code your application if you provided command buttons for your customers to use to scroll through records within the **Recordset**. Each procedure is based on the **Click** event of a command button. The **cmdNext** command button is used to move the user to the next row within a **Recordset**, while the **cmdPrev** command button is used to move the user to the previous row within a **Recordset**. The **If-Then** statement is used to determine if the **EOF** or **BOF** properties are set to True or not. While the properties are set to False, the row pointer will navigate through the **Recordset**. When either property is set to True, which means no more records are available

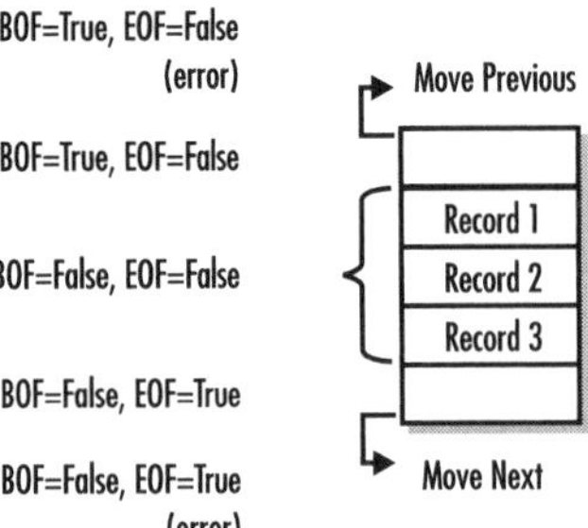

Figure 14.3 Settings of the **BOF** and **EOF** properties for all possible current positions in a **Recordset**

to be processed, the **MoveFirst** or **MoveLast** methods are invoked to keep the pointer on a valid row.

```
Private Sub cmdNext_Click()
    rsApp.MoveNext
    If Not rsApp.EOF Then
        cmdPrev.Enabled = True
        txtItemNbr = rsApp(0)
        txtItemName = rsApp(1)
        dtAuditDate(0).Value = rsApp(2)
        dtAuditDate(1).Value = rsApp(3)
    Else
        rsApp.MoveLast
        cmdNext.Enabled = False
    End If
End Sub
Private Sub cmdPrev_Click()
    rsApp.MovePrevious
    If Not rsApp.BOF Then
        cmdNext.Enabled = True
        txtItemNbr = rsApp(0)
        txtItemName = rsApp(1)
        dtAuditDate(0).Value = rsApp(2)
        dtAuditDate(1).Value = rsApp(3)
    Else
        rsApp.MoveFirst
        cmdPrev.Enabled = False
    End If
End Sub
```

Avoid Updating Through Recordsets

Ever since data-access object models were introduced, Microsoft has consistently made the **Recordset** object the most versatile object for storing data that's returned from a query and for manipulating database information. However, with great flexibility comes a cost on resources. When you open a **Recordset**, a connection to the database is created, and when you add, delete, and update the records within the **Recordset** the changes are immediately made to the database. Although updating the database through the **Recordset** is convenient, it adds additional resource overhead to your application because the **Recordset** needs to maintain an open connection to the database.

When developing your application, it's important to consider the number of users who will be using it simultaneously and the types of data interaction they will be doing against the data. If the application is going to be used by a small group of users, and the demand for data input is low, then speed and resource usage might not be that important.

In a high-transaction environment like the Home Shopping Network, where there are thousands of transactions each minute, you are really going to notice performance and resource degradation if you insert and update records through the **Recordset** object.

Rather than performing data inserts and updates through the **Recordset** object, it is much more efficient to perform those functions through the **Connection** object by executing SQL INSERT and UPDATE statements. In applications with a lot of database activity, it's a good practice to create a global connection to the database using the **Connection** object. To create a global connection, you first need to define a public object variable for the **Connection** object in the General Declaration section of a standard module, like the following:

```
Public gConn As ADODB.Connection
```

One of the first procedures that gets executed should instantiate the connection to the database. In your VB project, you can specify a form module or a procedure called **Sub Main**, which is defined in a standard module to be the module that gets executed when an application starts. The following is an example of the create a global database connection using the **Connection** object's **Open** method; it connects to an Access database, and the **Sub Main** procedure is the first procedure an application will execute.

```
Sub Main()
    Set gConn = New ADODB.Connection
    Conn.Open "Driver={Microsoft Access Driver (*.mdb)};" _
        & "DBQ=" & app.path & "\AppDB.MDB;UID=Admin;PWD=''"
End Sub
```

Design Tip *To make the **Sub Main** procedure the first procedure that executes when an application starts, you need to change the project properties' **Startup** object from a form's name to **Sub Main**.*

Through this connection, you can execute any SQL statement. In order to perform an INSERT or UPDATE statement, you would use the **Connection** object's **Execute** method. The following code is an example of using the **Execute** method with a SQL INSERT statement:

```
gConn.Execute "INSERT INTO CUSTOMERS " _
    & "(CustomerID, CompanyName, ContactName) " _
    & "VALUES ('ACMECHEM', 'ACME Chemicals', 'Roger Rabbit')"
```

Use Stored Procedures

Just as it's more efficient to use the **Connection** object to perform database manipulation, it's also recommended that database updates be done through stored procedures that reside on the database server. A stored procedure is a collection of SQL statements—often with variables, loops, and transaction logic—that are stored and processed as a unit of work on a database management system. Stored procedures offer many advantages over SQL that is embedded in your application.

One advantage is that stored procedures are precompiled on the database server. When you send a SQL statement to a database, the query processor has to parse it, analyze it, and create a query plan for execution. Not only does this slow down your queries, but it can create serious overhead when you multiply this by the number of users that use your application. Stored procedures are compiled, and their plan resides on the server.

Another advantage of using stored procedures is easier maintenance and security. Some developers use embedded SQL to keep the data access code with the application, but this is also a reason to move it out of the code. The smallest modification to your tables means searching your source code to find each instance where the table was referenced. By removing embedded SQL, you eliminate the tedious and inefficient task of formatting variables and SQL strings with single quotes, double quotes, so it can be read by the database.

With regards to security, users access the stored procedure, which then accesses the base tables in the database. In contrast, embedded SQL accesses the tables directly. Because stored procedures reside on the server, they remove the risk of SQL statements containing sensitive information traveling across the network.

Retrieve Only the Data You Need

When developers are first taught about querying data from a database, a lot of them learn that they can retrieve every column within the database by typing **SELECT * FROM *tablename***. The problem with this is that you probably only really need a few columns of information. Rather than using the wildcard parameter, it's best to specify only the fields you require in your SQL statement, like this: **SELECT CustomerID, CustomerName, MaxPurchaseAmt FROM Customers**. When it comes to database transactions, more is not better.

Handle Quotes Properly

When it comes to inputting data into a database, the character that causes the most headaches for database programmers, if not handled properly, is the apostrophe (')—also referred to as a *tick*. When you have names like O'Brian or O'Neil and you enter them into the database as is, the SQL engine will give you an error. In order to avoid this error, you need to add a second tick after the first one as part of the text string. The text should look similar to the following:

```
sInput = "Dennis O''Neil"
```

Adding the second tick tells the SQL engine that it has not received the end of a text string, and it then inserts the information into that database column and removes the second tick. The following code is a function that you can add to your project to help process the text.

```
Function CleanQuotes(sValue As String) As String

    Dim x As Long
    Dim RtnStr As String
    Dim bDone As Boolean

    ' Any data to process?
    If IsNull(sValue) Then
        CleanQuotes = ""
        Exit Function
    End If
    RtnStr = sValue
    x = InStr(1, sValue, "'")
    If x > 0 Then
        Do While Not bDone
            If x > 0 Then
                RtnStr = Left(RtnStr, x) & "'" & Mid(RtnStr, x + 1, _
                    Len(RtnStr))
                x = InStr(x + 2, RtnStr, "'")
            Else
                bDone = True
            End If
        Loop
    End If
    Debug.Print RtnStr
    CleanQuotes = RtnStr
End Function
```

To use this function in your project, you can use it within your SQL statement, like this:

```
sSQL = "INSERT INTO tblBLOB (ItemID, ItemText) "
sSQL = sSQL & "VALUES (" & txtID & ", '"
sSQL = sSQL & CleanQuotes(txtLastName) & "')"
sCon.Execute sSQL
```

Or you can use it when you read data from a control:

```
rs.Field("lstName") = CleanQuote(txtLastName)
```

Working with Binary Large Object Records

When Microsoft Access first came out, one of the examples showed employee pictures within a form, and the images were stored in the database. Since Access is part of Microsoft Office, this application was passed out to a large user base, and users figured that if you can do this with an Access database application, developers should be able to do the same thing with SQL Server. After all, SQL Server is an industrial-strength database management system whereas Access is more of a lightweight database system.

In Access, the data type that allows you to store large data objects such as pictures, documents, and audio files, is called the OLE object. In SQL Server, the data type is called Image, and in Oracle it is known as the LONG RAW data type. Regardless of the database management system you use, developers typically refer to this data type as a binary large object or BLOB. The following are some suggestions for using BLOB records:

- Using BLOB records in a database table will cause performance degradation at your server and add an extra layer of complexity in your application code that you can avoid. Rather than storing binary objects in the database, it is more efficient to store these files on your file system. If you store the files on your file system, you can then store the network's Universal Naming Convention (UNC) path for the file in a database. To access the file, let your code read the path and handle the file appropriately.
- When using BLOB records, you should place the BLOB column as the last item in your SQL SELECT statement. If you are in the habit of using **SELECT * FROM *TableName*** statements, and the BLOB record is not the last column in the table, you will receive a Null value for the BLOB record in your **Recordset**. You should change your query to something like **SELECT *field1, field2, blob1* FROM *TableName*** to explicitly reference each column and place the BLOB column at the end.
- When editing a BLOB record, you need to use the **AppendChunk** method. In addition, you should select at least one non-BLOB column as part of your **Recordset**. If you edit the BLOB column but not the non-BLOB record, ADO will not raise an error, but the data may not be saved back to

the table. BLOBs are typically not updateable with static or forward-only cursors on ODBC data sources.

- If you are trying to display a bitmap image in a **Picture** control that is stored in a BLOB column, keep in mind that the **Picture** control in Visual Basic does not have the capability of taking in a stream of bits via Visual Basic for Applications (VBA) code. The only way to place a picture into the **Picture** control through code, or to get the bits back out of a **Picture** control through code, is to use a file on the disk. You can also use the ActiveX Data Control (ADC) and bind the **Picture** box to the BLOB column. This works well for displaying a picture, but updating it in Visual Basic isn't very stable, due to problems in Visual Basic's binding manager. You should perform updates through code rather than the ADC.

When it comes to retrieving data from a BLOB field, it's not just a matter of using the **GetChunk** method. You need to tell the method how many bytes you wish to receive from the column at a time. Each subsequent **GetChunk** call retrieves data starting from where the previous **GetChunk** call left off. However, if you are retrieving data from one field and then you set or read the value of another field in the current record, ADO assumes you are done retrieving data from the first field. If you call the **GetChunk** method on the first field again, ADO interprets the call as a new **GetChunk** operation and starts reading from the beginning of the data.

The following code provides an example of a function that extracts BLOB data. The **GetChunk** method will extract 1,000 bytes from the **Recordset** column at a time, build the value into one variable, and return it to the called procedure.

```
Function RetrieveBLOB(ByVal BLOBField As ADODB.Field)

    Dim sChunk As String
    Dim nOffset As Long
    Dim nTotalSize As Long
    Dim nChunkSize As Long
    Dim nRemainder As Integer
    nChunkSize = 1000

    nTotalSize = BLOBField.ActualSize

    nRemainder = nTotalSize Mod nChunkSize

    sChunk = ""
    Do While nOffset < nTotalSize
        sChunk = sChunk & BLOBField.GetChunk(nChunkSize)
```

```
        nOffset = nOffset + nChunkSize
    Loop
    ' get remainder
    If Not nRemainder = 0 Then
        sChunk = sChunk & BLOBField.GetChunk(nRemainder)
    End If

    RetrieveBLOB = sChunk
End Function
```

In order to determine whether you need to use the **GetChunk** method to retrieve information from a column, you need to determine whether the database field is an OLE object, memo field, image field, and so on. To find out, use the **Field** collection's **Type** property. Table 14-1 lists the ADO constants and values that the **Type** property can return.

Constant	Value	Description
adArray	0x2000	A flag value, always combined with another data type constant, that indicates an array of that other data type.
adBigInt	20	Indicates an eight-byte signed integer.
adBinary	128	Indicates a binary value.
adBoolean	11	Indicates a Boolean value.
adBSTR	8	Indicates a null-terminated character string (Unicode).
adChapter	136	Indicates a four-byte chapter value that identifies rows in a child.
adChar	129	Indicates a string value.
adCurrency	6	Indicates a currency value. Currency is a fixed-point number with four digits to the right of the decimal point. It is stored in an eight-byte signed integer scaled by 10,000.
adDate	7	Indicates a date value. A date is stored as a double, the whole part of which is the number of days since December 30, 1899, and the fractional part of which is the fraction of a day.
adDBDate	133	Indicates a date value (yyyymmdd).
adDBTime	134	Indicates a time value (hhmmss).
adDBTimeStamp	135	Indicates a date/time stamp (yyyymmddhhmmss plus a fraction in billionths).
adDecimal	14	Indicates an exact numeric value with a fixed precision and scale.
adDouble	5	Indicates a double-precision floating-point value.
adEmpty	0	Specifies no value.

Table 14.1 ADO Type Values

Constant	Value	Description
adError	10	Indicates a 32-bit error code.
adFileTime	64	Indicates a 64-bit value representing the number of 100-nanosecond intervals since January 1, 1601.
adGUID	72	Indicates a globally unique identifier (GUID).
adIDispatch	9	Indicates a pointer to an **IDispatch** interface on a COM object.
adInteger	3	Indicates a four-byte signed integer.
adIUnknown	13	Indicates a pointer to an **IUnknown** interface on a COM object.
adLongVarBinary	205	Indicates a long binary value (**Parameter** object only).
adLongVarChar	201	Indicates a long string value (**Parameter** object only).
adLongVarWChar	203	Indicates a long null-terminated Unicode string value (**Parameter** object only).
adNumeric	131	Indicates an exact numeric value with a fixed precision and scale.
adPropVariant	138	Indicates an Automation PROPVARIANT.
adSingle	4	Indicates a single-precision floating-point value.
adSmallInt	2	Indicates a two-byte signed integer.
adTinyInt	16	Indicates a one-byte signed integer.
adUnsignedBigInt	21	Indicates an eight-byte unsigned integer.
adUnsignedInt	19	Indicates a four-byte unsigned integer.
adUnsignedSmallInt	18	Indicates a two-byte unsigned integer.
adUnsignedTinyInt	17	Indicates a one-byte unsigned integer.
adUserDefined	132	Indicates a user-defined variable.
adVarBinary	204	Indicates a binary value (**Parameter** object only).
adVarChar	200	Indicates a string value (**Parameter** object only).
adVariant	12	Indicates an Automation Variant.
adVarNumeric	139	Indicates a numeric value (**Parameter** object only).
adVarWChar	202	Indicates a null-terminated Unicode character string (**Parameter** object only).
adWChar	130	Indicates a null-terminated Unicode character string.

Table 14.1 ADO Type Values *(continued)*

To check the value of the **Type** property, you need to refer to the **Recordset Field** collection. The following code is an example of how to check the **Type** property of all columns in the NWIND.MDB's Employees table.

```
Dim x As Integer
Dim sCon As ADODB.Connection
```

```
Dim rs As ADODB.Recordset

Set sCon = New ADODB.Connection
sCon.Open "Driver={Microsoft Access Driver (*.MDB)}; " _
    & "DBQ=c:\progra~1 \micros~2 \vb98\nwind.mdb;uid=Admin;"

Set rs = New ADODB.Recordset
rs.Open "SELECT * FROM Employees", sCon

' Display the Column name and the column's data type
For x = 0 To rs.Fields.Count - 1
    Debug.Print rs(x).Name & " -> " & rs(x).Type
Next

rs.Close
sCon.Close
```

Most of the code for accessing the ADO object model should look familiar. First, you create the connection to the database and then create a new **Recordset** by selecting every column within the Employees table. Using the **Fields** collection's **Count** property, you determine the number of columns that are returned to the **Recordset**. Since VB's arrays are base 0, which means arrays start with zero, we need to subtract 1 from the **Count** property. If we didn't, we would be off by a value of 1, since the **Count** property starts at 1, not 0.

The following code snippet provides an example of how you could determine column type with the **Recordset** object's **Type** property and then use the **RetrieveBLOB** function, described earlier, that uses the **GetChunk** method. To provide some background, this code snippet is used to populate the **MSFlexGrid** control. Each **Type** property of the column in the **Recordset** is checked to see if it's a Long String data type, which is a Memo data type in an Access database. If it is, then the **RetrieveBLOB** function is used to retrieve the information using the **GetChunk** method, and the value is returned to the procedure.

```
Do Until rs.EOF
    For X = 0 To nColumns - 1
        cntl.Col = X
        cntl.Row = y
        If rs(X).Type = adLongVarChar Then
            sCellText = RetrieveBLOB(rs(x))
        Else
            If IsNull(rs(X)) Then
                sCellText = ""
            Else
                sCellText = rs(X).Value
            End If
```

```
            End If
            cntl.Text = sCellText
            cntl.CellAlignment = vbLeftJustify
        Next
        rs.MoveNext
        y = y + 1
        cntl.Rows = y + 1
    Loop
```

ADO Error Reporting

Despite your best efforts, you will still have to deal with errors from time to time. So when errors occur, what do you do with them? ADO has its own **Error** object model that can be accessed by developers to provide feedback to users about what might have gone wrong. Here's a list of some of the **Error** object's properties that you should consider using for database error reporting.

- The **Number** property provides a unique number that identifies the error.
- The **Description** property provides a description of the error for the given error number.
- The **Source** property contains the name of the database connection service provider.
- The **SQLState** property is a five-digit string that provides you with the ANSI SQL standard error-message number. For longtime database programmers, these numbers are what we relied on to provide us with database query feedback.
- The **NativeError** property contains the error number reported from the data source, itself. This number can vary from database system to database system.

When capturing an ADO error, you should have common error routines to handle all the information. This way it is centralized, and the error messages are displayed in a uniform manner. The following code is a procedure that handles the ADO **Error** object's error messages.

```
Sub ADOErrors(oConn As ADODB.Connection)

    Dim oErr As ADODB.Error
    Dim sMsg As String
```

```
    For Each oErr In oConn.Errors
        sMsg = sMsg & "Error #: "
        sMsg = sMsg & oErr.Number & vbCrLf
        sMsg = sMsg & "Description: "
        sMsg = sMsg & oErr.Description & vbCrLf
        sMsg = sMsg & "Source: "
        sMsg = sMsg & oErr.Source & vbCrLf
        sMsg = sMsg & "SQL State: "
        sMsg = sMsg & oErr.SQLState & vbCrLf
        sMsg = sMsg & "Native Error: "
        sMsg = sMsg & oErr.NativeError & vbCrLf
        ' Add an extra space
        sMsg = sMsg & vbCrLf
    Next

    MsgBox sMsg, vbCritical, App.Title

End Sub
```

To use this procedure, simply call it from any procedure that has an **On Error** statement subroutine, like this:

```
On Error Goto Err_ProcName
...
Err_ProcName:
    Call ADOErrors(rs.ActiveConnection)
    Exit Sub
End Sub
```

You might note that the parameter that is passed to the **ADOErrors** procedure is the **Recordset** object's **ActiveConnection** property. You should always pass the **Connection** object to this procedure, because you can't always rely on having just one connection.

Database Naming Standards

Just as it is good to have naming conventions for your application's variables, it's a good practice to have database naming standards to help your database administrators (DBAs) and programmers be consistent in naming elements and avoid integration confusion later. By creating these standards, everyone will be on the same page when it comes to dealing with the database objects they need to work with. The following are simply guidelines for database naming standards.

Experiment with them in your organization and find out what works best for you and your teams.

Table Naming

Tables defined in a database should have a prefix assigned to them. It may sound silly, because everyone knows what a table is, but can you really tell the difference between a base table versus a view table? A view table isn't really a table, per se. It may look and feel like a real table, but it limits the amount of data a user can see and modify. Views can include a single column of a table, the entire table, or even a combination of columns from several tables.

Why use views? Often you will have sensitive information stored in a base table, like an employee's social security number or salary. It's difficult to restrict developers from retrieving information from a table if they have access to the table. By using a view, you can provide access to the entire table except for the sensitive columns. Here are some examples of table and view names for an order entry system. Note that some are prefixed with *tbl* for table, one is prefixed with *tbl* but suffixed with *_v* for a view table, and another is prefixed with *vw_* for a view table. The last one, prefixed with *qry* represents a query in Microsoft Access. Unlike large-scale database management systems, Access does not allow for views, but a query is loosely related to a view table.

- tblCustomers
- tblCategories
- tblEmployees
- tblEmployees_v
- vw_Employees
- qryEmployees

Column Naming

When it comes to naming a column of a table, there are a lot of choices. You want to be as descriptive as you can within a short name. You should try to keep their names under 15 characters. As part of the column name, you should provide a suffix identifying what the column contains, like a date, time, timestamp, and so on. Table 14-2 offers some examples of some standard suffixes.

Suffix	Description
amt	Amount
cd	Code
desc	Description
dt	Date
id	Indicator/Identifier
qty	Quantity
tm	Time
ts	Timestamp
val	Value

Table 14.2 Examples of Column Name Suffixes

Common Columns

In any transaction-based system, there should be a few columns that are always included in every table for data verification. These columns are used to help track who made the last update to a record and when the update took place. This is more of a DBA issue than a developer's issue, but a good developer should be aware of it.

The following columns should be placed into each table of your database:

- LastUpdate_ID
- LastUpdate_ts
- Active_ID

The first two items are pretty straightforward—the employee identifier and timestamp identifying when the record was modified. The last field, Active_ID, might be foreign to you. Depending on the system and the line of business the software is developed for, you might be required by law not to delete any records within a database or overwrite any field to update a record. In this case, you would enter an "I" for inactive in the Active_ID column of an existing record, and write a new record with updated information (or write no new record to simulate deleting the record). In this situation, you will never issue a SQL **DELETE** or **UPDATE** statement directly to a row, or use the **Recordset** object's **Delete** or **Update** method, except to update the Active_ID column. If you ever need an audit trail, you can determine who last modified the record and when by looking at the most recent timestamp on the record.

Stored Procedures

Stored procedures should begin with a prefix of either *proc* or *spp*, followed by a name that identifies the purpose of the stored procedure. Table 14-3 lists some examples of stored procedure names.

It's not recommended that you use the prefix **sp**, *because that prefix is used by stored procedures that ship with SQL Server.*

ADO Optimization

Of all the data-access object models, ADO is probably one of the fastest to come out of the Microsoft campus. However, there are some optimization techniques you should consider to ensure that your data access is as efficient as it can be.

Transaction Processing

There may be times when you will be updating a set of values for several records inside some sort of loop. If you are, you should consider using the **BeginTrans** and **CommitTrans** methods around your loop. This can significantly speed up the update process. The following example shows how to use them:

```
cn.BeginTrans
Do While Not rsContacts.EOF
    rsContacts("AreaCode") = "626"
    rsContacts.Update
    rsContacts.MoveNext
Loop
cn.CommitTrans
```

Stored Procedure Name	Description
procGetOrderInfo	Get order information
sppLUPCategories	Look up categories
sppTransProcOrder	Transaction—process an order

Table 14.3 Examples of Stored Procedure Names

Use SQL Statements Rather than ADO Objects

The concept of using SQL statements when you have a perfectly good object to work through leaves a bad taste in some developers' mouths. The truth of the matter is that using SQL statements, and executing them directly, is faster than going through the ADO object. It's faster because every time you perform a SQL statement on an ADO object, it has to gather the data in the memory area that contains the **Recordset**, convert it to a SQL statement, and then send the SQL statement to the database engine. By using the SQL statement directly, you eliminate a lot of steps that ADO would need to perform.

This technique is best used on SQL **INSERT** or **UPDATE** processes because you don't expect to receive any data back, other than a confirmation that the transaction was completed successfully.

Cursors! Foiled Again!

A cursor is a pointer to a record in a returned **Recordset**. The cursor concept was introduced to SQL database engines to mimic record-oriented access methods. Cursors allow you to manipulate data by rows rather than by sets. The use of cursors allows multiple operations to be executed row by row on the results of a query. When you create an ADO **Recordset**, it's very important that you use the right type of cursor to ensure optimal record processing.

When opening a **Recordset** for populating a lookup table, grid, or any other read-only display, it's always advisable to use a forward-only cursor instead of any other cursor-type. A forward-only cursor will open about 25 percent faster in Access databases and over 80 percent faster in server-based database management systems. By default, the cursor type of an ADO **Recordset** object is set to **adOpenUnspecified**; therefore, you should set the cursor-type setting to the constant **adOpenForwardOnly**.

Summary

ADO is a very powerful data access tool. With just a connection and several **Recordset**s, you can do a lot of database-access processing. Keeping in mind the coding tips of using dots instead of bangs, remembering to use the **MoveNext** method when processing a **Recordset**, and making sure you check your **BOF** and **EOF** properties, you can save yourself a lot of debugging time. When retrieving information from BLOB data types, it's important to remember to use the **GetChunk** method, otherwise you will not get the results you expected.

When it comes to error handling, it's important to remember that ADO has its own set of error messages. You should not use the same error-handling routines that you've written for application logic. If you do, your users will be providing you with incorrect error messages.

Database naming standards can help make your job and the job of your DBAs a lot easier because everyone will recognize the table, column, and stored procedure names at a quick glance. Also, by using standardized names for columns, when you or your DBA perform joins on tables, there won't be much confusion as to whether the elements you are linking with are of the same data type.

PART IV

VB and the Internet

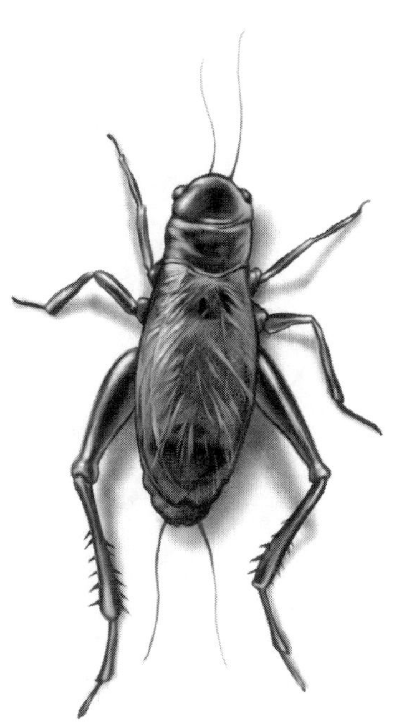

CHAPTER 15

WebClasses and DHTML Applications

Starting with version 6 of Visual Basic, Microsoft introduced two new types of applications: IIS and DHTML. More and more companies want to migrate their applications to a Web-based model, and these two technologies enable you to leverage your knowledge of VB and make your applications Web-enabled without having to learn a different development environment or a lot of new object models.

An IIS application is an application that is loaded and executed from a Web server. A DHTML application executes its code from within the Web browser. IIS applications require you to know some HTML in order to create user interfaces for your applications. DHTML applications require you to know some JavaScript terminology when it comes to designing events for objects on your user interface. There are some differences in design from what you are used to in VB, such as the way you should handle error messages and how you should segment your business logic. Other than those elements, however, these two technologies utilize nearly everything that VB has to offer.

IIS Applications

An IIS application, named for Internet Information Server, is a Visual Basic application that is accessed and executed from an Internet browser. It uses HTML to present information to the user, and compiled Visual Basic code to manage data and perform business processes within an ActiveX DLL. An IIS application project can consist of references to HTML and DHTML pages, standard modules, class modules, and WebClass designers. The *WebClass designer* is an ActiveX designer that provides a visual design window interface that references a special type of object called a ***WebClass***. A **WebClass** is an object that contains ***WebItems***, which are HTML pages, MIME-type files, or responses to an HTTP request, and the code that delivers those **WebItem**s to a client's browser. By design, for every WebClass designer, there is one **WebClass**. If you want to add more **WebClass**es to your application, you must add additional designers, as shown in Figure 15-1. The file extension for a designer is .dsr. One of the best things about IIS applications is that they are browser independent, because the application is executed on the Web server, specifically in Microsoft's Internet Information Server (IIS) or Personal Web Server.

The drawback to the IIS application is its development process. Unlike a project built completely in standard HTML or DHTML, IIS applications have to be compiled and then copied to the Web server each time a change is made to the project. Web-based applications developed completely using Active Server Pages

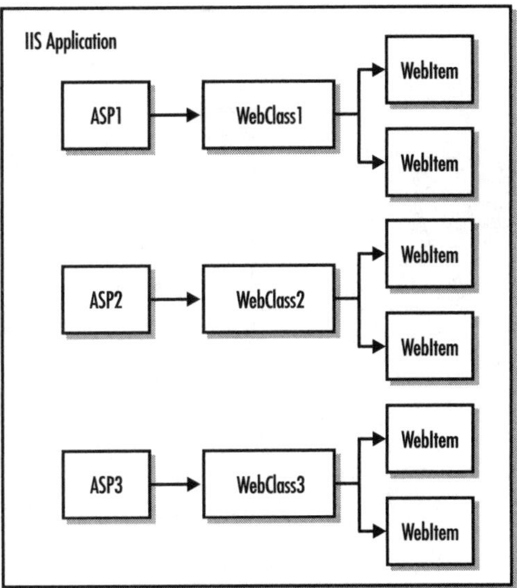

Figure 15.1 Architecture of the **WebClass**

(ASP) scripting are not compiled, they are text files that contain special tags that are processed through the ISAPI (Internet Server API), are executed on the server, and their result is sent back to the user via an HTTP response. Figure 15-2 provides an illustration of the request and response flow of an ASP page, as opposed to the architecture of an IIS application.

Note *Throughout this chapter, the terms "IIS application" and "**WebClass** application" will be used interchangeably.*

General Application Design Guidelines

There are a number of factors that you should keep in mind when developing your IIS application that are different from general application development guidelines. These factors need to be evaluated with your development team. Issues like file location, HTML coding standards, database transactions, and form-to-form navigation all need to be discussed.

File Locations and URLs

Developers all have their own special coding styles and methods of storing files. However, IIS applications are incredibly dependent on having a consistent directory structure, just like HTML documents. During the application

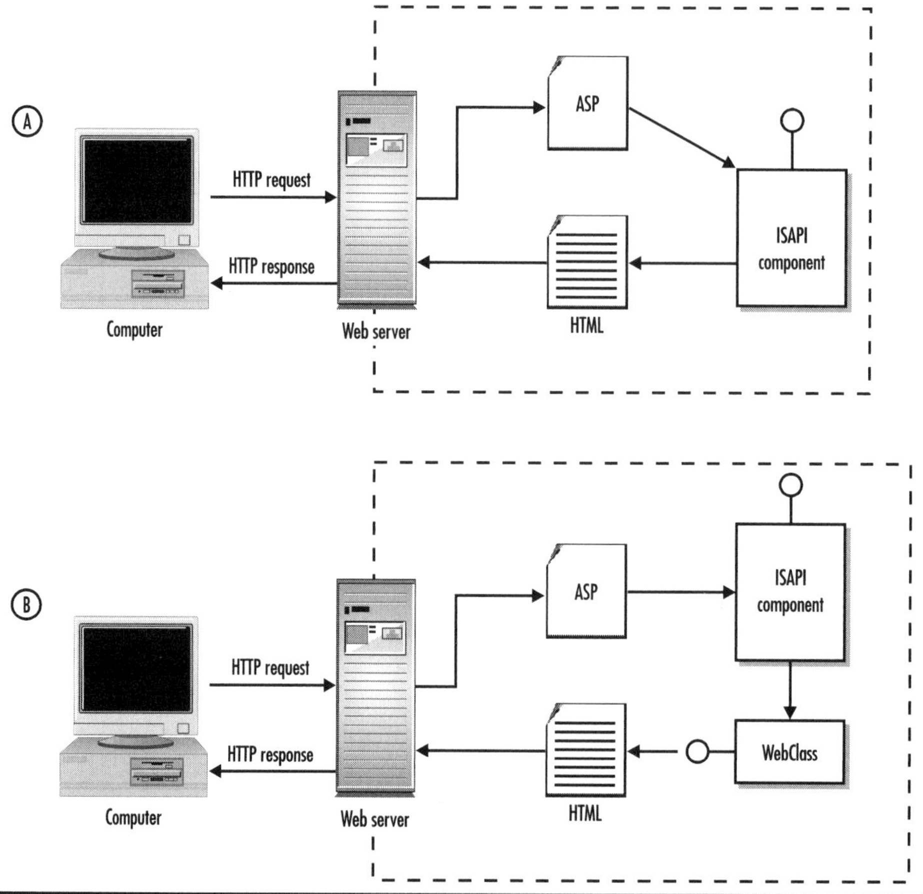

Figure 15.2 ASP application (A) vs. IIS application architecture (B)

development stage, you need to consider how your Web server directory structure will be laid out, because it might be different from your development system. Your project files, whether VB or Web-based, might be stored in a Projects folder off the root directory on one drive, and your images and other support files might be stored on another drive or even on a file server. It's a good practice to use relative URLs for images and related files because absolute URLs indicate exact drive letters and directories that your HTML pages will expect to find when referencing files. Relative URLs identify the name of the file and indicate its location in relation to your project directory, specifying how many directories up or down to move to find the reference. Table 15-1 provides examples of both absolute and relative URLs.

Reference Type	URL
Absolute URL	<IMG SRC="D:\WEBPROJS\IMAGES\LOGOS\LOGO.GIF">
	<IMG SRC="D:\WEBPROJS\BOGUSNEWS\LOGIN">
Relative URL	<IMG SRC="..\IMAGES\LOGOS\LOGO.GIF">
	<IMG SRC="..\BOGUSNEWS\LOGIN">

Table 15.1 Absolute URLs vs. Relative URLs

When specifying URLs within your **WebItem**s or pages, it's best if you use generated URLs rather than typing the full URL into your **WebClass** template or code. To use generated URL information, use the **URLFor** method as follows:

```
Response.Write "<A HREF=""" & URLFor(Menu) & """>Back to Menu</a>"
```

The **URLFor** method is used to create a hyperlink to the Menu HTML Template **WebItem**. The source HTML document will look like the following:

```
<a href="Webclass1.ASP?WCI=Menu">Back to Menu</a>
```

When the user clicks on the link, the Menu HTML Template **WebItem**'s **Respond** event will be executed, and it will be displayed to the user.

HTML Coding Standards

HTML pages can be created in a number of ways. Some developers use WYSIWYG ("what you see is what you get") editors like Microsoft FrontPage 2000 or SoftQuad HoTMetaL; others use text-based HTML editors like Microsoft Visual InterDev or Allaire's HomeSite, while true hard-core HTML-smiths use Windows Notepad. Regardless of what editor you use, it's important that your HTML pages are properly formatted and that nothing is taken for granted. If the HTML page is not formatted correctly, it is very possible that you will encounter errors when loading the HTML template into the WebClass designer.

So what is a poorly formatted HTML page? If you have a bunch of nested tables, it's probable that you might forget to close a table row or table data cell before opening a new table within a table data cell. If you've done any amount of HTML editing, you have probably seen instances where the HTML document will view fine in Microsoft Internet Explorer (MSIE) but part of the document might show incorrectly or not show up at all in Netscape Navigator. That's because MSIE is a lot more forgiving when it comes to sloppy HTML than Navigator is. Rather than viewing your HTML document in both browsers, it is best to run your HTML documents through an HTML syntax checker. The W3C

(World Wide Web Consortium) offers an HTML validator for every version of the HTML standard (http://www.w3c.org); Allaire's HomeSite uses CSE 3310's HTML Validator, which can also be purchased separately (http://www.htmlvalidator.com).

Design Tip *There are a number of fine HTML editors on the market today. Regardless of which one you like, it's best that you find one that can handle DHTML and XML tags.*

It is not recommended that you use HTML pages containing forms that use the HTML **Get** method. If your HTML page does use them and you import the file as an HTML template file, you will not be able to successfully connect events within your **WebClass** and properly run your application. You need to make sure that all template files you plan to use with your **WebClass** use the **Post** method for any forms.

Database Transactions

With any application, regardless of whether it is client/server based or Web-based, you really don't want your application to use too many database connections, because they will take up a lot of system resources, especially if your users are just browsing for data. Another reason you don't want to have too many database connections open is because a lot of database management systems (DBMSs) aren't sophisticated enough to only lock records at the row level yet. A lot of the latest incarnations of the popular DBMSs are now enabling row locking, but many companies haven't made the leap to those versions; therefore, they will still have to use page locking when it comes to securing data from other users' input.

An ADO (ActiveX Data Object) technique you should look into is using disconnected **Recordset**s. A disconnected **Recordset** is a **Recordset** that has been populated with data from your data source and is then disconnected from that data source. By disconnecting itself from the data source, it doesn't have the overhead of the connection to the data source; however, any updates to the data in the Recordset are not reflected in the original data source until the **Recordset** is reconnected to the data source and an **Update** method is invoked. If your IIS application is designed mostly for data lookup and inquiries, disconnected **Recordset**s are very useful because you can view all the information you queried, re-sort it, and narrow the **Recordset** without sending another data access command to the database server. All this data manipulation is done through the application.

The downside of a disconnected **Recordset** is that any changes made to the data in the source database will not be reflected in the **Recordset** until it is reconnected.

If data must be updated, the disconnected **Recordset** still has references to the source records. ADO makes the connection back to the database server as if you had never disconnected, and you can then update or insert any new information into the data source. Once the update or insert has been completed and you're sure that you're not going to update or add any more information, refresh your **Recordset** to retrieve all the changes you and anyone else have made, and again disconnect from the data source.

Application Navigation

It's difficult to predict exactly how your users will interact with a Web-based application. Unlike traditional client/server applications that rely on forms and structured navigation buttons to move between them, Web-based applications allow users to navigate more freely by letting them move back and forth at any time by using the browser's navigation buttons. Also, unlike a traditional client/server application, a user might close a browser-based application without completing a transaction, leaving open database connections and process threads on your server until they time out, if they ever do.

As much as you may try to guide the users down a fixed path, it's very probable that they will stray from the path simply because of the way people use browsers. To help remedy this potential problem, a lot more interface design time is needed for Web-based applications. You should structure your application so that users can navigate freely amongst the application's **WebItem**s, rather than assuming that they are going to follow a fixed navigational path.

When your users are performing any sort of data entry, you will need to consider how you plan to handle out-of-sequence navigation caused by the user's use of the browser's Back button and History menu. You need to consider this when your users are performing any sort of data entry. A user might go through a series of screens of data entry, click the Commit button, and while waiting for the transaction to complete, use the browser's Back button to go back to a previous screen to update some information and resubmit it, believing that the transaction hadn't been completed the first time. To prevent this from happening, you could try to train your users to not do anything after clicking the Commit button until they receive a confirmation notice that the transaction completed successfully or failed. Another technique you can employ is to always check to make sure that the record doesn't exist before performing any transaction, even if the user specifically chooses the Create New Record feature.

For security reasons, one technique a lot of ASP developers do is make all their pages non-cacheable so that Web forms aren't saved in the Web browser's cache. This prevents users from using the browser's Back button to go to previous pages to change information and then resubmit. This is not an absolute solution, though, because there have been instances where this technique does not work as planned. There might be times when the page becomes cacheable due to a bug in the browser or something else unexpected happening.

Performance Tuning

Because **WebClass** objects are components that are installed on the Web server, there are some developers who think that they don't need to worry about application performance any more. This philosophy comes from the notion that since the Internet is inherently slow, and people are used to less than stellar application performance over the Internet or even over intranets, why should they expect high performance from a **WebClass** application? That's definitely the wrong thinking. **WebClass** applications can have very acceptable performance if you keep the following techniques in mind. You will want to consider storing the state information, properly managing objects, and separating business and data services from the user interface.

Storing State Information

Due to the statelessness of Internet technology (Web servers are not capable of maintaining information between HTTP requests), you will want to somehow maintain state. A setting that is recommended in a lot of documentation is the **wcRetainInstance** setting in the **WebClass**'s **StateManagement** property; however, you should take care when using it. All ActiveX DLLs created with VB use apartment-model objects, and these objects are placed into **Session** objects when the **wcRetainInstance** property is used. This causes the Web server to bind the client to a particular thread in IIS, severely compromising the concurrency and throughput of your application.

Another method of storing state information is to put the information inside **Session** or **Application** objects. This does not require the **WebClass** object to be set to **wcRetainInstance**. Storing state in the **Session** object is as simple as in the following code:

```
<%
Session("soFName") = txtFName
Session("soUserID") = rs("UserID")
%>
```

To store state in the **Application** object, use code similar to the following:

```
<%
Application("aoTimeout") = 42
%>
```

You can also send information back and forth to the browser by either writing out your own cookie, using hidden fields, or using the **URLData** property of the **WebClass**. The **URLData** method allows you to pass information from the browser to the server by appending it to the URL itself. The caveat is that you can only pass about 2K worth of information in the URL string.

The problem with passing information through cookies is people's paranoia about security on the Internet. A *cookie* is a small file stored on the user's computer. Some Web sites use cookies to store your personal preferences for what is displayed when you go to the site. Other sites use cookies to store your user ID and password so you don't have to keep logging in to the site when you visit it. Obviously, if someone got ahold of some of the information stored in them, they could cause problems. There are a number of users who prevent Web sites from placing cookies on their computer altogether. If your users fall into this category, cookies probably aren't the best thing to use.

Object Management

Another performance-tuning consideration is to not create any additional connections to an object than you need. This is important, because each time you instantiate an object using the **New** operator or the **CreateObject** function, a new instance of the object is created inside the same process memory space of the **WebClass** object but in a different thread. To avoid this problem, you should use the **Server.CreateObject** method, because by doing so, IIS detects the thread model of the object and optimizes subsequent request processing. In turn, the object will be instantiated only as long as the **WebItem** is needed, then it will be unloaded from memory.

Business and Data Services

WebClass applications are great for building Web-based user interfaces (UIs) and for dealing with user interaction. Unfortunately, an application does not consist of just a fancy UI and screen navigation. Web-based applications are just like any other traditional client/server application; they're about solving problems. As with client/server applications, it's not advisable to put any business or data access services inside your user interface services—you should adhere to the same development methodology with **WebClass** applications.

It is strongly suggested that you write business logic and data access routines in ActiveX DLLs instead of in **WebClass** applications. Assuming that **WebClass** applications aren't the only applications you've deployed, you probably have a lot of ActiveX DLLs developed and deployed throughout your enterprise. Some may even be taking advantage of MTS (Microsoft Transaction Server) and MSMQ (Microsoft Messaging Queue) to run in a distributed manner. So why reinvent the wheel by writing routines that have already been written and putting them in your **WebClass** application. Once your **WebClass** application references those other ActiveX DLLs, all you need to do is add **WebClass** objects to run transactions and retrieve data you will parse into HTML.

Error Handling

If you've learned one thing throughout this entire book, it should be this: errors will happen regardless of how careful you are. This is no different with IIS applications. What is different is how you can display error messages to the user. Unlike traditional client/server form-based applications that can display forms either modally or modelessly, IIS applications don't have any forms. Since IIS applications are browser-based, you don't have the luxury of being able to display error messages by using **MsgBox** statements or functions. Like ActiveX DLLs, IIS applications need to run with the Unattended Execution option selected in the Project Properties dialog box, as shown in Figure 15-3. By enabling this option, all VB run-time errors and **MsgBox** function calls are recorded in the Web server's event log rather than being displayed to the user, regardless of the error routines you have in place.

To ensure that you capture errors when they occur, you should still use the **On Error** routine within your code. In your error subroutine, though, you will handle things a bit differently. Normally, your **On Error** routine would be something like the following:

```
Function DoSomething(Arg1 As String) As String
    On Error GoTo Err_DoSomething
    ...
    DoSomething = SomethingHappened
Exit_DoSomething:
    Exit Function
Err_DoSomething:
    Dim ErrMsg As String
    ErrMsg = "Something bad happened." & vbCrLf
    ErrMsg = ErrMsg & "Error Nbr: " & Err.Number & vbCrLf
    ErrMsg = ErrMsg & "Description: " & Err.Description
    MsgBox ErrMsg
    DoSomething = SomethingDidNotHappen
    Goto Exit_DoSomething
End Function
```

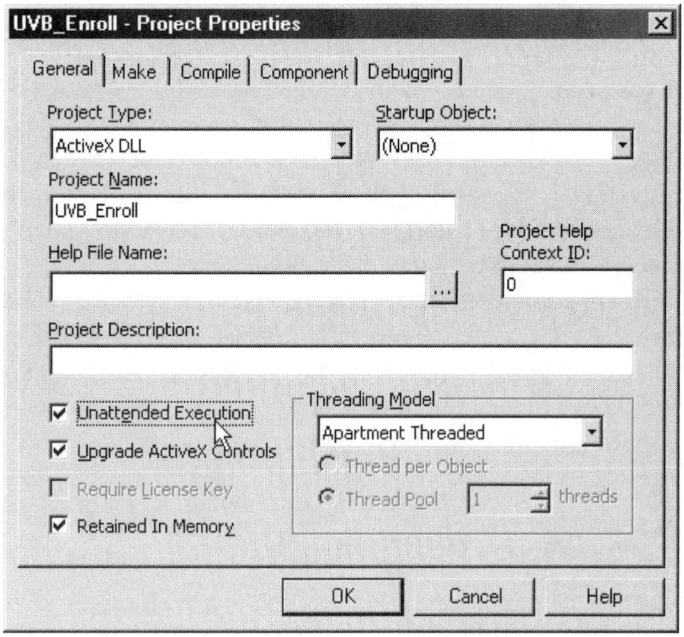

Figure 15.3 The General tab of the Project Properties dialog box for a **WebClass** with the Unattended Execution option selected

In a **WebClass** application, you still want to provide feedback to the user when an error occurs. Instead of using the **MsgBox** function to display an error message to the user, you're going to use the function's return value to pass the error message back to the procedure that called it. This means that the procedure that calls the function should be expecting more information back from the function than just a True or False toggle. The following code shows what this error function looks like:

```
Function DoSomething(Arg1 As String) As String
    On Error GoTo Err_DoSomething
    ...
    DoSomething = SomethingHappened
Exit_DoSomething:
    Exit Function
Err_DoSomething:
    Dim ErrMsg As String
    ErrMsg = "Something bad happened in the DoSomething "
    ErrMsg = ErrMsg & "function." & vbCrLf
    ErrMsg = ErrMsg & "Error Nbr: " & Err.Number & vbCrLf
    ErrMsg = ErrMsg & "Description: " & Err.Description
DoSomething = ErrMsg
Goto Exit_DoSomething
End Function
```

Deploying IIS Applications

In case you've had problems with the execution of your IIS application running on either Personal Web Server on a Windows 9*x* workstation or on Internet Information Server on Windows NT/2000, Table 15-2 lists the recommended files and their version numbers needed to run an IIS application. Earlier versions of these files might work, but in a production environment, you should use the recommended minimum version or greater.

If you don't have the latest versions of the files on your system, you should install at least Visual Studio 6.0 Service Pack 3. If you're using Windows NT, you should have Windows NT Service Pack 5 installed as well. Since the Windows 9*x* operating system doesn't have service packs like NT, you should install the System Library updates.

Microsoft recommends that version 6.00.81.69 of the MSWCRUN.DLL be installed on development systems.

When deploying an IIS application to a Web server, it may or may not have the required run-time resources, dependent files, or recommended minimum files; therefore, it's always best to deploy your applications using the Package and Deployment Wizard (PDW). Since developers should have the latest resource files outlined in Table 15-2, having the developers use the PDW ensures that the application is shipped with the correct resource files and that the target Web server will receive the minimum resources required to run the application.

Filename	Version	Location
asycfilt.dll	2.40.4275	Windows\System or WinNT\System32
comcat.dll	4.71	Windows\System or WinNT\System32
msvbvm60.dll	6.00.8495	Windows\System or WinNT\System32
mswcrun.dll (WebClass run-time)	6.00.84.50	Program Files\Common Files\Designer
oleaut32.dll	2.40.4275	Windows\System or WinNT\System32
olepro32.dll	5.0.4275	Windows\System or WinNT\System32
stdole2.tlb	2.40.4275	Windows\System or WinNT\System32

Table 15.2 Recommended Resource Files and Minimum Version Numbers Needed to Run an IIS Application

DHTML Applications

A DHTML application is a Visual Basic application that combines DHTML and compiled VB code to create an interactive, browser-based application. Unlike HTML, DHTML lets you add programs to your Web page that can change all aspects of the page. That's why the "D" stands for "dynamic." The page can change its layout, validate data, and so on, without having to transmit any information back to the server. What makes this possible is the introduction of an *object model* into the Web browser itself. As you might already know from developing in VB, an object model defines and exposes all the features of an object. The object model within the browser is called the *document object model* (DOM), and it is exposed when a Web page is downloaded and parsed by a browser. The one *big* caveat about the DHTML document object model is that not all DHTML DOMs are created equal, which means that Microsoft's implementation of the DHTML DOM is different from Netscape's implementation. This makes Web-based applications browser-dependent, because DHTML applications only work with Microsoft Internet Explorer's DHTML DOM.

Design Tip *In order to take advantage of DHTML applications, your clients need MSIE 4.01 service pack 1 installed on their system, or higher. This limits the effectiveness of deploying DHTML applications over the Internet, because you can't guarantee that everyone is using MSIE.*

In order to access the object model, you need to write scripts to manipulate the page. Microsoft's Internet Explorer 3.*x* and higher provides two built-in scripting language interpreters: VBScript and JScript. However, only version 4.*x* and higher contain the DHTML object model, so unless your organization has standardized on (or has access to) MSIE 4.*x* or greater, you can't take advantage of this technology.

In the past, most articles, tutorials, books, white papers, and so on, only showed scripting of DHTML using JScript, which is Microsoft's version of JavaScript. From all accounts, this was because DHTML worked better using JScript than VBScript. With VB now able to create DHTML applications, you can use VBA as your scripting language. If you wrote a DHTML application the old-fashioned way, using your favorite DHTML editor, and so on, the source for all your DHTML applications would be viewable by anyone who selects View Source in his or her browser. With a DHTML application created in VB, the source the user would see is the HTML used to create the page, and a reference to an ActiveX DLL. That's right, VB compiles all the DHTML scripting you write into an ActiveX DLL that gets installed on the client's system, and is then removed after the application terminates. Since it's deployed as an ActiveX DLL, you should change the DLL base address from &H11000000 to something more useful.

Note *The DLL base address is a memory address into which an ActiveX DLL will be loaded. The memory range is from 16MB (16,777,216 or &H10000000) to 2GB (2,147,483,648 or &H80000000), inclusively. The address must be a multiple of 64K. Consequently, the last four digits (in hexadecimal) will be 0000. By default, Visual Basic sets the DLL base address as &H11000000. Thus, there is a reasonably high probability that the DLL base address of &H11000000 will not be available and that a different DLL base address will need to be used.*

When Windows loads a DLL, it attempts to load it in at the specified base address. If the address is available, the DLL loads relatively quickly. However, if another DLL already is using that address, then Windows must relocate the DLL data and code to a new and available address. This is known as *rebasing*. Rebasing is time-consuming and also may complicate Windows' ability to share the DLL code with other applications. Obviously, rebasing is to be avoided.

Deploying DHTML Applications

In order to make your DHTML application available for use, you need to create a deployment package and place it on your Web server. To do that, you need to use the Package and Deployment Wizard that will create the necessary cab (cabinet) file with your DHTML ActiveX DLL application and its associated support files. A cab file is a Microsoft file format that compresses a number of files into one file, very similar to ZIP technology introduced by PKWare, Inc. Unlike IIS applications that are processed completely on the Web server, DHTML applications are very similar to HTML documents with ActiveX controls embedded in them. That means that since the DHTML application is installed on your client's system the same way an ActiveX control is, it's installed in the "Downloaded Program Files" folder inside the folder your Windows operating system is installed in.

Because the application gets installed onto your client's system through Internet technology, it's a good idea to obtain a digital signature for your cab files. A digital signature verifies the source of the application or ActiveX control/DLL by identifying the legal entity that created the software. If you plan to distribute your DHTML application to customers outside of your company's intranet, you should purchase the certificate from a *certificate authority*, which is a company that validates your identity and issues a certificate to you. (VeriSign and Thawte are two certificate authority companies.) The certificate contains your digital signature and is a verification notice of your credentials. In the event of any problems, the certificate authority becomes a witness to your identity. It sounds really complicated, but due to the lack of security when transferring files over the Internet, it's good practice to use a digital signature with all the components you deploy over the Internet.

For intranet use, you don't need to purchase a digital signature to sign your cab files or ActiveX components. With the Microsoft CryptoAPI Tools you can digitally sign files to be used with Microsoft Authenticode, and you can view and manage certificates, certificate revocation lists (CRLs), and certificate trust lists (CTLs). For more information about the CryptoAPI Tools and other digital signature technology offered by Microsoft, see the CryptoAPI Tools Start page at http://msdn.microsoft.com/library/psdk/crypto/portaltool_3u3p.htm.

Note *Microsoft constantly changes the links on their Web site. At the time this book was published, the preceding URL would take you to the CryptoAPI Tools Start Page. If they change the link again, do a search for CryptoAPI.*

Using the Package and Deployment Wizard

Under normal conditions, the Package and Deployment Wizard (PDW) allows you to create two types of packages: a Standard Setup Package and a Dependency File. (For more information on these packages, refer to Chapter 12.) When using the PDW to make a package that will deploy a DHTML application, a third package type called an Internet Package is available. This package is used to create a cab-based installation package that will be downloaded from your Web server.

In addition to the additional package type, there are a few extra steps for creating a DHTML application package. One of them is the File Source step (shown in Figure 15-4), which allows you to specify the location from which an Internet package should retrieve necessary files during installation. Files can be retrieved from the cab file itself, from the Microsoft Web site, or from an alternative URL location. Many of the Microsoft resources should be retrieved from the Microsoft Web site to ensure that the latest version of the resources is downloaded to your client's system.

The other step that is unique for creating Internet packages is the Safety Settings step, shown in Figure 15-5. This step lists all the ActiveX controls and

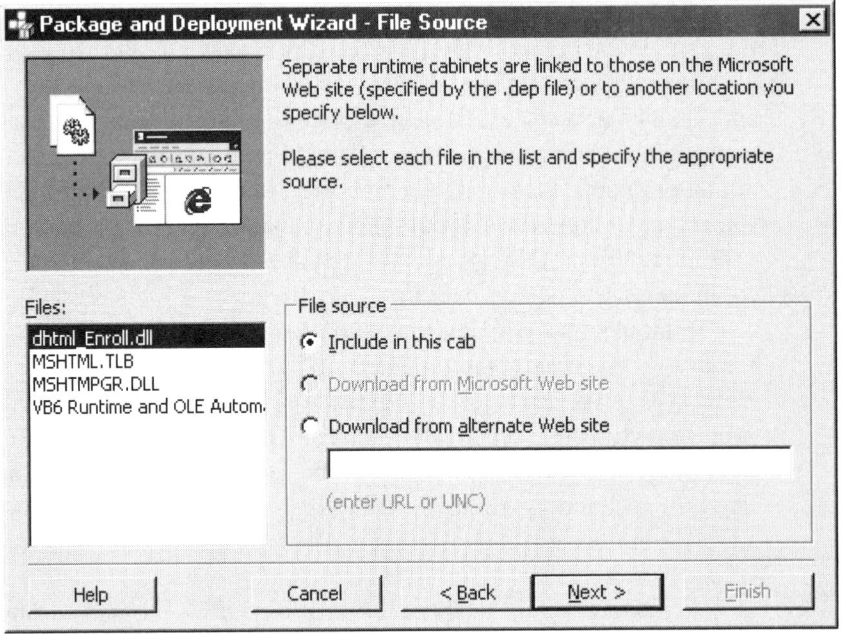

Figure 15.4 The File Source step of the PDW for Internet Packages

DLLs that are part of the project and lets you determine if they are safe for initialization and/or safe for scripting. By marking a component as Safe for Scripting or Safe for Initialization, you are guaranteeing that your component can never corrupt or cause undesirable behavior on your client's machine. Marking a component as either Safe for Scripting or Safe for Initialization implies that you are accepting liability for this guarantee.

Once you have created the cab file, use the PDW's Deployment feature to deploy your package to either the shared server or the FTP server that your application will be accessed from. To use the DHTML application, copy all the files associated with your application's HTML pages, such as images, to the necessary location on your Web server.

Summary

IIS and DHTML applications can be used to make some pretty powerful applications. Even though Visual Basic has gone through six major version releases, both IIS and DHTML application building are in their first iterations.

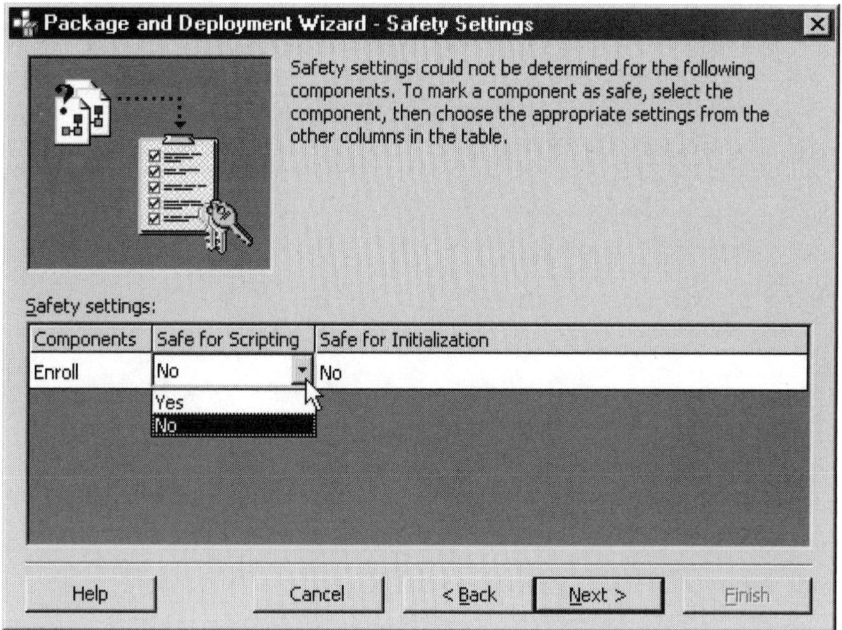

Figure 15.5 The Safety Settings step for the PDW for Internet Packages

If you haven't started developing applications using either of these technologies, you're not missing out on any earth-shattering technology. However, these two technologies are the precursor to what Microsoft has cooking in their development ovens for the next release of Visual Studio, which is technology that will allow you to program the Internet.

If you need to develop Web-enabled applications and have not yet embraced the IIS and DHTML application technology, then the best architecture design we can recommend is that you develop good COM and COM+ components for your business rules and data access, have them reside on your Web servers, and use Active Server Pages to instantiate them and produce the user interfaces. If you're completely unfamiliar with this concept, you might want to look into *Debugging ASP: Troubleshooting for Programmers* (Osborne/McGraw-Hill, 2000). To find out more about the next evolution of the Visual Studio and programming the Internet, read Chapter 16 of this book.

CHAPTER 16

Visual Basic: The Next Generation

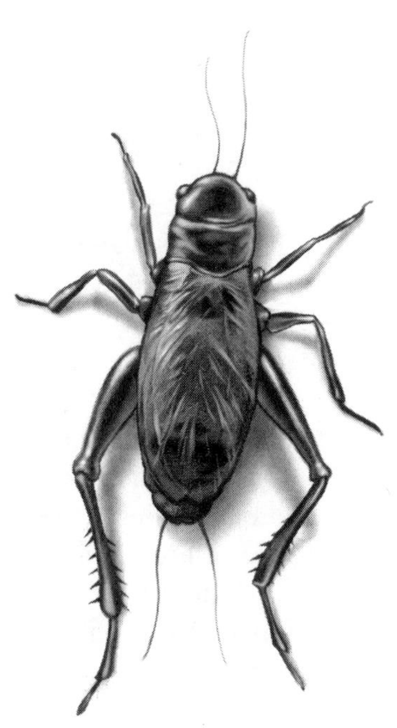

"With these new language features, Visual Basic will deliver all the power of C++ or Java while maintaining the instant accessibility that has made it the world's most popular development tool." —Microsoft's Visual Studio Next Generation Web site

Two young girls were discussing the size of dogs. One asked: "Can a dog be as large as an elephant?" Her friend responded: "No, if it were as big as an elephant, it would look like an elephant." —Stephen J. Gould, from Ever Since Darwin

Visual Basic's principal claim to fame is that it enables you to write a Windows application much faster and more easily than, for example, C++. Writing a "Hello World" application in Visual Basic is as easy as a single **Print "Hello World"** statement in the **Form_Load** event of a Standard EXE project. By contrast, trying to write even a simple Windows application in C++ can be frustrating enough to prompt the programmer to change the message to "Goodbye cruel world."

However, Visual Basic also has been regarded as not being a "serious" programming language because it is not a true object-oriented programming language like C++ and Java. In particular, Visual Basic has not supported inheritance. Visual Basic also has not supported other features auxiliary to object-oriented programming languages, such as structured exception handling. Instead, Visual Basic error handling relies heavily on **GoTo** statements, which have long been discredited, for good reason, in the "serious" programming world. For these reasons (and perhaps also jealousy over how Visual Basic eases development of Windows applications), academicians, programming purists, and some aficionados who use competing programming languages have looked down upon Visual Basic as a "toy" programming language.

As a Visual Basic programmer, you may not care, and properly so, about the snobbery of academicians, programming purists, and disgruntled C++ and Java programmers. However, Visual Basic's lack of support for object-oriented programming has more practical implications. An important benefit of object-oriented programming is that it enables you to model your code after the objects in the real world that are the subject of your application. This makes your code more accurately fit the real world problem that you are attempting to solve. Object-oriented programming also makes your code easier to understand and therefore to debug, maintain, and improve. As a result, large and complex enterprise and Web applications often rely heavily on object-oriented programming concepts.

With successive versions, Visual Basic has moved, or perhaps more accurately, inched towards becoming a true object-oriented programming language. Version 4 introduced classes, which are the foundation of object-oriented programming. Version 5 introduced the **Implements** statement, which supported a type of inheritance—interface inheritance. There have also been a number of other useful, albeit incremental, improvements. Still, through version 6, Visual Basic has not been a true object-oriented programming language.

With version 7, this will no longer be the case. Version 7 promises to support inheritance and a number of other exciting (for programmers anyway) features, including but not limited to structured exception handling, free threading, and overloaded functions. Programming language changes are often incremental and usually are not regarded as very exciting to anyone but those who teach or preach about the programming language. However, the changes to the programming language in version 7 of Visual Basic are nothing short of revolutionary, not just in terms of language changes, but also in your ability to extend reusable code components through inheritance.

While these changes to the Visual Basic programming language will enable you to write better programs, there is much new to learn, especially if you have not also programmed in C++ or Java. Additionally, the new features in some ways give you additional rope to hang yourself. For example, your newfound ability to spawn threads also places upon you the responsibility of ensuring that threads don't deadlock. Finally, and perhaps most important, object-oriented programming requires a new and different way of thinking when designing your applications. However, programmers should never be afraid of new challenges!

While the language changes alone make version 7 a significant upgrade, Microsoft did not stop there. In recognition of the pervasive influence of the Internet, version 7 introduces Web Forms and Web Services.

Currently, Web applications running on a remote Web server use Active Server Pages (ASP), involving HTML forms with embedded script. Web Forms, utilizing the next generation of ASP, appropriately named ASP+, still will use HTML forms. However, the code will not be embedded in the form, but instead will reside in a separate file. This will enhance the debugging, maintenance, and reusability of the code. Perhaps more important, the code will not be script, but instead will be compiled, which will speed processing by the Web server.

Code components, such as ActiveX DLLs, that provide a service to other applications reside on the same local machine or network as the application using the service. With Web Services, applications will be able to use a service (a Web Service) that resides on a remote Web server. As a developer, you will be able to reference and create an instance of a Web Service just as easily as you now can reference and create an instance of an ActiveX DLL. Indeed, though the Web Service will reside on a remote Web server instead of a local machine or network, your task of designing and deploying the Web Service to a remote server will be quite similar to your task today of creating and deploying an ActiveX DLL locally. This will enable you to use reusable code components in your Web applications just as you now can in your applications that run locally, through ActiveX Servers.

Caution *This chapter was written before the beta of Visual Basic 7 was released, and much may change between the first beta and the final release. However, Microsoft, at its Visual Studio Next Generation site (http://msdn.Microsoft.com/vstudio/nextgen/), has prominently announced the language changes, Web Forms, and Web Services, so it is likely that they will find their way into Visual Basic 7.*

Visual Basic 7's Support of Object-Oriented Programming

Encapsulation, inheritance, and polymorphism are the trinity of object-oriented programming. With version 7, Visual Basic will support them all.

Encapsulation

Encapsulation is the ability to contain and hide information related to an object. It often is referred to as "data-hiding." The data is hidden in the sense that other objects (that is, external applications that use these objects) cannot access the data directly. Rather, other objects can access the data only through the public procedures of the object that contains the data.

The information that is hidden often is a property that represents an object's state. You cannot guarantee the integrity of such properties if they can be accessed directly from outside the class. For example, an **Employee** object may have a **Name** property. If that **Name** property can be accessed directly from outside the **Employee** class, you could not guarantee that a blank name would not be assigned to the **Name** property.

Visual Basic for some time has supported encapsulation. In a class module, you can declare a variable as **Private**:

```
Private m_strName As String
```

A class variable declared with the **Private** access specifier cannot be accessed directly from outside the class. Instead, the class variable can be accessed outside the class only through a public procedure of the class. You can write code in that procedure that first validates the value proposed to be assigned to the property before actually assigning that value to the property. The public procedure usually is a *property procedure*:

```
Private m_strName 'class variable

Public Property Let Name (strName As String)
   If Not Trim(strName) = "" Then m_strName = strName
End Property
```

While property procedures usually are used for this purpose, a subroutine (to write the variable) or function (to read the variable) also can be used:

```
Private m_strName as string
Private Sub ChangeName(strName As String)
   If Not Trim(strName) = "" Then Me.m_strName = strName
End Sub
```

Note *The **Me** keyword refers to the specific instance of the class that is calling the **ChangeName** subroutine.*

While Visual Basic has supported encapsulation, its newfound support for inheritance affects encapsulation as well, as discussed next.

Inheritance

Inheritance is the ability of an object to obtain properties (variables) and behaviors (procedures) from another object and then extend or modify those properties and behaviors. For example, after creating a generic **Person** object that represents people generally, you can create from the **Person** object a **Student** object that inherits the properties of the **Person** object, such as **Name** and **Birthday** and the procedures to read from or write to those properties. The **Student** object may have its own additional properties, such as **Residency Status**, for calculation of tuition. The hallmark of inheritance is that the subclass or child class (**Student**) has an "is a" relationship with the superclass or parent class (**Person**), which means that a student is a person.

Until now, Visual Basic did not support this type of inheritance, often called *implementation inheritance*. Instead, Visual Basic has supported another type of inheritance, called *interface inheritance*. Some have argued that interface inheritance is "better" than implementation inheritance, and others have argued that interface inheritance is not inheritance at all. While this argument may be interesting intellectually, it is likely to disappear as a practical matter, because Visual Basic 7 promises to support implementation inheritance for the first time.

Version 7 introduces the **Inherits** keyword, which is used to show (to the compiler) that one class inherits from another. For example, the **Student** class would inherit from the **Person** class simply by adding the following statement in the General Declarations of the **Student** class:

```
Inherits Person
```

The advent of inheritance in Visual Basic affects encapsulation. Until now, the accessibility of a class property from outside the class was an all-or-nothing proposition. The class property was either declared **Public** or **Private**. There was no in-between. Nor did there need to be. Either you were accessing the property from within the class or from outside the class.

With inheritance there is an in-between—the inheriting subclass. As part of the concept of inheritance, the subclass is supposed to be able to access those properties of the superclass that the subclass is inheriting. However, the subclass cannot access **Private** members of the superclass because the subclass, while related by inheritance to the superclass, nevertheless technically still is outside the superclass. The subclass can access **Public** members of the superclass, but those members could be accessed from anywhere by anything, which is counter to the concept of encapsulation.

What is needed is a third access specifier that makes properties of the superclass public to the subclass but private everywhere else. Version 7 extends Visual Basic's support of encapsulation with the **Protected** keyword:

```
Protected m_strName as string
Protected Sub SetName(strName As String)
   If Not Trim(strName) = "" Then Me.m_strName = strName
End Sub
```

The **Protected** keyword will be familiar to C++ and Java programmers. The difference between **Private** and **Protected** is that a **Private** class variable is accessible only to member procedures of the class, whereas a **Protected** class variable is accessible to member procedures of the class and to classes that *inherit* from the class. A **Protected** class variable, like a **Private** class variable, otherwise cannot be accessed directly by external objects.

Inheritance: The Good, the Bad, and the Ugly

The Good, the Bad, and the Ugly was perhaps the most famous of the "Spaghetti Westerns" (the movies were filmed in Italy) and was produced by Sergio Leone, starring Clint Eastwood in his cowboy with no name role. In this movie, Clint

Eastwood, Lee Van Cleef, and Eli Wallach played characters that clearly could be identified as the good, the bad, and the ugly, respectively.

In contrast, inheritance plays all three roles.

An important benefit of object-oriented programming is *reusable code components*. Indeed, Visual Basic programmers, perhaps even without realizing it, use reusable code components every day, whether they be ActiveX controls, such as command buttons, or ActiveX servers, such as ADO for database access. Your ability to reuse preexisting, battle-tested code components speeds your application development, since you do not need to reinvent the wheel and can avoid the errors you might make in doing so.

Reusable code components are built on an object-oriented paradigm. ActiveX controls and ActiveX servers have properties and methods. These properties and methods are accessed by creating an instance of the object.

Using object-oriented programming makes the code component easier to maintain. With traditional structured programming, data generally is accessible throughout the program, so a change in one place in the code may have unintended consequences in another place in the code. This can result in run-time errors that are very difficult to debug. Additionally, the potential global impact of changing a line of code makes maintenance very tricky. By contrast, with object-oriented programming, particularly when a hierarchical, drill-down object model is used (as with ADO), it is relatively simple to identify a finite number of places in the code that can affect the given data.

While reusable code components are easy to reuse, they have not been so easy to customize or extend. That's where inheritance comes in. Through inheritance, you can reuse a functional, tested code component without being limited by it, since you can customize the code component to the extent you need.

While inheritance's enhancement of reusable code components is a very positive development, inheritance also has its dark side. Client applications access and use a class through the class's public interface, which is comprised of the publicly accessible properties and procedures of the class. The names and data types of these properties and procedures, and the procedures' arguments and return values, are hard-coded to the client. You can change how a procedure works, but you cannot change its "signature" (or remove the procedure) without risking "breaking" clients that have used that procedure.

This dependency on the public interface of the class is magnified by inheritance. With inheritance, subclasses as well as clients are dependent on the public interface of the class. A client application may be dependent on a subclass that in turn is dependent on a superclass.

These dependencies make good software design critically important. A poorly thought out superclass can result in the computer-programming equivalent of an impressive looking house with a shaky foundation. In other words, with inheritance it is easier to achieve a design that is ugly, perhaps not aesthetically, but functionally, in how it limits the extensibility of the applications that rely on it.

Polymorphism

Polymorphism comes from Greek and means "many forms." Polymorphism is the ability of two different objects, related by inheritance, to implement a specific method differently.

As discussed previously, a feature of inheritance is that a subclass inherits the properties and procedures of the superclass. Thus, if a generic **Employee** class has a **Name** property and procedures to read from and write to that property, a **NightShiftEmployee** class, by inheriting from **Employee**, inherits the **Name** attribute as well as the procedures to read from or write to that attribute, and can invoke those procedures directly:

```
'Class Employee

Protected m_strName

Protected Sub SetName(strName As String)
   If Not Trim(strName) = "" Then Me. m_strName = strName
End Sub

'Class NightShiftEmployee
Inherits Employee

Dim pers As Employee
Set pers = New Employee
Dim night As NightShiftEmployee
Set night = New NightShiftEmployee
pers.SetName "Jeff"
night.SetName "David"
```

Because the subclass is different from the superclass (otherwise there would be no point in creating the subclass), you may want a procedure of the subclass to do something different from the corresponding procedure of the superclass. For example, the **Employee** class may have a **PayEmployee** method that returns the product of the hours worked and the hourly rate. However, the calculation of pay may be different for different types of employees. For example, an employee who works the night shift might be paid time-and-a-half, and a salesperson might be paid a base salary plus a commission based on sales. The **Employee** class's **PayEmployee** method would not work for the night shift and commission employees.

The new **Overrides** keyword enables you to redefine procedures for derived classes. Given a base class of **Employee**, polymorphism enables the programmer to define different **PayEmployee** methods for any number of derived classes, such as **NightShiftEmployee**, who gets paid time-and-a-half, and **CommissionedEmployee**, who gets paid a commission based on sales. The **PayEmployee** method will return the correct result no matter which type of **Employee** object calls it:

```
'Class Employee

Function PayEmployee()
   PayEmployee = Hours * HourlyRate
End Function

'Class NightShiftEmployee
Inherits Employee

Overrides Function PayEmployee()
   PayEmployee = Hours * HourlyRate * 1.5
End Function

'Class CommissionedEmployee
Inherits Employee

Overrides Function PayEmployee()
   PayEmployee = CommissionRate * Sales
End Function

Dim nse As NightShiftEmployee
Set nse = New NightShiftEmployee

Dim ce As CommissionedEmployee
Set ce = New Commissioned Employee

Debug.Print nse.PayEmployee 'output pay based on hourly pay * 1.5
Debug.Print ce.PayEmployee  'output pay based on commission
```

Additional Language Enhancements

While inheritance may be the most significant language change, version 7 promises to introduce a number of other important changes to the Visual Basic programming language. While some of these changes, such as the ability to declare and initialize variables in one expression, probably are no more than a convenience, others, such as structured exception handling and free threading, may have a substantial effect on how you write your applications.

Parameterized Constructors

C++ and Java use *constructors* to create new instances of classes. C++ and Java also permit the constructors to have parameters (so-called *parameterized constructors*) so you can pass arguments to the new instance, usually to initialize its member variables. By contrast, Visual Basic has always required you to first create the object and then separately call a class procedure to initialize the variables.

Visual Basic 7 promises to support parameterized constructors. Parameterized constructors simplify code, and therefore code debugging and maintenance, by allowing a new object instance to be created and initialized in a single expression. Parameterized constructors also are an important part of object-oriented programming because they allow the creator of the instance to define the initial state of the created instance.

Initializers

Consistent with Visual Basic 7's support of parameterized constructors, which permit the creation and initialization of a new object instance in a single expression, version 7 also will support *initializers*, which enable you to declare and initialize variables in a single expression. Instead of code like this:

```
Dim X As Integer
X = 1
```

you can declare and initialize the variable in one statement:

```
Dim X As Integer = 1
```

Version 7's support of initializers, while not earth-shattering, brings it in line with C++ and Java in this respect, and will make your code easier to understand and therefore to debug and maintain.

Shared Members

C++ and Java support *static* class variables and functions. A static class variable exists independently of any particular instance of the class, and therefore is not accessed by an instance of the class. For example, while each instance of a **Person** class has its own name variable, since each person has their own name, a **Count** class variable that keeps track of the total number of **Person**s created should be shared among all instances of the class—it would therefore be a static class variable. Similarly, a **GetCount** procedure that returns the value of **Count** would be a static class function.

Visual Basic 7 will support static class variables and functions, though in Visual Basic they likely will be called *shared members*, referring to the fact that static class variables and functions are shared by all instances of the class.

Error Watch *While shared members is a useful feature, these members are independent of a particular instance of the class. This means that a shared procedure cannot attempt to access non-shared data members, since those members exist only in reference to a particular class instance.*

Overloading

C++ and Java both support overloaded functions. An overloaded function can be called by a single name to operate on different data types. Visual Basic already does this in a sense. For example, both of the following calls of the **SetText** procedure will set the text of the text box to the string "77", whether the argument is a String or an Integer:

```
Sub SetText(str As String)
   txtSample.Text = str
End Sub

SetText "77"
SetText 77
```

However, Visual Basic has not been able to react differently depending on which data type is passed. The **SetText** procedure is "one size fits all." Nor, until now, could you have separate **SetText** procedures to deal with the different data types, since procedure names have to be unique. Instead, you had to create distinct names for each procedure, even though they did the same thing:

```
Sub SetString (str As String)
Sub SetInt (int As Integer)
Sub SetDouble (dbl As Double)
```

Visual Basic now supports overloaded functions with the **Overloads** operator. With overloading, one procedure name can be used to display several different data types:

```
Overloads Sub SetInfo (str As String)
Overloads Sub SetInfo (int As Integer)
Overloads Sub SetInfo (dbl As Double)
```

Each "version" of **SetInfo** could have different code. Visual Basic will call the correct version of **SetInfo** based on the data type of the argument.

Error Watch *The compiler can differentiate overloaded functions based on the number, data type, or order of arguments. However, the compiler cannot differentiate overloaded functions based on the return value (or lack thereof).*

Type Safety

The Visual Basic language is very liberal in permitting one data type to be converted into another data type when assigning a value or passing a parameter by value. For example, the following code implicitly converts an Integer to a String so it can be displayed in a text box:

```
Dim num as Integer
num = 3
txtSample.Text = num
```

This implicit type coercion, while often a convenience, can make a programmer lazy. Even worse, an (attempted) implicit type coercion will cause a run-time error if the value cannot be converted without data loss. Of course, you (or your application's user) may not discover this until, unfortunately, run time.

Visual Basic 7 will improve type safety with the **Option Strict** statement, which generates a compile-time error when a conversion is required which could fail at run time or which, like the automatic conversion between numeric types and strings, is unexpected by the user.

Structured Exception Handling

Up until now, error handling in Visual Basic has required the **On Error GoTo** statement. **GoTo** statements are a relic from prehistoric programming, and they result in "spaghetti" code that is difficult to maintain. As the **GoTo** name implies, when an error occurs, control is transferred to a labeled location inside the subroutine. Once the error code runs, execution must often be diverted to another location, often via another **GoTo**, which may use yet another label, **Exit**, to get out of the procedure. Handling several different errors with various combinations of **Resume** and **ResumeNext** quickly produces code whose paths of execution are very difficult to follow and consequently leads to bugs. This becomes an even greater problem for larger, complex enterprise and Web applications.

Microsoft has recommended **On Error Resume Next** for error handling. This does avoid spaghetti code, and places error-handling code near the error. However, **Resume Next** does not always fit a given error-handling situation.

C++ supports structured exception handling, with the **Try … Catch … Throw** control structure. Visual Basic now has implemented this concept with the **Try ... Catch ... Finally** control structure, which performs as follows:

- **Try** You place here the statements that may raise an error.
- **Catch** You place here the statements that will handle the error.
- **Finally** You place here the statements that should execute if no error occurs.

For example, the following code attempts to open a file for output and then writes to it. If all goes well, then the file is closed with the **Close** statement. However, if an error is raised in opening or writing to the file, the **Kill** statement will execute:

```
Sub OutputFile()
Try
   Open "TESTFILE" For Output As #1
   Write #1, CustomerInformation
Catch
   Kill "TESTFILE"
Finally
   Close #1
End Try
End Sub
```

The advantage of **Try ... Catch ... Finally** is that it is a control structure that executes in both normal and error conditions. This avoids the spaghetti code that inevitably results from **GoTo** statements. The **Try ... Catch ... Finally** construct also makes it much easier to localize error handling around code that causes an error, making your code easier to understand, debug, and maintain. Finally, the **Try ... Catch ... Finally** control structure permits multiple error handlers in the same routine, and may permit nesting of error handlers.

At a preview of an early prototype of Visual Basic 7 at VBITS 2000 in San Francisco, Dave Mendlen, product planner for Visual Basic/Visual InterDev (who kindly provided the quote on the front cover of this book), proclaimed: "You never have to type another **On Error GoTo** again!" That indeed would be nice.

Free Threading

Visual Basic code usually is synchronous. This means that each line of code must be executed before the next one. This may be acceptable for small, single-user applications, but it is not for enterprise-level applications that require concurrent processing.

Visual Basic has supported apartment-model threading, but that threading model is complex and does not always fit a given situation. What was needed was the ability to freely spawn threads. Visual Basic now has that ability.

With the inclusion of free threading, developers can spawn a thread, which can perform some long-running task, execute a complex query, or run a complex calculation, while the rest of the application continues, providing asynchronous processing.

```
Sub CreateMyThread()
   Dim b As BackGroundWork
   Dim t As Thread
   Set b = New BackGroundWork()
   Set t = New Thread(New ThreadStart(AddressOf b.Doit))
   t.Start
End Sub

Class BackGroundWork
   Sub DoIt()
      'do some work
   End Sub

End Class
```

Error Watch *Free threading does give you the responsibility of ensuring that one thread is not a "hog" or that two threads do not, by calling each other, cause a deadlock.*

The preceding code (from Microsoft's site) also uses the **AddressOf** operator to return the address of a function. Apparently Visual Basic programmers will be able to use API functions that require a function pointer by using the **AddressOf** operator to provide a callback!

Visual Basic and the Internet

Unless you have been a hermit for the last several years, you could not have missed the growing and now pervasive influence of the Internet. At least every other television advertisement is for a "dot com." Even your formerly computer-phobic neighbors have a family Web site showing off their pet dog, which probably has its own (better) Web site.

The growing influence of the Internet shows no sign of abating. The main limiting factor has been bandwidth. Users, particularly residential users, have had to access the Internet through the dreaded POTS (Plain Old Telephone Service). However, bandwidth, or more accurately lack thereof, is becoming less of an issue with the growing availability of DSL and cable modems for the residential market. The increasing ease and speed with which users can access the Internet has contributed substantially to the recent explosion in the Internet's popularity.

Visual Basic has not been unaffected by the growing significance of the Internet. It is estimated that approximately one-third of current Visual Basic development is targeted at the Web. However, Web-based applications have lagged significantly behind their ActiveX Server cousins, which reside on local machines or networks. Many Web-based applications still are based on interpreted script embedded in HTML files, with the consequent adverse impact on speed, both in terms of application development and in processing by the Web server.

Microsoft, which did not get to be Microsoft by ignoring trends like the Internet, has been enhancing Visual Basic's Internet capabilities in succeeding versions of the product. For example, version 6 of Visual Basic introduced Web Classes, which enabled the extension, to a point anyway, of ActiveX Servers to Web-based applications.

With version 7, Microsoft has significantly enhanced Visual Basic's Internet capabilities with Web Forms and Web Services. The promise of these new tools is to extend services to the Web that up until now have been limited in location to the local machine or network.

Web Forms

Currently Web applications that are run on a remote Web server use Active Server Pages (ASP) involving HTML forms with embedded script. Web Forms, utilizing the next generation of ASP, appropriately named ASP+, still will use HTML forms. However, the code will not be embedded in the form, but instead will reside in a separate file. This will not only enhance the readability, debugging, and maintenance of the code, but will also enable you to reuse code components. Perhaps more important, the code will not be script, but instead will be compiled, which will speed processing by the Web server.

Web Forms will extend Visual Basic's rapid application development capability to Web applications. A Web Form will be to Web applications what a standard Visual Basic form now is to standard applications. You will be able to design a Web Form much as you can create a form in Visual Basic today. For example, just as you can drag an ActiveX control from the toolbox to a standard Visual Basic form, you will be able to drag a Web (HTML) control to an HTML page. Just as with a standard Visual Basic form, you can set the properties of the HTML page and its constituent controls. Web Forms also will support IntelliSense and WYSIWYG form design.

You can also double-click a Web control to write code for its events, as you can for a Visual Basic form. You can write the code in any of the languages in Visual Studio. Indeed, Web Forms will be shared in an integrated Visual Studio, so you can use Visual Basic and C++ code in the same form.

A Web Forms page has two parts. One part is an HTML file embodying the visual representation of the page. The other part is a source file that handles the page's events. Thus, you no longer need to embed script in HTML. The separation of the code from the interface means that your code will be easier to debug, maintain, and reuse.

Both the HTML file and the source file reside and execute on a server. The execution of these files generates an HTML 3.2 compliant document that is returned to the client. Since the client does not execute code but only receives HTML, a Web Form, like an Active Server Pages (ASP) page, can run on almost any browser.

While Web Forms are similar to ASP in executing code on the server and returning only HTML to the client, Web Forms, unlike ASP, do not use interpreted script. Instead, Web Forms, being part of ASP+, the next generation of ASP, use compiled code. This will result in a substantial improvement in speed.

Design Tip *While Web Forms are quite similar to standard Visual Basic forms, one significant difference is that with Web Forms event code has to be processed and returned by the server, perhaps over a telephone connection. There is nothing you can do as a programmer to increase the speed between the client and the server, unless you want to include a T1 line with your application, and there is probably little more you can do to influence the speed of the server. What you can do is minimize the number of round trips to the server.*

Web Services

Reusable code components, discussed earlier in this chapter, are commonly ActiveX DLLs today. Currently you can create an ActiveX DLL in an ActiveX DLL project, create a standard application in a Standard EXE project, and install both the ActiveX DLL and the standard application on the same local machine or network, and have the standard application access the public functions of the ActiveX DLL.

Reusable code components traditionally have resided on the same local machine or network as the standard application using the services of the code component. However, with Web Services, to be introduced in Visual Basic 7, applications will be able to use the services of a code component (the Web Service) that resides on a remote Web server. Just as a standard application can access a function in an ActiveX DLL residing on the local machine or on a network if the function is exposed with the **Public** keyword, a standard application can access a function in an application residing on the Internet if the function is exposed as public through a function tag tentatively named **Webpublic**. The **Webpublic** tag indicates that the procedure is to be exposed as a Web Service. The Web Service exposes its COM interface not just to objects on the local machine or network, but to any Web application that references its URL.

The following example (based on one by Microsoft) illustrates the process of creating a Web Service—in this case a service that will return "Buy!" if the stock is "Microsoft;" otherwise "Sell!" Of course, an actual Web Service would be far more complex. Additionally, while the following code uses Visual Basic, you also could use any of the other Visual Studio language products, such as Visual C++.

You would start by creating a new Visual Project, tentatively called a "Web Project." You then would add a new class to the project that would include the following function:

```
Public Function BuyOrSell(ByVal companyAs String) As String
   If company = "Microsoft" Then
      BuyStock = "Buy!"
   Else
      BuyStock = "Sell!"
   End If
End Function
```

When you build the project containing this function, Visual Studio will automatically create and publish to the Web the Web Service and the following XML file that describes the Web Service's public functions, the input parameters and data types, and the return data types:

```
<?xml version='1.0' ?>

<methods href='http://www.vb2java.com/stocks'>
   <method name='BuyOrSell' href='BuyOrSell'>
      <request>
         <param dt='string'>company</param>
      </request>
      <response dt='string'/>
   </method>
</methods>
```

Once you have built and published the Web Service, you will be able, in a standard application, to add a reference to the Web Service just as you now can add a reference to an ActiveX DLL. This is even though, unlike the ActiveX DLL, the Web Service does not exist on the local machine or network, but rather on a remote Web server. Indeed, Microsoft has indicated that Visual Studio will enable you to drag any exposed Web Service right into your application, creating a new class file. Then, just as with an ActiveX DLL, if you want to call a Web Service anywhere on the Internet, all you have to do is create a new instance of the Web Service class and call its exposed methods. Indeed, you would be able to use IntelliSense when you are writing code that references the Web Service instance. Thus, though the Web Service will reside on a remote Web server instead of a local machine or network, your task of designing and deploying the Web Service to a remote server will be quite similar to your task today of creating and deploying an ActiveX DLL locally.

The standard application will invoke the Web Service through the latter's URL. The standard application and the Web Service then will communicate with each other using HTTP. This will allow the standard application's requests to the remote procedure, and the procedure's responses, to pass through enterprise firewalls. If additional security is needed, the Secure Sockets Layer (SSL) protocol and standard authentication techniques are supported.

XML (Extensible Markup Language) is used to pass data to and from the service. At run time, all of the standard application's calls to the Web Service and the Web Service's return of information will automatically be packaged and handled through an XML interface and sent as XML packets through SOAP (Simple Object Access Protocol). The XML file that Visual Studio created when the Web Project was built is used to provide the necessary information about the Web Service. While this can be rather complex, Visual Studio handles the XML conduits between the Web Service and the application using it.

While Web Services holds great promise, you should minimize the number of round trips to the Web server, as discussed with Web Forms.

Summary

Visual Basic still is the development environment of choice for rapid application development. It is now a full-featured object-oriented programming language, as well. However, with that new power comes a new way of thinking about designing object-oriented applications, and the responsibility of using the new features wisely.

The addition of Web Forms and Web Services will let you create applications or services that run on a remote Web server as easily as you now create applications and services that run on a local machine or network. However, since both Web Forms and Web Services entail communication across the Internet rather than in a local computer or network, the importance of minimizing the number of round trips to the server is magnified.

APPENDIX A

Third-Party Tools

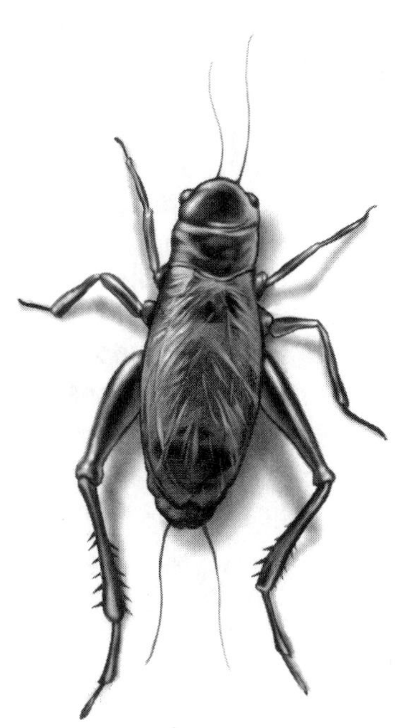

Throughout the chapters in this book, we discussed techniques to help you write bulletproof code within your application. As you get into larger software development projects, you will discover that techniques themselves are not enough to ensure rock-solid applications. There are a number of fine third-party tools on the market today that can help you write better code, find and fix errors more efficiently, and keep track of feature requests and error reports. This appendix provides information on various tools grouped by the following topics:

- Debugging and testing tools
- Source code libraries
- Version control tools for source code
- Software problem tracking tools
- Software deployment tools

Note In no way are the authors endorsing any of these products. The authors have used some of these tools in the past and found them useful, while others are tools they've heard of by reputation and marketing/press material. Many of the vendors' Web sites refer to other products through links. This portion of the appendix is just to give you a good place to start.

Debugging and Testing Tools

Visual Basic has a lot of really good features to help you with debugging your application during development; however, they are limited strictly to the VB IDE itself. Visual Studio is lacking tools to help you document your code for code reviews, application profiling tools for tuning and optimization, and automated tools for functional, unit, and regression testing.

NuMega DevPartner Studio for Visual Basic
CompuWare Corporation
http://www.numega.com

The NuMega DevPartner is a suite of software development productivity tools that accelerate the development of distributed and component-based applications using Visual Basic. Included in the product are a myriad of tools that touch all aspects of the development and product tuning cycle. For source code analysis, CodeReview examines your application's source code and attempts to identify potential problems before they can occur. For automatic error detection, the SmartCheck tool captures the VB run-time errors, diagnoses them, and translates vague error messages into exact problem descriptions. TrueTime is an application performance profiler to help you determine if one set of code executes faster than another so you can fine-tune your application. TrueCoverage analyzes run-time code and helps developers quickly identify code that has not been executed. Lastly, there's FailSafe, which captures the state of your system when your program fails, providing you with feedback on how your application interacts with your client's computers.

WinRunner
Mercury Interactive
http://www.mercuryinteractive.com

WinRunner is an integrated, functional testing tool for your entire enterprise. It captures, verifies, and replays user interaction with your application's user interface, helping identify defects and ensure that business processes work flawlessly. By having an automated tool such as WinRunner, you can perform functional testing on new application builds to ensure they work as they are designed to. In addition, the automated process can be used to perform regression testing to ensure that any new feature or bug fix added to the application didn't break something else in the process.

BugTrapper Pro
MuTek Solutions
http://www.mutek.com

BugTrapper is an error recorder that you integrate into your application so that if and when your application crashes, it traps the bugs by recording how and where the unexpected error occurred. This aids you in pinpointing the cause of the error in a reduced amount of time.

Foundation
Cirkadia Software
http://www.cirkadia.com

Foundation is an active error-handling expert that allows applications and components to recover from errors and exception faults and continue to execute, while keeping the client's environment stable, as if the error never happened. In all development environments, error-handling routines built into programming languages are reactive rather than proactive. Foundation has an ActiveError engine that takes control when an error occurs, unwinding the call stack through its TransActive Error Recovery schema, a propriety framework that prevents an error from occurring, records the error for debugging purposes, and allows the user to continue using the application.

SQL-Programmer
Sylvain Faust Intl
http://www.sfi-software.com

SQL-Programmer is a "test while you edit" development environment featuring a unique virtual editor. It replaces command-line ISQL programming with live editing, creation, testing, and impact assessment with all database objects, such as stored procedures, triggers, views, and so on. It features multiple SQLServer connections, with support for Sybase System and Microsoft SQL Server, including team programming. It has an Automatic SQL Server System Documentation generation feature that creates standard reports with the full transact-SQL scripts that can be used by other relational database systems.

SQA Suite
Rational Software
http://www.rational.com

SQA Suite is a complete set of tools that provide functional testing. The tools consist of the SQA Robot, which is used to record the tests you perform against your applications. The SQA SiteCheck is used to help you deliver Web site analysis, performance measurements, and repair technology for Web-enabled applications. For load, stress, and multiple-user testing for both traditional client/server applications and Web-based applications, there's SQA LoadTest. The SQA Manager is used to coordinate all the test planning, management, and tools, and the SQA Manager WebEntry tool is a Web-based tool allowing convenient data entry for recording and tracking software defects.

Rational Visual Test
Rational Software
http://www.rational.com

Visual Test is an automated testing tool that allows developers and users to create test scripts for applications. It helps automate the repetitive tasks of regression testing to enhance the effectiveness of your testing project. It also comes with redistributable components so that tests designed and developed by quality assurance engineers can be redistributed throughout your enterprise.

WebLoad
RadView
http://www.radview.com

As more and more applications are deployed over the Internet, you will need a tool to help you test your application's performance against simultaneous users, connection load, and stress testing. WebLoad is a test application you should look into. WebLoad is not one of those tools that was originally designed for Windows application testing and then ported over to handle Web-based applications—it was built from the ground up specifically for testing Web-based applications. Because of this, WebLoad validates the user interface against the browser's Document Object Model (DOM), which dramatically improves validation over testing HTML source code because DHTML- and XML-based applications rely on the DOM for interpretation of their functionality, rather than on a scripting engine. HTML source code is too ambiguous and there is no standardized way to validate an application by processing a bunch of markup tags. It offers the standard test session recording options for regression testing, offers stress and load testing, and more. Its performance monitor provides feedback on process and memory consumption on the application servers, and it offers real-time test analysis so you can monitor all results while the testing is being executed, rather than having to wait until all the test scripts have run their course.

Source Code Libraries

Books, magazine articles, Microsoft TechNet and MSDN, and VB Web sites are great sources of coding examples. However, unless you have all these sources in one place at your disposal, they don't do you any good.

Source code libraries are a great source of coding consistency and functionality reuse. How many times have you thought to yourself, "if only I could remember what application I used that code in?" If you've said this more than once or twice, you should consider getting a source code library. Good libraries offer you, the developer, the ability to add your own code routines so you can extend your library throughout your enterprise.

Visual Basic Annotated Archives
David Jung and Jeff Kent
Osborne/McGraw-Hill, 1999
http://www.osborne.com

Unique in its focus on advanced programming concepts, *Visual Basic Annotated Archives* explains how to extend and transcend the built-in limitations of Visual Basic using the Win32 API and subclassing. It also provides extensive coverage of cutting-edge programming techniques for using ADO, DHTML, WebClasses, and the Microsoft Transaction Server. The book's code components are ready to use for developing high-performance applications for the Internet, intranet, and client/server environments, and the detailed expert annotations enable you to customize the code components to fit your needs.

Total Visual SourceBook 2000
FMS Inc.
http://www.fmsinc.com

This product is probably one of the most complete code libraries for VB developers on the market today. It contains source code for every major area of software development, from ADO to XML, with over 85,000 lines of code, over 150 modules, and spanning more than 40 different categories. The product completely integrates with the VB IDE through an add-in, making the code just a mouse click away. Granted, the SourceBook can't have everything you and your developers need, especially if you have some standard code of your own. Fortunately, you can add your own code to the SourceBook and share it with the rest of the developers on your network, as well, making this a true repository for standardized code.

CodeAssist
Sheridan Software System
http://www.shersoft.com

Despite the name, CodeAssist is a template-driven code generation product that streamlines the data application development process and slashes development time. Using template-driven technology, CodeAssist helps VB and ASP developers create sophisticated data access routines faster, more efficiently, and more economically than ever. Developer modifiable code templates include a variety of VB, ASP, and SQL code for producing n-tier or client/server applications.

VB Advantage
Advantageware
http://www.advantageware.com

VB Advantage is a powerful VB development utility that will enhance your VB design-time environment. VB Advantage has many powerful, helpful, and easy-to-use features and tools that help you produce better code while saving time and eliminating those mind-numbing redundant tasks. It comes with over 100 design-time tools to assist in writing your code more efficiently and reducing redundant tasks, like remembering to put the **End If** at the end of the **If** statement, or the **Next** at the end of the **For** statement. The best part about this product is that the source code for each tool is included, and the environment itself, which is a VB add-in, can be extended and enhanced by you to include features you find useful. If you think other developers would be interested in your enhancements, simply send them to Advantageware where they will be made available to fellow VB Advantage users. If you've ever wanted to extend the VB IDE and didn't have the time or energy to write your own add-in, VB Advantage is definitely a product you should look into.

Version Control Tools for Source Code

When working on large projects, you will usually be developing in teams. Since a Visual Basic project is composed of different modules, it is possible to have developers working on different modules at the same time. You want to make sure that all the developers are using the latest versions of every form and module, and that they are not modifying the code that someone else is working on.

By using version control software, you can ensure that only one person is working on a component at a time. You can also share components across applications so that if you make a change to a shared component in one application, the other applications will also see the change. Trying to do this manually, without the assistance of software, can get out of hand in a hurry.

Visual SourceSafe
Microsoft Corp.
http://msdn.microsoft.com/ssafe

Microsoft Visual SourceSafe (VSS) is a source-code version control tool. A full version, single-user license for Visual SourceSafe comes with Microsoft Visual Studio, Enterprise Edition. Either as a stand-alone product or integrated with any of the Visual Studio products' IDE, VSS is an excellent tool for helping manage your development team's most valuable asset, your source code.

PVCS Version Manager
Merant Solutions Inc.
http://www.pvcs.com
PVCS Version Manager organizes, manages, and protects source code, supporting effective software configuration management (SCM) across your entire enterprise. It provides an effective tool for controlling source-code versions, tracing changes, and making code-sharing easier.

Software Problem Request Systems

A software problem request (SPR) system's focus is to capture application information, such as who originated a trouble call, to whom was it assigned, what was its severity, and to manage application bugs, request features, and request tracking.

TeamTrack Suite
TeamShare
http://www.teamshare.com
TeamTrack is a Web-based problem tracking system that offers scalability and customization to help you control, guide, and manage multiple projects and teams. Integrating features commonly found in project management applications with SPR systems, the suite offers a formidable solution for team-based workflow. Many products handle either project management or SPRs, but TeamShare offers both in the suite as tTrack and tSupport. Both systems feed off each other to provide a very integrated solution so that tasks in project management and features recorded as SPRs aren't lost or overlooked in the development cycle.

TestTrack
Seapine Software
http://www.seapine.com
TestTrack tracks bugs and feature requests, customers, users, test configurations, and more. It has additional features, such as e-mail notifications, e-mail bug imports, duplicate bug handling, and release note generation. You can distribute TestTrack's stand-alone bug report to your customers to automate customer

support, or you can purchase the Web licenses so all bug reporting is centralized on your Web server.

ProblemTracker
NetResults
http://www.netresultscorp.com

ProblemTracker is a Web-based defect tracking and change management system. It contains all the features you would expect from a defect tracking system such as e-mail notification, workflow management into project management systems, standardized and custom reports, and more.

BugCollector Pro
Nesbitt Software
http://www.nesbitt.com/

BugCollector Pro is a software bug tracking and feature request system. It helps manage details of the software development process and organizes software bugs and feature requests by status, priority, and severity. BugCollector can track multiple programs while keeping a record of users' statistics. It allows developers to attach screen shots and other files to individual reports, and includes a number of predefined reports and graphs.

PVCS Professional
Merant Solutions Inc.
http://www.pvcs.com

A complete package, Professional combines PVCS Version Manager, PVCS Tracker, and PVCS Configuration Builder. PVCS Version Manager is the source code management tool; PVCS Tracker captures, manages, and communicates feature requests, defect reports, changes, and project tasks with the entire team; and PVCS Configuration Builder automates and accelerates software builds across multiple platforms from a single point of control, saving your teams development time and eliminating build errors.

Software Deployment Tools

Once you have created your applications, you need to deploy them to your users. Whether your customer base is internal or external to your organization, you can never be 100 percent certain of a user's computer setup; therefore, you need to include every resource file and device driver your application uses to ensure that the customers have the same baseline of resource files you used for your application. The following are the most mainstream products for software deployment.

Windows Installer
Microsoft Corp.
http://msdn.microsoft.com/installer
Windows Installer is a new software installation technology from Microsoft that provides an installation engine that interprets and executes installation database (.msi) files.

InstallMaker, InstallBuilder, InstallMaster, and Wise for Windows Installer
Wise Solutions, Inc.
http://www.wisesolutions.com
Wise Solutions offers a number of software deployment solutions, all offering different levels of options, with each solution building on the next. InstallMaker provides the basic set of features available in all versions of the program, allowing you to quickly point-and-click your way to an installer executable in minutes. InstallBuilder is more for the mainstream developer who wants to customize the installation with more than just point-and-click options. It provides a scripting layer to provide finer customization. InstallMaster contains all the features of InstallMaker and InstallBuilder but also includes Windows CE setup features and installation packages for installing over the Web, and for distributing incremental updates over the Web. For Windows 2000 logo compatibility, Wise offers the Wise for Windows Installer solution that provides the wizards and easy-to-use interfaces that are consistent with their other deployment products.

InstallShield Professional, InstallShield Express, and InstallShield for Windows Installer
InstallShield, Inc.
http://www.installshield.com
InstallShield offers a number of software deployment solutions. InstallShield Professional is their most comprehensive product offering a full range of options for building software distribution packages. It allows you to create custom installation packages through its powerful scripting language. InstallShield Express offers many of the same features that its professional counterpart offers; however it's not completely customizable. For your applications to be considered for Windows 2000 logo compatibility, your software installation has to conform to the Microsoft Windows Installer specifications, and InstallShield for Windows Installer fills that niche.

Index

NOTE: Page numbers in *italics* refer to illustrations or charts.

B

C

E

J

K

L

M

N

O

Q

R

S

T

U

V

W

X

Z